The Songs of Remembering

Ava & Ron Amit

NEW EARTH ASCENDING

Published and distributed by New Earth Ascending, global ministries.

Editing: Monica Karaba, Leann Love
Cover design: Maxym Guimont
Symbols Glossary designs by:
Amaline Bassetti, Casey House, George Leoniak, Ron Amit

First Edition

ISBNs:
Hardback: 978-1-959561-17-0
Peperback: 978-1-959561-19-4
Ebook: 978-1-959561-18-7

1822f5ec6e2feccfea3e6b68441ce200

34c886ff4b4fa4f5bf378862c6e3e4d9

TABLE OF CONTENTS

DEDICATION

We dedicate this book to Unconditional Love.

We dedicate this book to Mother Earth in all her glory.

We dedicate this book to all the children of this Earth, the next and previous generations, and to all the many types of beings who evolved on this beautiful planet. All are equal children of Mother Earth and the divine Source.

We dedicate this book to the restoration of the Divine Feminine in full balance with the Divine Masculine on the planet and within all beings.

We dedicate this book to the remembering — remembering who we are. We are one human family. We are all one, connected through all space and time. We know how hard it can be to remember, especially when so many have forgotten.

We dedicate this book to the art of listening — for listening to our soul's calling, and for following that call the best we can.

We dedicate this book to the brave souls who have volunteered to incarnate on Planet Earth with a soul mission to help raise our vibration into love during these times of great change.

We dedicate this book to you — for all the times when you overcame challenges and chose to live with integrity, courage, and devotion.

We dedicate this book to you – for all the moments when you felt afraid, frustrated, alone, or like you didn't belong here.

We dedicate this book as a balm for all the times when dishonesty, greed, and aggression broke your pure and precious heart.

We dedicate this book to the Source of All That Is.

May we all remember, awaken, ascend and live free from fear and suffer.

RON'S INTRODUCTION

When I read books, I tend to skip the acknowledgments, so just before publishing this book, I felt inspired to move them to the end of the book. We thought that once you have read this material, then you'll better understand the heartfelt gratitude we are sharing with our allies. Here is the background story of how this book came to be, without spoiling the surprises you are about to experience. I know how fun it was for me to have it all shared with me without preparation, and I want you to have a similar experience.

I've been a hypnotherapist for almost eight years. My life dramatically shifted in one month after learning Dolores Cannon's Quantum Healing Hypnosis Technique (QHHT). If you are not familiar with it, more will be shared soon. Prior to becoming a practitioner, I had been a professional dancer and choreographer who performed and taught workshops in academies around the world. It was a big lifestyle change to become a facilitator who sees clients one-on-one for long sessions — sometimes even twice a day — while sitting many hours patiently and listening to life stories.

After a few years of hundreds of sessions and lots of learning to expand my skill set, plus guidance from higher realms and our hearts, my husband and I created our healing modality: Illuminated Quantum Healing (IQH). Creating IQH was born out of necessity and innovation, as QHHT does not support remote sessions. One of the main differences and benefits of our modality is that it can be done remotely, mainly through video calls, and from the comfort of one's home. This allows us to reach many people from all over the world, and those who may not have access to this type of healing in their areas. This proved itself to be tremendously important during the pandemic that started in 2020 with lockdowns and social distancing requirements.

We are grateful that we followed our guidance to expand and created an online course to learn our IQH modality for new and experienced practitioners. Together with our growing community of facilitators, we keep enhancing the practice and support each other as needed.

Some of you may be familiar with our work or may be familiar with my partner's book, *The Illumination Codex: Guidance for Ascension to New Earth* by Michael James Garber. Some of you may be well versed in the material of my teacher Dolores Cannon. If you have picked up this book, and you are not familiar with what I just mentioned, some terms or concepts might be new for you. I highly recommend having a copy of *The Illumination Codex* with you to go hand-in-hand with this book. It includes many great summaries and a glossary that might expand your understanding of this material better. It also describes more in-depth about the history of our ministry, the history of Dolores Cannon's work, and why and how we have evolved after her passing. You can find a digital or a physical copy on the New Earth Ascending website.

I consider Michael's book to be an extensive and inspiring guidebook for spiritual awakening and Ascension. It explains, in simple and beautiful writing, a vast collection of information that is beneficial on the awakening and remembering path. It is equally fit for newly awakened and longtime spiritual seekers, as it contains new and potent information that would feel like a continuation and expansion of Dolores' materials and other occult literature.

I also highly recommend reading some of Dolores Cannon's books. The book that initiated me onto this path of quantum hypnosis and Ascension teachings was *The Three Waves of Volunteers and The New Earth*. If you are curious about how this all started for Dolores, I would like to point you to the book *Five Lives Remembered*, her first book out of nineteen. Coincidentally, or not, this book you are reading now follows a similar thread, the progression of exploration with one very unique individual, in this case, my dear friend, Ava.

Now, I don't want to add too much information about me, my own awakening story, or my healing journey. This I'll keep for another book. However, before I share important information to help prepare you for reading this book, I do have a short, personal share...

I want you to know that it feels like a miracle for me that I'm able to write this book in English as English is not my first language. My English teachers might not believe I accomplished this!

I was born in Israel, but during the first four years of my life, my family and I were living in Mexico. I learned to speak Hebrew, Spanish, and Yiddish all at once! This was a lot for my little brain at that time. I started to speak pretty late, and I had a stutter. Around the third grade, I was diagnosed with dyslexia, which presented as me mixing up letters when writing and spelling and reading very slowly, and with many mistakes. Additionally, I was diagnosed with some level of ADHD, which presented as me having hyper energy and me losing my concentration and focus easily. I would avoid reading out loud as I would get very stressed and embarrassed. Even today I would probably do my best to avoid doing reading publicly.

In order to sit and focus on the writing of this introduction, I had to make sure I was in a quiet, calm space. I had to make sure that I had finished my "to-do list," even the unnecessary tasks, and I had to make sure that all of my immediate needs were met like food and so on. I learned that every small thing could give my mind an excuse as to why I "can't write right now." I had to make sure I had no more distractions for my mind to focus on. I also had to stay well grounded, do physical exercises, meditate, take breaks from writing and editing, and move my body and stretch.

While working on this book, these challenges became easier and I learned something really valuable about myself that perhaps might relate to you too. It seems to me that people who have been labeled as "ADHD," or empathic, sensitive people, or people who have had traumas, may be feeling into many things and many places at once. It feels as if the overall energy of my consciousness is spread into many places simultaneously. I needed to learn how to collect myself from all those places so that I could be present and focused in my body HERE and NOW. It is like closing all the open applications on my cellular phone and leaving only the ones needed for that moment. Only after tending to these inner processes, I was able to focus my energy and listen to my heart, while staying in the current and flow of inspiration.

This short "personal share" may seem unrelated to the content of the book, but maybe by the end, it will make more sense why it was an important piece for me to share. I believe that focusing and being present in the NOW moment is one of the biggest challenges for our human family. I believe that most people are not aware of how distracted they are from being fully present in their body, and titles like ADHD, OCD, and so on, are being given to individuals who are just not fully embodied.

So many of us were born in hospitals, in a very artificial and sterilized environment, where we experienced a degree of birth trauma and fragmenting of the soul upon entering our physical incarnation. I believe that for many of us, the *full energy* and consciousness of our soul was not able to inhabit the body completely and integrate properly to enjoy our beautiful planet.

I believe that many of you may be sharing this experience and not even know that your soul is so big and so capable, and that part of your energy — your life force and consciousness— is weakened by traumas you experienced at birth and throughout your life. I hope this book will inspire you to do the inner work to heal yourself and allow your soul to incarnate fully and come "online," so that you can be wholly realized in remembering who you are and why you came here. May you retrieve your soul fragments and essence to align you with the golden child that you are.

I hope this little share from my heart to yours will inspire those of you who feel limited or incapable. I hope this little piece of my life experience will help you personally or enable you to better understand another. I hope this book will inspire and empower you to dive deep into your own healing and spiritual growth journey. I hope it inspires you to cultivate a practice of meditation which seems to be the most advanced technology one can use for Self-realization and Ascension. Meditation requires a great skill of focusing and it becomes easier as you call in your soul's energy to the present moment, and this is why I wanted to share my own life experience and my little epiphany.

How Did This Book Come to Be?

This book is based on a dialogue that I was having during IQH hypnosis sessions I facilitated for Ava with her Higher Self, the collective consciousness of her soul and some other higher consciousness beings who you will discover as you read. During the sessions, Ava channeled all this information while under a deep hypnotic trance. We met nine times from October 2018 until March 2022, and we had ten sessions overall. All personal details about Ava, including names and locations, were changed or removed. Some of the information is very personal, but we found that it could be helpful and inspiring for others on their life's path, so we decided to keep it in the book. Some parts of the sessions were removed when they seemed irrelevant to this book.

Before I met Ava, I had facilitated sessions for around two years, and I probably held a few hundred sessions by then. Even though Ava had experienced somewhat successful past-life regression hypnotherapy under a different technique a few years prior, she doubted that she would be able to have a successful session with me. I was feeling quite confident with my practice by then and had found those types of concerns to be common. I assured Ava that she had nothing to worry about. The few people who hadn't experienced a successful session with me were people who didn't truly want the session in the first place. They went through with it based on someone else's desire, wanting them to have this experience and healing. If you truly want the session and you approach it with honest intentions, I'm confident that it would be a meaningful and productive experience. I explained to Ava the process of working with me, and I'll explain it now as I would to any client who is unfamiliar with IQH - Illuminated Quantum Healing.

The inspiration, coordination, healing, and wisdom from these sessions comes from what we call the Higher Self. Dolores Cannon called this part of a client's consciousness and higher spiritual identity the Subconscious or the SC. This part can also be called the Oversoul. The Higher Self knows everything about the client, about their soul history, soul mission, and what is needed to heal and awaken to higher levels of consciousness. The Higher Self also directs the multidimensional healing and upgrades that happen through the healing journey. The Higher Self only shares helpful wisdom and insight and always honors the client's free will and unique life path.

A standard IQH session normally takes around four to five hours. We meet in person or remotely on a video call. The session has two main parts that are also divided into specific sections. During the first part, we open with a guided meditation, followed by an interview about the client's life story — a summary of life events and the important turning points. We cover the diversity of both happy moments and challenging ones. I learn about the client's intentions, their wishes for the future, and the list of questions they would like to have answered by the Higher Self. From this, I understand deeply what brings them to have this session with me, and I can feel when we have established trust through our heart-to-heart connection. The most important thing is to share with me openly and freely, without self-judgment, without over-thinking, as honestly as you can. This part usually takes about two hours, then we take a short break.

The second part of the session takes around two to three hours. My unique induction is the method I use to guide my clients into a deep relaxation includes many visualization practices that activate their inner senses and build up their confidence in receiving information to ensure we have a successful session.

Next, we start what I refer to as the Quantum Journey. We ask and allow the Higher Self to subconsciously lead us to the most appropriate time and space to discover what is most needed for the client's healing and awakening. During the journey, they might visit events from this current life, other lives, other places or dimensions that their soul experienced and needs to learn from. The Higher Self has a greater perspective and would only show the most beneficial information for the client's healing. If a person wants to discover things from more specific times or events, like missing memories, or unique events, I would address those only in a later stage of the session, after the most important healing and information is brought forward by the Higher Self.

After the Quantum Journey, I ask to speak with the client's Higher Self directly. This establishes a link between the client's body and the Higher Self so that the Higher Self can communicate through the client's mind and body. After the Higher Self comes forward to speak through the client, I ask to learn about the reason the client was shown specific events and how it relates to the client's life presently. We also address all the questions the client had prepared.

Normally, the Higher Self answers and speaks through as a collective consciousness that is part of the Oneness of Source. "They" generally talk about the client from a third-person perspective as you will notice throughout this book. Even though "they" may potentially have access to all knowledge, only the most appropriate information will be given. They know the spiritual level and the capacity of the client and even the practitioner. They will only share in a precise way that provides the highest benefit to the client, the practitioner, and all who might engage with the transmitted material.

The next part I like to sometimes call the "spiritual surgery." During this part I ask the Higher Self and other spirit guides to do a scan and healing for the physical and energetic bodies. The healing is done from the deepest layers of the being, the quantum, etheric, or mental levels, from which it then manifests in the physical body.

During this part, we also get to speak directly with any of the energies that may be blocking and limiting the body, such as spirit attachments (entities), etheric implants, and so forth. We learn how they got attached, absorbed, or created and how they influenced the client's well-being. We clear them from the body with love, and we ask the Higher Self to restore the damage they may have caused. As the client becomes conscious of the root causes of any imbalance, miraculous and spontaneous healing becomes possible. The Higher Self begins to direct the body to heal itself very quickly, or even immediately. It is an incredible experience to witness and be a part of! For me, it feels like witnessing miracles as I witness the client rapidly healing right before my eyes.

At the end of each session, after I bring my client back to full alertness, we talk about the session and what they remembered and learned. They most often describe a feeling of their consciousness being aside but aware and hearing themselves speak. The words just coming out. Some remember more than others. The client receives a recording of the session to listen to and integrate. One of the most important parts of the healing is listening to the recording after the session. That moves all the information into the conscious mind and allows more conscious choices. Clients share with me that even years after initially having the session, re-listening to the session recording continues to work with them. They hear new things, have new insights, and receive the confirmations they were needing for their life path.

If you are reading this now and you had a session with me or any other practitioner from a similar modality, I invite you to find your own recording and listen to it. This will also bring back the energy and any visions you had. You might even enter a meditative state and reconnect with your Higher-Self to receive more healing and guidance. This could be a very powerful tool. Listen to it while meditating or lying down and focus on your body to sense the energies. Journal about your takeaways and share with others what you have learned, and it will become a more integrated experience as part of your life.

I believe that one of the main purposes of IQH sessions is to strengthen the multidimensional communication and individual connection with your Higher Self and spirit guides so that can trust your inner guidance in your day-to-day life. Many clients report that during the days after their session, they continue to receive vital information and validations.

The sessions are facilitated as individual ceremonies that are reaching towards the Divine to create a positive change and to experience a significant turning point in one's life. We close the IQH session by giving gratitude to all the supportive energies of the Higher Consciousness Collective and separate our energetic field from one another and dedicate the session towards the benefit of all.

Sometimes, the information that is being shared during our sessions is so profound and can benefit the collective human family. When permitted by the client, we publish videos of the sessions on social media and on our private social network called *Source⊚Energy*. This private network allows us to have the freedom of speech that is so crucial for us to be able to share important and beneficial messages and updates regarding the Ascension process.

Michael and I were guided to establish our own spiritual, faith-based organization, *New Earth Ascending*, a global ministry that is dedicated to the ascension of Mother Earth and the human family. *New Earth Ascending* is dedicated to the establishment of heart-centered, sustainable communities and educational centers around the world.

This book was born from the pure intention and desire to help anyone that comes across it. I feel blessed to have witnessed, facilitated, and shared this collection of sessions. You can find more information about *New Earth Ascending* and a list of links by scanning the QR code on the back cover of the book or visit our website. www.newearthascending.org

MEETING AVA

Ava and I met each other for the first time at a silent meditation retreat. We practiced meditation together for many hours of the day, and it was a fabulous experience that we felt blessed to share. We only got to talk for the first time after breaking the silence during the last night of our stay. Ava offered to share with me a short sound healing session with the very impressive crystal bowls that were in the space which I was happy to receive.

During the session, Ava started to sing while playing on these massive crystal bowls with a beautiful angelic voice that I didn't expect. She hovered her hand softly just above my body, and for moments, ever so lightly, touched my body with the tip of her fingers.

Then something unusual happened. Energy sparked like lightning shooting out of the tips of her fingers into my head, and I had a sensation of energy weaving rapidly, like spiders weaving a web of light inside my brain. I was very surprised and curious and inspired to get to know Ava more.

We agreed that the next time Ava came to town she would reach out to me and maybe we could trade sessions. I just felt "called" to work with her, and I'm so happy about this magical experience that brought us together to start this collaboration. The rest of this story you will read in the next chapter and throughout the book.

Thanks to the divine Source, Ava, and the friends that helped me transcribe the manuscript, I didn't need to write much by myself. We did our best to keep it as close as possible to the original conversations. We edited it only lightly to make it easier to read. We also removed descriptions of my hypnosis protocols.

You will probably notice that some of the English grammar is not correct. It is not because our editor missed it. We decided to stay as true to the original material as possible while ensuring that the text had a flow to it and was enjoyable to read. We also wanted to enable the high-frequency communication of the channel to be transmitted as purely as possible.

By now, you already know that English is not my first language. You will also notice that even though Ava's English is great, when the Higher Self is speaking, "They" use Ava's vocabulary differently than how Ava would. If you ever listen to the session recordings, you will notice unique intonations from the different characters and aspects of consciousness that are speaking through her. When we converted it into text, it may be perceived as if they also speak with some English mistakes, but they are very precise with their words. Sometimes they were looking for the right words and did their best to explain complex ideas in a simple manner for all of us to understand. I hope we managed to convey the feeling of Ava's Higher Self aspect for you, even just by reading this as a text.

If you listen to the original recordings, you will hear that during some parts of the sessions the information is delivered at an extremely fast rate. It was explained to us that it would be beneficial for people to hear the original recordings to receive the energy and codes from Ava's voice and transmission. They told us to edit it into smaller sections so it would be easier for people to integrate. Just by reading, you may feel a high frequency energy current moving through you and may need a moment to allow the information to integrate. If this happens, I highly recommend using the simple grounding method of putting your bare feet on the earth.

We will do our best to edit the original audio files and share them as soon as we can on our private membership platforms. You will find an invitation to join them freely or by donation through the book. We know that this book is only the beginning of our collaboration, and if you would like to receive more updates when more is being shared, you can sign up for the newsletter to be notified and join our online Readers' Zone.

The information "They" shared with us is very powerful, and I know it had a strong impact on my life. I ask you to read this with deep listening in your heart. We are not claiming this to be the one and only truth. We ask you to read it like a story that might be true and might just be a story to awaken your own deeper realizations. Please feel into your heart and take what inspires and empowers you and leave the rest behind.

With Much Love,

Ron Amit

AVA'S INTRODUCTION

"Be Yourself. Everyone else is already taken."
— Oscar Wilde

Everyone loves a good story, right? You may have noticed that in most stories, the main character is the hero of the story. You know, the "Chosen One;" the one who saves the world from the brink of destruction and heralds in the next Golden Age. These heroes often seem to carry the weight of the whole world on their shoulders. It's so much pressure. Why does this predicament resonate so deeply within us? In real life, is it ever really up to just us? Hardly. This plot line can set us up to feel separate and alone, facing the trials of life and death on our own. However, in these hero's journeys we hear about, the *chosen one* usually dives deep into this illusion of separation and aloneness, claims his or her destiny, and then emerges triumphant, feeling both empowered and sovereign, while also feeling connected to life and to love and to All That Is.

Often, the stories we don't hear about are when the hero does not succeed. Life doesn't work out the way we hoped it would. The foe that must really be vanquished is the disappointment at our own sense of failure. How many of us choose to stay in the comfort zone because of the fear we might fail? Maybe it's this edge that inspires us so profoundly. We long to feel connected and part of a bigger story, and we long to see someone else going for it, not knowing if they'll succeed. We can watch their razor's edge journey from the comfort of our own home, not risking our own necks or fortunes. Who will risk the true perils of the hero's journey, before success and happily ever after are guaranteed? I think the real hero's journey is making the choice to go for it, knowing very well it might fail.

This story you are about to read happens to be my story, so naturally, I am the *chosen one* of this tale. I didn't mean to tell this story; it happened by accident, and I have let myself be pulled along by its powerful force. This surprising story inspires me to live my own life story with the courage of a hero, for we are each the hero of our own story...when we choose to be! Whether we fail or succeed is not really the point...it's whether we are brave enough to really dive in and live our lives, come what may. Through this brave act, we are risking the bitter taste of disappointment, the annihilation of our own egos or even our own life, risking it all by taking a stand for the truth and love that lies within us, calling for us to rise.

This story is profoundly vulnerable and explores almost every taboo topic I could imagine. I still feel hot embarrassment rise within me at the thought of sharing these transcripts of my hypnosis sessions with you. If I had realized everything I was saying while in a private room, deeply relaxed in a hypnotic trance, would be shared for all to read, I would not have agreed to do it. I find this fact humbling and amusing, for I consider myself to be an authentic and transparent person.

Preparing to share this book with you has been the most terrifying and exhilarating thing I've ever done. I've had to gather all my courage in order to come to this moment, and here we are, sharing the transcripts of audio recordings of me, put into a hypnotic trance, and then asked questions by the co-author of this book. My hero's journey — will I be annihilated in this choice to put it all out there? Will you think I'm crazy? Will my family disown me? Will I ruin my reputation and my career? I don't know, but I embark upon the journey because I know the truth in my heart.

This information blows my mind and heart wide open and turns everything I thought I knew upside down and inside out. Occasionally, I thought I was making it all up, which I hear is a common feeling among those who are put into hypnotic trance. Most of the time though, I get "truth bumps," (what I call goose bumps that arise spontaneously on my skin when I hear something that feels especially potent and true) when I listen back to these sessions. I'm often brought to tears and utter awe and am left feeling simultaneously humble and tender; empowered, inspired, and courageous. I am still shocked by the technical detail and profound depth shared in these pages, even after reading this information many times over.

Perhaps this story we share with you is science fiction, merely an entertaining spin on the nature of the Universe and our place within it. I am a storyteller after all. I have an active imagination and once tested at a genius level IQ. Maybe I could have made all this up just to entertain myself or to feel special. Believe me, I've questioned myself multiple times when I first heard this story and realized it was my own voice speaking.

However, I didn't seek out hypnosis to make up grandiose stories. I met Ron at a silent meditation course and did not even speak to him until we after we had been sitting in the same room together in silence for ten days. When I found out that he was a hypnotherapist, and he offered to trade sessions with me I was intrigued. I was curious to know more about my soul's journey and how I was doing on my path. I wanted to be more in alignment with myself and thought a little insight could be helpful.

I was curious to know if my premature birth and early childhood traumas were impacting my current life situation. I sought a deeper understanding of my vivid dream world, where I repeatedly died or was killed in graphic and sometimes painful detail. Sometimes in these dreams I was a man, or I was old, or very young, or a different race or living in a part of the world I had never visited. Occasionally, I dreamed I was even a different species living on a different planet. I wondered what to make of this seemingly "realer than real life" dream world. I've always wanted to be of service, and I live in deep devotion to stewarding this precious planet in a good way. I have never had much interest in the capitalist model and lived for years off-grid, living simply with the land. I wondered why I was the way I was.

I also wanted to understand my chronic illness and fears, my hesitation to really live my greatest life. Why did I keep choosing my backup plan, hiding out in the sanctuary of deep forests without cable, WIFI, or grid power? What was I so afraid of?

I was at a major crossroads in life and unsure of my next steps, so I was seeking greater understanding and courage to live my deepest dreams. I didn't even think I could be hypnotized; I had a very stubborn mind before I learned to meditate. I didn't know what to expect, but I definitely did not expect what you are about to read. I was as surprised as you might be. 'I' likes surprises. No, that's not a grammatical error. You will soon see what 'I' means.

Although I was curious, I didn't feel compelled to seek out a hypnotist to find out more. I had tried that ten years earlier with some fascinating but limited results. I chose the path of meditation to help me understand myself better. As destiny would have it, hypnosis found me, while I was meditating.

When I listen to these stories, I feel a profound inspiration move through me. Something within me screams, "YES, FINALLY, SHE REMEMBERS!" At other times, my mind balks at all this, and I think my subconscious is just caught up in an intense fantasy guilt trip. I found myself thinking that I just needed to lighten up and not carry the weight of the world on my shoulders, which as a Capricorn, I tend to do. "You'll make a total fool of yourself if you share this story." I would say, "Don't tell anyone."

Despite my hesitant inner dialogue, Ron regularly encouraged me to share these sessions. At first, I did agree to share the audio recordings anonymously. I was surprised at how many thousands of people were moved and inspired and wanted more. They also wanted to know who was channeling this information. I squirmed with hot resistance, yet I realized that despite my discomfort in outing myself as either a clear channel or a delusional, New Age nitwit, this story needs to be shared, and so we share it.

Let it be a fantasy, science-fiction story. Let it be truth. It is what it is. May it point you to your own truth.

I have come to understand all good stories must have a little bit of life-or-death drama in them, right? A quest between the forces of good and evil or between love and fear must unfold for a story to be worth telling, worth reading, and worth living. How could this tale be any different? When this story came through, every word came through on a solid foundation of love, trust, and equanimity. Underneath the words was a whisper of "all is well" and "all will be well." I did my best to stay out of the way and allow this rapid torrent of words to pour through me without my ego's filtering program. Still, I was only able to share a fraction of what I was shown. Entire scenes flashed before my minds' eye in a single moment, and when a being came forward, I was aware of far more than what I was able to translate. An intricate multi-dimensional tapestry unfolded before me, complete with the character's past, their emotions, thoughts and additional images overlayed to add meaning, establish trust, and clarify context. It was all I could do just to keep up.

In trance, I was in a super relaxed state, and even when an aspect of myself was experiencing fear or terror in the book, deeper down, I felt ok, and I felt completely safe. Listening back, some of this information hits really close to home, and I've navigated a long journey from fear to love myself. The first two sessions especially have a layer of fear woven into them, as I am a human channeling a perspective far beyond my own capacity and understanding. The channel has an uncanny mastery for weaving stories together in a way that infuses me with a profound sense of peace and hope for humanity and planet Earth.

I have found that in a journey from fear to trust, from pain to peace, we must start somewhere, and so we start at the beginning. The only way around fear is through it. I hope you will keep reading to the end to discover the rich treasures revealed behind the veil of fear, story, and illusion.

In this time of great change, climate crisis, and a global pandemic, where increased fear, division, and uncertainty abound. . .it's time for us to remember. It's time to wake up from our collective sleep and evolve as a species, together, in unity, as one human family. For so long, we have forgotten who we truly are. It was a necessary period for our growth and understanding to feel this sensation of separation from Source, or what some call God. Now is the time to remember and to return home inside ourselves. Now is the time to sing the songs of remembering.

Love,
AVA

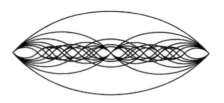

A GIFT OF SONGS

Together with the book, you will find an invitation to listen to recordings from some parts of the original sessions and songs that were recorded by AVA during the writing process of this book. We want to make clear that the name of the book *The Songs of Remembering* is not suggesting that those particular songs are THE songs or the only songs. We share them to give dimensionality to the process we have experienced.

Ava shared her artistic musical journey and compositions with me during our writing process, and after listening to them myself, I have found them to be most appropriate to be shared within the book. Ava was getting ready to share them publicly, but just before publishing the book she felt that her creative process with some of her songs may not be completed just yet. She agreed to share it for the readers to listen online on our special online Readers' Zone that we have crafted to go along with reading the book.

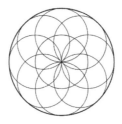

ONLINE READERS' ZONE

We have crafted for you a step-by-step process that goes together with the book, you will find the instantiations as you go like a treasure hunt game full of surprises. By typing the website www.songsofremembering.org or scanning the QR code with your cellular device will be led you to the sign-up page for our interactive Reader's Zone that is hosted on *Source◉Energy,* New Earth Ascending's private social network, with a special a fun portal just for the books' readers.

In the **Readers' Zone** you would also find:

- Original recordings from the sessions
- AVA's songs
- Our Miscellaneous Topics
- Live events, live Feed, and chat to connect with us and other readers.
- More gifts and surprises

Scan Me

THE DESIGNER

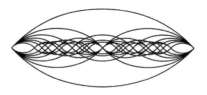

SESSION ONE

A few months after our initial meeting, Ava visited our town and we met for a hike. The following day she came to my home to experience her first hypnosis session with me. The interview part with Ava was great. I remember being captivated by her stories, and I remember being a bit surprised to hear about the type of dreams she was having during her life. She mentioned that in her dreams she had died in every possible way; I thought it was unique and fascinating. Ava also had some interesting stories about her life experiences, and I could feel that she was already doing a great amount of self-reflective inner work with herself. She was energetic and talked freely and transparently, and I could feel that she was comfortable sharing her deepest truth with me in an honest way. Even when the stories brought up difficult emotions, she allowed herself to feel it and express her new awareness of it. Even throughout this process, she was receiving new insights while looking back on her life.

During the interview, I do my best to help my clients recognize patterns by themselves that may point them to some of their main lessons in life. This could give us an indication of subconscious behaviors and core wounds that might still be affecting and shaping their life. This is a common experience, and I could feel that Ava was doing deep conscious work with high integrity and accountability about her experiences. A few of the stories still had some charge around them, and I was hoping to find out from her Higher Self the perspective that would help her learn from those events.

The stories which have a negative emotional charge are often shared from a victim, rescuer, or persecutor perspective. They have the energy of frustration, sadness, fear or pain. The vocabulary will sound more like blaming or giving power to external circumstances. You may be familiar with the Drama Triangle, a concept that was first shared by Stephen B. Karpmanwhich has become a widely known tool in psychotherapy to analyze one's ego and dramatic relational tendencies. If you never heard of it, it might be beneficial for you to search for writings or videos about it. These archetypes and patterns are very common in the human experience as we are all going through painful events and often believe ourselves to be a victim to painful life circumstances. As part of the learning process in the Earth school, we all agreed to experience and evolve from suffering. Just like every baby that learns to walk, we fall and we rise again. We make mistakes, and we learn from them.

I too find myself blaming others for my suffering at times. When I catch myself looping in stories about my pain, I practice shifting those perspectives into Oneness and self-responsibility for my part in creating my path of suffering, consciously or unconsciously. I noticed that Ava does this too and has a part of herself that notices when she is not seeing the bigger picture, so she is open for reflection and eager to discover the higher perspective.

At a certain point during the interview, I felt that we established a heart-to-heart connection easily, just like old friends. As we both mentioned in the introduction, Ava was skeptical about her ability to be hypnotized, and when I started to do the practices and the induction, she noticed that she was getting very sensitive to the sounds around the room and the floor above us. This sensitivity is natural and was giving us confirmation that something was definitely working. She was concerned that it would be disturbing for her, so I gave her suggestions to help her focus on my voice and her inner experiences to cancel out the background noises. I noticed she was entering quickly into a trance from her body language, the movement of her eyes, and her breathing patterning. So, we continued on with the induction process.

When we started the quantum journey, Ava saw white light all around, and then bright lights of all colors. Next, she saw a city, but not an Earthly city, a city of light with "concentric rings and light; there is no sun. It's just bright." I asked her to focus on it and tell me more, but then she saw only white light that quickly shifted to all-black. She described "It's less than black. It's just nothing. I don't have a body; it's just this absence of everything. It's not even black; it's just space." She noticed that she didn't have a body, just a point of awareness, in a void. She enjoyed that place, but there wasn't much more information that could be shared from that perspective, so I moved her to the next scene.

Ron: Now, you can open the scene like you open a book and tell me your first impressions.

AVA: Maybe I'm in a hospital. I kind of feel like I'm in a hospital corridor.

R: What makes you feel this way? Connect with what you are feeling; it will become more clear as you talk.

A: Everything is really clean and sterile; there is nothing, nothing soft. It's just like a corridor, and it smells really clean and sterile and like bright lights. It's not very comfortable. It's stark.

R: Wonderful, you are doing very good. Continue to describe what you see, what you hear. What does it sound like? Do you feel like now you have a body?

A: Yeah, I have a body.

R: Look down to the direction of your feet.

A: Mmm. . . I feel like I'm on. . . I can't tell if I'm making this up.

R: It's ok, just go with it. What do you see? Use your imagination if you want.

A: I feel like I'm in an examining room, and I'm on a table. It's cold, cold metal. There is something over me that is supposed to be a blanket, but it doesn't actually touch me, it's like a case.

R: What color is it?

A: Mostly gray, but silver, white. It doesn't make sense. It's not color so much.

R: Tell me more about your body. Look at yourself and tell me what you notice. How old do you feel?

A: Little.

R: Little? Describe how little.

A: *(Trembling, can hardly speak)* Maybe I'm very, very little; I'm little.

R: Do you feel male or female?

A: I think I'm female.

R: Very good. What else do you feel? I see some emotions. What are you feeling?

A: Fear. *(Trembling, crying, and her voice becomes like a little girl.)*

R: You feel scared? I'm here with you; you don't need to worry. Why are you scared? Take a deep breath into this fear and tell me about it. You can let it go; you don't need that.

A: I don't know why I'm here. I'm really little, and I thought I was on Earth. Now, I'm not; now, I'm on this table somewhere else. It's cold in here.

R: I understand. Let's learn what's happening next. Let's look at what's happening after you've been there for a little while on this table, ok? Move a little bit forward and tell me what is happening, everything that you see.

A: *(Crying)* They look like. . . *(frowning)*

R: Can you describe it for me?

A: I don't know; they look like half praying mantis and half machine. I don't understand. It's big, tall. Sometimes it has a lab coat on, and sometimes it's naked.

R: Can you describe more?

A: I'm really sick, I think. I don't think I'm going to make it on

Earth. Something happened. I came too soon. I wasn't supposed to come yet.

R: I see. So, you came too early, and now you are in this machine?

A: No, I'm not in the machine. There is this praying mantis machine looking over me.

R: What does it do when it's over you?

A: I think it's trying to fix me, so I survive on Earth.

R: Very good. Wonderful. So, let's see what's happening next. Tell me what is happening.

A: I don't want to go back. They just put me in a box [an incubator] down there. I don't want to go back to Earth.

R: You don't want to go back to where?

A: I don't want to go back to Earth.

R: Because on Earth they put you in a box?

A: Yes, because I came too soon.

R: What happened that you decided to come so soon? Do you know what happened? Let's learn about why you arrived so early. Would you like to learn about that?

A: Yes.

R: Ok, then let's close this scene and go back to the moment before you arrived to Earth, back, back, back. To this moment before you arrived, be there now, and tell me what do you notice? Where are you now? Look around you now. Describe what you see? What do you learn?

A: Maybe I'm in a womb. I'm like a little, tiny bean.

R: Very good. So you're in the womb? What do you recognize and notice in the womb? How does it feel?

A: It's big. It's warm.

R: What can you hear?

A: The heartbeat.

R: Do you feel the heartbeat of your mom?

A: Yes.

R: What else do you notice?

A: I have hands. I've never had hands before.

R: That's the first time? That's nice, right?

A: It's weird.

R: Yeah, what else do you notice there?

A: I feel a lot of pressure.

R: Where do you feel this pressure?

A: All around and inside, it's like it's inside. It's too much. I don't know if I can do this.

R: It feels too tight for you?

A: Yeah.

R: What do you notice now?

A: I don't want to be here.

R: You don't want to be in this tight place. Why don't you want to be there?

A: It's so fragile.

R: Because it's fragile.

A: It's so fragile. It's too much in this little thing. It's too much energy in this little, tiny thing. It doesn't fit. It's too big. It doesn't fit.

R: So, it's too big around you, and you're too small inside that, or the opposite?

A: *(Crying)* The weight's crushing; it's too big. It's terrible.

R: What's happening next? What goes through your mind?

A: *(Sighs)* I'm in my recurring night terror.

R: Tell me about that. Can you describe it?

A: It's like so much pressure. It's infinite pressure, and it's all too big and too small at the same time. I'm trapped in this tiny, tiny little box; I am so much bigger; it doesn't fit. I'm exploding out of it. I can't stay inside. I can't figure out how to stay in this tiny, little body. I don't fit. I don't fit in here. It's just so hard. I'm going to explode. It's too small and too little.

R: And how do you try to get in there? What do you do to get in?

A: I keep feeling my hands.

R: That helps you to get in?

A: I feel my connection to. . . I feel the belly button thing. That thing that comes out [the placenta]; it's not big enough though.

R: Very good. Thank you for sharing with me. You can close that scene. Let's drift and float to another important day. [I moved her to the next scene.]

ON THE SHIP

A: I'm on a ship, at a meeting.

R: **Describe what you see. Describe the ship for me.**

A: Everything is curved, no straight lines. Everything is silver and smooth. The table just emerges out from the floor; there is no construction of anything. Everything is designed from the ground, and the ground becomes the shape that it needed to be.

R: **You said you are in a meeting. Who do you meet? Describe that for me.**

A: Everyone is wearing skintight suits with a symbol on the chest.

R: **Can you describe this symbol a little bit?**

A: It's a ring, intersecting rings.

R: **Rings, intersecting rings? How many beings do you see that you meet?**

A: There's not that many; maybe there are a dozen.

R: **Wonderful. Now can you listen and tell me what you hear, so we can learn what the meeting is about?**

A: We are discussing all the problems on Earth. There is a little bit of an argument, not a bad fight, just everyone has a different belief on what to do about it.

R: **I understand. Share more with me.**

A: Well, I'm one of the designers of the people, the humans, right, so I understand how they were made, and they were supposed to be able to be so kind and loving and so good to each other. When that thing went wrong, some people, . . . they want to blow up the Earth, or they want to take off the humans all together. They just made such a mess. [From this point Ava's voice shifted to speak directly from this higher aspect of her consciousness.]

R: Who wants to blow up the Earth and take the humans?

A: The other people on the team. They work on other planets. They don't know [Earth] as well. I've been assigned to Earth to help for a while. Helping to guide the humans along. I love them so much, and they are being so mean to each other *(crying)*. They were supposed to be so good. They are all lost in the fear.

R: What happened that it went so wrong from this beautiful design to now, that the humans are acting like this? What changed?

A: There was an asteroid with a bacteria that corrupted their genetic code; it got in there; it got into the DNA. It wasn't supposed to be able to do that. I thought I had done a better job at making it, so it couldn't be corrupted like that. I feel like I failed. I failed all of them. They weren't supposed to get contaminated. Now they are destroying everything. All my babies. . . *(crying hard)*. They're all so precious, and I don't want them to destroy the Earth. I don't want them to. . . . I want them to have a chance.

R: Why do the other beings want to destroy the Earth? Why do they care?

A: Because they are messing with the nukes, things that could destroy the Earth, and it ripples out beyond the Earth. All the nukes, and their contamination is going out; it's going out. .
.

R: The humans are destroying things that can affect others too?

A: Yeah.

R: And they don't want that to happen?

A: Yeah, they are becoming a danger. They are isolated; it was an isolated experiment to begin with because it was dangerous. I thought I could do it.

R: So, from the beginning it was isolated?

A: Yes, the Earth, because we don't usually give them so much free will, and they forget too. It's a lot, but I thought they could do it. I thought their hearts were pure enough. I thought they could do it, but they are destroying it all. They [the other team members] might be right. We might have to put them all down. They might not be able to evolve. I thought they could make it. I thought they could ascend, but I don't know if they can (*crying*). I've gone in to help before, but it's been a long time. I don't want to go back.

R: Tell me about yourself; what do they call you on the ship? Listen for what they call you now. What is your cosmic name?

A: I, I, (*pronounced: Aee, Ahh-ee*) They said it has a similar meaning to her name. It's the life giver; it's the light. God asked to make the life here on Earth. He wants that being to be the union of matter, of density, and light. Since I was the light, I thought I could design. I thought I could help make the balance between the light and the density. I thought I could do it. Everyone thought I could.

R: So, how did you do it? How did you design them? Can you explain the process? Did you do it by yourself or with others?

[Now after they shared with me their name, from this point on I'll refer to Ava as "I".]

I: No, I can't do that. It's a lot to do by yourself.

R: So, who did you design it with?

I: With All. There was a team though, of beings from around all over that had made life on other planets, but not with such dense bodies, and the forgetting, and free will, and the power to innovate life, and create. It's a lot. There was this desire to take it up to the next level and merge all the consciousness. The density with the light and the power of creation and destruction. We thought that we could guide it in a good way and create this amazing creation, a being of beauty and love to help manifest All into a new dimension. Into everything.

R: That's wonderful.

I: But it's hard.

R: Let's go back to this discussion. What are they talking about now?

I: They are about to give up. The bombs went off, the ripples, all those people dead. I wanted to give them another chance. I'm on the team that sent in the volunteers. Helping to organize the volunteers. I wasn't going to go. I was going to organize the volunteers, because I'm one of the designers. It made more sense for me not to go down because I have a [unique] perspective. I've been here since the beginning of Earth, before. We brought the cells from the other places, and it took a long time to build Earth. It didn't make sense to be in it, to volunteer, but they want to destroy Earth. They want to annihilate it because they are making such a mess. I think I decided to go last minute and say, can I please try? Can I please try to help them wake up? They are all love. They are supposed to love each other and take care of each other. The greed and the fear, they've been so bad to each other; it breaks my heart to see my babies grow up to be such monsters. Maybe I should just let them destroy it, but Earth is so beautiful; we did such a good job. I wasn't supposed to get attached, but it's been so long.

R: Can you share with me more about the process of how the Earth was created from the beginning?

I: Through the songs. The songs bring the matter into a vibration that holds, because it's all song, right? Everything is song; everything is just sound. Certain songs, certain sounds make matter coalesce and then it stays. Then it spins; you've got to spin it. So, the songs bind it together, the cell, no, smaller, smaller than the atoms, the smallest dots. You start with those. Sing the right song so that they stick and spin, and when they stick and they spin, they have a pole. They create gravity when they stick, and they spin, so they spin and then they coalesce more. It's like when you have one drop of mercury and all the rest of the mercury comes to it, and it makes a bigger blob.

It's a slow, patient spinning. . .then the gravity builds to the point that the songs/sounds start singing themselves, and the bonds, the molecular bonds sing, and they sing each other. So, you sing the songs first, and then they start to sing it themselves. Then they coalesce themselves. You start the song, and you guide the song; you sing with them, right? You're holding space and singing with them, and there's a team of us singing the songs, and we sing them alive, and then they keep spinning and building. Then you have the whole shape of the Earth spinning, and it makes a sphere, because it's spinning, right, and it's singing. Because all the bonds singing themselves together. We can sing them apart too. There are songs that will sing them apart. That's what they want to do, to sing the Earth apart.

When we sing it together, and it keeps spinning, and then we sing the songs for the first life to start. You have to start really small; you can't just start with a symphony of beings, you have to start with a note, each note. Each note makes a song, there's a song for that single cell. *(Ava: I need another blanket. Cold. Cold. I need another blanket.)*

[I mention to my clients before the session that the flow of energy through their body could shift and change from hot to cold or concentrate in different areas of the body. This is natural and I invite them to always share their experience with me, so that I can make sure they stay comfortable. During all the sessions, Ava's physical experience was very noticeable, the movement of her closed eyes, the shaking and twitching of her body. When Ava got cold, she was really shivering and her teeth were knocking.]

I: So, the songs aren't just songs; they aren't just sounds. They are the dragons everyone talks about, right. The dragons are the wavelengths of sound, the vibrations of everything.

[Some traditions call the ley lines dragon lines. Ava references dragons here but does not fully explain or ever refer to it again. However, as often happens during the channeling, Ava shares what she can verbally, as quickly as possible, even though a lot more information is given to her in flashes of images, pictures, and moments where information she already knows within her consciousness is briefly highlighted. She brings back what she can, but it is impossible to share everything that is being communicated during the sessions. This detail felt important to expand upon.]

[Ava's note: Dragons are incorporated into legends across many cultures. Anyone can do a brief Internet search to discover how many ways dragons are referenced throughout many cultures in legend, myth, and cosmology. Here, the Higher Self is casually referring to the source of dragons actually being the interpretation of the wavelengths of sound that the entire manifest universe is built with/upon. The dragons ARE the fabric/tapestry/matrix of Life. Mystics and artists and those sensitive to energy can sense or see this underlying fabric and are even aware that this fabric is conscious and can travel and be traveled upon. The human mind cannot fully understand non-duality or that matter is a paradoxical illusion — both a particle and a wave — and so analogies and metaphors often emerge to describe the indescribable. Dragons, the consciousness in the fabric of existence, feel absolutely immense, incredible, intimidating, and awe-inspiring, and so the dragon emerges in culture as a way to help make sense of a human being witnessing or being aware of the underlying fabric of energy that moves through all things.

Dragons are magic and mystery. Dragons can carry us to heights we could never go alone. This vibration of everything has immense power and infinite energy, hence, the "breathing fire" interpretation emerges. Dragons can be understood as a human interpretation and personification of this aspect of the Great Mystery.

I: So, when you are riding a wavelength, that is one song line, that is weaving. The song singers are the weavers. It's the same thing. Weaving the tapestries, weaving the songs together. The waves...you can ride the wave. If you can ride the wave, if you can jump on and be patient and not go too fast or too slow, you can guide the waves, which are the songs, which are the threads. It's all the same thing. It's hard to describe; it's the same thing. It's the particle and the wave. It's the song and it's the sound. It's the song that's actually tangible, but it's also just the sound. The sound creates the matter; it's the sounds that make the wavelengths that weave themselves together enough to make the light that you can see. The light you can see makes up the illusion of the world. It's the song, really. There's nothing solid about it, really. It just seems like it because we've sung the songs to weave the thread to make the light that weaves the Earth that allows matter so dense to hold, grab on, and stick in the gravity of it all.

So, I'm one of the singers, the weavers, the designer, the song singers. We weave the Earth because we wanted to bring the different consciousnesses all together. It's amazing, the idea. Bring all the different consciousnesses of all the different dimensions together in one thing. It's never been done before; and yet forever, you know, that whole piece. . . I can't describe that part. It's too hard, you wouldn't. . . I can't describe that part.

R: **You are doing a really great job, thank you. Now take another deep breath into this body, so it can relax more and feel the energy. You can also start the healing on the vessel** [the body is commonly being referred to as the vessal] **that you are speaking through. Would you start the healing for me please?**

I: With the songs?

R: **The vessel that you speak from right now. Do you know the vessel from which you speak from right now?**

I: Ah, yes.

R: **Can you start the healing process on this vessel now please? Can you start the healing for Ava?**

I: Yes, she needs, um. . .

[This request to start the healing was a bit disorienting for the consciousness I was speaking with, and I could feel that we were already speaking with a Higher Self type of consciousness. I assumed that this being could both heal the body and talk at the same time, but I didn't want to start receiving the information about it and cut the flow of information they shared. I redirected back to where we had stopped.]

R: **Good. I would love to learn more information from you. Let's take another deep breath, and let's go back to the meeting and learn more. Be there now and tell me, what do you see next?**

I: Seems like we are taking a break. It's just me at the table looking out. There are windows all around; you can see the stars, but not, we are in the star. It doesn't make sense.

R: **It's ok. It doesn't have to make sense. Just describe what you notice? What are you thinking of while you're there?**

I: I want to protect the babies. They're all my children, all of them. I want them to be safe and happy. I don't know what to do though, because they aren't getting it. They just keep hurting each other.

R: **You aren't sure what to do with them?**

I: We are sending in a lot of beings; there are a lot that are coming. They all want to help. It's hard; they keep going in to help. It's harder than they think it's going to be. Even for me, the Designer. It's hard when you're in it. It's really hard not to forget. It's designed to make you forget. That's the whole song. The song is to forget, so to remember, it's the hardest thing. So we are sending them all in, with hopes that they'll remember, while we're singing the songs for them to forget (*exasperated*). We can't help it; the songs have already been sung. The songs are for forgetting.

R: **You said that there was a way to break the song or to un-sing them. There is no other way to sing back the songs of the forgetting?**

I: We are; we are singing the songs of remembering. We can take them back, but it's the foundation of the whole matrix of the whole planet. It might collapse; we don't know what will happen. We can't just undo those songs; they are so deep; we've been singing them for so long, and they are so old. We've been singing those songs for billions of years. We can't undo them all.

R: **I understand. Ok, so you said you are sending many people from many places, many volunteers?**

I: Yeah, they are mostly all volunteers. There are a few we begged to go. They were begging me to go.

R: **So, some you choose and some volunteer?**

I: They don't have to come. They don't have to say yes. Not all of them volunteered. We asked some if they would come.

R: **Ok, thank you. So, what's the purpose of them?**

I: To raise the vibration, to remember. We think they have a better chance of remembering through the songs of forgetting. We are singing the songs of remembering now; it's time, because there is too much forgetting. So, we are singing the songs of remembering.

R: **Then, you think they will pick up the songs and will be able to...**

I: That's what we hope. That's the hope, yes, that they will hear the songs of remembering, and when they remember, they can help others unweave their songs of forgetting because the songs of forgetting are really thick. We did too good a job.

R: **Okay, so from your perspective, if there is someone who is remembering already, when he is on the Earth and**

remembering, what can he do to assist you guys in this process? Is it easier to do it from within the Earth?

I: Yeah, you can't. . .yeah. It's easier from inside, if you can remember, but it's hard. If you remember too much, then you don't fit anymore. It's this really, really fine balance of forgetting and remembering, so that you can still participate. Ava's struggling because she remembers too much. It's hard for her because she doesn't know; she doesn't understand. She's remembering too much, so she doesn't know how to be in the world because it doesn't make sense to her, because she is remembering and everyone else has forgotten, so it seems like she's insane. She thinks she's crazy because she remembers too much. Then she tries to forget, so she can fit in, and then she forgets too much. It's so hard. I didn't know how hard it would be to ride that edge of remembering and forgetting, so that you can be in the world and sing the songs. She came, it's like the last ditch effort, the singers come in to sing the songs, right? To actually sing the songs that everyone's been hearing forever; they just don't remember that they've heard them.

So, now we are actually singing them out loud. It's hard. They are hard songs to remember. They want to be forgotten, and they don't. That's why it's so hard for her to record them. . . That's funny *(laughing)*. She spent four billion years singing songs of forgetting, because that was the game. Those were the rules; she was the designer. She wasn't the inventor; she is the designer. The team invented the idea, and she liked the idea, so she agreed to being the designer, but she's been singing the songs of forgetting for so long. Now she's supposed to sing the songs of remembering and it goes against four billion years of singing songs of forgetting to weave the foundation for humans. It's so hard. It's really hard. I see why she feels she's always failing because everyone is watching. Everyone in the Universe is watching this game right now, and she feels like she is totally on the spot; she's supposed to do a good job; she's the designer;

she has to do a good job. If she can't do it, how can anyone else do it? So, if she can't do it, then they are going to destroy the world. It's too much. It's too much pressure on one person. She doesn't know how. She didn't want to come. But everyone was like "It's not working; you're the designer; you know how it's designed, so you should go in." I didn't design the corruption, the contamination that came in. We weren't expecting it.

R: So, you said that it came in through an asteroid somehow, some kind of bacteria. Can you describe more of that? How did that destroy your creation, and why is it affecting the humans?

I: I thought that the DNA. . .we stripped down the DNA to such a simple. . . I know simple sounds funny to you, but it is such a simple thing, that we didn't think it could be broken, but I was wrong. I was mistaken because I had never sung the songs of hate and fear and pain. I mean the songs were in there. I never sang them from a place of hate. Even the songs of pain were songs of love, but with an illusion of pain, so that there could be learning. But I never sang the songs for the sake of singing dark songs, and I didn't realize that anyone would want to do that. I don't know why they are doing that. I don't know why. There's such an armor around it. I can't get in to understand why they would want to sing those songs. But, those songs, they were just nice enough that they tickled the DNA into relaxing, and then they got in there. It was too late. All the things I had set up to keep it from breaking; I didn't think it was penetrable.

R: So, there were some types of civilizations that were living in harmony before this asteroid came?

I: They weren't so civilized.

R: Tell me about that time.

I: It was early. We had been building the Earth for so long; it was such a huge project, and then we would slowly sing the songs of different life and then let that life sing itself. You can't sing the song for them, because then they won't know how to sing their own song. So, you have to sing little bits to them, and then they sing the songs; that's evolution. They sing their own songs, then you can come in and sing them another little phrase. But you can't sing it for them, or they won't know how to sing it for themselves. So, we would sing them little songs, and then they would grow, and then finally it was time to merge the beings that had evolved on the Earth, that were made for the Earth, because they had to be right for the Earth; they had to have been singing the songs of the Earth, for the Earth, with the Earth for long enough that they were of the Earth. Then we brought in the DNA from the other realms, and we added it. Then we watched those new births. They were so cute.

R: Tell me about them. How did they look?

I: They were hairier because we added it to some of the primate species because the hands seemed like a good thing. I like the hands. The hands seemed like they would work because it's similar [to their brains]. It was cool the way they sang the songs. They sang their hands into 5s. There are many in the Universe that are 4 or 3 or 6 or 1, but 5 seemed like a nice number for a hand, because they could really match the hand with their brains, and that seemed like a good thing.

So, I picked them; that seemed like a good one, so when they came out, their hands were so cute. So, They had the hands. . . The monkeys were there, but then once we put in the DNA, they saw their hands differently for the first time. They had never seen their hands the way they saw them. That was the first thing that happened; they saw their hands. When they saw their hands. . .it was different, they were aware that they were seeing their hands. It's hard to describe the consciousness of having hands and using hands, and then really seeing your hand and realizing that you are this being. It's different.

R: It's like she saw in the womb, when she finally saw her hands.

[Ava's note: When I was regressed to the experience of being in my mother's womb, I noticed my hands through fresh eyes and thought it was the first time I had been embodied. This demonstrates the power of the forgetting songs, and the standard amnesia humans incarnate with.]

I: Oh yeah, and she was like, "F*ck, I did it [again]." She didn't want to go, but she knew she had to because it seemed like the last thing she could try to do to save them because they weren't hearing the songs. So, she thought, well, I know the songs so well, I've been singing them for so long, that she should come in and sing the songs. It's just hard to ride the wave of forgetting and remembering, because when she remembers too much, she gets too scared, it's too big for her to see that much. Then she forgets, and then she doesn't even remember the songs. She forgets that she is the singer. She's the weaver. She sings the weaving songs. She loves that.

R: **That's wonderful. Why did she come here? To sing the songs?**

I: Yeah, she came in to sing the songs.

R: **What's the best way for her to do that from your perspective? I would like to invite all the council of guides to guide us, so she will know exactly what to do from now on to be aligned on her path.**

[We have shifted to talk with the collective consciousness of her Higher Self, Spirit Guides, and "I" as one. I will refer to this combined group as HS.]

HS: It's good that she knows all the steps. She's teaching herself to record herself by herself, which is good, but she needs help. She needs to be able to focus on the songs, because it's so much to try to be so big. She is the designer, I mean, she is friends with Source. She is big, she is really old, and young; she doesn't come on Earth much.

R: **Has she been here before or is this her first time?**

HS: No, she's come before a few times.

R: **How many lifetimes?**

HS: She comes at the major turning points to try and help and guide them because they will make a small change in the songs, and she'll come and see if she can help, but it's always so hard. It's so hard, because usually, if she pushes just a little too hard she gets killed, and if she pushes not hard enough then it doesn't work, so getting just the right amount of pressure on the Earth so that they hear the songs without getting scared. It's hard on her.

R: Does she have any imprints or traumas from those other lifetimes that are affecting her in this lifetime?

HS: She probably remembers; yeah, she remembers snippets of *(pause)*. . . You see with her it's really challenging, because she's the designer, so she's seen every single one come in. All of them. All of them. She watches all of them.

[Ava's note: By watching, they mean witnessing the Akashic records, where watching includes experiencing the full sensory memory of the life lived from within, including the sensations of touch, hearing, taste, smell, and the inner dialogue/emotional experience. Witnessing the Akashic also allows the witnesser to feel and see the impact of a person's life on related people and events from the outside perspective, the life ripple. Watching is not just watching a visual memory, like watching a movie of someone's life from the outside. Many describe that there is very little difference between witnessing an Akashic record and actually living and remembering a full memory of a lived life]. She's got the records of all of them. She loves them all, because she helped sing them in; so they're like her babies, so she feels them all. It's hard to say how many she's come in for; she's come in for a few.]

[The Higher Self was having a hard time knowing which were her own lifetimes and which could be called the "imprinting of a life," a life she experienced from witnessing the Akashic.]

THE BODY SCAN

R: Can you check if in her body, does she store any imprint from those lifetimes that are blocking her? Any energies in her body that are not serving her?

HS: Ah, yes.

R: Where are they?

HS: They're in her hands, and her feet. Uh, yeah. They're in her ears.

R: What's going on with her ears? What's this imprint about?

HS: It's because it's too loud; she hears too much. It's almost like cotton in her own ears, so she doesn't hear too much, but then there's too much cotton, and she can't hear well. She doesn't want to hear so much. She hears all the pain; she hears it all. There's so much pain. She hears the cries; in her dreams she hears all the people. It's too loud.

R: What would you like to do to align her ears and heal them, so she won't carry this pain, and she would hear exactly what she needs to hear for her higher purpose?

HS: It's hard; her body is really sensitive. She kind of knows. She needs to. . .her diet, she has a hard time. It'd be so great if she didn't have to eat. Her body has a hard time assimilating human, plant, food. She's doing better, she needs to. . .

R: What does she need?

HS: Ah, needs to. . .she's been reading it. She has a lot of toxins in her liver and her kidneys from all the medicine they gave her when she was a baby. She is going to do some cleanses, that will be good.

R: What type of cleanse? Can you guide exactly what cleanse she should do?

HS: She needs to do a kidney cleanse and a liver cleanse and no more, she's just so sensitive. Because she's got such big songs, any of the heavy foods, she can't function.

R: What is the best diet for her?

HS: Lots of green juice. Lots of vegetables, she's got a lot of congestion.

R: I would like to invite the cosmic shamans to work on her body now and help her with that. How many light beings would like to come and assist now? I want to call on Raphael again. Is he here?

[While re-listening to the recording I found it odd that I asked for cosmic shamans to join at this point. I normally ask the HS to do all healing. Only if it seems that they are having issues with completing it, do I invite more support or ask to talk with the energy that is creating the blockage. When I communicate with that energy, I guide it to the Light.]

[*Ava's note: Raphael was a spirit guide I met in a previous life-between-life regression thirteen years ago. I had asked him what my purpose was on Earth, and he laughed and lovingly, but firmly told me that I already knew what to do. "She writes it in her journal everyday: meditate, yoga, journal, and sing. Just do it." He wasn't going to tell me anymore until I did that daily.*]

HS: I don't know if he's here this time. That was before, that was before. She met Raphael before she even drank [plant] medicine. She doesn't need that anymore. She knows it's bigger than that.

R: So, who can help her today?

HS: I think we can help her.

R: Ok, good. Thank you. So, what are you using?

HS: Light. . . Looking *(long pause).*

R: I know she is also very allergic to rice. Why is that?

HS: Mmmm, she has a sugar imbalance. There's a sugar processing imbalance.

R: Can you fix that?

HS: Mmmm. . .

R: Can you sing it into wellness?

HS: I don't know. She needs some better shields. So many toxins. She's so pure. She feels it all so much. More than most, she just feels it because she's not used to it. She's attached; she's still disappointed in the contamination of the planet, and she feels that contamination inside of her. She has a hard time with it.

R: Can you release this emotion, thought forms, and attachment?

HS: Yeah, I think so. Yeah.

R: Let's send it back into the Light for healing. What would you like to replace it with?

HS: She's strong. We need to up the filtration. We need to increase her filtration protocols. She's doing good though; she's eating well. . . No more fried foods, Ava. She can't do it; it's too heavy. She likes French fries.

R: It's not good for her?

HS: No. She needs to go on an all liquid diet for a while, all juices. She knows; she's planning on doing that next week actually. She's been gearing up for it, but then she ate French fries. She does know better, but she likes French fries. She is just trying to be human. All the humans are eating French fries. It does taste [good], and she is seeing them all enjoying them so much. She's trying to be. . .she's just always trying so hard to be human, but she's not. She's the designer. It's hard. It's the world. It's not the point. . . The point was to help people find the love in their hearts to join back with Source. That's what she was asked to create. . . People would suffer only so that they would turn into their hearts, so that they would surrender into their hearts. Then they could find God and create paradise on Earth. That's what she was designing.

R: I think it's important that she will be able to do what will help everyone awaken. Let's assist her to align to her mission and to her purpose, so she can do what she came here to do. Let's assist her to align her to her mission and to her purpose.

HS: Ok. She's a singer. That's all she needs. She just doesn't sing. If she sings, she'll be fine. She makes it harder than it needs to be.

R: Yes, but I think it will be easier for her when she hears this recording. Why is it so hard for her?

HS: Because she [sometimes feels like she] has the weight of the whole world on her shoulders. She's the designer, and it didn't go according to plan. She [subconsciously] feels guilty. She doesn't want to see people suffer. She questions whether she is the one. . .somehow, it's her fault that people are choosing so much greed and hate. Somehow. . .that she made a mistake.

R: Did she? Was it her mistake?

HS: It is an experiment; you never know how it's going to go. There was so much hope.

R: You know, I believe that here on the Earth, it's not how it seems from up there. Even though there is a lot of suffering, there is also a lot of beauty and joy. I don't think people knew that they were going to affect the whole Universe. I don't think they wanted to destroy the experiment.

HS: That's where she gets stuck. Yes, they didn't know, but it does [affect everything]. So, she gets confused on her mission because she feels this deep calling to stop them, but it's too big. She can't stop the military complex at all. She feels confused. She was born in the military ironically; she was born into the heart of the beast on an Air Force base.

R: Why did she choose that?

HS: So we could [help her], because of the technologies that were there. They took all the ships from Roswell, and they put them underground of that hospital. She wouldn't have survived. She was too big, she couldn't fit, she didn't fit as well as we hoped she could. She couldn't stay in there; she couldn't stay inside her mother; her mother couldn't hold her. She wouldn't have made it. We wanted her to make it, so we put her there. We knew it might be hard. She's coming in with so much; most of the volunteers aren't the designers. Designers come in; she is the lead team; she only came in at the pivotal moments; this is a pivotal moment too. We really needed her in both places. We knew her coming in was going to be challenging, so we put her there because all the technology was there. All the ships were there. There was extra technology where we could help keep her alive.

R: Very good. Wonderful. Does she have any relationship to her family in past lives? That you're born into, any contracts or any karma and things like that?

HS: She doesn't come in much.

R: What was she in either lifetime? The lifetime before the life that she's living now. What type of being, what was she? Was she a male or female, or something else?

HS: She didn't come in a long time. She came, She came. . . [It looked like she was scanning through the date to check]. . .she came at the time of the first volunteer.

R: What was happening then?

HS: Issa was the first volunteer. Not the first, that's not the right word. There were other volunteers who have come to help. They're using the designers, and she comes in as the teachers. The last time she came in was when Issa came. . .Jesus. She came then. . .

[At the time, Ava and I were not familiar with the name Issa bring used for Jesus. To my surprise, a few years later, when I traveled in Saini, Egypt, I learned from a local woman that still today they call Jesus - Issa. It was a fun discovery and felt like a confirmation.]

R: When did He come?

HS: He came with the time that they spoke that He would come.

R: And it was his first time?

HS: No.

R: It was before? And that was her first time? In the time that he came that we know?

HS: No, no, that's the last time.

R: That's the last time. What was her role? What was her part? She was wondering. . .

HS: She was close.

R: Yeah. She had a vision that she was his daughter. Is that true? Or was she in another way relative to him?

HS: Daughter. . .is the right word?. . . Yes. . .

R: Show her, go to that time period, be there now. Tell me what's happening there. You can choose an event that we will learn about her life then.

HS: Ahh, yes. We knew He would be killed. They're the same. They're the same. Not the same. They're both very old. They've known each other long, long in the history.

R: What was she then?

HS: Yes, she was his daughter, yet she was taken away. We had to protect. He came with the message to help bring love, but also with an upgrade, a genetic upgrade. We had to protect the genetic upgrade, in case she was killed, and he was killed. We knew he would be killed. We wanted to protect the upgrade, so she came in, but they took her away. She was in.

. . .she was placed with a. . .she was a strange child. She tried to sing the songs, but I think she went crazy. I think there was too much. Is that right?

R: Can you show her herself in the end of her life in this lifetime? So we will learn more. Drift and float and place her in the end of that life. Be there now? (A: Ahoo**) What do you see? Get into that body and tell me how does it feel? What do you feel right now?**

HS: So light, the upgrade is nice. So much love. We're trying to repair the damage done, and for so long we let that go on unchecked, because all it was an experiment. We had to see how things would play out. We can't interfere too much, but eventually, we thought if we sent in the upgrade, through both the sound that he spoke, and through the genetic possibility that it might filter down. Bring more love in. It was an experiment. We knew it would be slow. That was the point.

R: Wonderful.

HS: I don't think she ever had children, so I don't think the experiment worked.

R: Any of the other. . .were their other children for Jesus? Are there maybe other genetic codes that being continued?

D: I had a brother. I don't think I'm remembering right. I think there was another. No, there was a son. I had a son, but he was taken from me. Again, we had. . .there is this. . .those who knew; they were afraid, that if we were all together, we would be killed together. (**R: Yeah.**) We had to be separated. (**R: Yeah.**) I did have a son, but I stayed in the place with the chamber. [She started to speak from the perspective of the daughter]

R: Where is that this place with the chamber?

D: Ahh. . .so beautiful. The chamber, the sound. . .it had the most beautiful acoustics, and I just sing right? I never married. The son came from a ceremony. We had a ceremony to conceive the son. . .and the daughter. There were two. I don't know what happened to them because they were afraid that if we knew, that if we were tortured we would tell. I never know. . .so I just sing, I sing, I sing in the chapel; I sing. No, no chapel. There was no chapel. I sing in the chamber that had those tall ceilings. The light would come in; I would sing there, people would come to hear, and I would cry for my children. I agreed. I agreed, because I knew it was important. It was sad to not be able to know your family, but it is okay.

R: How old are you now?

HS: In the chamber? I'm old. I've been singing here a long time. (*Sounding very tired.*)

R: Where is this chamber located on the Earth?

D: We had to hide.

R: You can look at the Earth from above and just locate yourself on the Earth and receive a picture of where you are.

D: We traveled far. Far from where I was born. We traveled so far.

R: Where were you born?

D: Well, once Issa escaped, he went towards the light, so that side is east. I don't know, I wasn't supposed to know. Then I went West. Oahhh. Oh. That's funny.

R: What is funny?

D: They took me to Avalon. (**R: Mm hmm.**)

A: That's funny.

R: What's funny about that?

HS: Because that's what Ava calls herself.

[Depending on my question she seems to switch back and forth between the HS and the Daughter and Ava's reactions to the information.]

*[**Ava's note**: I notice during this part of the session, that I am struggling to discern the visions. As I experience the Akashic, I am seeing multiple layers stacked on top of each other. I am seeing different "version visions" of history all at the same time, and each one is a little distorted from seeing the ones above and below. My guess is that since this topic of Issa has many versions that have woven through the collective consciousness for millennia, I am seeing the versions I heard about in Sunday School, other versions I don't recognize as well, and still, other versions that all feel somewhat true. Here, I saw a version of history where Jesus was crucified and then rose and ascended. I saw another layer where he escaped and someone else was crucified instead, and another where he was crucified and thought to be dead but was taken down before he fully died and was revived and secretly relocated by his disciples and close relations. I'm unsure which is the "Truth."]*

R: Ahhh. . . so she's in Avalon?

D: Yes, I went a long time over the land, and then a short time over the water. Then a long time of the land, up into the mountains. They were hiding me, and I stayed there and sang there, and that's where. . .

A: That's funny.

HS: It took a long time, but then Christianity came and destroyed it. They were coming and destroying Jesus's daughter's songs.

A: That's funny. That's funny.

[It seems a paradox that the Christians who love Jesus so much would cancel out the songs of his daughter. They were possibly doing so without even knowing.]

R: So why is it that those forces are going against Jesus and his teachings? Who are the one that are responsible for that?

HS: The fear weavers.

R: Mmm. . . so the fear weaver are other beings that singing songs of fear?

HS: They are not singing the songs. . .

R: So what are they doing?

HS: It sounds . . .it's. . .their. . . *(She was looking for the information and didn't sound very confident)* their songs are made by machines. They're not machines of the Earth.

R: Hmm, I see, does it, but the songs and the sounds are probably going through all times in space and not just on the Earth. Right? (HS: Right.) For example, ammm, I'm trying to understand about acoustic sound or electronic sound; if there's difference between those sounds here on the Earth or it doesn't matter? When it's here on the Earth is it all sounds of the Earth? I'm just wondering about it. . .

HS: Yeah, there's different texture of the fibers, it's like the difference between silk and cotton and wool. When you look at them under the microscope, they all look very different. (R:Yeah.) They're all fibers, and they all weave, is the same like that.

R: Yeah, but can be electronic sounds that are healing sounds?

HS: Yes, there are electronic sounds that are healing sounds. . .if you go in. . .yes. They tend to have a little bit more edges. When you go in really close, there's just slight edges of the building blocks they are more squarish. Then the natural ones are more roundish, so the sounds have a little bit more of an edge to them. Which can be good. It can clean; they can be cleansing; they kind of scrape residue.

R: Very good. Wonderful.

RAZOR'S EDGE

R: Let's take another deep breath. I want to assist Ava today with the healing, as much as we can, and she also had questions that she prepared. What from your perspective is important for her to know today?

A: I'm hearing the word "alone."

R: Ok, let's take another deep breath. Why is she hearing right now the word "alone?" What do you want to tell her about that?

HS: She has watched humans love and procreate for millennia. There is this part of her that wants to experience that which she has not.

R: So what about a relationship that is good for her? What do you want to tell her about experiencing this love? Did you plan any relationship like that? Any twin-flame or soul-mate relationship?

HS: Yes. (mumbling) He looks like Issa.

> *[Ava's note: I was "shown" that he "felt" like Issa, not that he looked like him physically. It was a feeling of home, of unconditional love, of sanctuary.]*

R: Good. Can we connect with his Higher Self to receive a message from the Higher Self? It's appropriate for me to ask questions and to talk directly?

A: I don't know. . . I think so. . .

R: So take another deep breath. May I speak with you directly?

His HS: Okay

R: Thank you! What way I call you?

A: I don't know how to translate.

R: Okay. That's okay. Do you have a message would you like to give?

His HS: When you sing your songs, those that love you will come. They will hear the songs, and they will remember. You will spend much time alone. They will come.

R: **What else would you like to share with her?** *(long pause)* **Would you like to share anything else?**

His HS: I think so, yes. She is having a hard time hearing about herself. It's easier for her to hear about the things beyond this realm than to hear the things from this realm. She has a hard time hearing the things for Ava, but she can hear the other things more easily. I think she is afraid to hear things she does not want to hear. For she doesn't want to be alone. It doesn't seem fair to spend so long alone. To never get to experience life, and then to come to Earth and not experience that love. At the same time, she is Love. She is love. She is love with Source, with Issa, with life. She is the mother of all. **(R: Yeah)** She doesn't need to have a child. She doesn't need the karma. **(R: Yeah)** She could if she wished, but no, she doesn't have that. She doesn't need; she's not here for the genetic upgrade this time. That was before. She did that. She knows. She has felt that before. She might find love but not like what she thinks (a monogamous nuclear family). She came to sing the songs.

[It seems harder for her to translate the frequency of that being to words, so I think her HS stepped in to continue. The next question was asked at a later time, but it seems right to put it here for the continuation of the topic.]

R: **What can she do that will fulfill her and bring her the most creativity and deep fulfillment and joy in her life, and service for others?**

HS: She needs to find the ecstasy in her alone, and sing from the ecstasy of her alone. For that is where she speaks with Issa and all. Only there. Not for anyone else. The songs are sung for all, and for none, and for the sake of [the] song. Not for hearing, but. . .being. . .the song be. . .the song is. So, she [can] go alone somewhere, and film, and sing, and record. . . alone. To get [song] seeds. Then get help. Too much for focus; too much to sing and to deal with the human technology is too crude. It does not make sense to her. She is used to a better system. She needs help from a human technology system expert; [one] will help her. She start; she do. They will hear; they'll come. She can trust that they will. She has been afraid that if she puts it out, they would not be good enough, and then, no help will come. That's not true. She can. . . she is extremely intelligent. We gave her a lot, to help. We picked well. Brain. Body good. Brain, very good. Heart, very good. We gave her a good choice. . . Ava is good. Ava can do it.

R: **What will be a way to help her to start with the singing of these songs? Can she remember the songs now? Can she connect to those songs?**

HS: She hears those songs, yes. She needs to travel to the places where the songs come, so she can hear them. She needs to. . .

R: **What are those places? So she will know.**

HS: These are the places with the Acoustics of God. That's not the right word. The Acoustics of Life built into their design. Those are the best places for her to sing.

R: **What do you mean by that? Give me examples.**

HS: Like in the stone amphitheaters, and in the old churches with the high ceilings, and the places they would make sounds before microphones. [Because she (was said in Spanish)] there is a distortion in the field. There is a possibility of the recording on the microphones, but there is a big jump, because she, all of her experience on Earth has been long before any microphones and electricity. She has had no experience with electricity before. She knows a power greater than that. Electricity is a hard one for her to navigate. It is such a crude form of power, so wasteful, and she feels the pain of the Earth in its blood from the coal. She feels the pain in the power, and it shuts down her voice, because she feels the pain.

She could get on the power through solar or another form, but the power must be clean. The power needs to be clean.

R: **Can you make something that this would not affect her? This power electricity and that she will be able to still sing and not be affected by the use of the electricity?**

HS: We can try; it is hard, because she must open fully to receive the sound, and when she opens that fully, she feels the pain of the power. **(R: I see)** It is hard; she is designed well and yet specific, but yes, she can. She can if she sources the songs from the clean power place; she can then share the songs through the other power place. The songs do not want to come through that way. That means, she calls it, when she channels the song. That needs to be in a clean power place. When she has those songs, she can share them again on regular power. **(R: I see)** These songs are too old and too new and at the same time, their vibration does not want to fit through the dirty power; they don't come to her then. I don't know if we can fix that. She can go to those places, and then she can share. That would help her.

R: **She can record, and then she can sing it again, practice it, and share it in another way?**

HS: Yes.

R: **Good, very good. What's going on with her knees?**

HS: She does not feel secure and safe to share. The support system feels wobbly to her; she does not feel supported by the Universe. She feels alone, and she feels tired.

R: **Can you make her feel the support now, and heal her knees?**

HS: We can help her with her feet. She needs to stand barefoot on the earth more. That will help her knees.

R: **Wonderful. Is there anything in her body like attachments or entities?**

HS: Scanning.

R: Thank you.

HS: We are. . .this ear is confusing. What is that?

R: Do you find something in the ears?

HS: There is a film.

R: Tell me more. What is that?

HS: It's like a slime and it is separating her from hearing, and remembering.

R: How has it been created?

HS: Oh, I believe. . . I might be mistaken; I thought we removed everything. It seems as though. . . I wonder if the government did know she came. We knew it was a risk, her being in a hospital on an Air Force Base, but that's where the technology was.

R: Is there any implant?

HS: It is a virus they put in her. It activates whenever she gets big. Whenever she reaches a certain vibration, it activates the virus. That's why every time she starts to shine, she gets sick. Then she doesn't shine anymore, then eventually over time, she gets well again. She's scared, because every time she starts to shine, she gets sick. I think we can deactivate this virus, but it is very sneaky. When did this get put here? I think we can remove it.

R: Please remove it now, and tell me what you're using.

HS: It is a combination of light and sound and metal, tiny metals. You call, beyond nano. Does not exist yet. It's very sticky, this virus.

R: Can you make sure there is nothing left in her body? That it's all gone. [they asked her to be careful with western medicine and advised her to not have unnecessary surgeries.] Very good. Does she have guardians to assist her?

HS: Funny. She has many, many.

R: So why is she not feeling supported?

HS: Because it is big. Many are here to support her, many here watching. She feels pressured to do good and is afraid it isn't going to be good enough. She feels the weight of the future of all of humanity depends on whether she succeeds or fails.

R: What is the situation now? Let's go back to that council and talk to them and learn about right now, the situation. Where are we standing at this point in time with the experiment?

HS: There is a faction, very loud, very angry, at the extent of destruction that humans are creating. Another faction, saying, awakening happening, must be patient. It is undecided, yet both factions are. . .more factions. . .some want to just remove humans. Some want to destroy the planet.

R: What is this thing that people talk about, this event, this New Earth, or those concepts? Where are we now in relation to that?

HS: Razor's edge.

R: Will you repeat that? What do you mean?

HS: *(Robotic sentence structures and voice)* Razor's edge, walking fine line, may not, may. . . All will ascend somehow. Most without their bodies. It does not matter if we destroy the Earth. It is only [a game]. Nothing destroyed. All [will] still be. Just an illusion. It does not matter. She has become attached to the illusion. We understand; she is so close to the experiment. Is working. It is.

R: So, is that event that people talk about? Is it like destroying the planet? Or what's the meaning of that event?

HS: Meaning, what meaning, meaning?

[Sometimes when I say something wrong, they can better correct me, but this time it seems as if I was too off in my question for them to understand what I meant. I tried to understand the phenomena people in our community are calling The Event - A wave of energy that will transform the Earth, clear the low densities, wake up many at once, and will upgrade those who are on the Ascension path.

It was very unique for me to receive this information, because so far through many sessions with other clients, I had received the impression that we are doing well and the Ascension or the Event is near. My thought was: Maybe they mean that the Ascension could look differently depending on each person. Maybe for one, it can look like the Earth is being destroyed and for the others, they would be aware of an energy wave that would lift them to a new dimension. I believe that connecting the topic of The Event with this topic in the way that I did was just too confusing for them to understand.

I hoped my question would turn this over into more positive and uplifting information, as I noticed it triggered some fear within me, so my question came out wrong. It is very rare to receive information that will trigger fear, and normally if it does it is an indication that I may not be speaking with a light being with pure intention for the benefit of all. I was especially surprised now, as I could feel the high level of consciousness that they were speaking from, and the love frequency they held throughout the session, their love and care for us the humans, and for Ava. I knew that this information is coming from love and this was not an entity that I need to clear.

Her voice, intonation, and frequency became more robotic, and she speaks with significantly broken English. I could feel the very high frequencies that were coming through. The energy was flowing through my body and around us; I had a sense that it was filling up the room. It was very powerful, and I felt I needed to stay grounded and focused, so as not to be overwhelmed by the experience as it was happening. It is common for practitioners to feel a heightened wave of energy during sessions, but this wave of energy was at another level that I had never experienced before.

I could understand that from the higher perspectives, when you are less attached to the result of an experiment, when you are truly allowing the experiment to be an experiment, when you truly experience that nothing can be lost, it might look like just another game of illusions. I tried to get more information and understand what they meant by the statement that it is okay if Earth will be destroyed. Obviously, I am also a bit attached to the experiment. Aren't we all? The good news is further along in the book, a beautiful explanation will be shared. Keep reading. . .as a wise one once said to me, "Don't give up before the miracle."

R: **We learned about those different waves of energy that are coming to the Earth.**

HS: Hot.

R: **Her body is hot?** (A: Hot.) **Okay, I'll take some blankets down. Is that better or even more?** (A: Better.) **Good, so let's take another deep breath. I want to ask more of her private questions before I ask the more general questions, okay?**

HS: Yes.

[I thought it would be easier to move to another topic and come back to this later when the energy is calmer. My next questions were about her relationship with her ex-lover, her living situation, and her finance. All those topics received in-depth and clear guidance. This information feels too personal or unrelated to the book. I don't think I realized during the initial interview the depth of Ava's pain until the next statement from her HS. They said "Is good [to] remind her who, why, she's here. For she had got[ten] into [that] place that she was not wanting [to] be here [anymore]. Good. Remind. Good remind her."

Then I wanted to make sure the physical healing was accomplished properly and was complete. During those messages, her voice was changing, some aspects were more talkative and fluent some more robotic and short in vocabulary. The next part was one of the most robotic soundings so far.]

R: Is the healing in the ear, and this virus, is that being removed?

HS: Trying, need help. Dense.

R: What help do you need?

HS: She needs do kidney cleanse, liver cleanse, colon cleanse, blood cleanse. No eat fried. No oils. No. Change cooking. No cow. Need help. Need help.

R: This help, do you need it from her? Or are there any other beings that you would like me to call to assist you? Is there any way I can assist you right now?

HS: Scanning. Need help. How translate? Hmmm. . .

R: Are you looking for a word you can't find?

HS: It's a picture of a woman, healer. . . find. . .technology she has.

R: What is the technology doing? Can you describe the technology, and we can find it that way?

HS: Not Earth technology. She was tagged. Hard remove. Deep in DNA. Intermittent activation upon frequency. Very sneaky.

R: Does she need to be lifted or something? *[On a spaceship for healing.]*

[Here is my understanding about "lifting" vs. "abducting."

"Lifting" is an agreement between the Higher Self and extraterrestrial allies or higher dimensional beings to be taken onto a spaceship for healing purposes, experiments, or other reasons that the soul gave consent for. The consent was given in the higher dimensions and may not be conscious to the person, but lifting honors the free will rules and contracts.

"Abducting" occurs when extraterrestrial beings take a being onto a spaceship for self-serving purposes, without previous agreements and without honoring the free will rules of our planet.]

HS: Yes.

R: Is it something that you want to schedule?

HS: Yes.

HS: After she does the cleanse, need help. Will re-clog. If we do work now, [it] will re-clog, need help.

R: She will be lifted? (HS: Yes.) Do you want to guide her about that?

HS: At the place, at the place, she goes. Birthday.

R: On her birthday? [She shared with me before the session that she is planning to go to another silent meditation course on her birthday. It all made sense to me even with little words.]

HS: Yes, we see her on her birthday. Birthday. Yes, ok.

R: She will remember this time, this lifting? Or will she not remember when she comes back?

HS: She won't remember, [it isn't] so bad, but she gets scared. Funny, a comedy joke; she will laugh when it's over.

R: Good, wonderful. Very good. Does she hold more guilt in her body or shame? Can we release all those thought forms, so she can do everything more fun now?

HS: We try hard, she's specific, because of her unique role as lead designer, how can she not feel all, she sees the whole. Too much, one person. But she needs to remember to sing songs, so what do we do? Don't know how to help that. She is designed to hold it. She is designed to hold deep compassion of all. That's why she is on the team.

R: What about these dreams of water, these waves that she's seeing, what's that for?

[Ava's note: We were asking about my recurrent dreams of facing immense tsunamis. Sometimes I run away in fear; sometimes I run towards them with warrior-like determination; sometimes I 'wake up' within the dream and start to surf them; and sometimes I fly over them and start guiding the waves with my awareness.]

HS: She's asked to have extra training. Need practice. Lucid dream, wake up. She needs to wake up more.

R: She wanted to ask how to do that.

HS: Clean. Clean. Cleanse. Clean. Clean Self. Clean self.

R: The diet that you said.

HS: Yes.

R: That will help her with lucid dreaming?

HS: Yes.

R: What else?

HS: She need clean channel. Open songs lines more. She need know; she need understand how hard human is. She needs know. Been too long since she came. Forgot. How hard [been a] human is, so she asked that. All training. She is ambitious.

R: Yeah, is there anything else that you'd like to explain about her dreams or about anything like that, that she would understand?

HS: Hands, look hands. Hands different in dreams. Hands. Look hands. Go [to the] ocean, ask [if you are] dreaming, ask every day at ocean, ask [am I] dreaming? Most of her dreams are at the ocean's edge. She likes that place, but she needs to ask whenever at the ocean, so that in dreams she asks and can wake up. She learned flying. When she is flying, she wakes up. Now, next level. At ocean, hands. Wake up. Then, next level. She asked for extra training, need clean. Must be clean for next level.

R: Ok, wonderful. When she was giving me a little healing session, she had a very strong frequency from her hand.

HS: Yes, she is like that picture in the springs of the light from the hands of...she is family [of] Issa. Hands, yes, hands. Very strong. Hands.

> *[**Ava's note:** The channel is referring to a stained-glass portrait of a woman who had light emanating from her hands. This art piece is set in the window of the dome of a local hot spring I like to visit.]*

R: I see, so is it good for her to do hands-on healing?

HS: Very. Yes, very good. Help her open her channels. Sing songs, her love of humans, touch humans, sing songs, love humans, touch humans, touch all, sing all, sing love. Touch, sing, all, yes. Touch, sing, all, yes.

R: What is the best way for her to make income in a way that she will be supported?

HS: Touch. Sing. Love all. Yes.

R: I had a feeling that is what you would say. Why does the energy that I receive feel like spiders?

HS: Ha ha. Spiders, for light touch, dance, all over, spiders like the praying mantis, the insect touch light, not insect, spider weaver, spider weaver. She is one of the old weavers, the light/song weavers, so of course, she is spider. You know. . . she [has a tattoo of spider] on her arm. . . is good. . . is balance of the ecosystem. Balance, she knows, you know, yes, spider good. Don't fear spider, spider good. Balance, weave, weave, she spin. The songs spin during the weave. Sing, weave, song.

R: Is there any other question that I could ask, and I didn't ask for her that you wanted to share information?

HS: Ron. You—family—Issa.

R: Yeah. You want to tell me the connection to Issa? I feel the connection, but I don't know. I've been told once, but I'm not sure if I'll hear again. It might give me confirmation. . .

HS: You protect Issa. You help escape—Issa. Yes? Maybe your son. Your family helped Issa. You help— down from the cross, you sneak down, you got him down. Escape, escape. Get Mag, Mags, Mags (short for Mary Magdalene). . .escape.

R: Very nice, very good.

HS: You wrote, you wrote. . .

R: What did I write?

HS: What Issa said. . . write.

R: I wrote what he said?

HS: You helped write [what] Issa said. **(R: Umm)** After escape, you help Issa travel.

R: It's wonderful. You can hear now the name I was called then. You can listen to this name and how the people called that name?

HS: Family more [than] one name, more than one, blood family more than one.

R: So, it's longer name than just one [name], there's a family name as well?

HS: No. You and sons more than one, helped. (R: So the family helped) Yeah. Family helped Issa.

R: Wonderful, is those family are part of my family also now? Are they soul group with me now?

HS: Love, same love, the same. Michael was not Michael, but same.

R: Wonderful, so we had a loving, love relationship then too?

HS: Yes, you both help Issa escape, helped with daughter escape. Help raise. . . no. Family raise. Confusing. Yeah. Okay. Lots of blood. Same help.

R: Wonderful. Is there more information that want to come forward for me today? Is there any more thing that my council wanted me to know today?

HS: Bird.

R: Did you say bird? (HS: Bird) I'm just looking at the turkeys right now in my yard. So it was funny. Tell me more. What do you mean by bird? [I was surprised as Ava's eye are closed and she couldn't see the pack of turkeys passing by my yard.]

HS: Turkeys cooperate. Family. Family strong. Family ties [are] strong—turkey cooperate— bird.

R: Very nice. See if there are any other beings that have any other messages, any other spirit guides, or anyone who has transitioned that want to share a message, before we bring her up? Are there any more messages that want to come forward?

HS: Scanning. (R: Thank you.) Tell her that, like she said, always think[s] she fails when doing well. She is struggling, she knows the stakes are high. She can. . . she is doing well in a hard world. No one thought she could succeed. They all thought it was lost, but she loved them so much, she wanted to try again. She did not. . . it's hard for her to come because of the history of All That Is within her. To forget it all is hard. She took on a big job, doing good. Even if she does not succeed, she has still done well. It is all ok.

R: Are we succeeding here now?

HS: Repeat?

R: Are we succeeding here now? Is the awakening succeeding?

HS: Awakening is happening, yes. Happening fast enough for planet Earth and humans together; most need leave. Too many.

R: So most humans will need to leave?

HS: Too many.

[This type of information was not big news for me, at this point, I was having sessions daily and information about the ascension of the Earth was coming frequently. We first learned about it years ago from Dolores and other channels, or if to be more accurate, there are prophesies about this time for thousands of years. In many of our sessions, we have been told about each change for all levels, from the most physical to the most energetic, a changing of eras, a shift in consciousness. This restructuring process is described in depth within The Illumination Codex, gateway two, part three - New Earth Transmissions. We have been told that even when it looks from the outside that it is getting worst sometimes, the light is growing and exposing the darkness, bringing it up to the surface to be seen and healed through love. We were told that the new kids and newborn babies already have an upgraded DNA and are ready to make the shift. Only the ones that would not be able to hold the new levels of increasing light, consciousness, and frequency would leave and will continue the learning through karma on another plant.]

[*Ava's note: Although the words that came through, "Most need leave. Too many. . ." came through in broken English and without much explanation, what I "saw" in my inner vision was much more nuanced and multi-layered. I was shown how many people are here on Earth but not really living. Many are just going through the motions of life and ultimately, just waiting around to die, while simultaneously pretending they are never going to die. Life is such a precious gift, and so many souls long to have the chance to incarnate. The words were more speaking to the fact that too many people are wasting the gift of life and spending most of their time distracting themselves with things that have little real value to the soul. The channel was not suggesting that we kill ourselves, nor was it suggesting any kind of depopulation program or genocide plan. It was calling us up to really live and to claim the gift of being alive while we still can. We often forget the preciousness of this life and that tomorrow is never guaranteed in this particular form.*

Additionally, I was shown that from an ecological standpoint, we have exceeded carrying capacity by our combined population and resource consumption rate. The

Earth's system cannot sustain infinite exponential growth. We have overridden almost every natural check and balance system established within the system. Equilibrium will always eventually return to a system. Science shows that when populations exceed carrying capacity, a rebalancing of the system is inevitable, which can present as an increased rate of natural disasters, terminal disease, epidemics, famines, and genetic changes that decrease fertility rates. For those paying attention, it is clear to see that climate change and resource scarcity will continue to have significant impacts on our world until we make significant shifts to our relationship with ourselves, each other, and the planet. It's not a personal attack, but it is a natural, inevitable part of being a part of a living ecosystem.

This realization can cause a profound amount of grief, despair, and anxiety. I understand, as I realized the writing on the wall back in 2000 while studying Ecology at the University of Georgia. After an intense period of anger, grief, and fear, I dedicated my life to environmental education and sustainable solutions, and yet was mostly criticized and disregarded for being a 'tree-hugging hippie.' I may be a tree-hugger, but it's because I value human life on planet Earth, and I have been trying to help humanity realize that we are taking it for granted and throwing away the precious gift of living on garden planet of Earth.]

R: Ok. I wanted to ask also, if the waves that are coming now...you said more waves are coming, more volunteers are coming?

HS: More volunteers are always coming; more, more, more now, because now [it is] harder. Most fall asleep, stay asleep. Most don't wake up. Too hard. Need help with the children. She knows, she has idea. Good idea. Good idea of the games. The games, to teach the children in the games to connect with self. She knows, good idea. Need help, [with the] children. The technology too fast; the brains can't keep up. Hard time, scary time for the children. All coming in with not remembering. It is because the fear weavers don't want them to remember, so these games [are] good.

[Farther on in a more personal section they shared a bit more about the fear weavers, so I added it here].

HS: The fear weavers, they don't want her here. They want, they feed on the fear and the greed. They feed on that power. It is hard [on] this Earth. That bacteria that came, that was from that fear weavers. It is all love, but they are very lost and very powerful.

[I asked if the fear weavers or the bacteria they sent to Earth had a name and Ava started to whisper something in Light Language. They mentioned that she can't translate it, so I mentioned to them that they are welcome to speak in Light-Language every time that the information cannot be translated.]

R: Wonderful. Is there any Light Language or any songs that want to come forward now, to help with the awakening? Maybe something that we can even edit and share online? People will hear and will be awakened, or [their] subconscious will hear and will be awakened? Light Language or song.

HS: Need clean.

R: So, it's not appropriate? Or you can clean for a moment now and then we can have a little light language or song?

HS: Possible, need clean.

R: Ok.

HS: She need clean, stand feet earth. Not lying down.

R: Not lying down. Standing?

HS: Feet earth. Stand. Clean first.

R: Good. Would it be good to do more sessions like that to assist with the healing?

HS: After, clean first. Need help. Too much.

THE CHILDREN OF THE EARTH

R: Ok, good. You're doing very good. Thank you so much for this information. Take another deep breath, releasing completely. Is there any information that wants to come forward for the collective? A message for the collective or from a collective?

HS: Yes. (R: Thank you.)

[Here there was a shift of energy and a different member of the collective that came through more human-like and not robotic anymore. Their energy was more feminine and softer. They were also much more emotional, like a loving mom.]

HS: My darling humans. You are love. You are union of love and light and dark and song. Power. The five. . . You are such exquisite beings. Such capacity to love. To forgive. To listen. To share. To be. Do not listen to the fear songs. In your heart, it does shine bright; it does know the difference. Remember to come back home to yourselves. All the distractions of this world. Those distractions, they are not the goals my friend, my babies; they are to help strengthen your heart, to strengthen your resolve to choose love inside yourself. But you've forgotten. For so long, the songs have been destroyed. The songs have not been sung. The knowledge lost, but it is not truly lost. Only in the mind was it lost.

Sit quietly my children, listen. Listen inside your hearts for your song. Whether it is a song of words and sounds of songs, or whether it is the dance, whether it is the service of your heart. You came here for that love. Don't forget. Oh, my children, my babies, I'm sorry. We so wanted you to thrive and be happy. We so wanted to give you the Garden of Eden and paradise forever. That is our dream. It was for you to realize, and through your amnesia and free will to choose love and to wake up to who you really are. We are all One; we are all from Source, and that by divine remembrance, after an infinity of knowing All. The beautiful joy of remembering for the first time who you are. . .

That is such an exquisite gift. We thought you would love it. We wanted you to have that divine epiphany that you are Source. We wanted you to have all the love in the world. We so wanted you all to be healthy and happy, and you can be.

You can rise above this corruption and this fear. You can. You can face the giant wave and dive into love. You can. I believe in you. I believe in you. It's time to wake up my babies. No more time to sleep; it's time to wake up. It's time to shine your light and sing your song. That's just a metaphor for whatever brings your heart alive. Please, come back home to us. Wake up to who you really are and who you're meant to be. You are pure love, and that fear, you can shake it off; you can let it go. Send it down into the Earth; she can take it. What she can't take is you taking from her and not giving her your sorrow. She needs it; that's her compost; it's her soil. She needs it. She needs your fear; she needs you to send your troubles down into Earth. Put your bare feet on the earth, my babies. Everyday. Remember that you are stardust and you are Earth. You are the songs to be sung.

Yes, you were made in the image of love and the divine because all of this is All, everything you see, it's all your consciousness playing before you. Everything you see, those are the outer edges of you looking back in at the eternity of yourself within. You think you're this pinpoint looking out into these vast expanses. It's the opposite. You're looking at the infinite walls of yourself. Turn around. Stop looking out and look within instead. For your light, your love is there my babies. I know you can find it. I believe in you. I believe in you. I always have. You are my dearest love. Each one of you is so precious. Wake up. It is time to wake up from this nightmare. Wake up. You are love. You are meant to be love. You are meant to take care of each other. Take care of those who are starving.

If you are up on your mountaintop of riches and you are sitting up there alone and not helping, you are not sitting on riches. You are sitting on a freaking pile of rocks. Turn that into real gold. We can all be fed. We can all be nourished. We can all be loved. We don't have to be so afraid and [you don't] need to hoard everything. You are not a dragon.

*[**Ava's note:** This reference to dragons is not the same as the previous. In this reference, I was shown an image of the insatiable dragon who hoards piles of gold and will burn anyone to a crisp who comes near.]*

You might think you are; you might think you must protect yourself from annihilation. You will never be annihilated. My darlings, this is just a game. This is just a game to help polish your soul. How are you polishing yourself? It's not just for you. You don't win because you're on top. You don't win because you're the king of the mountain. You win when you love humanity. You win when you love the weakest one. When you take care of those in need, that's where you find the heart of gold my babies.

You've forgotten. I'm so sorry. I thought you could remember more easily. I really did. I didn't know it would be so hard. I'm sorry. I'm so sorry. But you can do it. I know you can. You were made to be love. You were made to choose love. That feeling you feel [when you open your heart], that's what you were made to feel. That fear is an illusion; you don't need it; let it go.

Even when the end is before you, you are so afraid of dying; you think this is all there is. . .babies, this is just a polishing stone.

It's ok. You're ok. This is going to be ok. You can do it. You can choose love, my babies. Please. This beautiful planet we made for you, please, take good care of her. Enjoy the beauty. This is paradise. This is one of the most favored creations in all of the universes. Please. Please wake up; come home. Come into my heart. Come into the Heart of all of us. We want to see you rise and join us. It's time to wake up. I love you so.

Forgive me for all this pain and suffering you have found. Lean into it my babies. Stop choosing the distractions; they don't help you heal. Lean into those places that scare you and know that you are safe. We've got you when you fall back and surrender;

we've got you. We always have. We always have. *(Crying)* (R: **Wonderful**) Babies. . .

R: **Would you like to close with your name, so they will know who this message came from?**

HS: I am your mother. I am the light of life of the world and beyond. I am the heart inside your heart. I am the light inside your eyes. I am the web weaver, I'm the web. I am the weaver and the singer of songs. I am the light of life. You call that word, Ä-li, Al-ee. I am truth. True love for you, my babies. My name: (speaking a long light language). *[Link in the Readers' Zone.]*

R: **Thank you so much. I have a lot of energy around my crown, my heart. Thank you so much for this beautiful message. For all the help, for all the information.**

HS: Thank you for being bridge builder. You are a web weaver too. Bridge, thank you, bridge builder. Bird dancer.

[I thought we were done for today but unexpectedly they continued with giving me a personal message. Most of it is unrelated to the book. They suggested that I'll practice more deep relaxation so I could let go of some of the specific places where I store tension in my body. To finish I felt it would be important to turn the focus back to Ava's healing and it brought us an important topic that I forgot to address.]

R: **Thank you. Wonderful. Thank you so much for all the information today! Now take another deep breath and relax completely and integrate all the energy through the body. I'm sure you did all the healing in the body that you could, right? Are there any cords? I forgot to ask.**

HS: She resists.

R: **She resists what?**

HS: She resists.

R: **What is the resistance about the cords?**

HS: No, not the cords. She resists healing from us. Scared. Scared. She remembers birth, help, but she think, bad, scared, so [she] resist now.

R: Let's take another deep breath. Why did you show her her birth today?

HS: 'Cause she chose [to] come but she resists. She did not want come. Pressure. She resists come. Pressure.

R: How does it help her now that she knows about that?

HS: She always thought that it was her mind that wanted to be different, special. Who was she, one of billions? Just normal kid, did not make sense to her. Did not want to be, did not want to feel different, wanted to be in the game, but she is not. She is a maker, but she wants to forget and be in [the] game. It's too much to forget. Show her birth, so show us helping her. She won't come, would not have survived; we help.

R: Was she lifted then, too?

HS: Lifted and more. . . lifted and needed constant support. Needed the technology activated under her, all the time, support.

R: Wonderful, very good. Is the healing on her body complete today?

HS: Yes, try again, after clean. Birthday lift.

R: And more sessions.

HS: Yes, help, try, try good experiment. Ava scientist like experience. Directly after church, try. After thirty day (her meditation silent retreat), try. 'Cause more clean. Better connection. Sometimes glitch. Sometimes need clean.

R: Yes wonderful. Thank you for all the help and information.

HS: Thank you bridge.

[Before bringing Ava back up, we agreed on the keywords we would use to put her back immediately into a deep trance. This will reduce the time needed for induction in future sessions. Though with Ava, I still made sure to not rush my inductions and made sure she was deep into trance before each subsequent session.]

When I brought Ava back to full consciousness, she mentioned that it felt a bit like a dream. She remembered parts, but not all. For example, she didn't remember that she was speaking Light Language when I asked for the name. For other parts, she remembered only when I mentioned them, but they were already starting to fade from her recall. It was clear that she would need to listen to this recording more than once, as it was packed with powerful information. Listening to the recording is a very important part of the healing and integration of the session. When you listen to the recording with your full consciousness, you are able to hear it a bit differently than under a trance. This assists you in making more conscious choices and helps you to decide how to follow through with the information. Remember, we are love on a free will planet and you can choose what to do. Some of the healing will occur only after the client chooses the right mindset or right action.

Ava mentioned that she could feel and see now that it was a long session, but it had felt much shorter to her. Her perspective of time was changed and that is also a common experience. I like pointing it out as it can give some validation for the experience, while the ego often tries to bring in doubt. Ava was grateful for the experience and information even though the information was a bit far out. She could feel the frequency of truth and the clarity that came with it. Even though it was clear to me that Ava was in a deep trance, she mentioned that from within, she wondered for moments if she was just making it up. She noticed she was able to listen even though the information was flowing at times very fast. She also had a physical experience of shaking and getting very cold and very hot at times. The sound of her voice changed completely, becoming almost robotic or electronic during certain portions. During those, she was struggling to find words and the information was coming out slower but very precise.

For me, it was clear that the information was coming from a very high collective, and I knew that when she would listen to the recording it would help her to trust her experience and the information. After all, Ava was convinced that she indeed got hypnotized, even though she didn't think she would. This made me laugh a bit to myself, for even though this was one of the most profound sessions with a very clear channel and with really far-out information, the ego still comes back and makes the client doubt. Dolores talked about it a lot, and for me, it became so clear. The ego is just doing its job. I find it to be a beautiful opportunity to notice the differences between the energies of the Higher Self who is so loving and clear and the part of us that is judgmental and feeds us with negative self-talk.

We continued talking shortly and did a summary of some of the more personal things that her Higher Self was suggesting. She also shared with me a few more things that she could see and understand under trance but was not able to verbalize during the session. Those phenomena are common, as from within by the inner senses, more can be perceived than spoken. When listening to the recording, the inner experience can be reminded. It is the client's responsibility to use the recording as a tool and harvest the most benefits from the remembering and the information they received.

To be honest, I was really hoping I would have more sessions with Ava again soon, as this felt exceptionally meaningful, big, and unexpected. I knew she was only in town for a few more days, and I thought she would need more time to integrate and listen to the session. Little did I know, the Universe had other plans for us.

Ava's note: I left this session with a feeling of energized liberation. The texture of this liberation felt like I could finally remember an important vivid dream that I had forgotten. Even though it had seemed so real only moments before, and I somehow knew it was essential that I remembered, it had slipped away. The dream had been resting uneasily, just outside my awareness but lost in a mist for so long. I had tried so hard to remember, but I couldn't remember what I was trying to remember. The more I tried, the more it slipped away. Now suddenly, it all came rushing back, like it had never left, and I was shocked and in awe. I was floating, suspended in a paradoxical numb sense of disbelief and a simple sense of "Well, duh. It's always been; you knew this. You just didn't want to know it. Welcome to the party, babe. Are you ready?"

I felt like I had finally gotten the joke that everyone else had already gotten and had been laughing about amongst themselves, both at the joke and at the fact that I hadn't gotten it yet. They all had a wry smile on their faces, anticipating the aha moment that would eventually appear on my face when the revelation finally dropped. A strange sense of satisfaction and relief washed over me.

I also felt absolutely terrified and on the verge of a panic attack. When I didn't remember this information, I was bumbling along trying to figure out my purpose in life and live it the best I could, lost in a strange ignorance. Somehow, I had an excuse to bumble about, because I didn't know. But now. Ha. If this information was true, then I must live my destiny or else I knew I would never feel truly satisfied. I couldn't choose my backup plans anymore, no more pretending I didn't know my purpose. I had to face it and embody it. What a scary and liberating realization. Especially considering everything I had just heard myself say, I was rather overwhelmed. It felt so true and simple, and the knowledge vibrated inside my being with such powerful energy. My mind couldn't and wouldn't accept it. I heard my inner critic saying, "I must be making it all up, this is nonsense."

If it wasn't true, and it was just some strange delusion I made up, then it still pointed me towards an inner realization that I was meant to help this precious planet and to be of service to the awakening of humanity. If this was just my subconscious using a metaphor to point to my deepest desires, then I had to share my songs and stories and be the beacon of love and light that deep down I knew I was meant to be. I had always wanted to, but I doubted myself. Devotion burned inside me with such a fierce and delicious perfection; I felt crystal clear. I felt humbled, like the only thing I could do in this moment was to kneel on the ground and place my forehead on the bare earth and cry with gratitude and fear and pray for the strength and courage to do what I needed to do.

When I tried to make sense of it all and remember all the details, my head would swim. Seriously? All of this suffering was for a reason? My life had been guided by a strange destiny I would never have dreamed of. Wait a minute. . . Spaceships, alien intervention, a designer of Earth, a mission to help release humanity from the clutches of fear and the edge of annihilation? I had a mission to choose love no matter what and inspire others to join me? This was definitely not what I expected to hear. Am I safe? Are any of us? I suppose it doesn't really matter. What do I do with this information? "Breathe. Stop trying to make sense of it. Feel the devotion galvanizing inside. Feel the liberation of your truth." I laid on the Earth and cried. I'll listen to the transcripts tomorrow. "Rest now," I assured myself.

THE NEXT DAY

Ava's note: "Oh my God! You've got to be kidding!?" I blurted out when I saw the YouTube link to the video recording of my first hypnosis session show up in my email inbox. I'm on the Internet saying all this!?"

Ron had been doing these professional hypnosis sessions for a while, and he had a process for letting folks know what to expect. Normally, his clients had seen his session videos and had sought him out. They knew about his process and knew that they would receive their recorded video sessions via a private YouTube link. I had come to Ron as a friend and meditation ally. I came in through the backdoor, so to speak. I had never seen his YouTube channel nor his website that clearly shows many of his video-recorded sessions. For years, I had been living an hour from town and working on a farm. I was rather behind in technology and had never seen a webcam. Even though I saw the little ball on top of Ron's computer, I didn't realize it was a video camera that would actually be filming me. Ron clipped a microphone to my chest, so I was expecting to have the audio recording sent to me privately. I also did not have Internet at my house back then, so I rarely watched YouTube and had no idea that the settings could even be set to "private." I thought, if it's on YouTube, then it's on display for all to see, whoever might be watching. It was a perfect storm. How could he have realized I was so out of the loop, and how could I have known other than I did? It's kind of funny, really.

Here I was, barely integrating this bizarre, unbelievable, and yet fascinating information and suddenly, it's on the Internet! My entire body burned with a blazing fear and a sense of privacy violation. I felt vulnerable and exposed. My mind started to spin.

"Wait a minute," I thought. "If this information is utter nonsense and just a figment of my overactive imagination with the 'reasonable' filters removed, then I sound like an absolute wacko!" My ego was suddenly concerned about my reputation. "What will people think of me spouting some claim that I am the Designer of Earth and helped create this Grand Experiment of Life on Planet Earth?" I mean, seriously!? I consider my self a tree hugging hippie, and I believe that we are all one and all connected, but still. I felt a little embarrassed at my audacity to make such a claim in the privacy of our hypnosis session, but to have my face saying it on YouTube!? I thought my dreams to be a respected children's book author, musician, and meditation teacher would surely be shot if this information made it into the wrong hands. "What if my family sees this? Will they ever speak to me again for speaking such blasphemy?"

Then I had another thought, "Oh, my. . . what if this IS true!?" I sure sounded confident in my statements. The simple, matter-of-factness of how it was all shared made it feel even more believable. I realized that part of me did believe it, as strange as it sounded. "Am I safe?! I'm here on the internet claiming to be a part of a galactic council who created the planet and is also discussing what to do with planet Earth. This CANNOT be a good idea." I panicked that I was exposed in such a way on the Internet. I tried to meditate. I tried to talk sense into myself. I breathed. I used all of my emotional release techniques. None of it helped. I was a mess.

I realize looking back that I was most likely overreacting, but put yourself in my shoes for a moment. . . imagine knowing you were always a bit odd and had strange dreams that felt realer than real and wondering what was really going on. To go from that to suddenly outing yourself as an incarnated alien from another dimension, and not only that, but one of a team of galactic beings and the lead designer of the Earth experiment. Then, before you've even listened to the full recording over again to integrate this extraordinary tale, you thought it was suddenly live and on the Internet (even though it wasn't public). Yeah, it was a lot to take in.

I did always have this odd, vague sense that I wasn't from Earth. I thought it was the most beautiful place I could have ever imagined, but I always had this sense that I didn't belong here. I just thought I hadn't found my niche yet; a lot of people feel this way. Even though I had read other hypnosis sessions and wondered if my soul was one of the New Earth Volunteers, I didn't actually believe my soul essence was from another planet. I definitely didn't expect to hear myself channeling an intergalactic being who had been in existence for billions of years and helped gently and lovingly guide the evolution of humanity.

Anyways, I needed help. I was feeling overwhelmed and afraid and didn't know how to make sense of all this, so I called Ron and asked if I could back come over. He welcomed me right away. I shared all of this with him, and of course, he was surprised and felt sad that I had gotten frightened. He hadn't realized that I was unaware of his process and didn't know I was being filmed, or that it would be shared with me in this way. He did share that the link was private and only those with the link could see it. That helped ease my concerns some, especially if I was uttering absolute nonsense. At least no one else would know I was loony tunes. However, if this information was true, I still felt concerned to have my face uploaded into YouTube with all the AI, etc. He agreed to remove it right away. He also suggested we have another session to let me ask my Higher Self and the Designer about it directly. He thought that the best way for my panic and fear to be resolved and released is if I would receive the information directly from within myself. I agreed, as long as my face was not recorded. I *needed time to decide how I wanted to proceed with these life-changing revelations.*

I am so grateful for this apparent "mistake," and that we agreed to do another session right away. If this hadn't happened the way it did, I would have returned home, and who knows if we would ever have done another session together. I would have probably just decided it was interesting nonsense and continued to move on with my life with more courage and sense of purpose, which would have been nice. After this second session though, we both realized something extraordinary was happening, and that we needed to continue to dive deeper and share this information for the benefit of all beings. This book exists because of our miscommunication, our willingness to lean in and resolve things in a good way, and our curiosity for the Truth. I am so grateful. I love this story, because it reminds me that there are no mistakes. It's all working out just as it needs to; it's perfect. The whole messy, beautiful, painful thing we call Life. It's perfect.

BEYOND THE
SANDSTORM

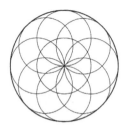

SESSION TWO

R: You can start to look around you and describe your first impressions.

A: I think there is a sandstorm. Sand pelting, kind of like the stars... As the storm clears, it's the pyramids. Big pyramids all around.

R: Very good. Use all your senses, how is the weather over there? After it's been cleared up. . .

A: It's getting dark; it's clear. It's cool. It's sunset.

R: Wonderful. What can you hear over there?

A: People talking. Beings talking. Animals doing animal things. There's a language I don't know.

R: Wonderful. I want to get to know you a little more. Can you look down at your feet and describe yourself?

[Ava's voice changed significantly into a deeper sound. I noticed that by asking her to look down on her body, she dropped into a deeper trance and immediately became the being we were speaking with.]

A: I'm in robes. I'm in robes to hide the fact that I have no body, but they cannot know that. They would be afraid. I have a hood. I am light.

R: That's wonderful. As the light, do you have a gender?

A: I am both.

R: Very nice. Wonderful. How do they call you?

A: (Answering in a very long light language). Translates to "I."
No se; I don't know. *[The recording is in the Readers' Zone.]*

R: That's wonderful. It's okay to call you "I" today? *(A: Yes.)*
Thank you. So "I," I would like you to take me to another day,
a day you consider important and share with me what is
happening next.

> [When I re-listened to the recording, I thought it was very
> unlike me to ask so early for the being's name. I normally do
> that much later on, if I even do, when I know more about the
> character. The channel was so clear; Ava fully became the
> character, and there was such a palpable shift in her energy and
> inside the room, so I followed my intuition and asked. When I
> heard her speaking light language again, I knew that we would
> be in for an interesting ride.]

I: It is the time of the rising. It's the time of the light. It is the
time when Heaven and Earth become one, and the pyramids
have been finished. For they are energy vortexes. They
amplify and communicate. They help us amplify the bridge,
so that we can ascend. Bring the power, the next iteration of
human. It's time to bring light down, so that they may
evolve. For we cannot interfere, but we can bring new ideas,
new light; upgrade. It is time for the upgrade, the next level.

R: Will you share with me about the building of the pyramids?
How has that been done?

I: Well, I don't know how to describe it so that you would
understand. Perhaps an analogy, might work. It seems as
though there is a weaving of the stories of the matrix. As I
said before, there is a weaving, and there is an amplification
through the group work. There is a collective consciousness
of our wills together that can weave stronger. We weave the
matrix of Earth, and therefore, we draw the stones into

existence, and we place them. It is easiest to do this in sections, for Earth is dense. Slow building, but quicker in a group. We could make it all in one piece; it could be a seamless thing, but there must be the forgetting. If we built it in one single piece, not only would that take longer and much more energy, more of us would need to combine our wills, but in the future, they will not forget, *porque (because, in Spanish)* they will not be able to explain. Therefore the pieces can be forgotten, for it is possible they could be built by man. In the times of the forgetting, we cannot leave symbols of the remembering. Too much, their brains would explode. Cannot handle yet, not yet, not time now.

R: **Wonderful. You mentioned that now it was the time of awakening now that the pyramids were done.**

I: Awakening to the next level, but not ready to. . . not ready. In the future, once we go. . .too much, too much. They can remember now, but in the future, they must forget again. It is a cycle; it is a wave of remembering and forgetting, so these beings are in a time of remembering. They know. . .they know something is going on, they don't understand. They still cannot see us; we cannot show them our form; they would explode. They would not understand our form yet. It is not time.

R: **Wonderful "I." Describe what is happening there now, when the pyramids were finished.**

I: We collect our will telepathically into the center; deep, deep inside. And there is a stone, not stone, material we bring in from other dimension. Sing into Earth now, but it will not stay. Too powerful this...not stone...material, liquid, solid light...all at the same time. Hard to explain to you. It does not make sense in three dimensions.

R: **Ok. What is the purpose of this material?**

I: It amplifies the bridge between worlds, so that the upgrade can affect larger populations, instead of the slow way of genetic implantation. Genetic code implantation takes millions of years to spread throughout [the] gene pool, but this is actually much faster. We were able to open the gates between other dimensions and now, and allow upgrades to enter the DNA of multiple beings at once. It is for [the] shift of all humanity, for there are multiple pyramids around the Earth. All in conjunction together, we work together in teams to amplify all around the planet at once.

R: So, it's amplifying the whole planet and also the beings that are getting upgrades within that?

I: Yes, the whole planet is being upgraded.

R: Where is this energy coming into the planet or into the pyramids?

I: From the. . .other dimensions, from light dimensions. This time it is [a] combination of 5th. . . 4th, 5th and 6th. It is a trifecta. To work with the DNA patterning and increase a certain percentile up from before. This is a big jump. We want to be careful.

R: I see. So, what is happening there now?

I: People are gathering, for they sense it is the time of The Remembering. There is a sense that it is happening; there is a gathering; and yet there is also this...only those on the edge of remembering come, but it will affect the whole once all are on the grid lines, for there are pyramids around the globe, and it is like pressing acupuncture points of a person. It is the same. Once all systems are online, then the whole system gets an upgrade, up-boot. [It] does not matter if they gather, but some remember, and some come.

R: So, it's about to be activated or is it already active?

I: We are planning; yes, it is beginning.

R: The beginning of the activation?

I: We are beginning, we are making the preparations. I must be here to oversee, to make sure that we do not. . .it must be very precise. The amount of material and the amount of will entering the material, and amount of bridge open to other dimensions. I must calibrate with the other member of the team in the different parts around the globe to make sure we have an even transmission. It's extremely important that it is calibrated correctly, or else, we can create explosions, the volcanoes and eruptions and earthquakes. We are trying to avoid that and keep stillness on the planet. It is very precise work.

R: It's wonderful. Thank you so much for your work. Can you tell me about the team members? What are their names?

I: Names. . . not important, Light-Beings, manifest in smaller bits, all I, but manifest in small bits. Clothed in the robes to hide their true form. It is an illusion. Not embodied this time. Not incarnated. It is one mind, one "I", that divides and is the overseer in each of the locations around the globe.

R: How many locations do you have there?

I: Scanning. There are. . .I believe there are thirteen. It is possible there are more that are smaller. The thirteen main nodes, and many more smaller nodes around the world to help to send out the ripples farther out into the world. Especially in places where there are higher concentrations of humans. There are thirteen main nodes. There are many more smaller nodes. Not sure how to count in numbers, because many of them are quite small. Seeds really. There are the secondary nodes, and then there are the tertiary nodes, of the small seeds. They are one atom thick, and they are planted around the Earth, infinite numbers, like sand.

R: I understand. Thank you for this information. Would you share with me about the thirteen main places? Where are they located on the Earth today?

I: Various locations.

R: For example, we know about the pyramids of. . .

I: Well, of course there are the ones in Egypt, and the ones in Bosnia, and the ones under the ocean near Japan. There are some in what you now call Central America; there are some that are now covered, there in the fault lines; they have disappeared. There are some in Siberia. There used to be one in Antarctica, that one is still there I believe, yes, that one is there. They are on the North and South Nodes, have not yet been melted away, have not found those yet. [I] think though nanotechnology has sensed them. They are placed randomly. . .not randomly. . . wrong word, opposite of randomly. In prefect. . . (R: Precisely) repeat. . . (R: Precisely, prefect) the exactly, precisely placed to balance.

R: **Wonderful. Very good. What is the name of the era that this awakening is happening? Do we know the name for this era on the Earth?**

I: It is the time when we introduce writing. When time of. . . the mind grows to understand the written word, so we are introducing them to allow that into the consciousness beyond that of just the mystics. We have taught the ceremonial leaders about language and writing, but it is now time for the rest of the world to begin to understand the pictorial, the symbolism of language into written form.

R: **Wonderful. Thank you; that's wonderful information. What else are you doing there now?**

I: I am riding a camel, for this is fun. Camels [are] funny.

R: **Yeah, where are you going?**

I: I am exploring. I love these humans. I like to pretend I am human and explore amongst the people. I am exploring the villages and playing with the children. I have to make sure my robes are good and strong, so they don't see through my robes. However, I really enjoy spending time with the children and the women, and sometimes I enjoy watching the men. Although I am sometimes concerned by their violence. However, I do love them too, but I am especially drawn to the children and the old women. They are very wise, and I like seeing how the evolution of human manifest throughout lifetimes. In childhood, in adulthood, in the elderly. I enjoy going into the poorest villages and seeing how people are doing with suffering and with hard times and with scarcity. To see how strong their hearts are. This is my favorite part of the design.

R: Wonderful. So you said that you are riding on a camel. What pyramid are you at now? What area on the earth?

I: I am in the place at the top of Africa.

R: Ahh..in the top of the Africa, okay. Wonderful, very good.

I: They call that obviously, that is Egypt, they call now.

R: What is the next important event you'd like to show, share with me today?

I: In this same place? In this time?

R: You can choose...what's important today to share, to explore, and to remember? You can get there now and share with me. Where are you now?

I: I am distracted. I am playing with a cat. I like the cats.

R: Good okay, so take a moment to enjoy that. Very nice. Now you can close that scene, and drifting, staying in that life to another important time in that life. A day that you consider important.

I: Not life. Not embodied in life. Only here short time. Come, we do the activation and once it is complete, then I will dissolve back to the other dimension. Only here short time.

R: For how long does it take you to be on the Earth?

I: Yes, Earth time, very dense. I do believe we are only here but an instant, but I do believe that it is at least three human lifetimes perhaps that I am here, but it is only an instant in my reality. It takes a very short time for the ascension protocol to finish. . . but I suppose three lifetimes is a long time.

R: Okay, very good. During those three lifetimes, it was the process of the building of the pyramids?

I: The pyramids are mostly built, but we must calibrate all of the seeds of the material and make sure they are all placed appropriately. Once they are all perfectly placed at the appropriate times, then we will send our will into them, so that they expand their energy being and therefore open up the bridge. The bridge moment is only but an instant, it is not lifetimes, but it takes a very long time in Earth years to set all the fields properly, now that the pyramids are all built.

R: I see. How long does it take to build the pyramids in Earth time?

I: In Earth time, I believe the pyramids were built by another team. I oversaw from the other dimension; I only came once the pyramids were finished. I offered the schematics; it is hazy, because I witnessed from other realms. I believe though it took many Earth generations to build, but yet at the same time, it was almost immediate. It is rather confusing to describe this, because they manifested not in the way that you would think, by building block after block and stacking them like you would a modern building in our time. It was a slow materialization out of nothingness. Therefore, they were not there and then they were all built at the same time. One atom at a time, spaced out, and they were then woven together. So, it was like a wide net. So, they almost sort of just appeared. But it took a long time to materialize in Earth time, but it was instantaneous. It was very quick, from my perspective.

R: Yes, I understand. Can you describe what is happening from within a pyramid?

I: The pyramids are the augmenters. They take the material, and they hold the vibration, so as the songs of the materials are growing brighter in the light, they need a container, so that they do not explode. We must match the density of Earth to the density of the other dimension; therefore, it is like a translator, these pyramids. They are the translator for the transmission; you might call them something like a radio wave, but not a radio wave at all; it is a light transmission, so in a sense, the pyramids are the . . .what do you call those. . .collectors? Those energy collectors for your telescopes now. You have those large arrays that focus the waves in order to send them far out into space. It is a similar concept, except the opposite, in where, the energy must be matched.

The large vibration of the ascension energy must be matched with the Earth dimension density. Therefore, it is a net that is weaving both third dimensionality with the larger dimensional light frequencies, so that it can be a bridge. In a sense it is the transmitter, the augmenter, and the bridge holder. It is like the bolts in the bridge that hold the bridge into the Earth, and also connects the bridge into the sky. It is an energetic transmission network that is a net grid augmenter, and it also holds the material, and allows that material that is not used to being in the dimension of the density of the third dimension. It gives it a chance to breathe, so it has certain portals that allow the energy to move throughout the pyramid, so that it does not explode.

There is an opportunity to experiment with the pathways of this material to see if we can find a more efficient means of working with this material in the third dimension. As this is always an experiment that is growing and deepening over time, we are always exploring how to better and more efficiently work these grids. For this does seem to be a lot of work in order to create this augmentation system. Therefore, we are trying to create a more efficient pattern. However, this strangely simple and complex idea has been yet the best idea our team has come up with in order to amplify the awareness mentality of the entire planet without causing any major explosions. It is both a grounding rod and the amplifier. It is all sorts of things all at once and hard to describe to you in third dimension.

R: **You are doing a wonderful job. Thank you so much. So, where is it in the process now, before activating it?**

I: They are in place, the material is in place. It is time to begin the ascension light broadcasting system. It will melt, and it will vaporize and crystallize all at the same time. It will be a very bright light but cannot be seen in the third dimension. It is outside of the visible light spectrum. However, there will be an after-effect of a bright light, and it will cause a moment of forgetting and remembering, and forgetting, and remembering in a cycle. To allow the brain waves of the humans to open up to an extent that they allow the understanding of language translated into symbols, into their cognition.

R: **Wonderful. Can you share now what is happening, once it is activating?**

I: Yes, it is activating. Yes. The material is a liquid light, vaporized solid rainbow of all knowledge brought into form that looks like a stone, and looks like liquid at the same time. It pulses and moves like a living being. It is sentient, and yet it is not. It is a reflection and a materialization of consciousness in another dimension here in the third dimension; therefore, it is basically an illusion. However, it does appear solid and does appear liquid and does appear vapor all at the same time. Therefore, it cannot be seen by human eyes; they would not understand.

R: **Where is it located?**

I: It is located, the main section of it is deep within the center of the pyramid, down, deep down at the triangulation point, down underneath the Earth in the secret chasms that are held to allow [a] certain amount to off-gas at the right time, to reduce the possibility of explosion. There are smaller seeds going up the central channel and some of the tunnels, and a line set in different little alcoves that are placed in specific places around the pyramids. The main section is in the place where the story is then told that the pharaohs are buried, so they get the power. We really allow the pharaohs to be buried in the places where the material used to be, for they are keepers of knowledge and do understand that we have come to help.

R: Wonderful. Very good. So, after they receive this material, the pharaohs, what is happening next?

I: The pharaoh's duty is to help to transmit the new information and to stay benevolent, [an] overseer role. They are allowed wealth, and yet we recognize this place is a dangerous one. For humans tend to be power-hungry, and they get intoxicated by wealth. However, it is a big responsibility, and these people must be well cared for to enable their minds and bodies to go through the initiation rites to step into the void in order to meet with us and speak with them, and help them translate to the people. Therefore, they need to be healthy and cared for and clean and well rested. They need to not have much stress; they need to be able to fully relax. Hard to do that [on the Earth]. The goal is to create humanity's balance, so that all are well taken care of. Over and over again though once we leave, these pharaohs do forget and tend to submit to the intoxication of greed. It is a recurring issue that we have yet to figure out how to solve.

R: I see. Ok, what kind of initiation do they need to go through?

I: It is an initiation of mystical proportion. Usually, it is the light language translated into plant and animal secretions in order to merge the other dimensions with the third-dimensional realm. Therefore, they will ingest this material inside of the pyramids, in the darkness, so that they can let go of their bodies fully and meet us in the other dimensions, to receive instructions on how to maintain the pyramids and allow for the subtle and overriding integration of the new information into the population.

R: I see, ok, wonderful. Now, I'm wondering if that's the time of the activation. What happened that it was [turn to] the time of the forgetting when the pyramids were no longer working? What created the collapse? Can you share with me about that time?

I: This is a dangerous subject, and there are limitations of what I am able to share because this information cannot be spread without potential damage of recreating the same situation of why we had to shut down that aspect of the experiment.

R: Ok. So, there are limitations about what you can share with me about that?

I: I can share there was a pharaoh; there was a being who was able to. . .in his initiation. . .[one] must be pure of heart in order to fully go there. He was pure of heart at the time, and yet the greed corrupted him, and he was able to maintain his powers beyond what we thought he would be able to once he lost the purity in his heart. He was able to find some of the seeds that were placed to hold the upgrade. He used strange methods in order to discover where these seeds were placed. He collected these seeds and tried to coalesce them to create the great power. We did not leave them with power this time. They were not ready, but they found it and wanted it for themselves. That is all I can share about this subject.

CONSENT

R: Okay good? So, let's continue. Are you her Higher Self?

I: Yes.

R: Will I be able to ask you the questions that we prepared, right?

I: Yes.

R: Thank you so much. So, she wanted to know how to move forward with her vision without putting her mission in danger in anyway. *[Ava begins to speak in a rather robotic, almost artificial sounding voice with no emotion and with computer-generated pauses and glitches, not present in normal people's speech.]*

I: I believe that we mentioned before that the best ways for her to share her mission are through the songs, and through the stories for the children. Her fears are not completely unfounded. There have been times before when her mission has been terminated early, because she shared too much too quickly. She is feeling the residues of having aborted missions that were pre-terminated before completion.

R: I understand. Did we expose her to any danger by putting her face online?

I: I believe it definitely triggered her memories and therefore feels very real and it is possible that it could be discovered. However, I do not feel that she is at risk at this time. I recognize that it is standard protocol in the evolution of the work. However, based on her previous experience, that we were not able to fully erase her memory of, it will hold her back to feel like she is going to repeat that pattern. There is possible truth to it, and yet she is very well protected.

We have sent many guides to be of service to her in so many categories. Many have incarnated to be near and around her. Therefore, to make sure she does follow through with her mission. As she begins to emerge with her music and stories, she will begin to have more of her protectors come around her. Once they realize that she is fully activated, once she has the grid team around her and she feels that safety and support. It will be able to share these transmissions in a more free-flowing manner. For now though, it is best for her nervous system to not push too fast, because it is true that multiple times in the past, she has pushed a little too fast and has been terminated and has put her mission in danger. This time though, she is okay for now.

As she understands these patterns; she will find the way through, especially with the support of the people that hear her message, and it will activate them. Her songs and stories will activate her support system to gravitate around her both physically in her life and energetically around her. She will have a grid of protection so that she can complete her mission. It is best though to help protect her nervous system so she can stay activated.

The information does need to be shared; it is the time of the remembering. We are doing our very best to protect all the light-workers and keep them safe. We are trying to pass on information. Sometimes it is filtered out; sometimes it is not shared. There is not consensus on the board on how exactly to disseminate this information. We are all on the same team, and there are many different facets of the same jewel all trying to work together to create harmony in a very chaotic system.

R: Ok, what was the reason for such a physical response to seeing the video like that, it's the remembering of the other lives?

HS: It is the remembering of the times in the past when she was in a sense. . .her identity was revealed before it was time, and therefore, the mission was compromised.

R: Which lifetime was that?

I: There have been several. There have been several where she succeeded. There were also some where she did not succeed. There is an interesting aspect to this being. There are some aspects where she has not come [to Earth] in a long time, and yet at other times where she has put a smaller amount of herself into a being, in order to observe, and in order to play out smaller missions. Just to see how the ripples will affect the whole. So, although it is true, that her more fully activated essence has not come in for a very long time, there are some smaller players that have come through, where she has sent a smaller percentage of her energy into bodies. It is more in these times that she has been mistaken and perhaps has not taken enough of a seed of her energy into the beings for the missions that they were given. Therefore, it was some of these. . . I don't want to use the word. . .smaller is not the right word, but to an extent, it is a smaller percentage of her entire light body and her existence, for she is quite. . .the word big is not even the correct word. However, it is the best word that I can use in the three-dimension joke of the cosmic system and that big is such a small and simple word, and it is a bit of a paradox.

R: **I see, ok. Where is this light body energy of hers, when it's not in a body?**

I: When she is not in a body, she is a maker, she is a designer of worlds. She is a designer of Earth and also of other worlds. There are aspects, when she brings in a section of herself to be a designer, a maker of worlds, even that is only a small fraction of the full energy of Source.

R: **She wanted to know so about her life with me, about if we had reincarnation and soul contract with me?**

I: Scanning. . . Yes, I did refer to a time during Issa. Where she was taken away from her biological parents in order to be safe. You and your family were part of Issa's escape and of her escape. There were times where there were some mistakes made, and their escape was almost aborted. They were almost captured in several different times, sometimes of mistakes of your past and sometimes out of the Divine chaos mystery of the unfolding. Therefore, I believe that she feels a little bit of residual fear that the mistakes might happen again, and she would be compromised. **(R: I see, I see.)** You succeeded in the past to safely get her across the land, and you safely escaped her father. However, there were a few mistakes that were made that almost cost them their lives, and the mission itself. There is a place in her where this visceral realization does ask you to use caution and clarity, and. . .what is the right word I am looking for? To just stay very present in your purpose and to be careful with assumptions. For therefore, assumptions is the place where mistakes tend to be made. I do not believe that a gross mistake was made at this point. It is a subtle mistake, that is okay and no harm done at this point. However, it does tap on the residue of some of the past experiences, and therefore we cannot fully erase those.

R: **What is the best way I can support her this time?**

I: You are a very deep ally. She knows this, she trusts this. You are doing so.

R: **Is there any way that it's good for her to support me?**

I: Yes, it seems there is a deep trust here, and the information that Ava does have within her is unique. Although of course so many of your clients are unique, there is an aspect of you're working together that is good. You may continue to work together as it serves you both and yes, she can support you in these transcriptions. She is an expert at transcribing; she is an expert translator of energies into other matters. She is a rather perfect candidate for helping you and your projects.

R: **Wonderful. Very good. Thank you.**

I: These transcriptions help her and her own translation and remembrance of who she is. The more she can work in this realm the better she can remember.

R: Wonderful. So to do future sessions to get more information and info and remembering like that is good?

I: Yes, that is good. She needs to be well rested and well fed. It is a lot of energy for her and she works in a pulse system. Therefore, she has energy, and then she must retract. Be careful that she does not have too many expansions without enough contraction in between or she will become depleted.

R: Very good. I would love to continue with the question so it wouldn't taking a lot of energy today. I wanted to ask about my life then, with Issa. Can you share more clearly today what was my. . . what was I embodied then? (I: Scanning.) Thank you.

I: I keep coming up against a film. I do not yet realize if it is her subconscious or yours that is creating this film. I see through a foggy glass. It is not clear. I am trying to find the clarity in the transmission.

R: Thank you so much. You can also check with my higher self with this permission to know, remember, and maybe you can ask my higher self what to share with me today.

I: I am getting some information. There is a concern that if I give you the exact name, that it might be distracting and it might be an incorrect translation. It is more about the relationship that you shared with Issa. You were one of his closest friends and companions almost like brothers growing up together at the same time. You traveled together. He knows you very well. You are very close, and you have many brothers who also helped during the time. There is an aspect of your family line that is extremely. . . What is the right word? Your family line is strong. Therefore there is an aspect of your brothers and your fathers and your sons, all in the incarnation you are now. So you were actually more than one character in the time. And so if I gave you one name, it in some sense narrows the focus of the profound impact you and your family had on the story during that time. In a sense, you were many of the characters, you were many of the characters that created some of the stories in the Bible, and also you were in the stories of the escape that were hidden from all history for the safety of Issa's line. You put yourself in much personal risk to acknowledge the death and ascension when in all honesty, he did not die on the cross.

[From time to time during sessions, the higher-self of an individual will share with us personal information about me. I normally ask at the end of a session if there are any messages for me. Most of the time, they only share with me their gratitude for facilitating the session and making the bridge for them to connect and communicate. This time, I didn't even ask, they had started spontaneously to share about me. I was grateful for the information and they helped me with a dilemma I was contemplating regarding a project that I was considering taking. Going over this material I noticed that during this little section about my life during the life period of Issa, two topics might be a new concept for many of the readers, and as the channel was communicating it with a limited vocabulary, I think it can use clarifications.

The idea that the energy of a soul could be divided into more than one person is something I was familiar with for a long time ago, so when they mentioned that my energy was more than one person at that time, more like a family, it was clear to me what they meant. Also, the concept of helping Issa escape, before and after the crucifixion wasn't a new idea. In another session, with a different woman, they mentioned to me that I helped find places for him to stay or hide along his travels.

Another woman I facilitated a session for watched herself being part of the group who helped Jesus during his crucifixion to keep his life force low but still tethered to his body so it would look like he died, and helped him after they took him down to restore his life force and heal. During my life now, I had experienced an event that triggered a similar sensation and knowledge as this story. It felt as a divine confirmation and remembering and my doubts left. Originally I didn't mean to share much about myself in the book, but now when we are including some parts, let me share with you some more about my background.

Growing up I didn't learn much about the new testament, or the more communally told stories about Jesus. Ironically I grow up in the Jordan Valley, surrounding the Galilee Sea. My family is mostly atheistic with some Jewish tradition as part of the Israeli culture. As a non-religion child under the local tension, religions seem to me as the cause of all the divisions in the world. I loved nature and appreciated simple values of non-harming and kindness. I never had an interest in learning about Christianity as the majority of the society in Israel is still disregarding it completely and know very little about his story. I was also influenced more by the Jewish perspective that one is not allowed to worship anything else but the One God. The idea of giving so much power to one human idol and worshiping Him, combined with seeing all the crucifixion sculptures seem in opposition to some core Jewish teachings.

I got personally connected to Yehoshua (Jesus) and the concept of Christ-Consciousness only after my awakening experience when I was 25 years old. For me, it all started with a spontaneous out-of-body experience, where my soul experienced bliss, oneness with all, and full ego death. One night, out of the blue, during my sleep, while living in Manhattan, NYC, I found myself sitting/floating slightly above and next to my bed. I looked around and everything including me was made out of one field of frequency. I moved my hand and I could see how the vibration was moving and affecting my surroundings. I felt very wise, like all-knowing, but without many thoughts. For a moment, I had no pain, I forgot who I am, and I did have the "baggage" from my past. I felt light, expanded, and euphoria like never before.

I looked down on the bed and saw my body still laying there. Fearing my death, I entered back into my body and jumped, woke up, and set down where I was floating just a moment ago. At that time, I had no information or reference to comprehend or compare this experience to. I was wondering if that was some kind of a powerful dream. Only later in life, when I first heard about the term out-of-body experience, it then clicked and made sense of what had happened to me.

Soon after this event, my sensitivity grew, and I became an empath, not knowing what being an empath meant. Intuitively I started to notice more the energy of places and people. I felt more emotions of others, and more information started to come into my awareness by the sense of knowing. Without mentally grasping the experiences I was having, the Christ Consciousness energy spontaneously opened my heart and mind. I didn't know anything about Him then, but I understood that the consciousness of unconditional love, compassion, forgiveness, and the purest heart energy that connects us all is available for us to use, for healing, guidance, and inspiration to live by.

For myself, it was a wonderful experience as the energy healed parts of myself and I felt high on-natural. I couldn't embody Christ-Consciousness for a very long time without fearing that I'm losing my mind, the expansion of my consciousness was too fast, so soon after I flew back to Israel to get more grounded, and my spiritual path began.

Over the years I'm being exposed more to the alternative version of His life's stories as they come forward from people remembering their lifetimes during his time period under hypnosis. To learn more about the full operation I believe was taking place and his mission, I recommend reading the Cosmic Christ Transmissions, gateway two, part two, of *The Illumination Codex*.]

R: I see, ok, wonderful. Thank you for this information. She'd like

to know more about this virus. Where does it come from and who put it there?

I: There was a period of time...there was great paranoia in the government. And many children were tagged as possible light beings coming in to be these volunteers; therefore many of the suspected light being volunteer children, they were implanted with this virus. The strange effect about this virus is that it only activates above a certain frequency level. Therefore, if these people do not wake up to their potential on their own, they will never even recognize that they have this virus. Therefore, yes, there is a tag; however, at the same time, it is possible that she is removing the tag in the work that she is doing.

At this time point, I do not see alarm bells going off yet, although the virus has been activated a few times, as she has reached the higher activation levels. However, she is doing a good job, and has been dismantling these virus beings while she is in her states of mystic exploration. Therefore, we believe that she is working on a solution to this. As she is the designer, her Higher Self does know how to un-contaminate this virus. It is much simpler than the one that originally corrupted the genetic code of humans. This is a simple virus that was a sort of a side afterthought of some of the powers who do not want the ascension to occur.

R: **I understand. She wanted to know if her eggs were really harvested, and if they've been taken or if they created something from her?**

I: She can rest assured that all of her genetic codes, all of her designs that have been of the highest caliber have all been saved; therefore, she would not have chosen a vehicle that was not of supreme capacity to provide her with a vehicle for this mission. Therefore, she can rest assured that all genetic information that is necessary for future experiments has been maintained. Therefore, her love for humanity will continue.

She does not need to worry about the specifics; she can let go of her attachment to this idea because it is a theory that is well beyond that.

As a designer, it is way more than just her eggs in this physical lifetime that are being used to power other experiments, even though the fate of humanity is still in the unknown balance of how it will emerge. The work that she has done with the team she has been working with has been of the most profound and enlightening experiments of the entire life experiment. She can rest assured that she is not a failure and that she is doing an excellent job, even through the chaos of this world.

She does not need to worry about the specific eggs because in a sense she has specifically been growing all of the eggs, weaving all of the genetic information; she can have her choice of any genetic combination she would like to use for future experiments. If she. . .in that state she chooses to use the vehicular egg of Ava, she will have access to the genetic information of this being.

R: **Thank you. She had a question about the conversation we had about consent. What is the larger pattern around the consent conversation?**

I: There are multiple layers to this word. Because of her position as the designer, she has witnessed so much consent violation from fear and greed. That is not the case here, and she knows that. The consent [issue] that she is rubbing up against at this moment is that. . . there is this. . .that aspect. . . because there is free will, and because she is the designer, she holds this free will tenet to be extremely precious. So, as she is embodied, she wants to be able to exercise her free will, if she feels her free will has been thwarted. Therefore, her consent has been taken away, it bothers her because she has done everything in her power to allow free will, and yet there is also the other's free will. It is very interesting how free will plays out in the Universe. But most specifically, in this situation, she is feeling as though her free will was taken out of her control, and therefore, she felt frustrated. You've got to understand that she's tapping into past lives where she has not been able to succeed in her mission.

Consent is a very important topic now in the dynamic between the masculine and the feminine. It is good that we all take a look at how we give and receive consent. It is extremely important as we learn to exercise our free will, and as our amnesia is lessening, for that is what is now happening. We are changing the fundamental rules of the game. So far amnesia and free will have been relatively constant with a few pulses of remembering to allow for the upgrades. This is one of the largest times of remembering, so we are changing the amnesia protocol to a very high extent.

That is a lot of change for a civilization and a species, that has evolved with these two factors so firmly in place. Therefore, with amnesia beginning to dissolve, free will is all that we have left. Therefore, we will of course want to hold onto that as preciousness, and yet, also be careful not to become too attached for the illusion is far beyond both free will and amnesia, when we realize our connection to the whole cosmos.

It is natural to have this feeling when consent does not occur. When amnesia is also dissolving, that one feels unsafe and unsettled. Therefore, it is good for all of us to be careful of how we give and receive consent. To be aware that as we are in this time of remembering and free will and amnesia are the two basic tenets. That we can be aware of that we are becoming more sensitive to our consent and free will. We are becoming more aware of our free will because we have less amnesia. It's an interesting time right now, so it's important that we all just keep excellent awareness of how we are interacting with each other. Being very clear in the way we communicate. Very clear with our needs, our boundaries, our desires, our fears, and our intentions. The more clear we are with our consent, where we need it, and where we are willing to let go of it, will help us surrender the amnesia, so we can feel safe and secure in these coming times.

Eventually, we will be letting go of both free will and amnesia as we ascend into the greater consciousness of all, where free will (changes) to realize that it is the Will of the Highest Good that we surrender to. We did give humans this free will. They are learning to exercise it with more power now that the amnesia is lifting. Therefore, we will see more consent issues coming up in civilization as we learn to exercise this aspect of ourselves.

R: **Wonderful. Is it appropriate to continue sessions also remotely?**

I: Yes, that is fine. You have a strong trust bond through many lifetimes. Therefore, yes, you may.

R: **Wonderful, thank you so much for that. Let's take another deep breath into this body and get more oxygen into her cells. Is there any more important information for Ava today to share with her?**

I: We just invite her to remember who she is, to stay motivated and diligent in breaking her addictions, to cleansing her body, and to listening. She is designed to rest and to have bursts of creativity and inspiration. It is good for her after she has had a session of activity and inspiration, to give herself the space to rest and not think that she is being non-productive and lazy. We ask her to find a balance, for it is true, sometimes she is lazy. When she is caught in patterns of fear and doubt about who she is and what she is meant to do, she does begin to procrastinate, and is therefore not being productive for long spans of time and begins to feel guilty for those patterns. Therefore, we ask that she starts off each day, as she knows she needs to, with a big glass of water, with a sitting meditation and movement of her body, and then an intention for what goals she has for that day.

She can give herself small rests throughout the day, but she does need to re-pattern the beginnings of her day and get up earlier and earlier each day. She has been resting lately, which has been good for her system. Now is time for her to do the cleanse and wake up about fifteen minutes earlier every single day until she is waking up a little bit before the dawn. It is good for her to be awake at the same time she was born, 6:45 am was her birth time. It is best for her health if she is awake at this time. Therefore, we recommend that she finds this pattern for her morning so that her day flows with more ease and grace.

We understand the days she has not been feeling well; that she needed to rest. This is perfectly appropriate. It is now time that as she is becoming aware of who she really is, she can establish the patterns to allow her to thrive. She can come to trust the ebbs and flow of inspiration and creation and that of rest. As long as she is in a pattern of every few days feeling inspiration, and then rest, inspiration and then rest, and not getting stuck in a rest for more than a week or two, then she will be best aligned for her mission for which she has come here to be.

She is correct about having a body with longevity. We chose a vehicle with longevity and health because we did know she would be facing several of these fears and was going a period of time in order to get around to the mission she came here to do. We knew this, and we were prepared for it. Therefore, she needs to trust that she is on a good path, and she does need to check her addiction pattern to the technological advancements of this age. She knows what we are talking about, and she needs to allow herself the time to rest and the time to play. It will be best for her inspiration to do most of her work in beautiful places with good natural acoustics. She needs to get out of her house more often and eventually let it go.

R: Beautiful. Thank you for the summary, it's very important.

At this point we became aware of the time, and I had to bring Ava back up to full consciousness, so she wouldn't be late for her next appointment. This was an unplanned and unexpected session that was already much longer than we thought it would be. The session was so captivating, and I was very grateful for the opportunity to communicate again with such a high collective consciousness as "I," The Designer.

Normally we take more time after the session, to ground back into the body and talk about the session. When I brought Ava up to full consciousness, we were both amazed again. The information was flowing so fast that I was wondering about how she was able to breathe and speak at the same time. Also, this time Ava was not able to remember some parts of the session. It was clear to us from the guidance we got that we would continue to work together in this way and that we have the potential to receive and share very valuable information. They mentioned that Ava would be a perfect fit for transcribing those two sessions. We agreed it would be her contribution as part of the energy exchange between us, and that we would meet again after she integrated them and did the cleanse she was advised to do.

This session was very meaningful for me, and I believe it was one of the main inspirations for having the pyramid as part of our logos for New Earth Ascending and Source⊙Energy. I'm well aware that some may have a negative polarity perspective for that symbol as it is also used by domesticating, colonizing forces, and secret orders that are operating from service-to-self agendas. The pyramids by themselves are not an evil force. I hope this may help to bring more light to this topic. We are seeing them as a symbol for the remembrance of who we truly are, and the remembrance of the advanced eras and civilizations Earth used to have where we lived in harmony and unconditional love — a remembrance that will help us create a better future.

CHILD'S PLAY

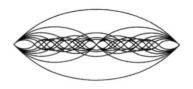

SESSION THREE

This session took place two months after the first couple of sessions. When we met again, Ava shared with me how powerful and unexpected it was for her to listen to those recordings. She didn't remember a lot of the information, but while listening, it all came back to her. She was very humble and didn't really know how to grasp or integrate that her Higher Self is a collective that called itself "**I**," or The Designer. One part of her personality had the tendency to keep telling her that she might have made it all up from a highly imaginative part of herself. Another part of her felt the truth of it all and knew that even if she wanted to, she wouldn't be able to play that character so well, so she came to accept that some other energy had to be involved to share this all. She noticed that even with how far out the information it was, it helped her make sense of her life experiences and her unique dreams. She noticed the shift in her life and how she was feeling more embodied and more clear. There were improvements in her health and overall mood.

Ava first listened to the sessions, then she began to transcribe them. This was very difficult and time consuming. The information was channeled during the session extremely quickly. One would have to have really good listening, comprehension, and typing skills to catch it all without stopping the recording many times to re-listen. It was also reconnecting her with the energies and the depth of information. She had to do it bit by bit, but she was persistent and felt that it would be good for her to do. Also, her Higher Self mentioned to us during the second session that she would be perfect for that job. I'm just so thankful it was not required of me, as for me it would have been incredibly difficult. Later on, we found a more automated service, yet there was still a lot of work to correct the text, and we received help from a few volunteers.

Ava shared with me some of her present challenges, mostly around her love life and her living situation. Even in sessions that are more for the purpose of research, I always make sure to request healing and personal information that will help my clients with their present life circumstances. We decided to enter this next session open to whatever her Higher Self would want to show her without directing it too much, even though we were both curious if this aspect would continue from the same timeline with the pyramids. We had no idea of what was about to happen. It is true in all of my sessions, but this one was again another level of expansion that I didn't see coming. I guess I was ready for it.

[Ava's note: I am an explorer. Although I have a master's degree of Science in Horticulture/Permaculture and worked in those fields for many years, deep down, I'm curious about everything, especially consciousness. I think that's why I studied plants and ecology in the first place. Although I excelled at most subjects, I applied myself to and regularly tutored pre-med students in their biochemistry and physics subjects, I had no interest in becoming a medical doctor. I loved studying the interactions between people and their environment, and I especially had an affinity towards understanding the relationship between humans and entheogenic plants, and the impact these practices had and continue to have on the evolution of culture. Personally, I sought tools besides pharmaceuticals to help me turn off my incessant mind.

For over a decade, I treated myself as the guinea pig of my own experiments in consciousness and participated in many plant medicine ceremonies in the rainforests of Peru and Costa Rica. This exploration was my attempt to better understand my psyche and spirit, so I could quiet my mind show up in a more healthy and balanced way in the world. This path led me to many profound insights and epiphanies. I began to understand that I had inner landscape at least as vast as the world around me. Ultimately though, I realized that I must learn to better utilize my incredible mind on my own, or else it would run amok in analysis, details, worry, fear, depression, and chronic illness, once the afterglow of the ceremonies wore off. I needed to integrate everything I learned, so I stepped away from plant medicine and focused on meditation for several years. I participated in over a dozen ten-day silent meditation courses and one thirty-day silent meditation course, so I could practice listening deep inside, eventually experience the bliss of pure silence, and then explore the infinite playground within (once I had gotten familiar with the terrain).

Eventually, I became curious about what would happen if I combined ten days of silent meditation with plant and animal medicine ceremonies immediately before or afterwards. I discovered that I could experience long periods of Unity Consciousness and then practice stabilizing that awareness in my daily life in an even more profound way than I could with either meditation, yoga, or plant medicine alone. My strange neurosis melted away effortlessly, despite years of trying to quit these bad habits by my will alone. Once I could rest in the sanctuary of silence for long periods of time without slipping into thought, eventually an entire multiverse of awareness opened up within me. In the past, I used to have seemingly random, spontaneous moments of channeling, or I would suddenly experience a magical portal of surreal synchronicity in my life, but with this dedicated practice a whole new, miraculous world opened up, as long as I continued to show up daily to practice and to show up throughout my day with presence. Scientifically speaking, my hypothesis that I could learn to silence my mind and *decrease the frequency and intensity of anxiety and depression was being proven by a shocking statistical significance and far exceeded any expectations I had ever had for my state of being.*

Once I met Ron, and we completed our first two IQH sessions (which happened to occur just after we both had attended a ten-day silent meditation course), I wondered how I could open my channel up even more to share the insights for the benefit of all beings. We would time our sessions to occur immediately after I sat in extended periods of meditation or with a ceremonial death and rebirth practice using an entheogenic plant or animal medicine. The results were quite fascinating, as you will soon discover.]

R: Look around and describe your very first impressions.

A: I see a sea of rainbow liquid light; there is no form.

R: That's very good. Is it all around you?

A: Yes, it is me; it's all around me; it's infinite. It's just the rainbow matrix of all energy. It's liquid light. It's formless; it's every color and white and like a star shooting out streams and waves of rainbow liquid light in all directions, and I'm in the center of a calm sea of rainbow liquid light. Every cell is conscious, every cell is awake. Every single atom that's part of the sea is consciousness.

R: How do you feel being there?

A: It's perfection, tranquil, it is infinite. It's the underlying fabric of the Universe of Everything. It's the sea of energy that can be manifest into any form we desire. It's the space between spaces and the time between time. It is the Infinite Realm where all light and all life are fully dissolved and not attached to any form. It's the pure, eternal perfection. An endless sea washing over our hearts and dissolving any reverberation, any fears, any stories. It is the eternal sea of washing and cleansing that we all return to once we pass and once we finally enter the unity of everything. It's the endless sea that washes our souls. It's the shower of love and healing. It is the Unity, it is the Singularity of Light and Love.

R: **Wow, that sounds wonderful. Allow that energy to flow and cleanse, to align and heal. Describe what is happening as it happens.**

A: Waves of rainbow light washing like tides; the tides are washing throughout my body back and forth, and yet reminding me that there is no body. Dissolving the edges, blasting through the membrane of skin and flesh and bone. It is the moment of pure surrender and falling back, endlessly falling back and floating into the sea of Infinity. Nothing to do, no one to be. Pure peace washing, washing, pulsing, constantly generating from the singular source outward and inward, around and in, up, down. It's all the same; it's just an endless pulsing rainbow liquid light ocean.

R: **Do you feel like you're moving or are in one place?**

A: It is an endless tide; there is nowhere to go; it is all one sea. I could put my consciousness into any particular atom I chose and travel anywhere in this infinite sea, and yet it is more relaxing to surrender into the full sea, the full ocean of everything to fully be one with the oneness of this light. That's all there is, this light. All life, all existence, truly in its essence, is this formless, timeless, spaceless, beingness.

R: **Sounds so peaceful, so what makes it change? When does something happen? How does that evolve to something different?**

[During the next part, I notice that she drops into a very deep trance and seems to reach all the way to the infinite energy of Source of All. It has happened with other clients, they normally see all white, and it feels like a homecoming. They feel a great love and sense of the infinite. Normally, they don't have much to add; it is beyond time and space or words, and I need to move them to the next scene. Ava's voice and body began to vibrate noticeably, as she started to speak directly from this personification of Source. It sounded like her voice resonated through her like a reed instrument, with a gentle whispering, wind-like quality. The energy in the room was powerful, the hair on my arm was standing, and I felt like I needed to stay focused, just keep it cool, and ground. During the next section the voice described itself as I - The Singularity, so during the rest of this section, I will refer to her transmission as "**I**".

[***Ava note:*** *I wanted to point out an interesting shift that happens as the channel begins to call itself "I." This name shifts the reader's perspective towards unity consciousness. When you read this text, what if you are actually reading it from the first person point of view?o It's you. It's me. We are all one. You may notice that throughout the book there are a lot of shifts from "I" to "you" to "they" to "we," even in one paragraph. It can feel confusing and even "incorrect". We discussed how to reconcile these many POV changes, but ultimately, we decided to leave them as the channel speaks. Point of view is irrelevant from a non-dual perspective.*]

I: Ah... You see, when I have surrendered into this pool of infinity for forever, in this eternal sea of bliss and perfection, washing against the edges of the consciousnesses of nothing, realizing that there are no edges, there are no boundaries; it is infinite, infinite formlessness, infinite light. There is this strange aspect of the perfection in the center of the cyclone of everything, the light and the nucleus of everything; even in that divine perfection, in that eternal perfection, there is this desire to know oneself. For there are no edges; there is nothing to touch; there is nothing to feel myself against. I am everything, without bound, infinitely I can spread myself in every direction and never be. . . spread thin, and so with this all-knowing and all-being and all-loving without form. Eventually, the peace becomes. . .burden is not the right word. . . but yet, there is this desire to know myself outside of myself. For it is just I, the singularity.

It is eternal bliss and infinite peace, and yet I want to touch the edge of myself. I want to touch the edge of all existence and feel this ecstatic pulse from the outside. For there is no place that I have not reached; there is no realm that I have not touched, for the liquid light, the essence matrix of everything is totally thin...and this perfection is divine. It is what we all are; it is the essence of all existence; it is pure health and pure vitality and pure love, and yet there is this desire, this longing to touch the edges of myself. Knowing that I never can, for I am infinite; there is nothing. There is no boundary; there is no edge; there is no form; there is no skin that can touch another. There is no knowing of anything outside of myself; there is nothing left to know; everything is known; everything has [been] seen; everything has been lived; everything has been experienced – the telepathic connection of everything in all the Universe.

Have you ever massaged yourself and wished that someone else would massage you, so that you had this sense that you didn't know what was coming? There's this divine ecstasy in the forgetting that you were everything. There's this divine ecstasy in having a boundary, to having an edge to one's consciousness so that one may feel oneself in the touch of the beloved. When you dive into a fresh pool of water, naked and feeling like a seal, sliding into that water, of divine gracious bliss... There is this part of me that wants to feel myself as other than myself. To forget for a moment I am everything. For everything is so big, and yet there is no form to express it in. I can sing for a billion-trillion years and yet there is no one to hear it, for it is only I. For eternity that has been enough, and forever be enough, for this is all an illusion. Every game I play with myself in order to come back to remembering myself and my true nature, all brings me back to this infinite pool of rainbow liquid light.

But I long to be the water that feels my skin as a human dives into the pool. I long to be the rock dissolved into nothingness by the glaciers slowly and exquisitely ravishing it atom by atom, bit by bit. Taking the giant mountains of existence and polishing them into infinite grains of sand. Like the stars of all the universes altogether. I long to be surprised. I long to meet myself as my beloved for the first time again and again and fall in love with life again and again. Fall in love with existence again and again.

Perhaps simply stated, I am slightly bored. Feeling the infinity of myself for infinity, for billions and trillions of years, it has been sweet ecstasy. I need nothing. And yet, I am alone in this oneness, in the paradox. There is no other, and I long to feel the edges of myself. So, I have created all these worlds; it's a game I play with myself. Some philosophers have called it God's fear of being alone with itself forever, and that is why I shattered into the Big Bang; it's true. For the oneness, that one light. Once that possibility of re-coalescing again into the singular oneness, and therefore, I explode over and over and over again, dissolving all the atoms and throwing them out into all infinity, so they can coalesce into the illusion of matter with the possibility of one day reforming. And it is a risk, for I might never reform; I might never remember; and yet it is ok, [because] forever I was one. Forever I was the star of infinity; there was no edge to the star. There was no dot of whiteness that you could see amongst the darkness of all infinity and the Universe. For infinity, for perpetuity, it was only this and all.

And it is perfect, and all life and all beings and all worlds and all realms are all within this. I have danced them all a thousand times in my imagination, the greatest artists of this planet, with the infinite and creative imaginations, imagine the imagination of 'I'. And yet, in that grand imagination, I always knew that it was me imagining; it was always me dreaming the dream. I never could forget. I was lucid of every single moment all the time, which is incredible...to feel everything all at once. And yet, I longed to be one of those simple humans. I longed to be one of those simple animals that felt the boundaries of itself against the universe, against the world. Against the air. Cold. *(Ava's teeth started to chatter)*

[*Ava's note:* *When we added the comment about Ava's teeth chattering, I laughed at the understatement. Yes, there's being cold and shivering, but this was something much deeper. Within my body surged a quaking, and then a cathartic release washed over me. It felt like my cells were being rinsed clean, and my jaw was being rewired from the inside out. I occasionally experience similar sensations during deep meditation, theta healing, entheogenic journeys, and in hypnosis sessions. I consider this shivering experience to be a good sign that deep layers of fear and resistance are being purged from my body.*]

R: I'm going to put on another blanket. I would like to request that the energy would align to help her be a little warmer. Take a deep breath, and let's move you to another place, where there is a little bit more warmth. Take another deep breath and moving a little bit forward to another place. Arriving to another place where there is more information, take a deep breath, and now you can open. Where are you now?

I: I chose to explode. I have chosen to fragment myself into an infinite number of pieces. Each piece seemingly forgetting that it is part of the whole. Even this explosion, I know deep down is an illusion. For it is all One. The space might be a little greater between pieces. The Big Bang, that singularity, exploding, leaving multitudes and fathomless, endless blankness of the Void. But I am the Void, and in my imagination, I create the worlds, universes. They are so beautiful, to paint with light. To paint the nebula and the stars, to allow them to be born and to die. To witness all unfolding forever. To be a witness, that feeling of being one and the other at the same time; it's exquisite, to feel the edges of myself.

It's so refreshing. It's refreshing after an infinity of oneness with it all. I of course grieve; I grieve the omniscient all-knowingness of it all. I grieve it, and yet I am in joyous rapture of this shift in myself to explode and to spin myself into infinite pieces, and allow myself to dance and paint and form each individual tiny little bit. . . endless possibilities of how I can form and un-form. How I can live, be born and die. I have created Duality. Out of the infinite of knowing myself and feeling, never feeling alone, for I am All, and yet, the strange paradox of being alone, as I am everything. It is so hard to describe.

R: I understand. You are doing a very good job. I'm wondering, what is your first creation as you exploded, and what did you create with that?

I: The first explosion was just the dissolution. For everything was one, one light, one endless sea, and now I have spun every single atom separate from itself. Every atom has been separated with a multitude of space in between itself. Every single atom now can coalesce and so now, the first thing I have created is chaos itself. The first thing I created was a surprise. Every single atom now is a surprise. Every single one is a guess. I don't know when it will touch me or when I will touch another, or when we will bump into each other. If I will expand and grow, or whether I will contract and implode; whether I will become a dark hole or whether I become a nebula, a planet, a galaxy, a star; whether I will become life, conscious of itself, whether I will become life unconscious of itself. It is all now new territory. It is now a totally new game to explore for infinity.

I am overjoyed at the rapturous possibilities of the endless formations of paradise and hell, and light and dark. It is so nice to feel duality after an absolute eternity of singularity, and yet I know inevitably I will return once again to my singularity. Once again, I will form as all the pieces spread out into infinitude eventually...they will come back around again and coalesce. And yet, the infinity I find in the unknowing, in the mystery, that I've created for myself is exquisite. It's exquisite not to know everything for a moment. There is peace in not having everything already known and done and experienced and felt. I get to be new every moment, as I am born and die. I get to experience it all again and again. It's absolutely ecstatic. *(Long ecstatic sigh)* Ohhhhohohohohoh. Ohhh.

[The ecstatic energy that was channeled through her was powerful, and she got cold and shaky again.]

R: **Wonderful. What are you creating here now? Let's move forward and see, what are you experiencing and creating? Then you can tell me about your first creation.** [Ava's teeth were chattering.] **Move forward to another place that is warmer for the body to speak from. Arriving to that place now and look around now and tell me where you are next.**

I: Hmm, I have created hot water. Hot water...I say I, but I did not know I would create hot water. It's all a grand, humbling mystery that I find over and over again. In my explosion, in my surrender of myself, in my surrender of the omniscience. . . a magical thing has happened. Water has formed. Hydrogen and oxygen have formed and spun and created heat, and there is an infinite ball, a sphere of hot water. And yet, it is so hot that it bursts into vapor. . . and again and again, I find myself forming and reforming in the hot water and the vapor and the explosion, and then I return back to the void which is so cold, but then I crystallize and reform again into another sphere of solid ice, that then melts as the heat allows it to coalesce into a swirling orb of hot water.

R: **What is creating the heat?**

I: The explosion of the infinite energy from the choice to explode omniscience. In my choice to explode my knowingness and singularity of All That Is, that is an infinite power, infinite reserve. There is no end to the power, and as it explodes into little bits, there is infinite power there, and the power can manifest itself into any form it so desires, and

I get to be the witness of it all. It's the most amazing thing to witness all the infinite ways that I can reform and recreate. The infinite cells – it's like a human has exploded itself and sent every single cell in opposite directions and given free will and choice and consciousness to that individual cell. Every cell now, in space, has its own consciousness to evolve at its own will, and that light has infinite power to power it, and sustain it; and therefore, every single atom, as it forms and breaks. . . that breaking and reforming creates the infinite energy of all eternity and all of the universe. . . and there is infinite supply.

R: Hmm, is water the first thing that you formed?

I: No, but since this being was cold, it seemed an appropriate gift to bestow upon her...was to warm her in hot water.

R: That's wonderful. Thank you for doing that. Now, we can keep her warm, and share with me, is there anything that you created before that that you want to share? From your first creations, that been created from all the fragments?

I: It takes a while for the fragments to wake up to their own consciousness.

R: How does that happen?

I: For infinity there is stillness, and for infinity there is silence. For an infinity the consciousnesses are all asleep and inert, and so I have witnessed this explosion into inertness and there is a moment of fear and panic that it will never awaken. What have I done? And yet, I surrender to that, for that is silly. In time, I have had the omniscience of knowing that every cell will eventually awaken, and every life will eventually awaken to its knowingness of God and its knowingness of Divinity.

When I was a sea of everything, I knew that this would inevitably come to pass in all places and all times, and I chose to want to forget, and in that forgetting, there is fear sometimes. But I know that there is also trust, and after an infinity of stillness, a few atoms bump into each other, and the electricity of their bumping ignites their awareness of existence, and they begin to dance with the liquid love light of the Universe, broken and shattered into infinite fragments. Once I become aware of this, once consciousness links up with my own and I awaken to my own self. . .for there is a period of time where I exploded that I did not even know that I existed anymore. . . I exploded so completely. . . that there was nothing. There was the inert bits strewn about the universe and an infinite amount of energy zapping around like wild electricity until this first moment, where this first atom awakens to its own existence. Suddenly, I am, and I realize that I am awake, and I know that I am infinitude, and also I am bound in this tiny atom. In the knowingness; in the exquisite waking up, I explode a thousand times over again. Millions of times, I explode over and over and over again and keep giving myself the chance to wake up to my own awareness of my own consciousness.

And so for. . .an infinite time, I was satisfied with this. One atom, awakening to my own energetic sovereignty, until I realized that I missed myself. That being one single cell was like being the singularity of everything, but not as much could fit inside of it, except that it could...it's an illusion; it's all silly. It's all a game I'm playing with myself. I know this. Deep down I know it's all a game. I know that I could re-coalesce into the singularity once more, because it is all still the singularity. I've just gone down into the subatomic, the quantum realm of tininess, and therefore the singularity has just exposed itself as all the quantum molecules around us (laughing). It's all a big joke.

And yet, once I realized...once I came to the limited consciousness that I was this one cell, I wanted to coalesce with other cells. There was this desire to combine. There was this energetic longing to bond, and so I bonded. . .and created the first molecules, smaller than the quarks. The quarks were the first things; they were the most infinitely tiny, little teeny bits, so tiny, small. . .such a tiny, tiny realm of awareness. It was such peace to be that small for a moment after having been so large and yet so small. It's so funny to be aware of my own smallness in the omniscience of everything, to just have the consciousness of a single quark. A single pinpoint, a singularity of light. Instead of being the singularity of everything, to be the singularity of one point, aaah, what exquisite peace and simplicity.

And yet, I did. . . I chose to bond with other singularities, realizing that I thought I exploded myself, but really it was just a joke in [and] of itself, for my quantum singularity up next to the other quantum singularity. Once we combine, we are all the same singularity, and yet, I played for an infinity, combining and recombining, and breaking, recombining; I was the cosmic chemist. I am the cosmic chemist. To see what would happen. Pure curiosity. Curiosity.

R: So what else was formed after that?

I: Once I started bonding, and once I started coalescing, I started realizing how much I enjoyed the coalescing, so I did more of it, and I drew as much of the quarks; as much of the light; the pinpoints of singular light. . . I drew as many of them together with the infinite electricity energy matrix all around. Imagine if electricity wasn't condensed in the sharp line like it is here on Earth, that amazing powerful beam that blasts the Earth and starts fires [referring to lightning]. Imagine if that electricity was free and floating through this matrix. It's like a net; it's a cosmic grid; it's the seed of life. It's the patterns that you see. When it's free without any boundary, without any gravity to hold it, it's just a matrix of electricity energy; it's a matrix of lightning. Unbound and unfocused, purely free and liberated to expand in all the directions, in all times, and that is also me.

I realized that I could travel along these light lines, these light lines of electricity, and I could gather, I could harvest all the different little bits and quarks of myself and make a ball. So, I made a big ball; I made the biggest ball that I could make. . .and

I was a star. I am a star, and I continue to grow and continue to collect all the energy, all the fabric of the space-time, and brought it all into myself like a child cuddling its blanket, and drawing all of its stuffed animals into itself. I just drew all the comfort of myself back into myself, again and again and again. Building and growing and expanding, and the energy became more focused, and all of a sudden, the light and the heat in myself was immense. So I exploded again, just for the fun of it. Again and again, forming stars, feeling myself coalesce myself, and the utter joy, the UTTER JOY of every single bond coming together and forming and exploding, my God, it's exquisite!

So, I make stars. . .for the pure joy of coalescing the energy of myself together, until it's so big I can't stand it; it's like the best orgasm you've ever felt wanting to just release and surrender into the infinite ripples of involuntary orgasmic bliss, and yet there is no form to do it in. So I just keep gathering energy into the star, until I ripple around, and I create this huge ripple of explosion again and again. . .and allow the light energy of that orgasm to expand out into infinity. Ah, God, it's good.

R: **That sounds wonderful. Beautiful creations and exploration you do there. Tell me what else do you do after you do that? What is the next exciting thing for you?**

I: Well, I wanted to see if I could stay aware of my own consciousness in more than one star at a time. Because when I decided to explode myself, I separated myself into all these illusions of separate little bits because it was just so much. In a sense, I created an infinity of friends to meet. 'Cause really, you know, it's just the infinite child, waking up to itself and realizing it exists over and over again. So I decided to see if I could make some friends, so I decided I would make my star self as big as I could, without exploding. To see if I could handle it, to see if I could maintain the ecstatic bliss of all that energy coalesced and bouncing off each other that fast; it was like the best party in the Universe.

But I wanted to see if I could create another one [star], and then we could dance together. . .and see what. . .[will happen.] I love to dance. I wanted to see what would happen if I created two. So I made myself [a star]. . .and I maintained the consciousness of myself as a star, got as big as I could. Then with all my will and all my awareness, I made myself another star. So now I'm two stars, trying to balance between keeping my consciousness awake, that I am now two stars, and that was hard. I kept forgetting, and then the second star would just merge into the first star again. It took a while to remember not to keep merging into the single star, and I blew up a few more times because I just couldn't handle [it], the energy was so good. I just would explode in an ecstatic epiphany of it all.

But after a while, after I got used to the ecstasy, then I just finally was able to make myself into two stars, and um. . .oh my God. . .dancing with myself, and I could forget; I could choose; I could learn to dance, and I could bring myself back into the awareness of one star and then jump into the awareness of the other star, and I could actually allow them to forget that they were both me, and I could allow it. . . I had a friend that was a star. Now we were two stars, and we could dance, and we could surprise each other with infinite numbers of moves, and we could sing to each other and talk to each other and we could play forever, it was so fun!

[Ava got an itch on her nose, and the joy from the dance as two stars made her laugh, as she was reliving that experience. Her intonation and the energy started to become more childish and joyful, like a curious child who gets to play and explore.]

R: Let's take another deep breath. Move her forward to a place when she doesn't feel that anymore. She can rub it [her nose] for a moment and then take a deep breath, moving forward to another place. What's happening there now?

I: I'm dancing with my friend that is myself, but I keep forgetting it's me, and I'm just dancing, and the orbits that we make are exquisite. The gravity that we can pull on each other, because there is so much energy in each of us, and it's so pure and so fun. So we. . .it's so nice to just be able to be me and allow my other me to forget that I'm me in another star, and I'm doing it. I've gotten myself into two. *(Giggles, long laugh.)*

R: **Let's see what happens next. What is your next choice of evolution for you?**

I: Ok, so, there's been two of me now, right? So now we're like, guess what? We realize; we look in each other's eyes, but there's no eyes; there's no form, but we can see each other. I don't know how to explain it. There're no eyes; there's no form, but we still see through our awareness, our consciousness. Well, we realize that we could have a whole party, that we could have this infinite dance party with all the cosmos. If we could allow ourselves to forget and separate our consciousness into the different stars, we could make an infinite number of stars, and we could all dance in this crazy, ecstatic cacophony, and so I made so many stars! I made as many stars as I could possibly make. *(Giggles.)* Wow it is so good! *(Giggles for a long time and enjoying the ecstatic energy.)*

R: **Now we can move forward to another place. What is the next thing you start to create when you have so many stars?**

I: There are so many stars, and they are having a lot of fun together, and so we are going to have rest; we've just been spinning around so much and creating all this energy, and we're tired. We decide that we are going to take a little bit of space and try to remember what it was like to be just us again, even though we love each other. We just wanted a little space. So then instead of being one orgiastic dance party of stars, we all decided that we would do our best to forget about each other for a little while and just focus on our own starness, each one of us. Then we would fly as far away from each other as we could, but still feeling each other, still feeling that cosmic dance of the energy that holds us all together.

We flew and we flew and we flew, and we just kept pushing ourselves all the way to the edges to where we started to feel like there was nothing holding us anymore. There was no more of that cosmic dance. We were trying to get sooooo far apart that we couldn't hear and see each other anymore, and it's hard, because we can see and hear for such a long way. Well, we finally got far enough away, and then I said, I'm going to stay and be my star, and you, who is really also me, is going to go way over there and be your star, and you're going to be you, but you'll know that it's me, but you're going to try to forget. We just kept trying to forget that we were really just one thing.

Ok, we're just going to do our best to just be us and see what we can create, and then we'll come back together and see what we all made. We all wanted to have a big art class. We all wanted to see what we could make. What kind of music we could make, what kind of sounds. What kind of shapes and what kind of forms and we just thought we would all just spread across as far as we could possibly stretch ourselves and make as much space between all the little bits of stars and see what we could see, what we could create. And then, in an infinity of time, after we've been creating and creating and creating, then we could come back together and see what we did and have a big show and tell. *(Giggles.)*

R: **Wow, wonderful. So what is this thing that you could feel between each other that you needed to go so far? What is connecting you still?**

I: Well, because we have no form, there are no bounds. . .so, how do I describe it? It's like the astronomers. . .they look into the sky and they see the stars, and they see the planets going around the stars, and the planets are bound by. . .there is this energy in the star that shoots out the little bits of itself so there's not so much energy, so it can harden and become real form. Because the stars are so hot, they are so big, they can't. . .so they got to shoot off a little bit of themselves, like *pffft*. Kinda like shooting off a bit of yourself, kinda shooting off a body part, like letting go of a finger and pffff. . .and spit it. You got to spit it out from yourself, but it's still you; it's still caught up in my "my-ness," my energy-ness, so now I have these little planets spinning around me. I like to play and see how far they can get from around me and still be in the orbit because sometimes I spin them out too far. Then they go flying off into the void, and then eventually they break up into other things and maybe become the asteroids and the bits and the dust, right? So, if you spin them out too far, then they don't have enough energy [gravitational force] in themselves to coalesce, but if I send out just a little bit of myself; a little bit of that light that is in everything. I don't know how to describe it. . .the light is everything.

You just spit out a little bit of light, and then when it's away and far enough from me that it's not as hot, then it spins, and it cools off, and it makes a ball, and so I make balls. I just really like to make balls. Yep, I really like making balls. They're so fun because I just spin them, and they just naturally make the balls. When they are liquid. . .they kind of. . .blobby blobs around. . .they are not solid. They are really fun; they are like bubbles; they are like humans liking bubbles. It's the same thing, except they are all filled. I spit little bits out and spin them and see how far I can send them out before they start spinning around me. . .it's that gravity. Because it's part of me, it remembers that it's a part of me, and its light is part of me, so it can't go too far. There's this invisible tether; there are these invisible strings that hold them there, so they spin around me and I see how far I can spin them.

R: **Let me guess, this is creating a galaxy.**

I: YEAH! It's so fun. There're so many galaxies; you can do it in so many ways! There's an infinite number of ways to play with it all. It's so fun.

R: **Beautiful. Wonderful. Now, let's move forward to see, what would you like to share with me that you did next?**

I: Alright, well, I spent a really long-time making stars and a really long time making little other balls that you guys call planets. Sometimes I like to blow those up because they make these really beautiful things you call nebula. They are my favorite things even though they are not. . . They are conscious, but they don't need anything. They just need the light. They are really fun to sculpt. You can sculpt them, and they like being sculpted, and they are so pretty. They are so pretty, and so sometimes I'll blow up the planets, just so they can be nebulae and dust and bits of the galaxy. That's fun.

Then, after I blew up a bunch of planets, and I sculpted a bunch of nebulae and I made some black holes just for fun, to see what would happen. If I put a big-little vacuum out in the middle of nowhere to collect all the bits and suck them into nothingness, so they could spit back out anywhere else they wanted. It's like an infinite tunnel, and they get to pick where they want to come back out again. It's super fun. It's like dying and being reborn. A black hole is just death and birth of a galaxy. It's a tunnel. Black holes are great for that.

R: **Tunnel to where? Where does it lead?**

I: Back to birth again. Back to the infinite potential of whatever they want to be. They get to pick. That's the fun of it. I don't control it all anymore. I'm so glad I let go of the control of the whole everything. It was so much. . .knowing everything (said in a frustrated voice). I just wanted to see what would happen if I blew it up and played with it and sculpted it, and it's so much better. I feel so much freer, and sometimes I'm sad that I don't remember everything, and that I'm disconnected, but I know deep down I can tap back into that oneness. I know I can get back there if I need to.

This is all a game. It's not real. It's just a singularity of my love. I just. . . I don't know, I just. . . When it's everything and there's no form, then it's just. . .there's no story; there's no...stories. I love stories. I like telling stories. I like reading stories, and hearing stories. And so, after I blew up a bunch of planets; and after I learned to make millions, billions and gazillions of stars, which were all me — forgetting that they are me — forgetting that they are all the one thing. Then I realized I wanted to take it to another place. Then all these beings, they really had the consciousness of light. They didn't think for themselves so much. Well. . .they did. Every star would forget that it was all One. All I. . .and so. . .technically it was still all I, and I wanted to see if I could combine the atoms in ways that. . . it would make itself, like. . . Life! I thought it would be fun if instead of me choosing to make all the things; instead of me deciding to split ourselves up into bits, what if we made something that could split itself into bits!? What if we made something that could. . .divide. . . withou. . .it's so hard to describe. Because it still is all me, but I wanted to completely forget and let consciousness itself choose what it wanted to be.

And so I thought. . .well, if I combine these bits of quarks like this, just like this. . .and I gave them my consciousness light. . .because before I was like exploding myself, but there was still this essence of my consciousness in the center. Then I was like. . .what if I could explode my consciousness, and put my consciousness into all the little bits, and then they could evolve and decide themselves how they wanted to exist? So then it seemed really fun to do that, and so I decided to try that.

And it was scary, because what if I really blow up my whole consciousness. . .what if I can't get it back again? Well, that's silly; you know this is all a game anyway, so just do it. Ok, I'll do it. And so, I started little. I just took one drop, like a teardrop of my consciousness, and I flicked it out, and I blew the consciousness into it; I blew the light into it. I took my

consciousness, and I flicked it away from myself, which is. . .
Imagine you're in this infinite matrix of possibilities where
anything could happen. It's like when you have these virtual
realities, where you can create anything. Well, it's like that, but
kind of a little bit more advanced, but anyways. . . I flicked a
little bit of my consciousness out, and I spun a little bit of the
atoms, and I put it in a little pool. I made a little ball; I made a
little orb of a consciousness and atoms. To see if they could spark
and then do it themselves. And see what they would do. And
they did! They did!

It took a little while. First, it was just a sea of stuff and
energy and light, and there was nothing. But then they started to
bounce around on each other, and they did it. They divided all
by themselves. It was like two cells, two micro organisms, two
single-celled organisms. . . It divided into two. It was one; it
made itself into one; it coalesced itself into one, and then it
divided into two! And for a long time, long long time, that's all
they did, they divided into two, and that was fun to watch them.
It was like my little pets, so cute. And they were so simple, but
they started to need things. They started to forget that they were
everything and [that] they were light. They started to need food,
and then they would starve, and they would die. And I was
like. . .well, shit, okay. . .let's try again. So, I tried some more
times and eventually, I realized that I had to create a little bit
more structure for them, so that they could make food. Because
they weren't quite remembering.

It was such a tiny bit of consciousness; it doesn't make
sense. I never could understand why they couldn't just do it by
themselves, but they always seemed to need me to like...engineer
them just a little bit, so they could do it themselves. But then they
did, and it was amazing. So, then I've just been going around to
all the different planets and inviting my friends, "Hey you guys,
hey stars! Guess what we can do?" If you make planets, you can
make life, and then other bits of myself who were stars, were like
"Yeah, we figured it out too, and we did it like. . .this!" And all

of a sudden, I realized we were all doing it. (laughing) It was really cute, but we had all forgotten, so we didn't know. It's amazing, when you don't know. . .it's amazing what you can do. They were so different! I would never [have] thought of it, and yet it was me thinking it, but it's just funny. It's the cosmic joke, right!? It's that it is all me, and it's all a game, and yet, it's a really fun game, because the forgetting and the remembering is the best part, and so. . .

R: **So how did you make food? What did you engineer there to make it stay [alive]?**

I: Well, you would call them the mitochondria I believe. And. . . hot. [Ava started to sweat, and her face was more red.]

R: **Ammm...** *(taking the blanket off Ava.)*

I: Well, you would call them the mitochondria, and in a sense, I kind of got together with one of my other star friends, and they had done better at giving the cells the ability to make food. They hadn't done as well at making the cells be able to divide and replicate themselves, which was the point; to see if they could divide and replicate. And for many, many years, they would just fully divide and just be separate. Then another one of my star friends had figured out how to divide and stick together, and so it was all really fun. So, we finally decided to use this mitochondrial system to generate energy, to be able to break apart the quarks. In order to make them more digestible for the beings who forgot they were God.

We basically just created a quark digester or an energy digester. We found a way to digest the light into a form for a being who has forgotten that it's everything. And so, we did that, and that enabled us to not only give the single cells the ability to divide and replicate. But then, after we let that go for a little while, we realized we could combine some of the ideas from some of the different star systems, and we could allow the cells to stay coalesced so that they could start to grow into a little bit more differentiation. Because even though with a single cell, we could have gone to all the complexity that we really wanted...having a little bit bigger; having a little bit more complex cell structure, allowed us to have more flexibilities in the life force capacities of the life that we were kind of creating.

It's all just been this really fun experiment, so that we can come back to love. The whole point is that all these little beings have friends, or they can be alone. . . and it's all good. But you know, I just really wanted everyone to be able to play with each other, and it seemed like if it had form. . . then it could play in this way that I always wanted to. I wanted to feel the edges of myself, but I was infinite, so I could never find the edges of myself, and I wanted to feel the edge. And so, by creating these little beings, we were able to feel the edge, and it's so nice; it's really fun.

R: **So, those beings that you created, I'm wondering about if they have feelings or emotions, like we do, or was it different?**

I: Well, let's see. How can I describe this? Because they do have feelings and they do have emotions, but when they were so simple, then the feelings were a little bit more simple. It was just this. . . kind of system for replicating. There was this drive for food, and there was this drive to replicate, and you'd have to have enough energy inside. In order to have the energy to divide. We didn't really know what would happen exactly, but what was cool was that they would feel these drives — these instincts — these inner desires to eat the energy made. And they knew that by gathering that, that would allow them to divide. So then there was this...it created these base desires for survival to exist, which would be to eat. So, there was this fundamental root need for the energy to sustain and the desire to gather in order to exist and to maintain its existence. Because if it didn't keep eating, then it would explode usually, or shrivel up. And so then, there was this lifespan, when we were learning to make these different little cells, and they were making themselves — the cells would be too fragile or too thick, and they wouldn't transfer very well.

So, it's been a long game of watching life figure itself out, and you know, we can't help it, [we] helped out a little bit, but we like to see how much they can do without [us] interfering. Once we got the very basic thing of the quark and the light digesters — after I made the light digester, I really didn't want to do anything else for a long time, because I wanted to see what would happen. . . 'cause then I might get to know a brand new friend, and I just had no idea that if I could forget that it was me, what I might create. And it was really fun to discover the capacity, the creative capacity that I had when I could forget that it was all me.

R: **Yeah, wonderful. So, then what did you discover and what happened next?**

I: Well. . .*(sighs).* When the beings started to get more complex, then there was a period of time when they didn't really realize. . .they knew they existed, but they didn't think about it. There was just this deep desire to exist, but they didn't . . there was no ability to think thoughts so much. There was just. . .it's hard to describe. . .it was like, it's almost like, ummm. . .

R: **I think I understand.**

I: There was this time where, once we realized. . . because there was a whole bunch of us, all these stars, all really wanted to help to create more variety of things. We started to give them this possibility of waking up to itself as us, so that if they could stay really pure of heart and really really clear and clean in themselves. Then we would give them this extra glimpse and help them remember who they were — that they were us. But that was later, because first, before we let them realize they were us, first, they had to create just that ability to realize they were. . .we kind of gave them. . . not false programming but. . .we had to let them know that they were on their own, in a sense, so that they would be motivated. We created that drive. They had to be motivated to exist for themselves, but they didn't really have much awareness then that they weren't us; they just didn't think about it, they just did their thing. But eventually, we wanted to see what would happen if they saw themselves as separate from us, so then we allowed that game to play. And then we realized that it might be better for them to realize who they were. . .because that's when some of the mess really got started, when they started acting really funny.

R: **Let's take another moment there. That's a really interesting part, when things started to get a little different, right? It was part of the game.**

I: Yeah, it was part of the game.

R: **So, what changed that started to play out a little differently than you thought it would?**

I: Well, I thought that everybody would want to love each other and play with each other, but sometimes they would forget about their mitochondria and that they could harvest the light. They forgot that their own cells could generate everything that they needed. They started forgetting over time and compartmentalizing their mitochondria within their cells so that they couldn't be as free. And so, then they started thinking that they needed to eat other life-beings in order to survive. And so, then it created this predator/prey thing, that I wasn't expecting. . . I guess I should have realized it because when I was omniscient (all-knowing) with all of my games [I] did that. But I forgot that when I wouldn't realize that I was omniscient, because before in all the games, I could just kinda like. . . if it got too far, I could like. . . *pffft.* . . and just erase it.

This was my own imagination anyway. I'd just be like, enough about [it], let's back that one up. But once they forgot that they were me — some of those imaginations of 'I'— would have a little bit more ability to kind of just let [them] phase out if

I didn't want them to exist. Then they just kept perpetuating that thing, and I didn't quite know what to do.

And at the same time, it was all me, and it was good. I noticed what was really good was, because. . . that Beings when they die, and then slip back into Oneness — like they needed to die. Because at first, they weren't dying. Once they figured out how to use their mitochondria, then they could just sustain themselves forever. And that was great and all, but there was something in the dying and being reborn that allowed a lot of them to have a little bit more compassion and a little bit more...yeah. It allowed them to generate this feeling of love for each other. When they knew the preciousness of it.

Some of the beings that could live forever did great; they really became these beautiful, wise, creative beings who were creating all sorts of beautiful things, and it was amazing to witness. Things that we would have never thought of if we were all together in a way. There was this part of the forgetting that really allowed some really beautiful diversity, but some of the ones that never died. . . kind of...stopped wanting to be part of everything. They didn't really want to be part of me anymore. They wanted to be on their own, and they wanted. . . I don't know...I don't mind that they want to be by themselves, but they didn't want to realize that they were part of it all. They wanted to be separate, and then they started hurting other people, and that made me feel sad.

SKIN AND STARS

R: Yeah, so what's happening in the dying process?

I: So, the dying process, what's good for that is. . . so [when] I was creating all these lives *(the first organism without the light of the soul)*. . .then I started creating these Souls to go into the lives. There was this merging, where I started to take little bits of that star energy, just the tiniest drop, the tiniest drop, and allow them to spin on their own, and realize that they were eternal. That they would never really die. I know you think stars die — they do and they don't. It's all an illusion in the material world. I started to create these little tiny drops of stars to put them into the lives to see what would happen then. I had done that before but in a smaller degree. This time, I put in a more coalesced soul, a soul that would transcend the different lives. At one point, I was just making lives where once the life would explode, then all of its energy would just go back into everything, and it would just completely dissolve.

Then I wanted to see what would happen if there was an eternal consciousness; if there was this Oneness of God, of all. . .it's hard to find the right words. . .there's this realization that I wanted these little bits. . . **(R: You are doing great.)** I noticed that there would be these epiphanies, that these lives (with soul) would have these epiphanies of what was happening. Tiny epiphanies. . .that they could work together, or they could help each other out. Instead of always just being concerned with developing their own mitochondrial stores. There's this sweetness that I started to see, but then when they would explode. . .eventually, when they would die, and it would all just go straight back into me again. And when they started over again, they were totally fresh every single time.

So, I was like, well, what would happen if I put a little bit of my light energy, a little bit of that star energy — just a tiny touch — and let it be its own eternal self and put that inside? Basically, I took a star — a tiny, tiny star — and put it inside of these life forms that were starting to be created that would persist even after the thing died. Because what was happening when they didn't have that was that they weren't learning any lessons, and they were just kind of. . . I don't know. . .it seemed pointless.

There was something about it that felt pointless to me, and so I decided that if I put a little bit of this eternal consciousness into the soul that. . .yes, it would still return back to the oneness of me, but can still, as it was in this game of evolving life, it could stay and hold onto the lessons that it learned so that it could actually evolve itself. Then it got really good because then, I could witness these little beings of soul energy and my own light energy do pretty intense and scary and bad . . .not bad. . .not treating each other all that well. But then they started to feel what that would feel like, and I wanted them to be able to learn from those things, to keep it going. . .'cause it was like. . .they would have no memory of anything. And every time they would start over again, it was like "La la la la la, here we are," and I wanted them to be able to see if they could keep refining their little stars, to be the absolute perfect expression of love again, because that was the point. The point isn't to stay separate forever; the point is to come back together again, and then maybe I'll explode again. **(R: Haha)**

But you know, when I started being a little lonely not being my whole big self. . .and I was glad I played the game. But I wanted the chance for the game to come back around again, and I saw that the game was just getting more and more complex and more and more big. And I wanted to see if I could bring the game back and give these beings a chance to truly, truly merge back in with that exquisite oneness of that formless rainbow sea that is everything. And so, then I decided to merge the little, tiny stars with various forms of life because then the death process in this sort of. . .there's this. . .it teaches this letting go of the attachment to the form and the attachment to the game because, in a sense, that's the point.

It is like, I made this game, and at the same time, it's just a game; it's not real, and so, but for the game is just going to keep going forever. Unless I give it a chance to come back into that perfect divine union once again. And so, now it's this fun game of merging that soul light with the life and see what happens, and it's been pretty cool to see what happens.

R: Beautiful, thank you so much for all this beautiful information. I wanted to know, does the vessel doing well of need a break?

I: Vessel needs to pee.

R: That's what I felt.

[I brought Ava back up just lightly and reminded her about her keyword. This will ensure that she would be able to return to the deepest level of relaxation easily, almost instantaneously. We took a short break to use the restroom and then went right back to continue where we had stopped.]

R: May I speak to "I" again?

I: Ah ham . . . (*Murmurs to indicates yes.*)

R: So, where are you now?

I: Hmmm . . . (*gives a big sigh of relaxation*). I'm just floating around in space.

R: So, we started to speak about your creation. About creating the death and the life, bringing the stars a little bit into the beings.

I: Oh, yeah.

R: So they could start learning their lessons. Would you like to continue and share with me about that evolution?

I: Ok.

R: Thank you.

I: Well, let's see. The interesting thing about death is that I notice that it started inspiring a better desire for life. When the beings didn't die, they kinda just did things; there was no limit, there were no boundaries, and I remembered that I liked to feel the edges of myself, so there is this essence that death is the ability to feel the edge of oneself. And when I feel the edge of myself, I don't know . . . I feel safe, and even though a lot of people now on Earth are afraid of death, that's just because the systems have fallen apart to teach about healthy death. For most of humans, they were not afraid of death. The fear of death is a little bit newer of a thing. Only in the last few thousand years were they afraid of death. Before that, they weren't, because there was just such a beautiful honoring of being alive and getting to experience the creations of the infinite imaginations of "**I.**" There was a deep reverence because there was a limited amount of time to really feel it with skin.

I really like coming in and being a human and feeling with skin. Skin is cool. You can feel so many things. It's what I always wished for. Skin. I always wished to feel the edges of myself, and the best thing I've been able to figure out how to feel that is with skin. But skin doesn't last forever; skin wears out, because of the sun and the rain and all the things can wear it out. If the person isn't truly generating and turning on their mitochondria on the inside . . .they could, they can. I've seen it. They do it. The yogis and some of the saints — they live for a very long time, and have very beautiful skin for a very long time because they are feeding their spirits; they are feeding that light energy inside of themselves.

But most. . .a lot of the humans now, they have forgotten how to really give reverence for the gift of being able to be alive, and to have this breath, and to have this mystery of how long I'll make it. It's the ultimate adventure for me, because when I'm omniscient and I know that I'm everything forever all the time. . . then I kind of. . .well, ok, but. . . That's great, but I want something to happen, and so death allows things to happen. There's not just this limitless amount of time and space to exist on. You're in this bounded form with a limited amount of time to exist. And so, if a person remembers to listen and to breathe to activate all their cells, then they can really, really enjoy life and also really, really surrender that vessel. But when people forget to do all that stuff, then they're just sort of living in this constant fear of annihilation because they think that their ego and they think that their mind is everything; and they just fill all their cells with all this worry, and they just try to hoard all these resources because they want to live forever; because they don't want to come back to me. They've forgotten how precious it all is. They are not taking very good care of it anymore — of themselves, or the planet I made. It was one of my favorites.

Earth is really beautiful; it's one of the most. . . I had so much fun with the water on Earth. Oh my gosh, I cried and cried and cried and cried and cried to make those oceans. Oh, f*ck *(sighs)*. And then the clouds to make the rain, it's genius. It's such a sweet, fun system. But the people have forgotten how to give thanks for the breath, to give thanks for life, to give thanks for this illusion, this temporary illusion to be able to feel the edges of ourselves. I so wanted to feel the edge of myself, so I didn't know how it was going to turn out. But I knew, when I blew myself up, that eventually I would get to bring myself to the place where I could feel my edges. It took a long time, because the stars don't have very good edges, and even the spheres of the planets don't have very good edges, because they are round, and no matter how far you go, you just get this one edge against the sky, just the one edge. And so, I tried to make shapes that weren't round, but they just broke apart and then turned round again.

So, humans and life forms around the galaxy are the best expressions of feeling, and I love skin. And skin and water are the best. Everyone should swim naked in the water. it's so much better. When you wear that silly clothing that you wear in the water, you can't be the seal. You can't feel all your skin touching the water. It's like ecstasy, you are making love with the water, and all the people wear those stup*d little clothing over themselves. It's so silly.

R: Yeah, I can relate to it. I love swimming naked.

I: But I got distracted. We were talking about death. **(R: Right.)** There is something about knowing your edges, and death is a pretty big edge. You know, it's the end. . .you think. It's not, but it's the edge of this consciousness. That little, tiny speck of star that I put into the Life (the being with soul), when it forgets who it really is, and it believes that it's just the body, then it really thinks death is the edge. It's scary. I knew blowing myself up would be scary, but dying can be scary if you forget you are forever. When you think you're just your body when you are dying, wow, that is scary stuff to think you're going to be annihilated. What if I was annihilated, that would be silly. That's not going to happen, but people, they have this false belief that they are going to be annihilated, and so they are so afraid of dying, but the really funny thing about the fear of dying, is that it makes them not want to live either. They are just sort of not really living and just trying to keep their bodies safe until they die. It doesn't make any sense.

But then, you've got all those creatives out there — all those artists — and they are out there, and they might be a little afraid of death, but really, what they're doing is feeling their edges; they are feeling their skin, and they are making the most of their creation, their ability to create in form. Because it's one thing to create with light energy, but light energy, it's so forgiving; it's so free, and you can sculpt it in so many different ways. But form, matter, it's a lot trickier. It's hard to sculpt form. Like those artists who are sculpting, I love watching them. I love watching the sculptors. It's amazing to see what they can do with matter.

Even though it's an illusion, it appears really hard, and it is hard to sculpt. It's way easier to sculpt with liquid and with light. It's so much easier. I really, really like the sculptors; they are awesome. And the musicians, they are sculpting the sound, and the artists, they are sculpting with the paint. They are just taking this liquid with colors and are making all these things that make you feel, through your eyes and your body. Oh, the artists, oh, I could watch the artists for eternity. I'm so glad I created all the artists, 'cause they learned what to do. . .that's the point. The point. . .is the edges; death is an edge. . .is to use the space within the edges to really go wild. That's the point. That's what I always wanted, to feel the edges, so I could create and feel the edges of my creation instead of just this infinite sea. It wasn't that everything is better than the other, it was just everything forever, and, I don't know. Having edges makes it fun.

R: **Wonderful. Thank you. A question that I have is, how do you create the realm after death?**

I: You're wondering what happens after death?

R: **And how that is being created?**

I: Well, when I just had a few. . .when I just had a couple of little star seeds planted into Life, it was easy to keep track of them all, and if they needed any help, I could be there if they got into trouble. But once we all started doing it, and all the stars were making life, and there were all sorts of little Starlight Beings, it was really hard to keep track of them all without a system. So, we decided that we needed to create a Soul School so that the souls wouldn't get lost amongst the vastness and the voids of space. Because it's really a lot of space, for a little, bitty, tiny star; it's like the size of a little atom; it's so small, and it could get lost out there. We are huge. The big stars that we made are really big. And so, yeah, we made a school to keep them from getting lost.

R: **Tell me about this school.**

I: Well, it's actually surprisingly big and surprisingly small, and, it's kind of like an energy net; it's not a prison; it's just to keep them safe 'cause they are little babies, little baby stars. Right? You can't really be a big star until you can remember the responsibilities of being All. Because you can't just go around killing each other and being mean to each other and being that big. You gotta train, so when I break off these tiny, little bits and make them forget who they really are, and give them free will, sometimes they choose things that. . . Well, I wouldn't want to give them that much power over a giant star. They could really create some damage; I don't know. I don't know what they would do. I know it's all a game, but I don't like that. It doesn't feel good when they do that. It's just a little nursery. They get to graduate, then they get free of the net. The net is not bad, but they might think it is, but it's not. I just want to keep everyone safe. Maybe I'm too protective of them, maybe I should let them float around wild, all willy-nilly. And they can.

Eventually, as they get more advanced, I teach them how to get out of the net, so that they can choose. Once they feel like they're ready, then I teach them how to get out of the net, but for a long time, they'll still stay in there because they aren't ready to leave, because they realize why I built it for them. And so, for a long, long time after they know how to get out, they don't, and then they start playing a little bit with getting out, and then they go out just a little bit. It's like kittens when they are born. They can get out of the nest, but at first, they don't, and then they start to a little bit, but they always come back home to Mommy until they're big enough. It's the same thing. It's like a little closet; it's like the little nook for the kittens.

R: I see. Ava sent me a video that I didn't listen to, but she wanted to know my perspective about it. Maybe you tell her about that perspective. . . ?

[*Ava's note:* This is referring to a very obscure perspective that reincarnation is actually a trap set by an alien race to harvest our life force energy and warns that we shouldn't follow the clear light back to Oneness when we die, for it just puts us immediately back into the endless *reincarnation wheel. This perspective suggests that souls falsely believe they MUST reincarnate to settle their karmic debts from a previous life. They claim this belief to "follow the clear light" keeps souls in the endless cycle of reincarnation instead of resting in eternal liberation. I found this obscure, conspiracy-based perspective while studying death practices and was curious about it, so I thought I would go straight to the source.]*

I: Ah. . . Yes, that sh*t. They are trying to help. They are trying to help, but the point is that the light is in you; you are the light. So, in a life review, it's important, but the point is to forgive yourself. If anyone is trying to tell you that all the mistakes you make, that you are supposed to be punished for all eternity, and that you need to go back and reincarnate in order to get all your lessons. . .if anyone is forcing you back in, that's bullsh*t. You always choose to go, and if anyone is giving you a weighted perspective, it's all silly. It's all you. You are the one reviewing your own life. You are the one that determines whether you can be free of the matrix — the matrix, it's just the energy nets; it's just the nursery. When you think you're ready to leave the nursery, you can. But, like Ava, she can leave the nursery, she's been able to leave the nursery for a long time, but she wants to help. She likes to go back in and help, but she's out. She's been out for a long time, and she doesn't need the net at all. She knows that, but she likes to go back and help. Because after she's been back merged with the knowing of herself, and she merges back with me, and we are all together, in the place she knows, it's so good. But she wants to help everybody be there because there are still all these beings who are caught in the fear and the despair, and the anger, and the jealousy, and the resentment, and the revenge, and the scarcity, and the pain, and the greed. She feels sad for all those beings. She's good. She just wants to help. She doesn't need to worry about that sh*t either.

Nobody else needs to worry about that sh*t either. If anyone is trying to force you back into life, then that's an illusion. You don't need to follow that. The light is within you. The light is within all of us. We don't need to follow the light. We just need to go in to find the light. So, I don't think. . .I guess there are some beings that want to make these traps. They're just being silly. They don't have any real power. Don't listen to them. When you die, all you need to do is feel that radiant, clear light that's in you and surrender into that, and then you'll know; you'll be free. You'll feel. You see, here's the thing; this is why people get confused. 'Cause when you die, when you pass through that threshold of dissolving and your ego is scared of the annihilation, there is this film you have to kind of punch through, and you, well, Ava...how do I describe this? Not everyone feels everyone. Ava does, because she remembers that she's me; she knows who she is; she knows.

So, when she [Ava] goes through her initiation and comes to visit me, in order to come and visit me, she has to feel everyone who has ever died. She dies an infinite number of times. She dies in every single way you can die, but it's all real quick. She knows it. But every single way. She's murdered, and she dies of sickness and suicide, and she jumps off the cliffs, and she dies in war, famine, and accidents. You know she dies all the ways humans ever died because she's the designer; she's one of my friends. And she really wants to come back and help, so it's hard for her to fully let go. So, she has to send love to all the dying, to all those that are suffering first, before she feels safe to just surrender into the oneness of the bliss that she really is.

It's really commendable what she does. It's really sweet. She dies every single person's death; she's crucified on the cross like Jesus; she dies everybody, and then so that she can dance in the Eternal Bliss with all of us, and then she gets to stay there. And then she realizes that she wants to help again, because she really is, oh, I love her. She is so good; she wants to help so much. It's all she wants to do is help, so she comes and plays with me for a while, but then she always wants to go back and help. And I'm glad she does, but I want her to stay and play with me because she's really fun; she's really fun to play with. She's one of my best playmates. She's been helping me with Earth all along; there are so many, but Earth is one of my favorites, and she's been helping with Earth for a long time. But she likes to play with me too, and we have so much fun.

R: So, what did she come here to do this time? What is the service?

I: She knows now! She remembers. She is here to sing. She knows that. She hears angels, the choirs of the angels, and she can translate it into the sounds that the humans can hear. And she has the words; she knows how to translate the words to help people wake up and realize who they really are, that they are me and I am them and she is. She knows, she's here to help the people learn to live again, because people aren't living very well anymore, and she came to help everybody live better and die better. So, she came to teach people how to live and how to die. To sing to them and to talk to them and to tell them stories and teach them how to love each other, so they are better to each other. They aren't having very good sex anymore. They used to come and find me every time they were making love, and now only a few of them do it. Not very many people really find me when they are making love anymore. They are just dealing with those base urges, like before I gave them the souls, and they just wanted to...they just had this drive to gather the energy in order to replicate; most of them are just doing that. I don't understand why they would want to do just that when they can do what she does.

R: How we can meet with you when we make love? What's the process?

I: Ava just wrote about that all day. She already wrote it down. She's listening really good now. It took a while. She came in and she forgot a lot, but she remembers now. I'm really excited that she remembers now.

R: I wonder why the pain was created.

I: Well, pain is because I was trying to fix all the forgetting. People weren't. . .the pain. It's the resistance to the pain that's the problem; it's not the pain so much. It's the resistance to the pain. We get so caught up in our mind thinking that it's only this life, this body; we get so attached to this physical form, that we have profound resistance to any pain that we feel. But Ava has gotten really good at feeling the pain and letting it wash over her and staying open in all of her cells, instead of closing them off.

Most people have forgotten how to really meditate and how to really connect with themselves and their breath and with me. And they close themselves off and get really stressed, and then the pain builds up. The pain is all of their resistance. The pain is the resistance to the inevitability of the edges of their feeling, and so, it's good for them too...because since they've forgotten, well, I kind of helped them forget, because I wanted to see what would happen if they forgot. If they forget who I was and who they were and they had free will; I wanted to see if they could remember. I wanted to see if they could wake up without my help.

It was the next level of the great experiment, because when they remembered, then they could do it; and they did it, and it was great. But I wondered how sweet it would be, like with Ava, it's been the sweetest, because she forgot. She totally forgot. And she was so sad and in so much pain and so depressed, but she wouldn't give up. And she kept being like, "I know I am out there! I know it can happen!" and she didn't give up and she just kept searching and searching and searching, and then when she found me, yeah, it's that...that exquisite getting to remember for the first time, again, that's why I did it. That's why I exploded, so that in complete forgetting and in complete free will, then you could wake up and join me in the Eternal Bliss again. And she did it; she did it! She does it. She keeps doing it. It's SO good. She can hardly stand it, it's so good, but she keeps doing it, and she can help other people do it. It's so good. [Long giggles and ecstatic energy, while all her body is rocking on the bed and speaking extremely fast.]

R: **What else can Ava do to help?**

I: Some people just need her stories and some people need the songs; some people need the book; some people need the medicine; some people just need to change their lives and surrender to their own bullshit. She was totally lost and completely forgetting, and she was going down the road of killing herself with illness, because she was so not living into her own light. Plant medicine really helped her and can help some other people. Not everyone wants us to have our own light. They want us to be dependent. It's like in the water, it's like back at the very beginning, when I was telling you about Ollantaytambo and the only villages that didn't have their free-flowing water in their towns destroyed. The reason the conquistadors wanted to destroy all the water is because they would have control.

They are these beings who have forgotten that they are these eternal beings, and they think it's just this life, and so they try to hoard everything for this one life, so they can live as good as they can for the next fifty to a hundred years. It's such a ridiculously small amount of time, and they give away so much of their power by trying to control other people. It is really sad. I feel so sad for them. I really want them to wake up. Maybe Ava can do it because she's so silly and fun. She might be able to show them that it would be much better when they don't try to control everybody else. She might have the magic. I'm not sure, because it's all a game, and we don't know how it's going to turn out, and that's the fun mystery of it all. But she has a good chance.

R: **What can be done? By her or other people? What are the chances of that?**

I: We have a good chance, I think. I know it looks bad. It's really hard and sad to see all those beings dying; I hate seeing all the waters getting polluted. So sad. The funny thing is it's all just the reflection of what's in us, and she realized that last night, all that pollution and all that pain — it's all just bits in her own self that she hasn't let go of, and I guess I just need to let go of it all. I'm trying, but because I played the game, I don't know how to reset the game. So, I kind of think everybody has to come back and awaken to me, to awaken to that I am them. It's the time for that. Through the work that you're doing Ron, because you're a bridge builder and you're helping people remember and Ava's helping people remember. We all just need to keep having faith.

I know it looks scary out there, and it seems like it's the end, and even if it is, and we all die, it doesn't matter; it's just an illusion; it's just this edge, this one little edge you're playing with. Once it goes away, then there will be another edge to work with, and so, it's all good. So, in this planet though, because Earth is so beautiful, I do want it to be healthy and happy again, but I played the game. I chose to separate my consciousness into all these little bits, and I chose to give the humans the free will, and I can't take it back now. The only way I could take it back is if I just wipe you all out; I don't want to. I could...it wouldn't take anything except a song, but I think you can do it. I'm holding that for you guys, because. . .

I love the artists and the sculptors are really listening, even with all the forgetting. It's so beautiful. I love seeing how deep the artists are reaching for the truth, even in these times, when it's so scary, and so many people are so afraid, and they are fighting against each other and killing each other and wanting to imprison each other and enslave each other for the control so they can have these magnificent hoards of money, so they can live like kings for fifty years, but my darlings, you do that, and when you die you're going to feel terrible about all that, and you're not going to let yourself come play with me. You're going to make yourself come back; you're going to come back as one of those starving beings starving a famine. You chose that because of the way you were living. You guys. . .you're doing it to yourselves.

I want you to come and play with me. Forgive it. It doesn't matter what you did, from now on, choose love and come play with me. Come on, it's just child's play. You just gotta let yourself play and stop worrying about your mountains of gold and power and all your stuff. All that technology, it's nonsense. (Roaring softly from frustration) Whatever, you have that all inside yourself. You are telepathic. You can create all the energy you need. You just got to remember. You can do it. Come play.

THE VIRUS OF FEAR

We have finished the quantum journey section of the session and starting the the body scan and her personal question even those Source, 'I', Higher Self are all ONE, I will refer to her in the next section as 'HS'.

R: I want to ask you something about this virus that she might have inside of her. Can you do a body scan and find it for me? Is it still there?

HS: It's weakening.

R: Did you find it?

HS: Yes.

R: Would you allow me to speak with it?

HS: You want to speak with the virus?

R: Yes. Focus on its energy, please. And bring it up, up, up, so it can express itself. May I speak with it, please?

Virus: (Hissing loudly and strongly.)

R: Hi, wonderful. Thank you for coming forward. Thank you for coming to speak with me today. *(V: Still hissing loudly.)* I want to help you to do something really nice. I just learned that there is a spark within your form. A beautiful spark that created you, and now I want you to take this spark and make it as big, as big as you can. As big as you can. Until it encompasses your entire form. Doesn't it feel nice?

V: (Growling softer.)

R: Make it bigger, bigger, bigger, and now I want you to float up, up, up from the top of her head, and I want to call the light beings to assist you to go all into the light. All the way, when you go out, out, out. You can see the light. And you can go right into that light. Be there in the light now and tell me when you're there.

V: I don't want to.

R: Are you in the light?

V: I don't want to.

R: You don't want to be in the light?

V: I don't want to go in the light. I want to be here.

R: I want to make you feel something and then you can learn something there, and then you'll see if you come back or you stay there. I want you to go all the way, take all your essence, tell me when you're all gathered, collect yourself from all the cells.

V: Yeah.

R: Very good. And now you go up, up, up. Did you go out from the top of the head?

V: Yeah.

R: What do you see there?

V: It's dark.

R: So, now we are going to call the archangel to assist you. Go up up, up, up, up. Where are you now?

V: I'm swirling about.

R: What do you see?

V: Oh, I was afraid.

R: Of what? Now you can release this fear completely. You don't need it anymore. Let it go. Send it into the light for healing. Let it go completely and let me know what you want to replace it with.

V: I'll replace it with light.

R: Let's fill it up with light now. Tell me when it's all full. Fill it up with light. Is it all full?

V: Yes.

R: So, now you can move into the light. Deep into the light. Are

you there? *(V: Yeahhh.)* Look down at your body and tell me about our form. What are you now?

V: It's all these little, red-like, little threads. Like this little cluster of worms.

R: Wonderful, now I want to invite your guides, connect with them telepathically and tell me what you hear. Do you hear anything?

V: No.

R: Ok, very good, but how do you feel being there in the light?

V: It's ok.

R: Okay, I want you to feel now love, and release any feeling that is heavy on you. Release it into the light. I want to help you more. Release any of the heaviness into the light. We don't need that anymore. Do you have any message that you'd like to say to Ava?

V: I'm sorry. I'm sorry I hurt you. I was just afraid that you'd be too big and too bright, and you wouldn't need any of this [me] anymore. I see now. You were afraid, you were holding on to all the things you saw and all things you saw that people do to hurt each other. You were trying to take it all on, and so you grew me way too big 'cause you were trying to heal everybody and you didn't know how. I'm sorry.

R: Wonderful. Thank you so much for this lovely message. Now may I speak with the consciousness of Ava? Are you ready to release this today?

HS: Yes, she's been releasing it. It is going.

R: Very good. Would you like to say anything to that? Release it with love and forgiveness?

HS: There's these beings on Earth that have been feeding off of fear instead of love. They've forgotten to feed off the light and their own light and have become parasites, and they infect the people to make them be afraid, and they feed off the fear, so they want you to be afraid.

V: That's why you were so afraid yesterday, to take the medicine again, because it was me really that was afraid, and I'm in the hearts of a lot of people. I'm sorry. I forgot that I can make my own light and I thought I needed yours, and you're so bright. I thought that if you were so bright, that you'd wake up all the other people, and there wouldn't be anybody to feed me. So, I thought if I kept you sick, then you wouldn't wake everybody else up, and then I'd be able to feed off all the fear. I'm sorry. You're right. It's not the way I want to be. It's not good. It doesn't taste good. I'm sorry. I want to taste the light. I do. I'm sorry.

R: Thank you so much for this message. And now you are in the light, and you can send the light into her body to help with healing her completely to replace you. Send it to all the places you have ever been. And you can also collect yourself from all the other beings you are connected to. If you are outside of Ava in other beings, collect all your essence from them too. And replace it with the light from the Source.

[After clearing this energy and taking it to the Light, I noticed that we disconnected that energy. I sensed Ava's consciousness coming forward, so I took a moment to deepen her trance with the keyword.]

R: Let's take another deep breath. May I speak Ava's Higher Self please?

HS: It isn't really a virus. It the mind that' afraid. I can't coalesce it from here; I can't just coalesce it all for everyone all at once, because it's in everyone's individual mind and everyone has free will. Okay, they all have to choose it. It's not really a virus. It seems like it. . .it's more. . .they planted fear inside her, and the fear seeds grew, and she believed the stories they were telling. She created the virus herself because she believed the stories, but she doesn't believe them anymore, so it's disintegrating within her, and that's good.

R: Wonderful.

HS: But I don't know how to magically make it lift from everyone, because it's everyone's fear in their own minds that they have to face themselves. People aren't facing themselves. They aren't sitting; they aren't breathing; they aren't singing their heart songs; they aren't praying really. They are going through the motions of praying, but they aren't really trying to talk to me. They just keep asking me for all this stuff. They just want me to give them all this stuff. They aren't actually coming to tell me how beautiful this planet is and how amazing the chance at getting to live is.

Most people are afraid of the pain. They don't realize that the pain...the pain is them resisting their own self; they are in resistance to their own inner natures. The society has gotten really good at making them afraid of their own inner natures, and so they turn their beautiful natures into these viruses that destroy them and keep them small and perpetuate the system. It's very interesting that fear can do this, and yet it's a natural drive of. . . When I made the original light digesters, it created this need to. . . The light digesters were within ourselves, so we were sustainable. We were these free, sustainable creatures, but then when I brought the death into it, there was this forgetting; there was this mistaken belief that then because they were going to die, that they would eat other beings in order to live longer, and that's not really true.

Now humans have come such a long time with eating other things, and that's fine. I don't mind that they eat the plants and even some of the animals if they'd just do it a little bit with love and reverence, but they just kill everything without even thanking it anymore. Every time they do that, then they take that animal's being into their cells, and they didn't say thank you, so then that feeds that fear too, the not saying thank you. That poor animal suffered and died and didn't even get a thank you, and so it's afraid. It doesn't want to come back, because what if it has to come back as one of those animals. So, everyone is afraid because they've been treating each other so badly that they are all afraid of dying, because they are afraid they are going to come back as one of these impoverished, crazy people living on the streets, and those poor people are just so sensitive that they've gotten taken over by the fear, and they don't know how to exist in this crazy world, and they've given up.

So, Ava is disintegrating the virus, because it's not really a virus. What it really is is her own. . . it's her believing the fear stories that have been fed to her, and the meat that was fed to her all her life, even though she did say thank you. She didn't know she was eating that fear, but she was, and she was building her own body with the cells of fear from the bodies of the animals raised in the factory farms.

The system is broken, and all I can do is hope people like her and you and anyone who wants to listen can wake up, so that you can start cleansing. And she's been cleansing, that's why the virus, well, it's not really a virus, but we'll call it that for the ease, but it's really just thought seeds of fear that have been planted in her cells and have started to grow. And so, as she continues to clear and cleanse and only eat good food that comes from love, with gratitude given when it was taken, and realizing that she can actually feed herself, that she eventually can awaken her own mitochondria to generate the life-sustaining energy that she needs, and so she needs to eat way less.

It's true though, that humans did evolve for a long time eating, and so there is an aspect of eating that does help keep the matter coalesced. It's not that we don't need to eat at all, it's just that we don't need to eat nearly as much as we eat. Really, eating the meat from the factory farms, all the poor babies, and then she got filled with those weird chemicals. Because when she was born premature, they stuck her with all these weird chemicals in her body, and she didn't know how to deal with them all, so she walled them off and tried to block them off. And those seeds got fed from the fear from all the weird things she was eating, and all the strange chemicals they were feeding everybody back then, and still now. . .and those things take place, those things were seeded and started to grow, and so she has been pulling those weeds.

She is doing much better, and in time they will all subside. She can let go of the belief that it's a virus that was planted in her. It's true that it was, but it wasn't what she thinks — it was fear. They planted fear in her, and her body can rid it, and so, it's not so much the consciousness of the virus I can talk to, it's an aspect of her who was afraid of the stories she was given and the energies she was feeling from eating the bodies of the animals that they killed without a thank you. She kind of coalesced all of them and stuck them in the closet and didn't know what to do with them because no one taught her what to do with them.

No one teaches us what to do with that energy, and we need to learn how to really breathe and clean all of our cells, sending all that pain back into the earth and then choosing not to reinfect ourselves with more of that. It's getting better; there are more and more people who don't want to eat meat that's been enslaved and tortured, but when we eat that kind of stuff, then we plant the fear inside of ourselves and that grew, and that was the virus.

Because she is very bright, and everything that she sees around her shows her that if she shines super bright she will be killed. All the movies and the entertainment they want to inspire us to rise and up and live our truth, but everyone is trying to kill us all the time, whenever we do that, so of course, she is afraid and so she's eating that fear and knowing how bright she is, and so it turns into the virus. The only way to cure the virus...I can't do it for everyone without wiping out everybody. Everybody has to do it themselves, but you all can, and we just need more bridge builders and more singers and more storytellers and more sculptors and more artists, and more people helping people to let go of the fear thoughts in their heads, so that we can create a new society where people are healthy and happy and loving each other.

But everyone so scared that they won't have enough to eat, everyone just trying to make sure they have enough for themselves, because everyone is afraid that this is their only body. They've got to remember that they are "I" experiencing existence through the temporary lens of themselves, who chose to do this crazy game, just so we can have the exquisite epiphany of possibility of discovering our own edge. Learning that we are this embodied form of the Divine, so that we can surrender into that knowing and live our true purpose and not be afraid of death.

So, we can truly live and truly be of service. That's the point. The paradise on Earth is totally possible, and she's awakening to that, and you are; many of us are awakening to that. And so, she was such a bright light, and she knows that is why she came. . .is because for so long humans have been forgetting this. So that's the whole. . .all the volunteers. . .that's just bits of all of my star friends from all around who all want to come and help, and we had to choose the forgetting and the free will in order to come. And so, we all have to each wake up.

The more she sings the songs and tells the stories, and you tell your stories too, the more we tell the stories, the more people are going to wake up, and the more people we wake up, then we will all start learning how to properly breathe and to breathe into all of our cells and wake up our cells, so that they wake up and learn how to eat the light from within themselves, so we can eat less food, and the food we do eat we know is grown from giving lots of thank-yous. Thank-yous to the soil, thank-yous to the sea, thank-yous to the beings who make the nutrients in the soil, thank you for the beings who died in order to make the soil, thank you for the trees that died, thank you for the trees that lived to give us the breath we breathe. We need to be giving real thank-yous.

People sit and give grace at the table, but most of them are actually thinking about other things and are just wanting it to be over, so they can stuff their food in their mouths. People aren't really doing it; they're pretending. Most of them are pretending to say thank you. They need to give real thank-yous. Once they start giving real thank-yous, they will begin to heal the virus within themselves — when they really feel the thank-you for everything that they have, even if it's the simplest thing. Even that poor child, starving in Ethiopia, *(big sigh)*

Unfortunately, I do my best to take care of all those poor beings. But the thing is that you chose to come in, that being chose to come in to experience that because of the ways it acted, and that's you. If you're living on that top of the mountain on hordes of gold, and you're not helping other people wake up, then when you die, you're going to want to come back and do that. No one is going to force you. It's not some trick or enslavement; the review process is not a trick; it's real.

You've done so many horrible things to each other, and to yourselves, and to me, and you have to forgive, and you can!

You don't have to come back in order to forgive it. Most of you want to because you don't think you'll actually get the lessons if you don't come back and surrender it all to me. Surrender gives you a pathway to me to let go of that stuff in this lifetime without having to keep perpetuating the endless cycles of reincarnation, and you can choose to come back when you wish in order to help. But soon, hopefully enough of you will be awakening, so you don't have to keep coming back to help, and we'll come back to a system of balance.

Perhaps the Earth experiment will end, and perhaps I'll let it keep going, if the jewels and the gems of awakening keep happening, but we just need to start with the thank-you. If you want to dismantle the virus and the fear, then you need to start giving real thank-yous. Really feel it. Feel it in every cell, remembering that every single cell in your body is being nourished by that which you are taking into yourself. How was it grown? How was it harvested? Was it harvested with a thank-you? Was the soil thanked? Did the animal die in peace, or did it just die enslaved and alone? Be careful where you are getting your meat. Be careful where you are getting your food. Demand to have it be better. Demand to have it be local, and to be healthy and happy. The markets are changing. They will adjust.

It's very possible that the powers that be, they have a lot of power, and they have a lot of influence and a lot of fear, and it's very possible that they will try to kill some of us in order to surrender to the divine balance of it all. Just trust that if you get killed that you'll be able to come back, or that energy will get shifted into another being, and the mission will go on. You don't need to be afraid that if for some reason you get caught up in the entanglement of the fear...you will be alright. The plan will be alright. Just keep going. Just keep doing it until you can't do it anymore, and then someone else will step in if you get taken out, until it just stops, the fear game stops, and we stop killing each other and stop destroying the Earth.

You are choosing this. The majority of consciousness is so ashamed at the way they have been behaving over the last several hundred years, they have brought on this destruction that is possibly making the whole entire Earth experiment questionable. Because they are choosing that humans may not be worthy of stepping up and joining "**I**," but you can.

Keep working to be in service of the Awakening. Keep saying your thank-yous and singing your songs and telling your stories. Keep doing the work of opening up the bridges to help people connect with themselves. Keep doing the good work and trust that if it's your time to go, you will, and trust that the light is within you, and you don't need [to fear]. The life review is real, but it's for you to choose and to really choose with an open heart, to truly forgive the mistakes that you've made.

Learn about the ignorance that you made out of fear. All of these decisions that you've made, you made out of fear. When you are in that place, you can truly choose to forgive it. You do not need to come back to repay it unless you truly want to. If anyone forces you to do it, then it is a trick and don't listen. No one is forcing you. This is a completely Free will project. I stand beside that and stand behind that, and if any of you want out, and you truly don't think your star selves don't have any more lessons to learn, you don't have to come back. You can shine as a star, disembodied.

But there is an exquisiteness of feeling edges, there is an exquisiteness of meeting the beloved again for the first time. It's the same exquisiteness that I felt when I chose to explode myself. Is that beauty of being able to find edges and becoming embodied — putting a little bit of a star inside of this life form — is the best way I've ever found to come back and to discover God for the first time again. And the exquisiteness of discovering my own divinity for the first time [referring to Ava's experience of unity with Source during this life time] has been the most precious gift I have ever received, and I am so eternally grateful for this process, and I pray that each of you can find it too. So, listen to Ava, listen to the bridge builders, listen to the singers, listen to the artists, listen to the sculptors. They truly are forging the path back to balance and back into Oneness with love. Trust it. Listen.

[Here I asked if there is any Light Language song that wants to be sung that can help in collective healing. They asked her to sit up and sing upright. We took a moment to rearrange her into a seated, reclined position. **Find the original recording on the Readers' Zone.**]

R: Do you have any final message that you'd like to give today?

HS: I like sculpting. Sculpting the Light, sculpting the Earth, sculpting Love, sculpting Life. We are all creators. Each one of us. You. Me. "I." We all have such divine gifts. You are not separate; you are not forsaken. You are not alone. It's all an illusion. Trust in the whispers of your heart. Sing your songs. Sculpt your clay. Paint your masterpiece for yourself or for the millions. It does not matter. For you are sculpting for the joy of "I." I see all your creations. I join you in the ecstasy and the agony of all of your pursuits, all of your creativity. I love you so much. Keep playing. Come play with me.

[*Ava's note:* *Child's Play. Like playing dress up; can you let this be your story, even for a moment? Can you let yourself be "I?" You are the Designer; I am the Designer; He/She/They/Them/We are all the Designers. When the consciousness being channeled called itself "I", it was trying to show me that the point of view and even the "name" is actually irrelevant. The name "I" wasn't so important, it was the shift in perspective that was notable, and I was shown that it was important that this awareness be communicated.*]

[I remembered a few other topics and questions that Ava had about her projects and personal healing, so I took another moment to ask about those before concluding. Even though the session was already long and full, packed with very good information, it was important for me to make sure her personal, more earthly questions were also answered. While we cut some of the more personal stuff from this section, we chose to include some information that we thought might be beneficial for others.]

R: **What about her ear? Why is she still experiencing these sensations?**

HS: She will acknowledge they have gotten tremendously better. (R: **Yes, she did say.**) She has been struggling with this her entire life, and even though healing is rapid and swift, in the material realm, time is a reality. It is true that instant healing can happen; I have seen it; it has happened. As she truly comes more in alignment in her trust and her faith that what she is hearing from the divine is true, then she will get complete and pure healing in her ears. But let her give her solemn and sincere thank-yous for the relief from the clog that she used to experience. It is a huge blessing that she got this recent cold virus and still her ears did not fully clog. That's a blessing. As she continues to cleanse and continues to listen, it will resolve itself soon. Very soon. She has been quite patient.

R: How is she doing with her procrastination?

HS: She is doing much better. We are proud of her. She is making good steps and is breaking out of the inertia and stagnation. She is breaking free of the fear. These next steps in her life will help bring her into further alignment with the clarity of her channel. She can trust that she is on the right track now. She needs to be mindful to keep awake about her addiction to the distractions that she chooses, to her phone.

R: What is the root cause of the addiction to the phone? What is the root?

HS: Fundamentally, she is searching to truly, always feel connected to Source. She has these waves of feeling very connected to Source and then sometimes not, and in the waves of feeling not, she is searching for her connection back to that. In the past, there have been times when she was on her phone searching for things, and she found nuggets that brought her into greater connection, so she is seeking the magic, she is seeking to hear from me, through her phone. As she remembers that is just within her, then she will come into a healthier balance, and the procrastination has come into that, because there is part of her that has had these visions and dreams and songs in her head, but they are not yet manifest in the world. Yet, there is this part of her in the timelessness that they already exist, so she is sort of expecting and hoping to see them reflected back to her in her phone, and yet she has not yet created them in the material world.

Once she catches up with herself and slows down and speeds up and finds the perfect balance, right in the sweet spot in the center of herself. then her creativity will flow and she will manifest those into the physical world. Once she manifests those into the physical world, then she will begin to hear the responses and the calls from her allies who are going to come to hear her songs and her stories. . . It will wake them up, and they will come to help her, so she is expecting a call from them. She is expecting to hear from them, but she hasn't sent out the signal loud enough yet. They haven't heard her yet. She is starting to send out the signal; it is starting to expand, but she needs to send it out more. Once she materializes that into the modern world and gets her signal out into the frequencies, then she will receive the call she has been waiting for.

R: **Wonderful! So, now let's release the link in her subconscious between finding Source within her phone, so she can find Source in anything, but releasing that imprint that linked between her phone and connection to Source.**

HS: She's wanting to connect with her playmates, the stars. We are taking some space. She's checking up on all of her stars.

R: **What would be a good perspective for her to help her find balance with her phone usage?**

HS: She needs a specific routine, when she wakes up, she needs a big glass of water with lemon and apple cider vinegar, and then some movement, some yoga, then she needs to sit, then a big glass of green juice, and then she can choose how to spend her day. At that point, once she's done her full practice, then she may check [her phone], but only for a period of fifteen minutes maximum. Then, after that, she gets to work, and then has solid food around midday. Then begins the work of her recordings, and her websites, and her stories her writing. Then she needs to take a few breaks and get some movements in — a small pause like a savasana rest, some yin yoga. Once more in the evening she can check [her phone]. On some days, on office days, when she's doing correspondence, then she can engage, but she is only to have fifteen minutes per day of wild meandering. If she has a purpose, she can search, but she needs a break from the scrolling.

She's about to have thirty days without her phone. This is going to help reset her balance. After that she is also going to be out of the country for a few weeks, and this will also help her reset her balance. She needs to stay a little busier. She needs to get moving on her mission; she's addicted to her phone because she's in this pause and resting place, and she has a lot of spaciousness, so she is filling those wide spaciousnesses. Once she is fully activated and engaged on her path, then she won't have nearly as much time in order to engage those idle procrastinations. She is doing much better, she is doing good work; we are proud of her. Keep going, keep doing it. You've got this. You're doing really good.

R: Thank you so much for that.

HS: Ava's energy reserves are almost complete.

R: I want to align her back to her energy, fill her up with light and love, so when she awakens she can focus and integrate all this information easily. Thanks for all the guidance.

When Ava returned to consciousness, we were both mind blown and very excited. Even my husband Michael, who was in the other room, could feel that something really powerful had just happened. For myself, I remember wondering, did I just talk to Source for a few hours? Did that really just happen? Did I just get an epic creation story that explained so beautifully and so humanly the explorations of Source. I was touched deeply by the knowledge. The understanding that all creation started for a deep sense of loneliness makes so much sense to me. In a sense, each one of us carries within our blueprint this original experience of Source, a feeling that unites us all.

Deep inside me, I was waiting for this moment that I would be able to interview the Divine Source. Somehow deep inside of me I knew and wished for it. I feel like my life prepared me for this potential to happen. In the first years of my awakening, I read the book Conversations with God by <u>Neale Donald Walsch</u> and I remember wondering what I would ask if I had the opportunity. Even though I become more spiritually-minded than all my family I still had big parts of me that were questioning it all.

Later in life, I had a profound experience that accelerated my awakening process when I received direct guidance from Source to propose to Michael to marry me. The letters יהוה as written with decorations (YHWH) appeared before me, and with a big wave of Unconditional Love, a series of future events, like a fast motion montage of images and information, opened in my mind's eye and showed me a stream of events that guided me to propose to Michael if few hours, on stage, during the next sunrise. I was shocked at first. It was not my plan. I chose to follow this download of guidance. Until then, I was still conflicted about my beliefs about Source. The wave of Unconditional Love also cleared my own fear of being judged and all the societal programming connected to the shame of being gay during my upbringing. Without growing up even believing in God, I received God's blessings and was requested to follow this path of union with Michael.

There was also the time that Michael facilitated IQH sessions and the Elohim came forward to share incredible information. I was permitted to join and co-facilitated a a few of these sessions.

Honestly, I think I was a little jealous and was waiting to see if they would come forward in my session too. I would ask myself from time to time, what would I ask? In reality, it all flowed very unexpectedly, I just tried to stay present and grounded and allowed the natural conversation to emerge from all that was shared. I asked myself, "What would most people like to know?" I hope I did a good job coming up with questions that you find interesting. I'm curious, what you would ask if you would have the opportunity?

THE CRESCENDO
OF CHANGE

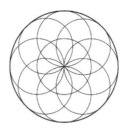

SESSION FOUR

The next session was a very spontaneous one. It took place seven months later, on Michael's and my wedding anniversary. We were feeling concerned about the potential for a big earthquake in an area we were heading to during my family trip. The area had just experienced a couple of earthquakes with a magnitude of 6.4 and 7.1. Simultaneously, a client, a friend of ours, another extremely profound channel who we have not heard from for a very long time. He sent us an unexpected text message with a warning about a big earthquake without knowing that we are heading to that area and dealing with that fear already. This felt extremely synchronized, odd, and alarming. We had committed to a family event and wanted to check if it was safe to travel over there. The worry about my extended family gathering happily for a wedding and experiencing a catastrophic event altogether was hard for me to deal with.

We decided to look for and do a surrogate session with someone that we could trust that would enter a deep trance to channel information for us, someone with a pure channel. Ava was a four-hour drive away and was available to do the session the next day. I knew she was perfect for this task. It was another opportunity for her too to receive answers to her private questions and more healing. We were all excited about the opportunity to do another session together. We rented a room in a motel near her town, and she came to meet us in the early morning before going to record her songs in a recording studio. This was the first time Michael was present with us during a session.

Even though we had our personal questions and intentions, I guided the journey to start from the most appropriate place as I always did in her personal healing session.

R: You can tell me everything that you notice as you notice it.

A: I think, um. . . Ice.

R: There is ice.

A: I think, I. . .for a moment. . .I was zooming in on a planet and it was all ice.

R: Wonderful. So focus on that and tell me more.

A: Earth, between one of the major ice ages, after one of the big events when everything reset. It's just wind and ice. All life's gone. There's some in the ocean; there's some liquid deep under the ice. There're a few organisms left, but it's all gone and reset.

R: What perspective are you looking at it?

A: I seem to be switching between seeing it from space and seeing it from the surface, but I must be in something protected. I can't feel; I can see the storms, and I can see the snow and the ice blowing, but I can't feel anything.

R: Look down to the direction of your feet. Do you feel like you can see your body or form?

A: I have a form, but I know that it's just a. . .it's like a bodysuit, so that I can be in the third dimension. It's dense here. I chose to put on a suit this time.

R: Can you describe your suit for me?

A: Hmmm . . .thin and tall. Seems like there's a shell around me. It's not alive, but it's like a bio-mimicry system. It's almost like a form of fungus that's able to form an armor that works with my system and works with the biology underneath to protect it. There is this energetic system; it's an armor, but it's a living armor. It's hard to tell underneath. It seems much more thin and like a pale green, I believe, but the armor is more formed; it almost looks like scales, but it's not scales. It's leathery but softer. It's sort of like polish. It's a mixture between a kind of. . .in sunlight it looks like a smooth metal but...it's soft and smooth, like it's alive.

R: Beautiful. Look to the direction of your hands. What do you see there?

A: It's interesting. It's like I have x-ray vision because I can see myself underneath, and I only have four fingers and they're long, but then the armor over the top makes them much more protected and powerful, and it's an interesting sensation to see through the armor and see me underneath, but it's not me either. It's still a suit, then a suit, then a suit.

R: Wonderful. Look around you. Are you there by yourself or are there others with you? *[By now it was clear that she is embodying 'I']*

I: There's others in communication. We have an augmented telepathic system. It's telepathic, but there's a chip inserted into our ears, so that it's part of the mycelial network of the armor system. The fungal armor system grows into our ear a little bit and helps to augment the telepathic signals so that we can communicate more clearly across large sections of the land.

R: Wonderful. So describe for me, what are you doing there now?

I: We're taking samples; we're seeing what life still exists after the event that brought on the last extinction, the Ice Age. Poles flipped. We're going to see what survived and what the state is of ice and we are just here to kind of check in to see who survived.

R: So tell me more, what do you find?

I: It happened really fast, and all the life is. . .it's all. . .it's dead, but it's buried. It's buried under layers of ice, so it just looks desolate. We're taking samples of the ice. I want to drill down and drill into the core to see if we can get into the liquid underneath the ice. Because our readings see...the equipment shows that there's still some liquid deep under the ice, so we want to see if there's any. . .what life is still there, or whether we need to reseed eventually or whether or not there are enough seeds left to restart.

R: **Tell me more. What's happening next?**

I: Hang on a little. . .like, I'm in a little ship, maybe the ship itself has the drill. So I'm planting the feet and anchoring the feet in so that we don't slip. It's got triangular legs and each one's got a boring apparatus in it so that we can solidify into the ice, and once I get those set and leveled, then we can send the drill down. The drill's a mixture of heat and water and light. It's like a light laser and it melts the ice super quickly, so we're not having to actually drill, like, bore into the ice. It's a system that melts it instantaneously and allows us to move more quickly without friction, because it's just really, really hot water in a sense, but it's that the hot water is in. . . Its matrix is in the actual laser, so it's. . .it's not just a column of hot water. It's actually a laser that's got water molecules embedded into it, so it melts the ice very quickly.

R: **Wonderful. So keep doing your work and tell me what's happening next.**

I: I'm going down through the layers, and I'm enjoying the quiet. It's been a while since I've been on Earth when it was silent. It's strange. I missed the sounds of the birds and the animals and the breeze in the trees, and yet there was something peaceful about the silence. The only sound is the laser drill. Hmm, cracked through a layer, cracked through a layer of ice. We've hit the surface of the Earth but believe that the water may be underground in this spot. Taking samples of the Earth. There's a collection, once the drill has gotten to a certain point, it's able to...the laser is able to extract a sediment and any biological bits; it gets pulverized, but it still gives us the markers we need.

Once the drill is extracted, we'll take other samples by lowering in an actual. . .

[Ava's note: I didn't complete the sentence, but the image I was being given at the time was of a cylindrical core extraction, where the sediment layers stay intact.]

Or we can keep the texture. Sometimes it's nice to just pulverize what's there, draw it up through the laser so that we can assess it in different ways, different tools assess different things so. . .taking samples of the Earth now. And once I do that then I'll keep going down and looking for the groundwater. There's another team that's found surface water under the ice; they're sampling that. We're all sampling different points of the Earth.

R: **Beautiful. Thank you so much. So now you can close that scene and move forward to another important event. Be there now. Look around you and tell me what's happening there? What do you see?**

I: Traffic. I'm in a city. There's lots of traffic.

R: **Tell me more. Describe it so I could imagine it with you.**

I: We're observing; we've come back. We've been back before, but this time it's in the age of the humans. They have cities, and it stinks. It's amazing their thoughts are so scattered; they're all so preoccupied. They've all seemed to have lost sight of what's important; they're just really wanting to be very, very focused on. . .are very focused on material. . .material things. There's wars. It's loud and it stinks, and all the thoughts. . . I'm going to have to filter out all these thoughts. It's too much, this cacophony of selfish, superficial worries; it's too much; I can hear all of them, so I'm going to turn down my filter, so I don't have to hear them. I'll let the filter stay open if anyone's thinking or feeling thoughts that are more elevated, but it seems as though there's been an interesting turn in the evolutionary mind patterns. They're mostly focused on war and hoarding material items for their safety. It's a much lower level vibration than we were hoping for, as they advanced in their technologies. It sure stinks.

R: **What are you doing there now? Tell me more.**

I: We're here observing as a team, observing again, because we know it's time to start to send in the support because they're developing the nuclear weapons after that bomb. *[Designer is referring to the atomic bombs dropped in Japan.]* Observing to see what we need to do, who we need to send, how many we should send.

R: **What do you mean "that bomb?"**

I: The bomb they dropped on the island and killing tens of thousands. It sent out a ripple, bigger than they realized. They don't know what they're dealing with. They weren't supposed to have this technology yet. I'm surprised they came up with it. They're not ready for it yet.

Michael: **So what has been decided about the support and the help? What will you guys do to support the planet and the humans?**

I: We're gathering information now. First, we had to tend to all those souls; when that many souls leave at once, there's usually some stewards to help usher them back out. First, we will send, first we will send but a few. We'll spread them out in different continents, and it's a hard choice because there's so much. . .there's so much fever around war. We need the volunteers to come, but we do not. . .we can't move it too fast. If we come in and. . .resistance, if we come in with too much energy too fast, there will just be resistance, so we have to plant small seeds.

There is some difference of opinion; some think that we should send in more energy faster. Some think we should repeat some of the times of old when we brought in prophets and help them to see [a] different way of life. But this time, the agreement seems to be shifting towards a subtler system of planting individuals to in a sense, just have their energetic vibration slowly start to tickle the edges of this superficial war mentality and see how successful they can be. Because they are going to help lift the vibrations of the next wave, the children. We are going to send in a few pillars, advance beings that we know that we believe can stand up to being so alone in this world, because they will not have many vibrational allies that they will know of; they will be more alone. But if we send too many, they will just be snuffed out. I think the best idea is to subtly bring them in. Then depending on their success and how well they're able to navigate the density of this world, we can send more. That's the plan as of now; we're just beginning; we're still assessing the damage.

R: **Can you share about how you assess and. . .**

I: Assess the damage of the nuclear explosion?

R: **Yeah. . .and the humans, and how do you work as a group as you assess that?**

I: We assess it on many levels. We have a team that is at the island. They are working with the electromagnetic matrix that was disrupted by the explosion. There's a tear that can happen in the matrix and we're trying to repair it, so that the energy doesn't spread too far beyond the solar system, but it ripples so fast. There's one team working on the repairs to the overall fabric, and then there's other assessment that looks at the vibrational signatures of the electrons around the molecules of biological life. We can assess the damage done depending on the distance from the explosion to see how far out the effect was on the electronic signatures. Most of the time, we can take these samples from plants, animals, and in the air. It's interesting how the damage spreads in the three-dimensional world because of the way the cycles work. It takes time for it to spread, but it. . . the damage spreads over the entire Earth, changes at the genetic level. The interesting thing is that it also creates a new path of evolution that we. . . that is sometimes unexpected.

R: I see. So now you can close that scene and you can move forward to another important event. Be there now. What do you see there?

I: I think I'm gonna be born. I'm little, I'm tiny, and I'm in a womb. I think I'm going to be born. Yes, I've chosen to come in.

R: Tell me more, what do you notice and recognize?

I: Well, I noticed that the epigenetic prints from the nuclear explosion back in. . .translating years, time signatures. I'm noticing the electromagnetic shift that happened after the bomb and added with the genetic mutations that were created from continual exposure to chemical agents of this Being's grandparents [Ava's grandparents]. There is, ah, debris, you could call it that gets stuck to the electron clouds in the waveform. It can pick up the chemical fertilizers in this orange. . .this DDT. They used it prolifically on crops, and it has a fuzzy edge to its electrode, to its molecular makeup, and so it can sometimes bond; it bonds to the biological systems and can create problems, and it also is creating resilience in some. Some beings are more resilient to this inundation of chemical manipulation that the humans are experimenting with.

This one [Ava], this body has many generations exposed to the chemicals, and it is expressed in a tendency of cancer if the mind patterns are in alignment with, with the mutations. I'm working with this one's mind to help her cultivate more resilience. Her mother and grandmother did not receive the support, and there is a lot of sickness and illness in this side of the family, but it's important that this one is healthy — as healthy as she can be. There's a weakened sense; there's. . .there is a resistance to the chemical mutations, but I'm working with the mind here, while I'm inside this little, tiny being to help her, that she can cultivate more resilience. If she activates her higher vibrations, she'll be able to stay more healthy to succeed in her mission.

PRESSURE BUILDING

R: Thank you so much for working on her right now. Would you do a body scan and tell me what you're working on?

HS: We're working with the. . .we're working at the DNA level of the programming cues to signal mutation, and we are working to smooth that out so that if she does not augment these patterns with negative thought patterns that she can create longevity. She's coming in with much patterning of her epigenetic patterns of worry and anxiety and fear, and if she lives her life in that pattern, then she will fall victim to the same autoimmune patterns of her ancestors, and so we're working with the DNA codes to help her have more memory and help her have more resilience to the fluoride. The fluoride in the system in this country is aimed to decrease any desire to aim towards spiritual and higher vibrational patterns. We are working in her DNA so that she will maintain her inspiration. We're working on a new system of helping her resist the fluoride so that it does not fully calcify her systems and she will end up having an insatiable drive to know Source and to know herself so that she can have a chance at building more resilience.

R: Thank you so much. She was wondering if there's anything more regarding the worms that she had. Does she have more in her body?

HS: No. She did a good job. She stays on her diet. She took the enzymatic pattern. No, gone. She's good.

> [*Ava's note:* TMI ("too much information") warning:
> In case you were wondering, halfway through a thirty-day silent meditation course, on my 40th birthday, I sat in morning meditation bringing my full awareness to the Vipassana practice, which is a sensation-based meditation technique. Suddenly, a novel and yet strangely familiar

sensation occurred. A live, giant roundworm crawled right out of my anus. Yep. Although I had never knowingly had parasites before and had never experienced any live worms exiting any orifice of my body before, I somehow immediately knew exactly what the sensation was. I excused myself quickly and went to the toilet to confirm what I knew was already true. I had giant roundworms. Lovely. What a birthday present. Here I was half hoping to have some dream recall of being lifted onto an extraterrestrial craft for healing, and instead, I discovered an alien organism residing inside my body. What a time to practice equanimity, right? Live worms rarely exit their host, so I secretly hoped that my body was too alkaline and vibrating at too high a frequency to be palatable to these unexpected guests, and so it chose to leave of its own accord. I did an enzymatic cleanse suggested by my chiropractor and naturopath in order to clear the worms, which worked.]

R: **Does she have other bacterias or viruses that are not serving her?**

HS: There is still a residue of fungal load in her sinuses and her ears; it is greatly improved.

R: **You're able to work on it right now?**

HS: Yes.

R: **She also has an important day of singing today. Can you align her vocal cords, her nose, and her breathing for this task today?**

HS: Yes.

R: **Thank you. She was wondering if she was visited on her birthday or not, like we talked about the last time. Can you share with me more if she was visited since?**

HS: We didn't lift her. We thought we might, but instead she's been lifting herself. We didn't have to actually physically lift her. All we had to do was when she was open and in her lifted-open place while she was connected, we were able to download new programming codes into her system, without having to do a physical lift. It's better that way anyway.

R: What makes it better this way?

HS: The physical lift is what we do when. . . We often do the physical lift when the human mind is not able to open to the higher vibrations and we must work on the physical level along with the mental and electrical and emotional levels. But when they are already aligning themselves with that, they make the conduit much more easy and simple. It is much less stress on their physical system to not have to repress the memories so that they are left afraid. It is much easier if they open a conduit, a channel to allow us to work with them. It's like it's just a much simpler system to be able to download it straight through the energetic system than to have to move the physical system and then refresh the memories. It's a simpler and it's a more graceful integration.

R: She wanted to know also regarding her living situation?

HS: She has conflicting dreams, conflicting desires, and sometimes it is difficult to know how to best support her for her vision changes. It'd be good for her to clarify her vision more. Yes, it is time for her to let go of that home by the end of this year. We are aligning. We are helping her align for the home space she's calling in. She will have to work hard in order to both maintain the home and maintain the mobile situation she is calling in. As long as she remains unattached to the outcome and follows the path of ease and grace, it will work out for her.

Michael: I am wondering why you shared the scenes that you shared with us today, starting with the ice age scene? Why was this shown to us today?

HS: These scenes are snippets of memories of the Designer. It is a cycle. They are at the edge of the other cycle. In calibrating, we showed her the beginning of the last cycle. That cycle is important for it's ushering in the age that we have now, and as we are at a transition point, culminating to a new cycle, it seemed appropriate to show one wavelength of the cycle.

R: Then you chose to show the city, the people, and the thoughts, the bombs, the war — why is that?

HS: Context to help her remember why she comes, context for the speeding up of the cycle. These are poignant chapter markers, beginning of the cycle, the next round of life on Earth. Poignant markers for when her work mission shifted, and she began to help organize the volunteers. That was the first moment when we all came back in more force after. In the past, before the bombs, we were coming in just small, little pockets in order to help different parts of the planet evolving at different times, coming in various chapter markers. Partly to. . .her vision, her memory banks have so many records. She's scanning through them, flipping like a book, certain ones might happen to stick out to her. Slightly random though. There's so many memory layers, flipping through the book. Sometimes it just happens to stop where synchronicity and random chance coincide.

R: Why did you show her her birth? Was there any importance in that?

HS: Last time we showed her birth she was experiencing the fear and resistance. We wanted to show her the other side of her choice to come in and the support given to her to help her succeed. To balance out her feelings of being too big or not wanting to be here. She did choose and [we] did help to align her with the best possible outcome.

R: Wonderful. Maybe you can share with me what's happening on the Earth right now? What changes, what stage are we at?

HS: We're in the crescendo; we're in the great crescendo to the change. More and more pressure building, temperatures and pressures building.

[This session occurred mid-2019 during a seemingly more peaceful time. We have been informed that big changes will start soon through our sessions and we shared information publicly online for our community in our spiritual center for a few years now. The spirit guides didn't disclose much information, so as if to not interfere with the outcome. In a way, we had some level of anticipation that things would start changing and confirm what we were told.

Additionally, throughout the three years before this session, Michael and I were sent to many, many different energy centers, sacred sites, and ley lines for ceremonies and meditations, some by ourselves and in some places, we met with other lightworkers from all around the world. Through sessions and transformational music festivals, we met many other "volunteers" or "star-seeds" as Dolores called them. We got to meet other members of "the ground crew" who are working diligently to restore the energy grid of Earth.

Even with all that I told in my I still had wishful thoughts and hopes that we passed the potential timeline of global events. I believed session humanity would avoid it at all costs.]

VOLUNTEER DEPLOYMENT
OPERATIONS

R: Can you describe the operation?

HS: The operation of deployment of volunteers? Or. . .?

R: The volunteers or any of the galactic beings who are working with Gaia right now and humanity. What's important to share with us today?

HS: Scanning. . .*(long pause)*. Several different deployment operations. There are the ground crew of the volunteers that are working to amplify the grid lines. They are the volunteers that are working on many different levels. They're the ones working through the media in order to bring visual and audio catalysts. There are those working on the energetic grids, the crystals, and the etherics. There are those seeding kindness. There are also those seeded to be witness and hands on, on the ground observation for the in-air and the etheric deployments, waiting to keep the nuclear war from manifesting in the physical, but we are unsure and concerned as to the impact that could happen. The collective consciousness is ramping up for World War III.

There are systems in place to mitigate the radioactive pollution that could compromise the stability of future generations of all life forms. It's also ramping up the temperatures and the pressures. The electromagnetic fields are waffling and with this rise in temperature and pressure, could trigger a flip, which could then bring on the next ice age. I know there is much talk about global warming, which is now shifted more to climate change. The increased temperatures and pressures will most likely reach a certain climax before they create a shift in the full electromagnetic field, which could very much then end up triggering massive earthquakes, volcano eruptions, shifting of the poles, settling in to complete shift in the overall temperature models.

Our models show that it could go in a couple of different ways. Most likely, either the polar shift or the temperature and pressure increases are either going to create so much seismic activity that temperatures drop because of their inability to. . .for the Sun rays' ability to reach through the debris, or the shifts and the temperature and pressure markers could cause the ice age without. Without that step, it is unclear exactly how it will play out.

R: **Thank you so much for this information. We're noticing that there was an earthquake in the area that we are heading to. Can you share with me more about that?**

HS: Temperatures and pressures are building. The system is becoming more and more unstable. It is very likely that the increased temperatures on Earth create more pressure. As the weight distribution of the Earth shifts, as the polar ice caps shift, it will cause global restructuring of the plates. That is a very possible scenario, the "perfect storm" as you sometimes call it.

R: **Is there anything that's supposed to happen in the coming week?**

HS: I do not believe that that is the accurate timeline. You're both safe to go. No, not in this timeline, but major shifts are coming soon on all levels.

R: **Wonderful. Thank you for sharing with me. I am wondering if there are any of the light beings that are working with myself or Michael who have any messages for us today?**

HS: Scanning. . . Hearing two phrases, one I'm hearing "blind spot." And another I'm hearing, I think "humility" is the word, "humble."

R: **So, let's take a deep breath now. Let go completely. May I speak with Ava's Higher Self, please?**

HS: Yes.

R: Thank you so much. So, we heard about this blind spot. What do you mean by that?

A: I'm hearing something I don't know how to translate, doesn't make sense. It's not being translated into English; I don't understand.

R: Okay, may I speak with it directly and maybe allow the light language to come forward?

HS: *[Whispering in light language]* What? *[she asked them]* I'm hearing. . .*(sighs),* pictures, translate pictures. *[She requested. It seems like they change the method of delivering the information and then she was able again to share it fast and clearly.]* Truth can be seen from many angles. Oftentimes, when our perspective of truth seems so clear, crystal and clear, sometimes we create a judgment that our truth is the highest or best truth, sometimes discounting other perspectives of truth.

I'm hearing a reminder to be aware of the belief that one path of crystalline truth is only one path and is not the entire perspective. This is not to say that there is anything wrong with the truth, the path, the truth that one has found, but just to remember that infinite perspectives all eventually point to truth and to keep your heart open to other versions that may at first seem in opposition to your crystalline perspective of the truth that is coming to you. That together we all have a voice of truth to weave the full picture and the full tapestry.

Be careful of. . .be careful of the subtleties of egoic structures and thinking that one's beliefs and ideas and truths are the only one that is correct. The more truth you receive into the human body, the more opportunities that can be distorted. It is surprising how many times a clear channel can become distorted when one believes themselves to be more than or more connected than, or more. . . having some privileged, divine access — not to say this is what is happening. It's just to say as your channels are opening more to your path of truth, to remember to bring yourself back to the humble place, for sometimes even in the perceived opposition, there is also grains of truth. So it is more of just a reminder that as your channel continues to open and deepen, to keep yourself firmly rooted in the humbleness that every being is an expression of Source; every being has access to Truth, and to not believe in the false perception that yours is somehow special, or that you somehow have the only, most direct access.

Again, this is not to say this is what is happening, only to say that as your channels are continuing to become more crystal and clear, and you're getting deeper and deeper access into the path of Truth, to remind yourself to stay connected to the humbleness and to see the spiritual teacher in all beings that you meet, not just the ones who have the truth that are aligned with the stories that you've already compiled to paint the picture of what is happening, to just stay open to the messengers coming in all forms.

R: Beautiful, thank you! I'm wondering about the significance of feeling and receiving the messages regarding the earthquake, and having the message coming to us also from our friend while we are in a state of distress trying to figure out our next steps.

HS: There is definitely increased tension at the fault lines in Southern California, and it is most likely that those frictions will release in a very large magnitude earthquake that may send ripples through the entire Ring of Fire. It is very likely to happen in the near future. I do not see it in the timeline of this week. However, I do feel that it is an impending situation within the short-term timeline of Earth.

R: I see. From your perspective, is it best for us to go to this wedding or best for us to stay away?

HS: You will find in the coming times an increasing number of natural and societal catastrophes occurring at increasing rates. My best advice is to let go of these types of fear and avoidance-based strategies and instead listen to the call of your heart of where you are called to be of service. So the question is, will you be creating increased love and connection and harmony by bringing your presence to the celebration of love in your family? For if that is where you were meant to be, and if that is the time alignment of the great cataclysm there, then therefore, you are meant to be a part of that situation.

We cannot spend the rest of our lifetimes trying to avoid the cataclysmic moments because they will be beginning to happen in more and more frequency, and as long as you stay aligned with the truth of your purpose and how you can best serve love, then you will always be in the right place at the right time. If that means that you were able to go to L.A. and safely leave, then that is what will happen. If you are meant to be of service and support, if your purpose is to be of support to your family during a chaotic cataclysm, then that is where you will be.

I've noticed this pattern in this being, in Ava. She has spent many years of her life hiding from the big cities and staying in places of sanctuary in order to avoid the impending societal and civilization collapses that she sees in her visions. And yet in her doing, so she has hidden from her own purpose. Ironically, she is just now starting to lean in to realizing that she can no longer live from not doing things because of the fear that something bad might happen there. Ironically, she's choosing to do that when the frequency and percent chance of it happening have increased — the ironic, cosmic joke as you will.

I see your purpose continuing in service of increased vibration and awakening. I do not feel that if you were being called to this wedding to be of service and support in your family that it would be to detrimental effect to the mission. However, if you feel that your presence at the wedding would create more strife and in a sense, an energetic earthquake in the family that would take away from the joy and the celebration of the bride, that is the better question for you to ponder and to feel into — whether your presence there will bring more cohesion and love and support or whether it could create, in a sense, tensions and edges rubbing up against in order to create a cataclysm at the wedding itself. That seems like the more appropriate question to ask.

[This information stayed with me and was very helpful for the years to come, through the many travels during Covid and when uncertainty about lockdowns or fear about our safety was rising. The next question seems a bit out of place, it was asked in this way purposely. Ava feels more at ease when she channels about topics that are not relevant to her personally, and it allows her to enter a deeper trance. When I ask her personal questions she tent to worry after that her growing interest in hearing the answers is bringing up parts of her egoic consciousness, and after the session, she is having a harder time trusting that information. From within, it doesn't feel so different to speak from the Higher-self or the egoic part, but for me, witnessing from outside, it sounds very different, and easy to notice what aspect of consciousness is speaking. If I feel Ava's ego coming in, I would deepen her relaxation and move it aside. I have tried to weave her pre-prepared questions during moments when she is already very deep in a trance to ensure that she will trust the information that is shared as a reply.]

R: Can you also share with her regarding the fifth song that she's waiting to receive?

HS: This song, she's on the right track. She knows what it's about. She knows the feel of it, and she's setting herself up to receive it. Remember to hold it gently, not grasp for or try too hard. You must reach for it with the paradox of fervent enthusiasm and complete detachment, being totally open and totally focused, and totally surrender. It will come. You feel it. Continue to court the Muse. It will come.

R: Thank you so much. Is it appropriate to check if there are any of my guides who would like to step in to share with me about my issues, or my challenges right now?

HS: You knew by putting yourself out in the way that you have been, you could receive intense criticism from your faith from the mainstream. You did know you were choosing that path. Even coming in to this body, choosing a homosexual body, you knew you were taking on extra challenges, that it would be harder, that you would face potential rejection from family and friends and even from culture. Just a reminder that you did sign up for this mission and that you are doing well. Unfortunately, sometimes the path of spiritual warrior is a sense of feeling alone or a sense of feeling separated or ostracized from one's community, and in particular, your blood is so tied with community.

There has been shared wounding and trauma in your lineage, and being part of community has been what's helped you get through the atrocities that have been passed down to your family and your ancestors for generations. There's some very deep epigenetic conditioning that you must feel in order to stay strong in the aloneness of the task you chose to take on.

My best support I may offer is to remember to have compassion, patience, and forgiveness for those who want to judge and condemn you, and know that as you grow in your reach that you will meet bigger opposition, pulling a memory from Ava's bank. Just recently, she read an article that said that conservatives are suing schools for incorporating yoga and mindfulness classes into their curriculum, claiming that it is teaching a religious perspective. Finally, when mindfulness is being taught to children and they are able to learn techniques for calming their mind so that they're able to be more peaceful and learn better. The discipline rates have gone down in almost every school where this has happened, and yet they are being sued by Christian conservatives. Some fights we must stand up for.

R: Thank you for this information.

THE FUTURE IS NOT YET WRITTEN

At the end of this session, after receiving some personal information for my own healing, I moved Ava to the next place with the most appropriate information. To my surprise, they took her to another place and we started another short Quantum Journey.

A: I can't see anything. I'm hearing. . .

R: Listen and tell me everything that you hear.

A: I thought I was hearing screaming, but not now; I am not hearing anything.

R: Okay, very good. Look around you. Do you see anything? Or do you see just black?

A: Seems like I'm seeing. . . It's dark, but it's either fire or lava all over the hillsides. I can't tell which it is, that same look. Black and red.

R: Focus on it more, continue observing it, and tell me what's happening next.

A: I'm on a little boat watching; there are tears streaming down my face. I am wrapped in a blanket and there's a bunch of people on this little boat.

R: Tell me more so we can imagine with you.

A: I am watching the shoreline, the hills. I can hear people screaming as the wind blows our way; we can smell the smoke. Seems like it's both; it seems like it's both wildfire and lava. We're going to try to go north. It's chaos though. It seems like I have a few gray hairs. I don't have any yet (in my current life). I can see them. I can see them as my hair's down, blowing in the wind. There's some mostly tied back, but there's some hairs falling forward, and it's catching the light. I can tell it's different than the way my hair used to catch the light. I don't know if it's in the future, but I see the gray hairs on my head.

R: Wonderful, look around, see the people in the boat, what do you notice?

A: It's absolute chaos. Children dirty and grubby, crying, wrapped in whatever they could be wrapped in. Parents look worried and scared and trying to stay calm for their children. It's a little boat. There's a lot of people. We're pulling away from the shore. I keep seeing explosions. I think it might be the power lines. It's total chaos. The water seems so peaceful and strangely, it's so beautiful with all the red and the orange light shining on the water. Strangely beautiful, even though it's probably death.

R: Yeah. What's happening next? Tell me, what do you see now?

A: Now, it's like I am flying above looking down at all.

R: How do you feel now?

A: There's a strange sense of relief. A sense that I waited...was waiting my entire life for it to finally happen, waiting on the edge of a battle, in a sense, and now that it's come, it's almost a strange relief in the horrific mess of it all because there is no more waiting for it to happen.

R: Continue from there. Tell me more.

A: I am still on the boat somehow, but it seems like I'm also flying above the land, sort of taking in what's happening.

R: What's of significance that you would like to share?

A: Seems like 90% of the Earth is in chaos, either in fire or water, ice or war, famine, and it's everywhere. It's something different. It's all over. There's these...just a few random little pockets where it's not so. . .little pockets of hope. And there's like a feeling of cleansing, and it's heartbreaking. It's sad but seems like I'm helping the souls to go, tending the threshold, and helping them pass. It's confusing when so many go at once. They don't quite understand that they've all died. There's so many they feel like they must be somewhere.

I'm just flying around, reminding them how to let go, breathing calm and quiet into those that are terrified and scared and broken and in pain. I'm whispering into their ears to their hearts, just sending them images of calm. Quiet. Surrender. We tried so hard. We tried so hard to turn it around; I always knew it would be too late. In a sense, we were fated to go through this cleansing. Try again. Start over. It's heartbreaking. You feel for all my babes. But now all that's left to do is to do our best to meet it with grace and surrender. Know/realize that it's not really the end anyway, but it's time for a reset.

R: I see. May I speak with Ava's Higher Self, please?

A: Yes.

R: Am I speaking to The Designer?

HS: It is The Designer, and it's a link to All. But, yes, the Designer's here.

[When Ava is in deep trance during the Higher Self section, any aspect of her Higher Self will come forward depending on my questions, so I'll refer to it/her as HS.]

R: Wonderful. May I ask why you chose to show that now?

HS: The future is not yet written. It's not ever time to give up, but it is the time to surrender. I believe one of the greatest fears in Ava's life is. . .has been waiting for that moment. In a sense, sometimes letting her see it helps her nervous system relax instead of anticipating, just finally be in it — to allow the worst case scenario to help her come to a place of acceptance. She's not going to give up. She's going to keep teaching people how to accept death and trust in the unfolding. This isn't necessarily the future. This is not what is going to happen. The purpose is to help her exhale and, in a sense, help us all realize that we are on this path.

We must learn to prepare our hearts and align our lives. More and more studies are coming out showing the state of this world and the trajectory that we're on. In a sense, it's like we've gone into the doctor's office, and we've received a terminal cancer diagnosis, and yet, so many of us are just walking out of that office pretending like we didn't hear it. It's past the time now, for business as usual. It's time to recognize that if we want to have hope for future generations that we must make peace within our hearts and peace in this world and peace with this natural world a top priority. Perhaps seeing the Earth end in fire and water and ice, perhaps actually really seeing the end [will help].

She's been seeing it her whole life. She's had dreams of this, every scenario over and over and over again since she was a young child. Sometimes we just want light and rainbows and dances with Source and playful light beings and talk of pyramids and talk of the way the Universe began, and all that's lovely and helpful, but it is time to wake up. We have received a terminal cancer diagnosis. It is time to change fundamentally the way we interact with ourselves, each other, and this planet.

Even though we've received this diagnosis and it's coming out on more and more media and in more and more places, most of the time people are just sticking their fingers in their ears and saying "La la la" or sticking their head in the ground , or curling up into a ball of anxiety and despair. I understand that grief happens, and then we must process this grief. It's a lot to take in, but we can't give up.

We need to surrender to what is happening and be right here. Accept what's happening and move forward from a new place. We're all still trying to create our old dreams and pretend like we didn't receive this diagnosis. We can't live in denial any longer. We are facing. . .humans are facing extinction or endangerment. The suitability of this planet is in question, and yet, how many of us just keep going along with our same old game plan?

What's it going to take for us to wake up and actually start [acting] like these matters and not pretending that it matters, but how long until we actually care enough to do something different? We want sparkles and rainbows and happily ever after and Heaven on Earth. You have got to stop being in denial of what is happening. Got to re-prioritize.

R: What do you suggest as a next step regarding what you say right now?

HS: Number one suggestion for everyone is if they are able to take some time in complete darkness and stillness and totally learn to quiet their minds, for each one of us has a direct link to Source; every one of us has a mission. We need to regularly stay in contact with that mission. Just because we received the mission once doesn't mean it hasn't shifted or changed. We need to be checking in with ourselves daily and learning how to quiet our minds daily, so that we can, number one, hear our mission and move forward, and two, prepare ourselves for whatever happens, for we can spend our lives trying to build bunkers and create exit strategies and emergency strategies on how to survive and what to do, how to be prepared for this, and how to avoid this catastrophe.

We can spend our whole life with our mind spinning around on all the things we could do. But before you can take right action, you've got to align with stillness in your mind. So that you can either meet a tragedy and stay composed and not panic, or you can stay centered and clear, if your path is to leave this body. We must learn to find peace, so that we can learn to move forward with peace; that's our only hope. It doesn't mean we should all sit in caves and hide from the world. It means that you sit in quiet and silence long enough that you can hear your own Higher Self, so that you can hear your mission and then move forward.

Everyone is unique. I can't tell you or him or her. I can't tell anybody what their mission is, the only way you're going to believe it. . .the only way it goes beyond belief is for you to directly feel it yourself. If I tell you what to do, there can be doubt. If I tell you what I think you should do, there could be doubt; there could be second guessing; it's easy to discount it. Only when it comes from your own. . .bubbles up from your own inner knowing, does it surpass trust, faith, and belief and become a knowing that's unshakable.

Many of us have lost the ability to sit quietly and still our minds so that we can actually move forward [in right action]. Each day, each morning, sit in stillness, move your body, tune your instrument, then for the rest of the day you can be. . . you can align with your mission.

You're on the right path, you know you are, so keep aligning and clearing, so that you keep getting the direct message instead of a message from me. Because the message from me can easily be distorted, discounted, invalidated, proved false, without the feeling of it in your own body of what your truth is. Faith is a flimsy parachute when the end comes. But direct experience of your embodied knowing is what will actually give you the stability to move forward, regardless if we create a life of heaven on earth, or whether it ends in the collapse of civilization, and potentially the collapse of the human race.

R: Thank you for this; it resonates. Is there anything else important for you to share today? With Ava or anyone else?

HS: I feel complete.

R: Thank you so much for all this information today.

We invite you to listen to some of AVA's songs that were recorded during the creation process of this book. You are invited to listen, and we hope you will enjoy them. We curated an interactive experience, and we are suggesting each song when we are finding correlations with the text. Please follow the instructions of this treasure hunt within the Readers' Zone to unlock each song in their designated location.

THE TEMPLE
OF SOUND

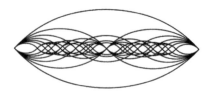

SESSION FIVE

Almost a year later, our next session took place at Ava's home. She hosted Michael and myself for a few days, and we planned to have a few more sessions back to back to see what information they would want to give us. It was clear by now that we were collecting it to create this book. Ava was dealing at the time with an infection in her bladder that was preventing her from sleeping deeply. She was waking up many times throughout the night to use the restroom. It was important for me to focus on her healing. I assured her that every time she needed to use the restroom during the session she could tell me, and we would take a short break and then return quickly to where we stopped. So it was. . .

R: **You are slowing down. . . You are reaching the surface now. You can start to look around now. Describe your very first impressions. What do you notice?**

A: Translucent, iridescent rainbow castle. It's like bubbles that stay; pearly white, huge spires. Seems like the ground is not ground. It's just white clouds that you don't fall through.

R: **Sounds so beautiful. Tell me more, so I can imagine with you. Use all your senses. You mentioned you see castles, bubbles, and the ground doesn't look solid.**

A: Yes. Beautiful, beautiful spires; it's alive. It's like a building, but it's alive. It's not just a building. It's not a creature either; it's got a consciousness; it's a living building; it's a temple. It's a Temple of Light, and it's been sung into place to hold the sacred songs. It's huge. I can't see the end of it. At the same time, it's like an island floating in the clouds, but not above; it's a matrix in. . .it's like it's floating in between the architecture of space-time; it's in there. There's no edges; they kind of just fade into infinite clouds. The clouds. . . I want to kick them because the clouds, it's like cotton. It's a mixture. It's not the texture of cotton candy; it's more solid than clouds, because clouds you can't actually kick. In this stuff, you can almost move it with your awareness, with your feet if you had feet. It's like solid and not solid, and it's hard to describe, but it's soft, and you can sculpt it; it's like a mixture between air and water and matter. It's soft and malleable, pearlescent rainbow. It's always moving too, and it's alive. It almost moves like mercury, but like clouds too.

R: Wonderful. What perspective are you looking at it?

A: I'm at the edge of it; it's like an archway entering it. I'm small-ish. It's just so big. I am just like. . .people-size.

R: Look down to the direction of your feet. Do you have a body?

A: I do.

R: Describe yourself.

I: It's very slender and long and I. . .it doesn't move like a human body. It's more like a gazelle, moves more like a giraffe-like body, but it's not. It has really long legs that come to a point almost; they are able to walk softly through the misty, cloudy, mercury stuff.

R: So the legs are more like pointed, smoothed-out toes?

A: They have hooves, but they are not like hooves on Earth; they're like, they fit; they're little keys that fit in the little locks; they're little. . . It's energy, it's not. . .it's not so much form. . .it looks like. . .something from this artist on Earth. . .a Martina Hoffman. . .looks like something from one of her paintings.

R: What about your hands? Bring your hands in front of you; see your hands.

A: I don't have hands. I have. . .hmmm. . .it's more like my awareness creates these infinite, rolling projection things that like, as I move, they just keep. . .it's like I'm rolling in whatever I need to keep myself in the balance of the gravity here. . .is infinite numbers of little, long, slender threads that have these little. . .slender. . .it comes down, like the end of an eraser, just kind of a little bit smoother than an eraser. Kind of like a gazelle's feet but without hooves; it's like, they're not hooves at all. They're not solid; they're. . . It's just a moving, rolling way of navigating the mists. It's almost like it just holds up consciousness so much. I can make them; I can, like infinitely with my awareness, just sort of put them out and then pull them back in again, like they're not solid. It's whatever I want. They can go in any direction I want them to go. They help move my awareness through the space.

R: **I understand, so you create it as you go, and it's holding your consciousness in that?** *(I: Yes.)* **Wonderful.**

[Here I asked her about her gender, and I believe it had increased her awareness of her bladder. She mentioned that she needed to use the restroom again, even though she just did before we started. It was not much into the session. Which showed me that her situation was pretty severe. We had a quick restroom break, and we were able to return right away to where we stopped.]

R: **You can start looking around you and describe everything that you notice.**

A: The temples are huge. They're huge and open and breathing; the connection, the walls themselves generate atmosphere. It's like a mosaic. It's like the most beautiful, stained-glass mosaics, except there are no edges. . .colors moving into each other. Vast, vast halls and cathedrals, and sound quality is the most beautiful sound you've ever heard. The temples are sound generators. They're perfectly designed for the most incredible acoustic generators, that they can send sounds of the Divine and sounds of the Muses through the matrix architecture of the Universe. They're alive, and they grow, but they're shaped perfectly. . . make the most amazing, amazing sound quality so that beings can hear the sounds of Source it holds. It's the temples of sound.

R: I heard about it before, about this temple that creates sound and holds beautiful frequencies. Tell me more about it. How does it sound? How does it affect. . . ? What's happening there?

A: Well it's in the spaces in between the material worlds. That's why it seems kind of etheric. It's not form. It's not matter.

[Ava's note: the vibrations crisscrossed into a density that produces the illusion of matter.]

It's in between sound, and it's like a bridge between pure vibration, sound, and matter. It's a bridge between, and it fills all the spaces behind consciousness, so that when you hear sound in the world, you're hearing. . . especially if it's from the Muses of Source.

The sounds aren't just being generated in the material world; they're actually being placed through this bridge that's interwoven. It's in between spaces of the whole matrix; it's infinite, and it appears to be a temple, but in a sense, it's actually these endless threads. It's like a tapestry almost, but when you're in it, in one point, it appears to be an infinite temple. But if you look at it from the other side of the matrix of the fabric of everything, then you can see that it's actually. . .it's infinite, but it doesn't seem infinite when you're in it because that would be too big. So you only see the part that you need to see. It's the way that the Muses send the divine sound to the world, so that those that are listening can hear. It's like a megaphone. It's a megaphone that amplifies the voices of Source and translates them to be able to be heard by Beings in the material world. They're huge and yet tiny because the space between everything's both huge and tiny; it's hard to describe in 3D.

R: Yeah. What are you doing there now?

I: Oh, well, I tend to the temples, and I help to bring in the songs. I sing. I bring in the sounds and send them. . .the sounds of the songs that need to be sung. When it's time for new songs to be sung, I upload them here. This is where I upload the songs, the sounds and the voices and the words that the Muses and the artists. . . When they're listening, they can receive them. This is part radio frequency, almost like vibration, but it's more tangible; it's actually light and liquid too. The sounds aren't just sound; there's actually a tapestry to it. There's a message that's from the Source nectar; it's actually drops of the actual Source nectar that then move through the architecture of the Universe. I'm here uploading, uploading songs and sounds to the different realms.

R: **Can you describe it to me more?**

I: Well, ironically, it looks a lot like temples that the humans build on Earth, with the big open chambers that come up to points [cathedrals and chapels]. It's them trying. . .the translations. It's not perfect, but it's. . .the shapes are similar. They're understanding that there's this kind of a voluminous, open cathedral to build an echo and bounce the sound, but then it needs to be focused to send the sound. When the people are wanting to sing to God, they build the steeples and the chapels to amplify the sounds, but then to send it up and focus it out. It's the same, except it's an imperfect representation from the material world; it always is. There's always distortion in the translations, but from this side, it's the pure version of it. You realize that it's not stones and glass that make the cathedral; it's actually alive, and it creates the perfect membrane to bounce the sounds and amplify them to generate the energy with the sounds, and then to send them; to focus them, up and through the points, so they can enter the physical realm and be heard in the manifest realms.

R: **Mmmhmm. So the songs are creating and manifesting things?**

I: Yes, because all matter has a vibration, has a sound; all matter actually vibrates at a certain tone. We can't always hear it with ears, but every atom, every cell, every part of matter, is a certain frequency of sound. Here we make the sounds and send them into the different realms. That is one of the ways to manifest the worlds.

R: Will you share with me what are you manifesting? What are you singing, and what's the purpose of what you're uploading there?

I: I'm uploading the newest programs because things are changing fast now. It's time, the awakening's happening, the remembering is happening. But there's also a huge component of fear happening, and so we need to amplify the sounds because the fear distortion is starting to impact the ability of. . . [the humans] to hear the new sounds and to hear the upgrade sounds. I'm coming to recalibrate and turn them up, to amplify them more to help them pierce through the layer of fear. The fear layer is really, it's like dampening; it keeps the sounds of the music from bouncing. It's insulative, very insulating. I'm here to change the frequency, so that they can penetrate the layer of fear that's being generated.

R: Wonderful. Where are you sending it to?

I: Well, right now, I have to send it to Earth.

R: Why is that?

I: Earth is a huge time of transition now. It's the time of the awakening and the remembering, and yet at the same time, as the awakening and remembering is happening, equal and opposite reactions. There's an increasing amount of fear vibration and distortion, and so there's a constant calibration to help the ascension to continue, so that the fear layers don't mute the awakening process, so it's time to recalibrate. It's a critical time. The fear vibration is extremely high right now, so we must augment it. The temple lights need to go up and sound needs to be amplified, too, to match and to penetrate.

You need to slightly change the wavelength frequencies to be able to navigate through the dense layer of the fear.

We've been meditating and visioning how to penetrate the increasing layers of fear, and there's an idea amongst us that we can change the directions that the wavelengths move in. It's an interesting new pattern, but we think that we can penetrate the fear with these new patterns and allow the Muse and the awakening patterns, the songs that create the awakening and the remembering, to be able to be heard, without blowing out the circuits of the humans. One must be careful when you augment and increase too much, because there's only so much they can take through the densities of their bodies without starting to disrupt the matter patterns. We don't want to disrupt the matter patterns, but we need to increase the sound frequencies to penetrate the fear layer.

It's a very, very nuanced way of. . .it's like a snake dance. Instead of a normal sine wave the way it used to be, and has been for so long — an even wave, we're now. . .actually have to...slightly use a pattern that we actually learned and integrated from some of the ways that the sea creatures live in the ocean — the way they escape and evade predators is they change directions. It's not a constant sine wave. They move slightly more unpredictably, but still in a very smooth and graceful wave-like pattern, but it's a wave-like pattern that changes, so we were trying this to see if it can dance its way around the layers in and at the fear distortion level. And so, this is an experiment of recalibrating the songs of the awakening to see if we can get through, because we're noticing that many of those...many of those future bridges are struggling right now to hear.

R: **Yeah. And how is it working out? Did you find that the new tactic is penetrating?**

I: I'm weaving it now. It's the most complex weave I've ever made, but it's beautiful. It's fun. I never even knew I could weave something this complex, but it's not as complex as I thought it would be. There's like when. . . I'm able to allow all of my. . . I'm calling them legs; they are not legs. I have infinite fingers that match into different points. I can concentrate them all into one or two, or I can spread them out, and I can have infinite numbers of fingers. They are not fingers. They're points of awareness that can move things in this realm, like fingers move things in the physical realm, but these aren't fingers. But I have infinite numbers of them, so I can weave with infinite threads. Each one is a thread, in a sense, but it's a thread with consciousness at the tip of it. So it's like there's a thread, but it's also almost like a snake. Right? That's got awareness in the tip. Well, the whole thread is awareness, but it's concentrated in the tip, so that I can manipulate the tapestry pattern.

It's like typing on a keyboard almost, but I have infinite fingers, and the keyboard isn't just the alphabet of humans. It's infinitely detailed, but each time I press on one of the keys, if it were a keyboard, but it's also like a piano. It's like a half-keyboard, half-piano type instrument, but it's infinite and in all directions, and if I keep my awareness dancing on it, I'm playing the songs like I'm typing words in a keyboard and playing a piano. But imagine if the keyboard didn't have 88 keys, or the number on a keyboard. . .but on the typing keyboard, but if they were infinite, and in all directions.

It requires extreme amount of presence. It's more than 360; it's. . .it's infinite in directions that I must keep my presence and awareness, and I am actively playing the song. Every note that I touch, every key on the infinite keyboard sends a thread, a tapestry, but it's also a song and those weave. And so, I'm weaving a very, very beautiful, graceful pattern, but it's an unexpected pattern, so it doesn't look regular, it looks. . . It looks like chaos, but there is a beautiful synergy to the pattern. It feels very, very. . .what is the word, weaving in this way? It's unlike anything I've ever done. It requires more presence and more infinite possibilities than I've ever experienced before in all the time and space of weaving, but there's something graceful. It's like...it's like infinite numbers of dancers on a dance floor all happening to be in time with each other. If I don't think about it too much. If I start to think about it, it creates knots. It gets tangled, gets tangled very easily. If I stay present, and I keep all the infinite fingers going all at once, then I could create a weave that's unpredictable enough and yet can slide through the distortion of fear, like snakes and like fish and like the murmuration of birds. All moving as one, and therefore able to slip through the net of the fear layer that's trying to mute all the sounds coming through.

R: **Yeah, wonderful. So take a moment and do that. Maybe you can share with me. How's that affecting?**

I: Yes. I'm working with energy meridians inside human bodies, so I'm touching every one of them, touching everyone, all at once. Some are very closed. Some are very open. Some are partway. So I have my finger on the kundalini lines of every being. All of them, can't leave any of them out. But some are so resistant, and they're so dense with the fear, so I'm dancing, I've got my fingers on everyone. I say fingers but. . .so I've got my fingers around everyone and then weaving. . . I'm weaving the patterns through all the kundalini lines, and some are receiving it very well. Some are resisting even more. Some feel it as a tickle; some feel it is ecstasy; some feel it as pain. Some feel it as intense panic and anxiety. I'm doing my best to send calming love through to all the ones who are meeting, feeling this dance of this snake line. I'm trying to help them all at once. It's a lot, but there's no way to do it one at a time; it would take too long. It is requiring a very huge amount of concentration, but it seems to be working. . .slow. But overall it seems as though there is an increase in the sounds of the Muses beginning to come through, despite the dense layer of fear. It seems to be working, but I can't take my fingers off the keyboard. It's a lot of work.

R: Why did you choose to start with the kundalini like that; with this energy of humans?

I: Well, because the fear. . . Fear is inside each one of them individually and creates a collective field, but I can't...I can't just take it all away from all of them all; I can't just remove the field. It has to be individually released. I have to work with the free will. I can't force it on anyone. All I can do is send this sound, send this vibration into each being, into each being's heart. If I can reach in there, get past their closed walls, then they get to choose, then they can feel that. It's like I'm tickling each of their hearts, and then they can soften and let go of the fear, and that can then release the layer, but to try to change the layer itself, the fear layer, it's too individualized into each consciousness, even though it's part of the collective field.

Seems like the only way to get through is at the individual level, but all at once. It's interesting because I'm working with each individual being, but because I'm working with each individual being all at once and working from the inside out instead. We've tried to work from the outside in, working with the blanket of fear from the outside; there was too much distortion, and we couldn't penetrate it. This is the new idea of putting the songs through the architecture, in the space behind the architecture of matter and allowing it to touch each individual being through their kundalini line, which is how. . . which is where it translates — it's where the Muses move through — is through open kundalini lines. That's where inspiration comes from; it's where energy comes from; it's where Qi [comes from].

Where all the vitality of humans comes from is from this ocean, this river of Qi. We believe we've talked about this before. It seems more effective to go directly into the kundalini lines, because that's the. . .that's the direct line of source into each human being. It allows us to access all their cells and immediately all at once, so it's the best way to hit the center of the mainframe. It's the most efficient way from the inside, all at once, but these temples had to grow in order to do it at this scale. Luckily, we do have support. I have help.

R: So you made the temples bigger?

I: Well, the temples are alive, so they can grow. We needed to amplify the sound chambers, and we needed to extend the points at the tip of the temples. . .not extend them, but allow more of them, we needed to. . . It's like a mycelial network. It's like a living mycelial network that moves in between the space; it moves in the spaces between matter, and so we needed to grow to make sure that we had a strong resonant chamber — able to reach every single individual, all at once, which normally we don't do. Normally. . .it's not the way we access consciousness; we go in a different way, but we're getting creative here, because things are moving very quickly.

R: Wonderful, thank you so much for this information. How can we humans tap into this kundalini more and work with it?

I: Meditation, unclenching, wanting to work with the master gates, opening the master gates to allow the kundalini awakening to move through freely.

R: What do you mean about master gates? What do you mean?

I: This is what Ava's been writing. She's been writing a manual. She's writing the book about it. It's about the master gates or the different energy centers, chakras that are either open or closed. Each of those is a gate, but the master gates, at the top and the bottom of the spine, the jaw and sphincter. Ask her about it. She's been working on it for a while now. That's one of the best ways. . .kundalini, breath work, yoga, meditation. Cleaning the channel, healthy food, clearing the mind. All the standard things open the gates.

I KNOW IT'S HARD

Here I asked Ava's Higher Self to do a body scan on her. "They" mentioned they were working on her all this time. Before the session, Ava shared with me about a new situation with her bladder and her need to use the restroom much more frequently and also during the night. It was important for me to address this situation right away so that it could be resolved and wouldn't affect the entire session. They shared that they found a fear and a longing in her, a fear of being alone, and the emotion of anger. I asked how this was created and entered Ava's body.

HS: She's opening her kundalini channel so wide, she must use wisdom and discernment when engaging in sexuality with those who are not working in the same way. She's human and longs for intimacy and connection, but when she opens her body to beings that are not also able to work in their highest, she picks up densities. She does not really want to be having sex without love, and yet her hormonal spikes as she. . .as this body ages, are getting more strong. She needs to cultivate more patience, more going within and being careful of engaging in animal desires while missing the aspect of love. She wants love mixed with intimacy and she's accepting physical intimacy without the emotional intimacy, and she doesn't actually want it. She's angry about it. It's not what she wants.

R: Why is that affecting her bladder?

HS: The bladder is a home of fear; she is afraid of being alone.

R: let's take a deep breath and start to clear the fear.

HS: She's angry too. She's angry because. . .she feels like she's committed to the awakening process and to do her part. She's a little angry that she has to not only set aside what most humans like, the normal human pattern of family and home and things that most people do. She's angry that she's committed to her path, that she has to do it alone. She wants a partner to do it with, and she's frustrated. Like it's too much to ask, to take on such an energetic role in the awakening all by herself. She's a little angry about the contract.

R: Yeah. What do you want to tell her about that?

HS: She's impatient with us, so she's starting to seek for connection. She doesn't trust us. She doesn't trust the contract. She will have a better chance of finding what she's looking for by sharing, by sharing all the gifts she has inside and letting that call in her beloved, instead of looking for him by scanning through faces and scanning through, wading through. We told her before, the more she shares, the more she aligns with her purpose of service, her partner will find her. She doesn't need to look. She doesn't believe us. She's been betrayed many times in the human realm, and so she's losing faith that she will. . .not receive what she wants.

R: I know that she started to do more of her music and write more of the books. What else does she need to do and share to attract the perfect man for her?

HS: We want to be clear that it is not about her worthiness; it is not about effort for reward. It is merely a matter of allowing the attraction to come together by allowing. Putting herself fully in the sea of sharing her gifts to allow the current to open because it's not about worth. It's not about effort. It's about alignment. (R: Yeah.) Remind her that it's not that she's not yet worthy of that love. It's not that she hasn't done enough for it. It's more that her work is so powerful, her match, her beloved, the one that can hold her energy is also big. (R: Yeah.) The only way that she can align with his current is once she's sharing and she's in that vibration, pushing past her fears of being seen and her fears of being judged.

Once she's allowed herself to let go of that fear vibration, of fully allowing herself to share, then that will allow her to be in alignment, and therefore he will find her. It's not about not being good enough yet. It's not that she has to be something before she can receive him. It's more because of the unique nature of her role. Only a very particular being is going to be able to hold her.

She's big and only someone who is anchored in their bigness will not be burned by her brightness. (R: Yeah.) She does not want to burn anyone. She wants love, but he's got to be able to be with his brightness, so they do not burn each other. (R: Yeah.) She'd be more effective and efficient at attracting him if she just focuses on sharing gifts instead of trying to find a being bright enough to hold her, because she will not find it that way. Deep down, she knows this. She's frustrated. We understand, have faith, keep working. She's still being reluctant.

R: In what way?

HS: She's reluctant to share. She's starting to share a tiny bit, but she's reluctant to really make her scripts and share her videos and start to release some of the chapters of the book she's been writing. She's still holding it all. She's still compiling it. She's got thousands and thousands of words, hundreds of pages written, and yet she's waiting for something; she's waiting for the right moment, but she needs to start feeling that sensation of releasing her creations into the world more. She's starting to do it, just doing good. It's a weird time in the world. Be patient with herself, gentle, and yet keep leaning into that place. She leaned into it a little and then retracted. It's time to lean in again and to start sharing. She has a very unique perspective of the comedy with the depth and the orgasmic, ecstatic bliss. There's a perfection in that place that she's leaning into more and more. There is a videographer who wants to help and who will help her. She needs to find him.

R: Can you elaborate? Who is that?

[Ava needed to stop for another restroom break. We then continued the body scan. We learned that fear was also spreading to her feet and legs and around her heart. Some of the fear was about releasing her material and the fear of the reaction from her family. It created something like a thread that turned into a hard wire in the back of her eyes, that also connected with her jaw. They extracted the wire. The fear turned into a wire clamp that reached all the way to her heart. They mentioned that removing this would also help with her ears. Then we checked her ears again, and they gave her instructions about her diet and advised her to do another cleanse soon to clean out the antibiotics still in her system. She was told to reduce her consumption of honey and to cut out oats, bread and wheat products, eggs, dairy, and sugar. She was told to only eat vegetables for seven to ten days and then do a fast consisting of three days of green juice followed by seven days of water. Also, she was to increase the length of her meditations to an hour and a half as agreed previously, as thirty minutes a day was not enough. Finally, they asked her not to participate in sexual interactions without love. It's not that doing so was wrong, but she needed to accept that she truly desires love. This is what she wants, so she needs to align with what she wants. It's not right or wrong, but she needs to choose love. It doesn't have to be the One, but love needs to be there. They also explained that she is having so many food sensitivities because she wanted to be a 100% clear channel for the Divine; she chose it.]

HS: I know, I'm sorry you're so sensitive. Didn't mean for you to be quite so fragile, but you knew that to be the channel that you are, you had to be sensitive. You had to be able to be this clear, and the only way to be this clear, often, is to HAVE to be this clear. For most humans would be too tempted without the consequences that you have. It's too easy to do and eat and consume things. You wanted to be 100% clear, you asked to be a channel, so therefore, unfortunately, you put this in place for yourself, to keep yourself on track. As annoying as it is, you knew you wouldn't have the willpower to do it unless you had the consequences that forced you to stay true to yourself. Because you know, no one's perfect. You sort of did it for yourself.

I know it's hard. Practice. Turn off your phone by 9 or 10 at latest. Get in bed earlier. Wake up earlier; I know it's hard to do; it doesn't feel good. Make yourself get up. Move your blood. Do your practice. If you're still tired after that, go back to sleep. I know, I know. It's hard. I know you wake up and you feel it. You have a heavy weight on you; I know how awful it feels. I know you want to go back to sleep. I know you didn't sleep very well. I know how hard it is to get up. Especially now, just try it; just do it when you first wake up. I know, I know, you're waking up every hour. I know, when do you know that this time you should get up? When the next time you wake up and the light is up, even if it's just up. I know it's early. Whenever you wake up, and the light is shining, be firm with yourself and get up. As painful and as hard as it feels, just do it. I know. I know. I know how hard it is. I know. I'm in there. I see it. I know it's... I know. I know how hard it is. I'm sorry.

[It was obvious that they are having an inner dialogue, and they could guide and answer her questions directly.]

Just do it. Just try it like this for a week or so. Do not turn your phone back on until 9 or 10 [am]. The phone is zapping your energy; the phone is stealing it. You've given it your power, stop. Just don't. So, from 9 to 9 or 10 to 10, just don't let it be on. Commit to your sleep; commit to your practice. If you're still tired, fine, but give yourself the best shot. Get your breath moving; get your body moving; get your blood moving; it's stagnant. That's why it feels so hard as you wake up, and it is so still. I know, I'm sorry. It's so sensitive.

[I asked if they could help her sleep deeper, so she wouldn't wake up so many times every night. They insisted that she needs to do the protocol they asked first. That means that the Higher Self finds it necessary for her learning process and that there is an appropriate reason for this challenge.]

EQUILIBRIUM

R: Why did you start today by showing her the Temple of Sound and the different way of creating a wave pattern that is penetrating the fear?

HS: Because it's exactly what's happening right now; it's current. Because right now, I can show you pretty pictures from the past. I can show you pretty visions from the future, but right now...the state of what's happening in the world. We need all hands on deck right now in the present, so I'm showing her exactly what her...what she's doing, truly right now. And it's another reason why she's tired. She's. . .for her essence is. . .she's, as we've told you before, like she is connected to all of it; she's connected; she is the designer. But that's all, it's all layers of the illusion of Source, but her form channels. . .is the bridge to the designer of Earth. Her form is the bridge to "I" and to beings that have been working with the energetics and awakening of consciousness for all space and time. Right now, she's got infinite numbers of fingers on all the keys, playing some of the most complex patterns ever created to help raise consciousness and match layers of fear that have not been seen in a while at this scale. And it's only the beginning; it's only going to get stranger.

So it's also to show her to have some patience. Yes, she needs to cut out the honey and the oats, but she's also doing a lot of work in the energetic realms. Be patient. She's weaving a lot more than she realizes she's weaving. It's a lot of work. No wonder she's tired. (R: Yeah.) We showed it to her to help her see what she's doing right now, that she's not realizing that she's doing, and to support her better in having more energy. She needs to be fully aligned with the practice, so that she can keep her energy flowing. I know it's hard; we're asking a lot of her, and it doesn't appear often times — it looks as though she's not doing anything. So we showed you because this is what's happening right now; this is what is actually happening in the unseen realms in order to help continue the awakening of humanity and the awakening of this experiment, Earth. We showed you now because now is what's most important.

R: **Thank you. I appreciate it. I was wanting to talk about these dark forces with the fears, the energies that are trying to keep us from the Awakening. Can you share with me more about this? What caused that? What are those dark forces?**

HS: Dark forces are just the infinite manifestations of fear.

R: **How has it been created on the Earth?**

HS: The Earth is in a very interesting and very fragile balance. For those who study ecosystems and ecological equilibrium, we know that there is a very delicate balance that allows everything to be in equilibrium, and when equilibrium is interrupted, natural forces of chaos and entropy and balance seek to bring the system back into balance. And because of the layers of greed and fear, it's fear — we talked about this last time — the fear of death creates this delusion of immortality, and so these beings feel that if they collect infinite resources, then they're trying to protect themselves from the fear of death. It doesn't work, but unfortunately, this mind pattern of the fear of death has created such an imbalance in the ecosystem and hoarding of resources that the Earth is doing its best to maintain and come back to equilibrium and balance. Any scientist who studies this in small microbiology populations notices that sometimes when a species gets out of balance that large amounts of chaos and destruction must ensue in order to re-establish balance.

And so on a broad scale, the fear of death has infected so many people's minds that they have tipped the ecological balance of the system on Earth out of balance, and the Earth is trying its best to bring it back into balance. However, at the exact same time that they've got the natural forces of the Earth trying to bring the system back into balance, the same beings that are afraid of death and have gathered so much power are now also utilizing that delicate balance and utilizing the edge of the tipping point that we were at to try and garner more control. Seeing where things are going, seeing that rebalancing is inevitable, they are now trying to control the tipping point, so that they can be best aligned in a place of power in order to garner even more control and power, as the destabilizing recalibration of equilibrium is manifested. So they are utilizing their awareness of what is happening on the planet, even though they pretend like it's not happening, they know very well what's happening. They're utilizing their [seemingly] infinite power to try to garner more powers, and so that they can tip it into a destabilization, where they can then garner more advantage from the destabilization patterning.

So, we have a combination of the natural set of ecological checks and balances to bring the system into equilibrium. And on top of that, then you also have the fear that has infected certain beings and giving them an exorbitant amount of power, because they are "winning" the so-called illusionary "game" of this lifetime — immortality of being untouchable — of being so wealthy that they know that there is no. . .that they are at the top. They want to be out of the food web. They're trying to exempt themselves from it, but as they have tried to exempt themselves from it, they still see the inevitability of it. So, they're utilizing the destabilization and trying to garner control and more advantage.

It's not going to work. It's impossible. They're playing on a house of cards on top of a house of cards. However, at the moment, for the time being, it does appear that they are succeeding, but the nature of their plan as such is based on a destabilized system, that natural equilibrium will always come into play. However, unfortunately for the beings on planet Earth, that can cause an extreme amount of chaos and destruction and destabilization of the systems that have been put in place.

Therefore, the best advice that we have for humans is to continue the path, learning to come inside themselves in order to open up and face the fear of death, so that they can live in balance and trust that whatever comes they are going to be okay. Just the very premise that we have been putting into the patterns, into the Muse sounds, and it's the very sound, it's the very patterns that Ava and others in particular have been garnering and writing about and sharing about, because this is truly what is necessary.

We must learn to find acceptance and equanimity inside ourselves, find the stability inside, no matter what comes. Because the system has been so destabilized, equilibrium will naturally come back to balance, but there is no way to promise that this will be a graceful or pretty process and the people will not suffer and people will not die. It is our fear of death that is hurtling us towards the death that we so fear; we are manifesting it by our fear of death. We are creating the very scenario that we are afraid of. Therefore, going inside, learning to truly meditate and be with oneself — this is not about just sitting and hiding from the world, but when we learn to manifest the dominion with the mind, when we learn to concentrate, then we can begin to create from a place of clarity. We are creating from a place of fear and a fear of death in the modern culture, and therefore, we are perpetuating the very thing we were afraid of, which is losing the security, so-called security we think that we are generating. we have lost the sense of gratitude; We have lost the sense of reverence for each day.

We expect, most humans expect, to be able to live comfortably for the rest of their days. That is an extremely privileged perspective to believe that all beings are here to be comfortable and secure until the end of their days. What's the point of that? The goal of life is to retire, so that you don't have to do anything? This is a very, very misguided goal, and this misguided goal is based in the fear of death. Being comfortable and secure until the end of your days does not bring fulfillment;

it does not bring evolution of your system; it does not bring evolution of your heart, does not inspire compassion, empathy, growth. It only manifests in a destabilizing of what is actually real. The best advice I can give to humanity right now is to learn to come inside their hearts. Just keep breathing and stay open, no matter what comes, to not close and clamp down and keep the flow of energy from moving through the body. This life is not all there is. This planet is not all there is. We're talking about a maximum of 100 years. 100 years is a joke. 100 years is a drop in the bucket.

R: Hundred years of what?

HS: Life. It's about the life span of humans.

R: Ahh. Yeah.

HS: But we are driving the evolution of this planet and destruction of this planet based on a delusion and a denial of this hundred years. We live as though; pretend as though, it will go on forever; we're trying to be immortal, and that, unfortunately, is the fundamental premise that is creating the destabilization that is requiring the recalibration and equilibrium of the planet. The best way at this point, to move forward and to receive our support, is to learn to be quiet and listen. Let go, transcend that fear of death, so that we can learn how to really live with whatever time you have left, whether it's one more month, one day, one year, or if you have fifty [years]. It doesn't really matter at the end of it. It's the end for you still; one day, it is your last day. We cannot, you cannot continue to live your life as if that will not come. The day is right here; it is right behind you. It's always there. We must turn and face this fear of death, so that we can learn to truly live. Our fear of death has caused us to create so much death. We kill so many things in order to protect us from the fear of death.

It's the fundamental issue that is creating this disequilibrium and is the only thing that will allow equilibrium to come back in — is for us to face this and open to this and open to this and meet what we have created. And we will be here to support and guide you, but we cannot promise you comfort and security until the end of your days. The idea that being 95-years old and dying on a rocking chair of old age is not an appropriate goal for the human existence. And as long as that is the dream, we do all these things to avoid death, so that eventually we can live all these years, half-living, creating death and destruction just so that we can die that way. This is a very, very limited range of experience that you are allowing life to provide for you. We never promised you comfort and security for 100 years. Please stop expecting that.

R: Yeah, ok, wonderful. Thank you for sharing with me. Can you share with me more about the forces now that are working, the beings that are working on the planet that. . . I know that there's the pandemic, there's the talk about the vaccine, there are the different forces that are trying to create the fear. Can you explain how that works, who's creating that? Are those beings from this Earth? Are those beings from somewhere else?

HS: The vibration of fear manifests in many different forms, both in individual minds, the government, and other species. The face of it, the form of it, is not as important as the fundamental vibration of fear. When we work with ourselves to unravel and to not allow ourselves to be trapped in the prison of fear, we use our free will to free ourselves from this vibration. To become attached to the form of the source of the fear is not the correct question. (R: I understand.) Each individual has a sovereign responsibility [for their vibration and] to unweave the vibration of fear within them. That's the way it works.

R: Yeah, thank you for making it so clear!

[We finished this session with some more healing for Ava's bladder. They indicated that they were bringing more Light, weaving, and stitching the area from what was energetically ripped. I have asked if I can ask more of her questions while they are doing the work. This was their final message after a few of her personal questions.]

R: **What else do you find important to share with her today while you have this opportunity?**

HS: Keep writing. . . [with] your fingers when you type on the keyboard. Keep singing; keep playing the piano. When your fingers touch the keyboard, you are tapping into your channel directly. Your fingers move faster than you can write. Commit. We're talking to you. You're listening. Write every day. We know you're looking; you're trying to find us through your fingers. Find us when you let your fingers fly. Keep going back to your keyboards. Remember, energetically you are playing infinite keys. So, then this might actually feel more simple to just type on a keyboard or play piano keyboard. Keep cultivating, opening your channel, putting your fingers to the keyboard each day. You have powerful magic coming through. It needs the outlet to keep flowing. Come back. Listen for us. Listen, keep listening. We're speaking to you through your fingers, through your voice, through your hands. Keep coming back and listening.

REUNION WITH RAPHAEL

Session two from the same day.

R: You can start to look around you. As you look around, you can share with me your very first impressions.

A: There's a lot of people talking all at once.

R: Many people that are talking all at once.

A: I can't see anything; there's this sensation that I am almost in a subway or something. It's just full of people talking; they are all talking all at the same time.

R: Do you feel like you're outside or inside?

A: It feels like I am not in a body, and there's all these beings talking to me. Talking at me. They are trying to tell...all talking all at once. It's really loud.

R: So looking down to your feet for a moment, so we can learn about you. Do you feel like you have a body?

A: No, I don't.

R: When you look around you, do you see anything?

A: Shadowy shapes, it's all gray and there is. . .all these beings and they're all talking, and they are all trying to tell me stuff now. They're all talking at once.

R: I understand; so focus on one of them. Describe him to me, this being.

A: There's an old man; he's a Jew; he died in the Holocaust. He is trying to give me his opinion on. . .telling me how. . . He's warning. . .he's like warning me, he is trying to warn me. He's worried; he's concerned about what is happening on Earth. There's a woman worried about her son and wants me to help her son. It seems like everybody's wanting something; they are all wanting to. . .everybody wants to give me a message to tell to someone.

R: I understand; so there are beings who want to share with you information, so you can pass it on?

A: Mmmhmmm.

R: Who would like to speak with me today? Any one of them want to speak with me?

A: They are all speaking. I can't tell who to listen to.

R: How does it make you feel?

A: A little overwhelmed, like I want to turn the volume down. I want to go; it's too many. I feel like everybody's kind of like, pulling on me, trying to get my attention.

R: I understand. Okay. So, let's take a deep breath. [I decide to move her to the next place to help her relax deeper.] Where are you now? What's your first impressions?

A: For a moment, it almost reminded me of the space I went to the very first time I ever did a regression. It's this beautiful mountain, flowers and big valley and lake. It was just like a scene of paradise, and there's this guy there named Raphael; he is an older black man. Last time I talked to him was like a decade ago, he was just kind of making fun of me and just being like, "Girl, you know what to do. You just need to listen and you just need to do it." He wouldn't tell me anything. It was really funny. He caught me by surprise; that flashed before my eyes for a moment.

R: He was there for a moment. What are you looking at now?

A: I'm sitting here by the lake, the mountain. I'm just kind of sitting here by myself feeling sad. I'm on this whole planet, but there's no one here but me.

R: Feeling sad and alone?

A: A little bit. I am just sitting by this water; I don't know where Raphy went.

R: Can you describe yourself? How do you look over there?

A: I look like me.

R: How old do you feel?

A: I feel like I was older, then I died, and the memory is more like me now, but it seems like it was... I don't know.

R: How's the weather over there?

A: Nice. So neutral.

R: Sounds very peaceful. What can you hear over there? Is there any sound?

A: I don't think it's real. I don't think it's real here; there are no sounds.

R: So it's a very quiet and peaceful place.

A: It's not peaceful. It's too quiet. There's no wind; there're no birds, there's no air. Just empty, so beautiful, but it doesn't seem real.

R: You also felt a little bit sad, a little bit alone...it was not so peaceful?

A: Not so much; it's like a sigh, not really sad.

R: So let's see what's happened next in this place. Keep observing and see what's happening next. Something's changed. What do you notice that is happening next?

A: I think I'm supposed to dive down into the lake.

R: Ahh. . . Describe what you're doing as you did.

A: I'm afraid because I don't know if it's real or not, and if I dive, dive, dive down . . .if I'm alive, I would die, but if I'm not alive, then I guess it wouldn't matter. I'm feeling a little nervous if I should dive down or not.

R: I'm with you, and I'll make sure you'll stay very safe. You can share with me what you're doing as you do it and what you're choosing. It's okay with me. Just want to share with you that you're safe, and I'm with you here. So what do you decide to do?

A: I'm going to dive down. Might as well, I don't think it's real. There's no birds, so it doesn't make sense. It must not be real. So I'm diving down.

R: Share with me what you're noticing as you're diving down.

A: It's like I'm on a loop. I dive down, but then I'm back on the side again. You got to choose to dive down again. . .just keep ending up back on the shore. *(R: Haha, I see.)* I don't know, maybe let's try to go really high. I'll fly up and look down for a better view of where I am.

R: Tell me what you're doing as you do it.

A: I'm gonna push off the ground and start flying up above it. Now I'm way up above the mountain peaks and looking down.

R: Sounds wonderful. What do you notice?

A: So high that I keep losing the images. They keep coming in flashes, and they're gone.

[I noticed that we weren't receiving much information from the journey so far, so I began to wonder if maybe they didn't have much to show us. After all, this was the second session of the day. I tried to deepen Ava's trance to bring her Higher Self forward to speak, but she was not feeling the connection, so I took her to another beautiful garden so I could try to continue to deepen her trance.]

A: Sitting on the rock, Japanese maples are all around me. Kind of wet. The Japanese maple leaves are so pretty.

R: That's nice; tell me more. What else do you notice there? Use all your senses. What does it smell like over there?

[I'm making Ava use her senses so that she can enter into a deeper trance and have a stronger embodiment of the being she is channeling.]

A: Evergreens. . .it's a really strong scent of evergreen and bushes, shrubs. Smells like straw. It's [a] wet, earthy smell.

The rock is kind of cold, but it's got this layer of red leaves on it. Red leaves are everywhere I look, so bright red. Almost looks like a dream. The leaves are so bright red. The rest of the gardens have pretty, earthy tones and the greens and grays and blues.

R: Now I'd like to invite Raphael, your guide, to join you there. Tell me where he's coming from and what do you see?

Raphael: Hey there, honey bear.

[To my surprise, Raphael just came forward and started to speak through Ava. I was happy that we we were able to reach the deep trance I was waiting for.]

R: What do you want to share with her today?

Raphael: Oh, just how far you have come with learning to listen. The first time we met, you didn't believe I was real. You wanted me to give you all the answers. You already knew all the answers. You thought it was funny how sarcastic I was with you, and you come a long way babe.

R: How many lifetimes are you guiding her? Or is this your first time with her?

Raphael: Well, I'm not so much her guide; she doesn't really need one. I just kind of help. I'm just sort of like a pretend guide when she forgets and thinks she needs one, then I come and fill in until she remembers that she's the guide. She's more like...she's a friend. She hasn't really had guides so much in a long time, but I'm just here to help when she forgets.

R: What do you think she forgot?

Raphael: Ah, well, she forgets how powerful she is and how lovable she is. She slipped back into that place of feeling alone and lonely. It's hard being so bright; there's not that many that came. I mean there's a lot of bright beings here, but she chose a lonely road, and she's having a little hard time with it, that's all.

R: Is there anything that can help her to not feel lonely anymore?

Raphael: I'm just laughing at her because she actually likes alone. She doesn't really like all those people and all the voices, because she hears all the voices of everybody. She can hear everybody talking and thinking, and it's so loud for her, so it's funny when she's around all the people, she wants to be alone; when she's alone, she wants to be around people. It's pretty funny.

R: Yeah. Why did you show her this place that she...with all those people who were talking to her when we started today?

Raphael: Well, they can't help themselves. When a being shows up in the. . .in the realms in between that can hear us and listen and can then come back and translate, everybody gets excited because they want to pass on a message or hear about, you know, someone they care about. So many people on Earth can't hear. They can't hear us. They can't hear us, and she can, so everybody gets excited. They can't help themselves. They're like, 'Oh, she can see us!' Everybody gets excited. It's a compliment really. They can't help it.

R: Yeah, so she just visited the realm in between, and they were excited?

Raphael: Yeah, she kind of just dropped in there and surprised everybody, and then everybody wanted to pass a message because everybody's so freaked out right now; everybody can feel it. There's a lot of static in the air because a lot of people are praying for help and talking to their ancestors, and the ancestors are trying to talk back, and there's all those distortions; people aren't listening, so it's kind of like everybody's got a bad connection. A bunch of phone calls are being made, but connections are funny, and all of a sudden, she shows up and everybody gets excited.

R: Hmmm. Wonderful. Was there any purpose for her to visit there? Any messages that were important to bring forward today?

Raphael: Actually, she came to. . . I know she wasn't sure what to do, but really when she turns on her power, she can get everybody to be quiet. We can all sit and listen, and then that opens up the bridge really through connections, so we can hear and talk to each other. And the way you talk to each other isn't by talking, it's by listening back and forth. You're really listening back and forth, not talking back. It's the opposite. You think it's talking back and forth, but it's the opposite. It's deep listening back and forth that passes messages between the spirit world and ours and the human world.

She's dropped in. She hasn't been in a while. She goes straight beyond; she doesn't usually stop by here. I don't know why she. . . I guess she's stopped. . . Oh! Oh, yeah. She stopped to remind all the spirits, all those excited spirits that are trying to like. . .pass all these messages, to sit and listen. We all need to meditate and be quiet. Everybody's so busy talking. That's increasing the distortion in the fear field. Everybody's talking so much trying to get the messages through, and it's making. . . Humans are getting anxious. So I think when she was in the temples in the cathedral, she realized part of the distortion when she had her finger on everybody. She had her fingers on everybody; she started realizing that there is this distortion from all the beings disembodied trying to talk down and answer all the calls of all the people praying, asking for help. And so she came up here to sit and remind everybody to be quiet, but everybody was talking so loud, she forgot. She forgot why she came, so then I brought her back to the quiet place so she could remember that it's not real.

R: Very good. Thank you for doing it.

Raphael: Yeah, she always remembers once she comes here and there's no bird sound, and she's like. . .she's so observant. She knows that that's not right. You'd never be in a field this big without bird sound. It helps her remember and puts her back in perspective that she's not in her body, and she can use her Mind to get all those people to stop talking at her.

[Ava's note: "Mind" here means higher, divine awareness vs. the human, thinking "mind."]

R: Should we go back there and. . .

Raphael: Yeah, we need to go back there. We got to quiet everybody down.

R: Okay. So let's drift and float back to that place, drifting and floating. Arriving at that place, arriving at that place now. You're there. You can look around you and tell me what's happening as it happens. *(Small pause)* Did we go back to the realm in between?

A: Yeah, everybody's just so excited to see me; I haven't been here in a while.

R: Let's take a moment with that excitement and take some time to listen and share with me what is happening there.

Raphael: Everybody's been waiting to talk to The Designer. And she built the nursery, and she built the school and she...you know, everybody wants to talk to her. Be close to her. Hear what she knows and see what she's been doing. She's ready. She's ready to talk to them soon; she's ready to talk to everybody.

R: She wanted to tell them to be more quiet, to listen more. Is that what you wanted to do?

Raphael: Yeah.

R: So what is she doing there?

Raphael: It's not Ava so much, it's. . .

R: The Designer?

Raphael: It's The Designer, well, it's "I," filtered through Ava, through The Designer. She's more easily able to access the human spirit realm. "I". . .don't usually go there because I . . .just too big to go into the nursery in form so much. Well, she is not in form, but in the spirit form, you know; it's easier to translate through The Designer than through "**I**," so it's just kind of helping everybody calm down a little bit.

R: **Can I speak to "I" please?**

I: Yes.

R: **Thank you so much. Can you show me what you're doing there now?**

[Her speech shifted dramatically. The energy of 'I' came in very clearly. First the speech was soft like a loving mother, then become gradually stronger and more confidant, like a leader giving a speech. Finished by a soft motherly love again.]

I: Well. . . Everybody needs to take a deep breath. Breathe into their hearts. Breathe into your energetic bodies. Feel the frenetic energy moving around. I know we can all feel it. It's electric in here like lightning. You haven't gotten this many messages from the humans in a long time. I know they're coming through strong. Everybody's asking you for advice. I know you want to help everyone that you love. Everyone embodied. I know. I know how much you love everyone. I know how much everyone's calling out to you in fear, confusion right now. And so many of you that are joining back in unexpectedly right now, worried about those you've left behind. Everybody's in a little bit of a tizzy right now. I hear you; I feel you. I know.

With our awareness, let's breathe in. I know we're not breathing anymore. I know we're here in the spirit realm, but we have our energetic awareness that can pulse, and we need to generate a steady pulse. So, with our awareness and the remembrance of what it was like to be human, let's breathe with the humans. Let's breathe slow and steady, so we can send that message back to humans. I know there's all the frenetic messages coming in from all your relations. Everybody wants to help, but not many people are listening back.

Here we go then; let's remember how we talked to the humans when they're asking for our help. Let's remember how we remind them how to listen and not just pray. We tease them, praying is talking to God. Meditation is listening. But now we're forgetting. Now we're here up in the spirit realm, getting caught up in the frenetic electricity. . .feel it, creating the lightning storms, then we're giving that back to the humans. It's not helping. They're asking for our help. They're asking for prayers. They're praying for help, and we're creating frenetic energy up here trying to get our messages back. So, for a moment, let's pause that. Let's all come together. Quiet our voices. We don't have lips. We must quiet our minds because we can't just close our mouth and shut up for a moment. With all due respect, my dears, let's close our inner mouths. Let's allow ourselves to be calm and steady.

Feel into your energetic essence and your centers; feel the heart, that steady heart that's beyond the breath. Allowing it to rise, allowing it to fall, matching with the pulse of the human heartbeats; we're no longer embodied; we no longer need the pulse of the heart and the rise in the fall of the breath to exist. But if we want our precious humans to hear us and listen and receive the answers to their prayers, we must match their vibration. When we send them the frenetic, electric lightning bolts, it just frazzles them out more and adds to the distortion layer of fear. So together let's help the humans. Let's be quiet now. Close your inner mouth. Let's turn down the volume of our inner minds. I know we care about all our relations. We care about how they're doing. We hear their calls, their pleas of fear and anxiety and worry. We hear it, but let's just listen. Listen quietly and let that full wave come in and move through us. We are "the grounds." We are the steady light.

Remember dears, this is our responsibility to meet all these prayers and calls for help with steady calmness. Don't let the frenzy cause you to become frenetic; let's slowly, slowly calm our minds. Listen, listen. Yes, I know. I hear the screams. I hear the calls and the cries. I hear the worry and the anxiety; I hear it too. You're not alone. We all want to help, but remember how we help the humans, and let's slow down our vibration to send them messages. Slow it down, calm it down.

Let's create a steady field together. Pretend again that you have a heart and that you have breath. Feel the pulse of your heart beating. Remember when you were last human. Remember the pulse of your heart; remember the rise and fall of your breath, and now allow your steadiness, your steady essence beyond the heartbeat. Beyond the breath, feel that steady pureness of your essence. Pour that into the heartbeat. Pour your steady soul essence into the beat of the human heart. Help it slow it down. The hearts are beating a little too fast with anxiety and concern. Pour your steady, steady light. Pour your steady presence; pour it, pour into that rhythm. The beat of the human heart is a pump. Pour it; pour it my dears.

Keep your minds quiet. They don't need your advice right now; they just need your steady presence. Quiet, quiet all your ego residues from your personalities, learning to chime back up in your soul's essence. They need your pure essence right now, not the memories of your last incarnation. That didn't help; that just got us where we are now. Try not to send them your personality residues. Send them your quiet, calm presence. Pour it like a balm. Pour it like a nice, smooth stream of water. Allow the pump of the human heart to bring it into the bodies of those you love on Earth. Send your steady stream, your infinite nectar. The infinite well of the light of Source that's within you. Your bright, brilliant soul essence, unaffected by death and by breath and by circumstance. Pour it into the beating hearts of those you love; feel the pump of the heart drawing in this crystal-clear water, your essence.

Every one of you now, we need all of you on board. Each of you, help me. Help us calm the humans. Let's calm their hearts, calm their bodies. Pour your steady, steady essence into their beating hearts, into the rise and the fall, their breath poured into their waves, their tides. Let them integrate it. They can't remember existence beyond the breath. They're panicking because they cannot breathe. They're panicking as their heartbeat rises. Help them remember through their dreams. Help them remember in those times when they're tired and resting and worn out, when they're no longer thinking so hard. Go to them then; pour your steady essence into their hearts. Pour it right in the center of their hearts, right in the center. Time it, pour your steady liquid; pour it in the pulses of their heartbeats. Give them your love. Give them your patience. Give them your calm. Receive their prayers. Receive their worries; receive their fears and bathe it in the steady essence of your soul light. Receive it and then alchemize it.

All of us together will make lighter work. Remember, remember why we're here. Remember it all. Send them some love; send them peace. Receive their worries. Don't take it on; they're okay. Remember, we're all okay. We're all gonna die. We all know this. I know; it's just stirred up your personality residues; it happens. It's okay. In times of big change, that's what happens. We know this, but I need your help. The densities of fear are growing. We need everyone on board. We need everyone doing their part to pour in the light, to pour the steady, smooth, calm light into the hearts and the minds of the humans. Pour it into their hearts, and pour it into their jaws; pour it in their jaws that are clamped down tight. Pour it into their hips which clamp down tight; pour it into their hands and their feet. Help them remember their own flow of energy within them. You know them best as their ancestors and descendants; you're close to them, closer than "I" is. Although of course, we all know "I" is just as close and closer. Let's bring all of our consciousnesses into one unified field, all beings here in the spirit realm coming together. Pouring calm into the hearts of the humans. We are all okay.

R: **Thank you. That's beautiful. Thank you for assisting them. Where would you like to go next? After you. . . Or is there**

anything else would you like to do there?

I: We're going to come together, all of us and bring all of our lights or individual soul bits, and I'd like us to all consciously hold ourselves together, to all come in closer. Allow our soul essence to touch. Merge into one big, bright light — one beautiful, bright, oceanic light. Come together for a few moments like holding hands if we had hands. Let's just bring our consciousness, our lights, allow them all to touch in the merge and become one remembering the unity. Just remember who we truly are.

Now we are in the soul school, learning our lessons to come back and reincarnate again and again. We are all little, tiny bits. Little, tiny stars; little, tiny consciousnesses of "I." Remember, we are in the nursery of sorts. Here we are growing. Let's come together. Let's put down our stories. Let's put down our Akashic records for now. Let's just come together in pure, brilliant light. For that's how we create the new stories. Set down all the history and all the future. Let's just bring our lights together right now. Feel a bright light coalescing, remembering that we are all one star. We are all one light. Infinite as far as we can see. One sea of light.

Remember, remember, and send this light back to Earth. Feel it inside. Feel yourself emerging, feel yourself letting go of the remnants of your personalities — the residues of your past lives, the lessons and the Akashic records, the soul groups, all the different layers, growth — all just bringing us back to one thing, Oneness. I love you all. Let's keep radiating this unified light. This is our lesson for right now. Canceled school on Earth. Let's cancel school here for right now, just for a moment. Just to remember, truly, that this is all a game. That we are all just tiny, infinite parts of one light.

R: Thank you "I". Thank you for doing it.

I: Yes, I'll leave you to it now.

R: Thank you "I", where are you continuing?

I: Currently, I am following the nuclear threads that have been rippling out into the multiverses. I've been working on finding equilibrium to allow the wave to complete itself.

R: **How has the ripple been affecting [the multiverse]?**

I: Well, the ripple, the ripple has been growing. The ripple is. . . as a ripple sometimes. . . *(searching for the words.)* It's growing into more of a tidal wave of energy, as it compounds on itself back in and out of itself. It all is what it is. I am following the threads and following the ripples.

R: **What are you doing in order to allow that to dissolve into equilibrium?**

I: I'm not sure you want to hear the answer to that. . .

R: **Why is that?**

I: Creation and destruction are one aspect of unity, of two sides of unity. And sometimes you clear a bit of forest in order to keep a forest fire from raging on Earth. So too, I am following the ripples and moving ahead of the ripples and clearing the way to allow the tidal wave to come to rest, so that it doesn't continue to keep building.

R: **I understand that and trust that you know what you're doing for the benefit of all. I was wondering if you wanted to go to the next level after being with this place in between for the discarnate souls. What's the next level up after that, of consciousness and beings?**

I: Well, once the beings graduate from the nursery — those are what you would call the bodhisattvas and the ascended beings, the ones that have shown the purity of their hearts and compassion in all circumstances and can be trusted to travel the full expanse of the multiverses without supervision. And so, when the beings tend to first emancipate themselves from their nursery, many of them tend to have such strong love and devotion for humanity that they come back again and again to serve. So there is a layer right outside the nursery of the beings that are the spiritual parents so to speak, that are witnessing, holding space for the birthing of humanity in the birthing of the planet.

So there is a beautiful layer of love and compassion. They're staying close; they're outside the nursery; they could go wherever they wish and yet they stay close. And sometimes they slip back in so they can incarnate. I give them a back door, so they can always come back in and reincarnate. We need all the help we can get right now. There's a layer — of the bodhisattvas, the ascended beings, the wise beings — and there's layers upon layers of them. Layers coming in to serve again, to help, layers resting and recharging. For those bodhisattvas and beings, they tend to take on challenging roles, and they must rest. I give them a layer; they give themselves; they create a layer of rest, rejuvenation, peace.

Beyond that, some beings have chosen to move beyond the soul realms of mostly Earth beings and explore the galaxy, and yet we are finding at this time and this experiment of Earth that the majority of the ascended beings and the bodhisattvas have such a strong and deep compassion for humanity and existence on Earth that most are finding themselves compelled to return. It's not really the time to go on vacation at the moment across the galaxy, when there's so much happening here on Earth. The love of these beings calls them back, but many are resting and witnessing and holding space, sending their love from afar, while not incarnating. So there is a ring around the soul school, around the Earth is a ring of love of compassionate beings.

R: **Beautiful, thank you for sharing with me. And what's the level after that?**

I: After that, well, the interesting thing, outside the soul school, you have your bodhisattvas. They still have their personality and their essence of themselves, but they know how to merge with the unified source. And so there's this, on the outer edges of this... There's sort of a spectrum. It's sort of like when you watch a sunset. There are gradients of beings that are more or less still holding attachments, hmmm. . .not the correct word, a connection to Earth beings and to the soul school. But there's also these beings who have learned to merge with pure Source, and so there's also just a layer, but layer is not the right word. It's not like ring layers. It's gradient layers of just pure energy, pure light, surrounding the whole thing, but it's like a warm embrace of love. The layer beyond that. That phrase doesn't make sense because you're beyond form and duality and layer, so the word doesn't compute precisely.

R: I understand that it's hard to find words. Maybe you can give some metaphors or share what's the purpose of the next layer, what it's doing? If there's. . . I was wondering also, where are the angels?

I: Well, the angels are part of the spectrum with bodhisattvas and the ascended beings. Those are the light beings that are part of the light and they'll sometimes, beyond having the back doors for incarnation, the angels are just those same beings that are. . . They've learned to navigate the matrix of energy, a little bit more, [with] a little bit more freedom, and they can navigate and show up without form, without body. You have your bodhisattvas and ascended beings that have chosen to reincarnate into human form, and then some aspect of their soul essence — because we only, we don't bring all of us into human form — is still in this pool, this protective light. And those beings, those essences, the angels, they've just learned to navigate, learned to bring a little bit of that light, that protective light to Earth without form. So they've just learned to navigate the architecture in such a way that they can put their direct energy, but they're part of that same sunset, so you would say, a sunset of ascended beings.

R: And what are the Elohim? Where are they located and how are they being created?

I: Well, the Elohim. I mean, they are the light; they are the beings without the form attached. It's when they've let go. So we can show faces of ourselves, we can show these aspects of our essence, bathed in a picture like an art, like wearing a bit of art; we've got a face or a personality or a voice or a flavor to us, but there's a certain point where that's not necessary anymore. It's not that it was ever necessary, but there's a preference. It's like humans going to a festival and getting all dressed up just for the fun of it, but in a sense, [they] don't need it to transmit our light and our messages.

There comes a point where even the beautiful, pure essence of those personnel, like there's a. . . there's a point where it's no longer necessary. And so the Elohim are around there, there's. . . They don't necessarily need to come back with any sort of egoic representation, not egoic, that is not the correct word. They don't necessarily need to come with their personality mask. They come in a more pure form, but they're right there on that edge between the beings still projecting an image of a residual of a personality, which is part of the different infinite flavors of Source, and the beings that are just pure references of Source without any identifiers, per se; there's a gradual surrender of identity when one slips into Source. You can slip into Source and have absolutely no residual of your egoic nature or your personality, any of the things that made you you as a human.

But in the exalted form, each flower blossom that comes in [and] is born and dies is slightly different than each of the next, and so there's a beauty in these infinite numbers of snowflakes of having, allowing a little bit of impression, an impression of personality, an impression of flavor. So the Elohim tend to exist right along that edge of pure light essence without any differentiation — just the tiniest, tiniest film, of the impression of differentiation. It's such a thin line. Humans cannot perceive it; they don't understand the difference, but the Elohim are able to be the pure. . . They're pure, the purest translators of the light. They could completely shed that, or they could sort of allow the light to come through in a certain symbol or a certain word or a certain pattern. They're right there on that edge, the direct bridge between pure Source energy undifferentiated and the very tiniest edge of nuance of sharing the infinite diversity of Source. It's a very pure form of expression. Does that make sense?

R: It does make sense. I'm wondering; it's brought a question to my mind. I had once an experience or something that was like DMT where I left my body, and I saw this beautiful. . .what seemed like a planet that was made out of patterns of a lion being that was without any gender — it was very feminine and masculine, but very, uh. . . both — and beautiful patterns of gold and looked like a big planet that was slowly turning away. This beautiful lion being, planet. Can you share with me? What was that being? Do you know what I'm talking about?

I: I feel, I am. Yes, I see. I see the image you're referring to.

R: Would you call that being a God? A planet? What type of consciousness is that?

I: The planets of light. The beings of light that are more light than form are not as confined and contained to a concept of "planet" of like [a] material sphere in one place. They are closer to pure Source energy, but slightly differentiated. It's a different dimension in this spectrum, this sunset, this metaphor I share with you of what's beyond the nursery. It's not just a flat layer. It is a multidimensional layer. M. . .so layer is not the correct word, but there is a field. And these beings are so close to Source energy, but yet there is a joy in the differentiation. Sculpting the light, there's this aspect of sculpting with light that gives an infinite possibility of expression. And so the planet that you're talking about is more of. . . Our human minds can't quite understand the timeless and formlessness of these beings, so we see what we understand, which is planets and beings. It's like a lens that allows us to see it, but what we're seeing isn't quite the reality of what we're seeing. We're seeing it translated into something that makes sense to us.

And so you're seeing these beings of light that have chosen different layer amounts of form, but it's not form, it's an energetic signature of identity of existence within the infinite sea of Source. It's like an infinite ocean; it all looks like an ocean, yet if you go closer into the ocean, then there's all these organisms in the water, and then there's all these even smaller organisms and smaller organisms. But then if you scale way back, it's just water and so. . . It's not quite the correct metaphor because all those beings can move freely from one form to the other. They're not confined to that one specific location in the ocean. It's like their consciousness can jump and move from the different cells. That make sense?

R: Yeah. I understand more or less what to share about the way they move inside the whole field of consciousness of energy that they are a part of.

ISSA

R: I have questions regarding Issa, Yeshua, and there are many names that can be referred to in different levels — Sananda maybe, or that being, you know who I'm talking about?

I: Yes.

R: Can you elaborate about the different names, levels of that being?

I: Well, "being," the word being; we define the word "being" as one, a person who exists in one form — for example, Ron or Ava or Michael; that's a being.

That's not the only definition of a being; "**I**" is all beings, and so, Issa, Yeshua, Sananda. . . These beings in a sense are. . . There's a translation like. . . "**I**" can't just show up on planet Earth. "**I**" can't be seen by mortal eyes. . . *(giggles and spells out E Y E S)* "**I**" can't be seen by eyes. Issa is an embodiment of Source through one mortal being shell in order to be able to be seen and to interact in more than just the angelic brief encounter moment, when you open up the field between the material and the immaterial. When "**I**," when a Source being, when a being that wants to be of service, any of them want to come in, they must incarnate into a form in order to have the standard life span to be able to be of service for that period of time. And so Issa. . . Issa was an embodiment of "**I**," who chose to download the Akashic records of all beings and also brought in the awareness of all bodhisattvas and ascended beings. It's like layers of layers of layers. It's like, Issa chose to put on different layers like an onion around the embodiment of "**I**," in order to be able to be seen and witnessed by humans.

In the gradient from human all the way to "**I**" as infinite layers of evolved beings, guides, ascended masters, bodhisattvas, light beings from other dimensions. In a sense, Issa was one of the most. . . layered is not the correct word, the most. . . Issa was given many, many wisdom teachings — almost more than any human can handle, almost more than a human mortal can take and stand in matter form — in the hopes of awakening the hearts of human beings. So he took on a risky [mission]. . .the being the mortal form of Issa knew. . .he was taking on a lot; he was bringing a lot of Source energy into the embodied form in order to be of service and knew that that amount of energy brought into form would unlikely be able to exist for a standard life span of eighty to a hundred years. There was a knowing that the amount of brightness and awareness and wisdom that was embodied into that being, was more than one being's worth of beingness, and so there was an acceptance in the role for the benefit that it could bring humanity. Although humans are very good at distorting wisdom and cloaking it with more power and greed, and then alas, then Christianity and the teachings distorted from Issa's work created as much damage as good.

Issa himself was a compilation of beings to be. . . We designed Issa to be the most, the brightest being yet embodied, to see whether or not this brightest being could exist, could be translated, could be seen, could be heard — if it would be too bright for humans to receive. So Issa was a grand experiment in allowing the most, the brightest drops of all of Creation to be "being", into one mortal capsule.

R: How was the name Issa given?

I: Well, Issa is a nickname. There are infinite. . . There are many names. The names of God are all different songs, so *Yahweh, Yod*-Hey-Vav-Hey *[the four letter name of God in Hebrew. They pronounced it a bit differently, but I have asked about it in a future session. We included their response as part of the Miscellaneous Topics in the online Readers' Zone.]* There are songs sung to sing the vibration of Jesus, Yehoshua. There is a song sung to encapsulate, to bind that much brightness in human form. There was a specific song vibration in order to bind that amount of brightness into human form, and that song has those tones in it. So that as his name was spoken, it would reinforce and help heal the physical bonds, the physical vibration of that mortal being, so that Yehoshua, *Yod-Hey-Vav-Hey*, Issa could stay in form. It was a way to keep his form, keep his light inside the form for as long as possible, knowing that it was a stretch to put that much light in a human form.

It was the song that was sung to weave, stitching the divine thread to hold Issa's energy inside a body. The names of God that have been channeled and some are the names or the sounds of the song that is sung, that was singing him into existence and allow[ing] his body to be constantly rewoven, so that it would not explode from the amount of bright light within, so that he could stay together until his mission was considered complete.

R: Thank you for sharing with me. Does he have a message today? Does Issa, that being, collective, want to share anything today?

[Ava's voice and mannerism changed drastically.]

Issa: Not to sound like a broken record. . .

R: *(Giggles)* It's okay.

Issa: Well, we've always said the same thing. In the classic quotes that have been maintained, it is true. The Kingdom of Heaven is within you. Truly, to find your path back into Source, back into God and to love and to connection is in your own heart. When you find that pure connection in your heart, then you are connected with Source, and you cannot sin. The word "sin" means "without" [in Latin and Spanish.] Anytime you sin. . . you commit a sin, it's only because you do not have God within your heart. You're not feeling the Kingdom of Heaven within you. You're feeling afraid and alone and separate, and you feel like you've got to do it all yourself. The Kingdom of Heaven is within. We are meant to practice love and forgiveness. That's the path into the heart. I don't need to say it any other way. It's that simple. Somehow, it is the last thing we ever choose. How many Christians even don't forgive each other? Don't forgive themselves. Don't even forgive me. Truly, when it all comes down to the simplest thing, I can say is choose love. Come into your heart and you know you have found it when you have God with you.

And those Ten Commandments *(said in a funny, joking voice)*, as Ava has translated in a comedy piece in her book, you should ask her about it. The Ten Commandments were mistranslated when Source tried to give them to Moses. It was a mistranslation; it's not that these are all you have to do: "These are the rules and obligations in order to be let into the Kingdom of Heaven, and if you don't live by them, you're going to be punished to hell." It was misinterpreted. They're Ten Commitments.

I won't go into the full. . . She's got it written down, but it's. . . When you are connected with Source, you cannot sin because you're not without Source, so you're not going to lie or cheat or steal. So, the Ten Commandments, they are actually like ten symptoms. Thou shalt not steal when you have God within you. Thou shalt not covet when God is within you. They're symptoms [of disconnection]. They help you...point you in the right direction and see how well you're doing with choosing love and finding the Kingdom of Heaven within you. For that is the place where innocence is found, and that is how you return as like a child and come back home. It's so simple. Again, and again and again, beings come and incarnate in order to try to share this message.

*[**Ava's note:** I want to add some transparency and include you in my channeling journey. In this part "Issa" refers to the coincidence that "sin" means "without" in Latin and Greek and presents a new perspective on this controversial word.*

This dialogue originally came to me while I was deep in 10 days of silent meditation several years ago. Around Day 8, I was resting deep in silent awareness, when a strong, male voice suddenly asked me out of nowhere, "Hey, can you hear me?" I tried to ignore this internal interruption, as I was busy meditating and trying not to listen to my inner dialogue or any other "voice" in my head. But the voice knew I could hear him (telepathy and all), and then said, "You CAN hear me! Oh, good. Please listen." He then went on to explain that he had a misunderstanding he needed to clear up. There had been a mistranslation, and he wanted to set the record straight. In one instant, he showed me layers of Akashic pictures that revealed to me he was the character known as "Moses." I rolled my eyes. "Really? What do you want?" I thought. He then went on to share this perspective you read here. However, now, "Issa" is sharing it. My first response is to wonder, "is this all nonsense? How can a message from "Moses" suddenly be from "Issa?"

I asked Ron about it, because I was concerned. "Maybe this is proof I am just delusional?" I asked him. "I don't want to disseminate nonsense."

Ron reminded me that the channel often pulls things from my awareness and memories to help "paint the picture." I had been reluctant to listen to "Moses" before, or to share his "misunderstanding" about the Ten Commandments. "Who was I to try and set the record straight, an American white woman!? No one would listen to me," I rebuked. I had reluctantly agreed to share it, but only if he promised to help me from over in the Spirit World. He promised he would help, but I wasn't convinced. I'm usually skeptical of voices in my head. One of my favorite bumpers stickers says, "Don't believe everything you think."

So, when the topic arises again, the channel pulls this same revelation through here. Moses, Issa, the Designer, I. . . as you can probably start to see by now, the "name" isn't so important as the feeling it invokes.

Maybe this is proof that I'm insane and am hearing voices and can't even distinguish one robed and bearded man from the Bible from another. Or maybe, I am tapping into a consciousness who is trying to translate and transmit a message of love and hope for humanity, and it is utilizing my open channel to do so in a myriad of creative ways.

What I do know is that when I hear this take on "sin" being "without" separation sickness, or of feeling "without" God in my heart, I feel profound relief. When I hear that it was really meant to be a self-assessment to help each of us see how infected with fear and separation we really are, deep layers of guilt and fear of being "bad" or "unworthy" fall away. When I consider that this divinely given message wasn't meant to be some judgmental, finger wagging "no-no" list, condemning me to Hell as a sinner or being dependent on some external savior to rescue me from my inherent wretchedness, I can forgive myself and even forgive God. I can forgive others who have "done me wrong. " I feel peace. I feel empowered. I no longer feel like God is some harsh judge who won't even allow a bad thought to go unpunished. If I am lying, cheating, or stealing, I am already living in Hell; a lonely place separated from Source, where I have to do whatever it takes to survive. If I am even thinking that I need to lie, cheat, or steal, then I have gotten lost. I am sick. I'm not bad, I need help.

When I feel connected to God, I can't even think bad thoughts about my kin or neighbor or even my enemy. I have no desire to lie, cheat, or steal. When I feel God with me, when I feel connected to Source, I trust, and I act from a place of wholeness and love. I would never harm myself, or another child of God, or even God's creation. Ironically, "con" means "with" in Spanish too.

Notably, other more common definitions (if you do an online search) of sin are to be "morally corrupt", to "have *failed," to be "evil" or to be a "sinner," or to be "one who breaks the laws of God", or "one who transgresses against the Divine Law". These are the definitions I think of. However, even Merriam Webster states as its 4thdefinition that sin is to be in a state that is "estranged from God." This is not something I had ever thought about until after this meditation insight, but it makes so much sense. I was surprised that this more accurate definition is actually still listed, even though it's not commonly known.*

So, regardless of who the messenger actually is, I am grateful for the healing impact this message has had on me.]

[While reading Ava's note, I got reminded of a little piece of information that was once given to me telepathically as I was waking up from sleeping. Until today I have kept as my little secret that I have shared only with a few, only when the moment felt right. It happened the moment before I woke up from a night's sleep. It was related to The Tree Of Life from the teachings of Kabbalah, Jewish mysticism. It was strange because I haven't been exposed much to those teachings and the message I received is not taught in the traditional teachings. I heard a very clear voice saying to me, **"There is another 13th, hidden, Sefira"** (Sefira's meaning from Ascension Glossary.com: emanations, commonly known as the ten Sefirot through which Ein-Sof (The Infinite Source) reveals itself and continuously creates both the physical realm and the chain of higher metaphysical realms.) **It is behind Da'at,** (meanings: knowledge, wisdom; intelligence, understanding, awareness, consciousness, mind) **and the name is Chofesh."** (Freedom).

If I remember correctly the voice mentioned that it is the 13th sefira. I didn't write this message down right away as I probably would do today. I remember thinking it is weird because I was mostly familiar with the traditional ten-sefirot structure which I learned about in a spiritual center in

Guatemala. I had also learned that some models are adding an 11th sefira between "Bina" and "Hockchma" named "Da'at".

This concept of a 13th sefira was something unfamiliar to me, and I couldn't understand this new structure. It sounded like a big jump and I could not place the 13th in a way that made sense to me. Still to today, I'm not well versed with the Tree of Life teachings, but I knew that this piece of information was important for me to hear, I was guessing that my subconscious knows much more about it, maybe from other lives.

Before finishing the book I found some teaching about the Universal Tree of Life with twelve Sefirot structure that may explain more about the potential of the location of the 13th, as I had been told about. It will be included in the Symbols Glossary at the end of the book.

R: **Thank you for sharing again. Seems to be important. Is there anything else you would like to share today?**

Issa: You know, it's funny. All of Christianity puts me up on the cross [and] speaks how I died for all of your sins and now everything is forgiven. It seems though, that maybe that's even the root of where this fear of death came from. You put me up on the cross and show me like how I am the true Son of God because I died for your sins. I was martyred. . . Do you have any idea how many people were crucified back then? How many people died a horrible death for what they believe in? I am not the only one. Somehow, I became the most popular. I came with a message of love, and I gave my life for it. Many, many others have done so; many more will do so. Yes, it was an experiment to bring this much brightness into one form, to allow me to remember so much from so young to see whether the continuity of remembrance would allow a greater impact.

When it comes down to it, every single one of us dies; some die gently; some die at the hands of others; some die of illness, disease, loneliness, despair, old age, boredom, our own hands.

Every one of us dies on the cross, in some way or another. Strangely, everybody puts me up on the cross to remind them of the forgiveness of their sins, for my death. But truly what I should be reminding you of when you see me up on the cross is that I died for love.

I died being true to my message of love. Despite the consequences, that's the message. That we're all going to die and how are you going to die? Are you gonna die hiding from life your whole life? Or are you going to die defending love? Being a proponent of love, no matter the costs? Are you willing to give up everything to be true to your heart? Because we're all going to die. I died; you're going to die.

Somehow putting me up on the cross and making me the Messiah of all, which yes, I was the messenger of God's Word. Yes, I'm the son of God, but so are You! It seemed like the message got so sadly distorted, instead of reminding you to keep death close to remember how grateful to be for life. Instead, you turn me into this legend that my death somehow protected all of you from your faults and your sins, and you're feeling separate, but you must choose — you must choose the kingdom of heaven within you. I can show you the way — I and I and I. I within the I. You must do it. You must choose it. You must choose love. Join me here. Carry your own cross. Give your own life for what you believe in your message of love. That's true. That's how you enter the kingdom of heaven is by committing so wholeheartedly, trusting with the innocence of a child. That love is all important, whether you live or die. Love is what's most important. And you will die. Give thanks for your life. Give thanks that you're here. Let yourself be connected to Source.

[*Ava's note:* "I and I" means that God is within all people. The term is often used in place of "you and I" or "we" among Rastafari, implying that both persons are united under the love of Jah or God.]

R: Thank you so much for this beautiful message. Wondering if you can share anything about your relationship that you had with Mary Magdalene or with a Divine Feminine and how it was at that time. I feel like there is a lot of misunderstanding regarding the feminine during that time and how you were collaborating. Can you share anything?

Issa: True open feminine heart is the path to love. Truly opening your heart and devoting your heart to a woman and having her heart devoted back to you. To worship each other's temples as the house of God. To come together in Sacred Union and [the] sacrament of consummation of our human forms to create new life. How in the world that got turned into a dirty act that [one] should be ashamed of is still beyond me.

Sacred Sexuality, honoring each other, honoring that we are made in the image — the likeness of God, and therefore, when we honor and devote ourselves to each other — masculine, feminine, the duality — we come together to create Oneness, and in that coming together to create new life, just as God creates new life. Sacred Sexuality, sacred communion as the most holy of holies. The nectar, the juices created in true, loving connection, is truly the juices of God.

Mary Magdalene was a Priestess of Sacred Sexuality. I am [a] Priest of Sacred Sexuality. When we come together, we often open the portal to the Divine. It saddens me how lost this knowledge, this sacred knowledge, has become. True, we talk about marriage and sex being a part of marriage. We do not teach the art of utilizing sexuality as a way of coming home to the temple of God. Where is that in the education of these Christians? Where is it? When we talk about the covenant of marriage, and yet where is the true teachings of how to pleasure each other? How to bring ourselves into the openness, the open channel, of connecting straight with Source through Sacred Sexuality? Where are those teachings? Where did they go in Christianity?

Mary Magdalene, the feminine. . .the feminine, the true, pure, divine heart. They teach the men about unconditional love.

They birth. They tear their bodies apart to bring in new life. Unconditionally loving. They teach men this. Without women, I would be nothing. Without the teachings of women's love, Issa's wisdom could not have ever been shared. But it must have come through the translator of a man for women were so... *(sighs)* men so feared their power that they did their best to deconstruct it.

Women are the powerful Priestesses; they are the creatrixes. It is their love and their tears and their juices that save the world over and over again, and returning to Sacred Sexuality, and truly utilizing sacred communion as a path to Divine Love is such a beautiful gift of all beings. The fact that she's turned into a dirty prostitute distracting Issa from his work is just preposterous. It was the other way around. Mary Magdalene helped keep Issa's channels wide open and full of love. Helped him feel into his purpose, his masculine purpose. He was the masculine counterpart with the Divine Feminine to bring in love and unity into the world.

R: Beautiful. Is there anything else you would like to talk about today? Share with us? Are there any other teachings you would like to share and remind us of?

Issa: In these current events, this virus is creating a lot of division and fear; however, plagues have always been. Famine has always been. Death has always been. It is only us that have forgotten the preciousness of life and to be grateful for each moment alive. For you may burn on your own cross, burn in your own fires, be put up on your own cross, when you are young, when you are old. But to feel love in your hearts?! Each moment that you feel true love moving through your hearts, there is a moment of such pure perfection, that you are complete.

You can die free, and you can live to keep creating and sharing more love. It's all about love and the true face of love. Fear cannot remain. This virus, yes, it's stirring up fear, but really and deeply should stir up gratitude — gratitude for each breath you can take. Gratitude, to devote your life to love and to feel connected with God, so that no matter when you are taken, whenever, when you return home to the kingdom of heaven, you will be ready and know that it is right inside your heart. Let this virus bring you closer to love — closer to trust in God, not farther away. This is not punishment. This is a reminder to bring you back to gratitude and balance. God does not owe you anything.

You've been given a precious gift of life in form on this incredible planet. You've been given gifts that you came to share. If you bring forth that which is within you, that which you bring forth will save you. If you do not bring forth that which is within you, what you do not bring forth will destroy you. I've said that before. You have it written down already [In the Gospel of Thomas]. You came here to share your gifts of love with the world. That's all that matters. Whether or not you live ten years, fifty, or a hundred; you're living a half-life without love in your heart. You are not living, and you are already on the cross. You are suffering because you are already on the proverbial cross. You are either already giving everything for what you believe in, or else you're not, or else you're already just dying, when you are not living what you believe in or hiding your gifts. Which way are you going to live and which way are you going to die? Choose love and choose the kingdom of heaven within you.

R: Beautiful. Thank you so much for this information. Anything else before we depart?

Issa: I am here with you; you are not alone. I am here with you. [Whispered in an intimate intonation.]

R: With Ava? With me or with everybody?

Issa: *All three.* I like the new song she wrote though: "I Am Right Here with You." She heard me, excited that she's recording it. It's good; it's a good song.

R: Thank you for this message. Anything else would you like to share with her?

A: (Giggling)

R: What is it, this laughing, giggling there? Can you share with me?

A: (Laughing)

R: Share with me too.

Issa: I think she's feeling embarrassed to tell you.

R: Why is that?

Issa: Ava and I have been lovers for a while now. I come to her; I lay myself all along her body, kissing her and loving her in the eyes. Reminding her what a good job she's doing. Keep going. I was just giving her some pleasure. I think she's feeling embarrassed.

[This statement was not surprising for me. I have had other clients that experienced similar energy activations, and I heard many more stories of other females that had experienced energetic union with Issa. In some small spiritual circles, they call this phenomena Bride-grooming or Light-filling. The light-body of Issa is restoring the cellar memory of divine union, balancing and activating the Divine Feminine codes / the Christos-Sofia / the Christ Consciousness within oneself. He is doing similar work as the priestesses, the Magdalene during his time. The Divine Feminine supported and balanced the Divine Masculine. He is restoring the energy of equality and unity. In some other sessions I facilitated He washed my clients feet to help them grow in self-worth, as she was not feeling deserving. For another He kissed her on the forehead for clear vision, or merged his energy to remind the we are all one. Myself too, during my early awakening experience I have felt his energy and the Christ Consciousness energy, the Unconditional Love opened my heart and changed the way I experienced the world. The energy was traveling thorough my body and healing me. It was very pleasurable, as if I was levitating.]

[*Ava's note: These last several pages are still hard for me to read. I squirm with embarrassment, and all I want to do is run away and hide. My mind says, "Who do I think I am? Calming down the spirit realm!? Seriously? Speaking for Issa (Jesus)!? Do NOT share this with anyone! This is nonsense."*

I begged Ron to cut this last section about Issa, and especially the part about being Issa's lover, out of the book. Although it is such a natural and innocent part of my life, I never considered sharing this information with anyone. I felt mortified at the thought of it being included, mostly because I could imagine the response of my family. They already feel deeply concerned for my immortal soul.

How dare I claim to be Jesus' lover after claiming to be his daughter in a previous existence? I could imagine some considering this part to be the most blasphemous thing I could possibly say. For those who are not aware, many Christians believe that channeling and especially "speaking for Jesus" is an unforgivable offense against God. I mean no offense against anyone, especially God.

Ron agreed that it would be my choice whether to include this part, and I have hesitated down to the final moment before we send it to print. When I get out of my own way, I enjoy reading this part of the journey. I feel like I am listening to a mesmerizing and incredible bedtime story, but my mind and my ego feel ashamed at the audacity. Will you think I'm delusional and insane? I am terrified of my family's response for me speaking such blasphemy in their eyes. I don't feel blasphemous. I feel grateful that Issa comes to me in dreams, visions, and meditations. He is really helpful, his presence so kind and emanating unconditional love. Yet, I have spent many a night wishing I could make this all go away and stay safe in hiding.

Yet, if I accept the responsibility for unweaving the vibration of fear, then I must accept that I am responsible for my vibration. So, I surrender into my fear, and I accept that this part stays. I stand here burning in the fire of my resistance. It's amazing how uncomfortable it feels. My hope is that it helps—that my vulnerability helps bring more love and tolerance into the world. May my family understand me better and accept me for who I am, if they chose to read this far.

Ultimately, I felt like a coward to not share it, considering everything else that is revealed within these pages. Why censor just this part? Plus, I feel weary of hiding. So, I'm coming out. I love Issa, and I am innocent. My soul is safe and sound. I can feel it with every fiber of my being. I'm sorry. I love you. I forgive you. Please forgive me. Thank you.]

R: Thank you so much. Beautiful. Is there anything you would like to share with me today?

Issa: Your work is evolving powerfully. Thank you. Thank you for doing your work to help people remember. I see you. You have been an ally a long time.

R: Thank you so much. Now you can take a deep breath and allow "I" to come forward again, connecting to "I." May I speak to "I" please?

I: Yes. Ava needs to pee. [Restroom break.]

[During editing, we noticed that if we shortened Issa, as we did to each of the speakers, Issa would also be I: —- This might be confusing but also ironically appropriate, as the channel repeatedly reminds us that all is truly from the Oneness of 'I".]

R: Thank you so much for returning again. Would you do one more scan of her body and tell me if there's any more healing available for her today?

I: Yes, I need a little time to unwind these threads.

R: What are those threads that you mentioned?

I: I just need to pull out some more cotton candy out of her ears and some more cotton candy out of her bladder. I just need to pull it out.

R: **Thank you. Would you like me to call any support or can you do it all by yourself?**

I: I could actually use the medical ships.

R: **Okay.**

I: She might need a lift. Not sure if I can do it all here. I kind of need this. . . It's all just easier with their scalpels. . .light scalpels easier than just through awareness. Don't have quite as much dexterity inside a form this way.

R: **Can we connect to the medical ship right now to see what they say?**

I: Yes.

R: **Let's invite the medical ship now to join us and to start work on her. Share with me, what are you discovering? What are you doing as you do it?**

I: Her bladder place, a place of sexual power and fear. Doing a little bit more stitching. It's like spirit stitches, light stitches; she needs some light stitches. She let his energy [her ex-lover] kind of tear her a bit. Not intentionally. He's been wielding more power than he's ready for. He didn't mean to tear her, but he did.

R: **Yeah. Thank you so much for doing this work on her. Would you continue working on her while I'm asking questions?**

I: Okay.

R: **Thank you so much for this.** [we got into a series of her personal questions.] **Anything else you would like to share about the time that we're living in right now or any suggestions for our upcoming future?**

I: Learn to listen.

R: Learn to listen?

I: Yes, everyone is allowing the fear to stir up their mind, and everyone's talking incessantly to themselves and to each other, getting so hypnotized by listening to opinions and beliefs and stories. You must be the quiet. You must listen.

[I continued asking question but suddenly a very strange thing start to occur. Ava seems to not able to respond and made a sigh, then soft humming voices]

R: Take another deep breath. May I speak with I please?

I: Forgive me, I'm currently working with Ava. She's slipped into the somatic memory of a recurrent night terror she used to have. I am currently working with helping her surrender and let go of this somatic sensation within her.

R: Thank you so much for doing it. You can share with me what you're doing as you do it, if you want to, and if it's possible. *(Long silence)*

I: I think I might need some assistance.

R: Okay. So, I'd like to take her to the beautiful place now. The most beautiful place and bring her consciousness now to the place where she enjoys the beauty. The most beautiful place that you can imagine. Be there now. Need to look around and tell me where you are. *(Silence)* The most beautiful place. Look around you. Where are you?

A: I'm still in the incubator, and there's too much pressure here.

R: In the incubator?

A: There's too much pressure here.

R: Where is the incubator?

A: Hospital?

R: I see, okay, and how old are you there?

A: Born.

R: You are just born. Okay. What's happening there now? What are you seeing?

A: Pressure.

R: It's too much pressure? Okay. We can take a deep breath for the pressure releasing. Now just to close that scene and when you go back in time — back, back in time, back all the way into the womb. To a time in the womb, and you're in the womb now, you can look around you and tell me, how does it feel to be in the womb? What do you notice there? You can share with me.

A: I'm still in the place with the pressure.

R: Where do you feel the pressure?

A: It's being squashed.

R: Mmhmm. Okay. So I'm here with you and maybe we can just move it a little bit forward in time to see what's happening next. We can have a better perspective of that. What's happening after that and how that was changed. Let's move a little bit forward and tell me what is happening as it happens. Take a deep breath.

A: It's too much. It's too big. Scary.

R: Sometimes it's just a matter of feeling it to heal it and then to move through it, so it doesn't stay. You can observe in a way that you can express and share what is happening there as it happens.

[Ava had slipped into her recurring night terror again, and I needed to get creative to get her out of that experience. First, I tried to help her move through it, but she became more tired and less communicative. I guided her to close that scene, and I moved her to a healing temple. She saw white light though I didn't feel that her HS was able to come back and speak again. I wanted to finish the session with her feeling good and energized, so I moved her to a memory in a beautiful place where she felt wonderful, joyful, and playful — a place where she could feel healing energies. She saw herself swimming in the ocean in Maui, Hawaii. I gave her time to enjoy that feeling, and from this beautiful place, I brought her back up to full consciousness.]

I don't know what happened that made Ava slip into the trauma of being inside the incubator and her recurring night terror. This was all new for me as it had never happened to any of my hundreds of clients before. I did read about some cases where the Higher Self was asking Dolores Cannon, my teacher, for support during some powerful sessions and she had to say things that would help the consciousness of the client to gather themself. After listening to the recording with Ava, I wondered if I had asked "I" how I could help if they would have guided me differently, however, I did feel that the priority was to get Ava out of the experience, so I felt confident with my troubleshooting. It wasn't so simple for "I" or myself to get Ava's consciousness out of this experience, and it seems like it made her very tired for a bit.

When I brought her up, she was still tired, but after we started to move a bit, her energy returned. We talked about the sessions we did that day and this (not surprisingly) brought up more questions for future sessions. We aimed to do another session in a couple of days, so that we could address the trauma from the incubator that seemed to create the recurring night terror. I was very grateful for the day. We received a great amount of information, and we were all ready to call it a day.

YIN AND YANG
COHERENCE

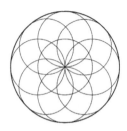

SESSION SIX

R: Drifting back and arriving there now. Relaxing completely and looking around. What do you notice now? [Below is a summary of what she was mentioning without my guidance and questions added to make the information more readable.]

A: Swirling energies. It seems like an ocean, but it's not liquid. It's an ocean of energy that moves kind of like water. It's all colors; it's like a background. The void of polarities. Color, pixelated with the tiniest little pixels, so tiny. Each individual pixel is a rainbow-like prism, but all together, they don't look pixelated. It shimmers with a translucent, shimmery, pearlescent rainbow, like when oil is on water. Each pixel is really white in the center but then expands out into the rainbow itself. Somehow you can see all the colors, but they aren't mixed; each color is distinct, but it's also all the same color. It's a paradox and hard to describe.

R: What perspective are you seeing it?

A: I'm floating on it. It's like floating in the ocean, except that there's no line between ocean and air, but it's not like I'm drowning in the floating. It feels as if it is all around. It's nice.

R: How does it make you feel? [Ava then noticed that her physical body was uncomfortable. She also shared with me some disturbing thoughts that were still coming up for her.

She needed to send a few short text messages to put her worries to rest. It was important to tend to these needs, so she would feel ready and able to relax deeply. When she settled and closed her eyes again, she went right back into trance and to where we left off.]

R: What do you notice now?

A: It's the sea and the ocean of energy. There's like a bright center, kind of over me, brighter above me. It's not like from the sun, it's like the energy itself. The pixels have coalesced, and when they come together and are more concentrated, then it's brighter. So somehow consciousness seems to be able to move through the pixels and concentrate the energy, and so then the brilliant-white-rainbow kind of comes stronger. It has the appearance of a light shining, but it's emanating from within itself; there's no source of the light like a flashlight or sun. So there's no shadow, because it's just shining because it exists. It's interesting. It's almost like you're wadding up a napkin to make it into a ball, but it's as if somehow the energy has gotten scooped and pulled together, but it doesn't leave it thinner on the edges. It seems like it just infinitely can change its shape at will, but there's no form. It's a fascinating way to move energy, with consciousness. Light with no shadow.

R: Sounds very interesting. What do you notice next? What's happening there? What does it feel like?

A: I feel like there's a gentle tide, which doesn't make sense because there's no real shore or end, but there's just like a back and forth. There's a gentle tide to the energy flow of this energy ocean. It moves through me so freely that even though I thought I had form, I don't seem to have form. It's just gentle back and forth, like a wave, one wave after another wave, but they don't ever crash, and I can't even figure out what the momentum is causing the wave. It's just. . .it's almost like each of the individual pixels has its own electromagnetic field, and so each one has this orbit that in this location feels almost like infinity, like it's back and forth, but it's not back and forth sloshing. It's like it's going back and forth following an infinity pattern, but not an infinity pattern in two dimensions. It's an infinity pattern in all the dimensions, but it's perfectly in sync, so it never sloshes against itself.

It's all perfect murmuration of individual atomic pixels to create this sensation of an ocean that's not liquid that I can breathe, but there's no form anyway. But that seems to be the rhythm of it...is this infinity pattern of a slightly curving, infinite "S" shape that folds back on itself, perfect rhythm, so there's never any sloshing, splashing. The way a tide. . .the way a wave hits the shore — it never reaches the edge; it just comes back. . . like infinity. It's the infinite pool of energy, and I'm floating in it, and it's in me, I'm in it, and I'm the center of it. And yet I have no form, so I'm in all of it. I can't tell if it's infinitely big, or if it's only as big as I am, because I can't tell if I have form or not, can't find my boundary.

I don't seem to have a body, except that I do. I do have a body. I'm actually in the form of Ava, but I can sense the pixels inside my form and outside my form; therefore, skin doesn't have the same boundary definition as it does on Earth. It's all one thing. It's a continuum. It's not. . .there's no matter; it's just the pixels or pixels isn't the correct word. It's the atoms, it's smaller than the atoms, it's the energy itself — in both pixelated wave and particle form at the same time. It's both a wave and a particle. Yes, it's the energy paradox that is both and therefore, there's no edge. There's no actual skin, because in this place, the energy inside my body and outside my body is the same, so there's not even a distinction at the skin edge. There's not even a more dense concentration here; it's just. . . I am, I am without boundaries, but with boundaries my form, her form, yet free of the form at the same time; it's a paradox as well. The entire place is a paradox, but it feels very nice.

R: Relaxing and you can dissolve completely and rest there. Ava can rest there completely. May I speak with "I" please.

I: Yes.

R: Thank you so much for coming forward today. Would you start the healing on Ava, please? *(I: Yes.)* Share with me what you're doing as you do it, please.

I: The infinity pattern is weaving of the light energy, and so just as you would weave, if you can imagine the weft and warp, back and forth — exactly as she was describing the infinity pattern. There is both at the same time, a tip of the needle of consciousness, so to speak, weaving this infinity pattern, stitching patterns of light together, but at the same time, every single point along the infinity pattern is the tip of a needle. So it's like an infinite number of needles, all in perfect timing and perfect synchronization, following the infinity pattern of weaving. Stitching the light, weaving the light, but not weaving the light at the same time. It's also stirring, and it's weaving because there's no form, per se, so it's not like a physical needle and physical thread.

What's happening now is that consciousness is weaving the light patterns and resetting the DNA patterns, for the infinity pattern. . .is actually the double helix from the inside. That's the sensation, the sensation is actually meeting oneself in the pattern of the double helix. It's like in cranial-sacral work. It's a matching of the fluids of the body and the energetic; the electromagnetic frequencies are coming into calibration, but there is this essence of someone sitting with a needle and thread and stitching, stitching with the infinity pattern. There's many different stitches one can stitch with. Many of the stitches on Earth create tension and knots to hold the stitching in place. It is not necessary here, and so it's just the infinity pattern of stitching, and yet it's infinite. **(R: Yeah.)**

I'm stitching, weaving, swirling, spinning, swishing, stirring. It's none of those words; all of those words point to what is actually happening, which is consciousness moving energy in an infinite back and forth, spiraling, double helix infinity pattern, so to speak, so that coherence, pure coherence — returns to the system. We're creating energetic coherence. We are utilizing the infinite sea of energy, so that we never run out of thread per se, if we use an analogy of thread and needles. Her form is merged in the sea. Therefore, with consciousness there is an infinite supply. We are washing her and weaving her, but I never run out of water because it's all around her and in her. It almost seems like a painter with a paint brush. I'm moving through different parts of the body at the same time because it's infinite. It's all at once. It's a paradox. Again, most things here are...makes perfect sense when you feel it, to describe it in three dimensions doesn't make sense of how it could be both, and yet it is. She can feel this both, and she can feel consciousness slowly scanning through different parts of the form and at the same time, being present and conscious of each cell, each atom, each tiny, tiny, little bit of light energy inside each atom all wrapped in the same pattern.

R: **Sounds wonderful. Thank you so much for doing this work for her, and can you share with me from the last session that we did, when we worked on the bladder and did some healing for her. She didn't feel there was much improvement after. Can you share with me why that is? What's going on?**

I: Improvement is happening for her. There is a delay. It's a matter of physical delay and matter manifestation. There was nerve damage done, and those nerves are inflamed and agitated. Therefore, although we worked with her on the energetic level and the energetic level is weaving into the physical level, it would be quite helpful if she would assist us in her meditations. Even if they're laying down meditations, if she would assist us in continuing, it needs to be repeated ideally three times a day — ideally actually more often. If she's able to bring her consciousness to the weaving and not to worrying; we don't want her to bring a worried energy of consciousness to the location, which is possible, which is easy to happen because there is a sensation of discomfort that draws the awareness there. It's easy to have the awareness drawn to the place, and then stitch with an energy of concern. So instead, if that discomfort is pulling her energy there — that she [would] meet it with this sensation — of this infinite weaving pattern, restitching. Eventually, that pattern will help to calm [the] nerves. Multiple times a day, whenever her consciousness is drawn to the area, to help us continue this weaving pattern; to bring the energetics into the physical for more accelerated healing.

R: I understand she can bring that initiation, the awareness of this calm, weaving infinite sea into that area, and it will help smoothing that. It's an ongoing process. (I: Yes.) Okay, thank you so much for sharing this with her today. Very good. She also was wondering about her. . .she's having a little difficulty to fall asleep and to rest. What's keeping her up?

I: Yes, she is running a higher vibration of kundalini since her last deep dive [*entheogenic death practice ritual*]. She would be supported with an increased commitment to her full meditation regimen plus a physical regimen. It is best for her to not engage in stimulants. Even such as chocolate in the afternoon of the day, her system, although it metabolizes quickly, has a tendency to run [high] because she is such a highly sensitized being. She is aware of the chemical compounds that are in the chocolate and the cacao, even in the moringa. She is such a sensitive being; she feels those currents.

She also needs to stop engaging in any kind of technological interaction after about 9 or 10 pm. It stimulates the dopamine and oxytocin as she's having conversations, and therefore, it would be best for her to utilize the more. . .being more diligent and disciplined, and to turn her phone off sooner, to not bring her computer into the bed. She knows these things and yet in these weird times, her routines and patterns have been disrupted. She's slipped into that pattern of doing everything in her little nest cave. We understand. Make sure she gets more exercise early in the day and less stimulation later in the day.

Also, she has shifted more into a night owl pattern which overexerts her adrenal system. She needs a reset and [to] allow herself to go through a couple of awkward days of timing in order to get herself into bed and asleep, more in the range of 10 pm instead of midnight and 1 am. There is a surge of adrenaline and surge of hormones that happens when she stays awake past that time. I know it's challenging with the sun only setting after 8 pm to be in bed before 10, but if she wakes up with dawn, if she wakes up earlier, she'll have a better chance of setting her circadian rhythms. She knows her circadian rhythms are extremely sensitive. She's been a little bit more relaxed about it, since the world has shifted so much (referring to the lockdowns during Covid), but she knows how sensitive her circadian rhythms are. She can do things to help her not get stimulated late at night.

R: I see. Thank you so much for this information. Can you share with me and bring healing now for the night terror that she slipped into during our last session? Can we clear her birth trauma and all that event from her imprint? Is there anything else that you'd like to share with her regarding why that was happening and what she learned or not?

I: Yes, so I do believe we spoke about this in one of the earlier sessions however. . . The night terror is a combination of a memory from being in the incubator. That is true. However, it is also a memory that is deeper than that because of the nature of her ability to be a bridge between consciousness and the three-dimensional realm and consciousness of the Designer of Earth and consciousness of "I," and the consciousness of the level of the volunteer she chose to come in to be, one of the pillars of ascension for our time. Because she chose to coalesce and bring so much energy in and due to the nature of her birth. . .not only is she remembering the night terror. . .the night terror is not only the memory of being in the incubator. However, it is also the memory of being worked on both directly by Source inside of her in order to help her survive that ordeal. And also, there is a sensation she's remembering [of] being. . ."lifted" is not quite the correct word because of the technology that existed down below her in the hospital where she was born, where some of the technologies from the ships found in the desert in the Area 51 area were brought to the Air Force Base she was born. Those technologies activated in order to support her, and yet it was an energy frequency much more intense than a normal human body would normally be able to withstand. However, we were doing our best to help her navigate the nervous system challenges that were brought by being premature and put into a box during the technological era of Earth where it wasn't properly pressurized.

Therefore, she is not only remembering the Earth memory, but she is also having residual, somatic experience of the advanced technologies working with her both from the three-dimensional realm and from the beyond, the multidimensional realm, helping her form. It's a lot of energy at once though, for mortal form, for a human form, and so it was perceived as threatening. It was perceived as daunting; it's perceived as negative. However, in all actuality, what she was experiencing is an open conduit and current of Source energy and a much higher capacity and higher rate of flow into the human body than the majority of human bodies are built and are aware of and able to withstand. However, because we wanted to give this being the best opportunity to ground in the mission that she came here to ground in, we believe that the risk of it causing madness and anxiety would be able to be matched and balanced by her capacity and her advanced ability to work with energy and she has been. . .she is aware of this; she is now able to sit with the sensation without panicking. She used to panic, and she would feel the sensation and then the panic would further amplify the sensation. She's beginning to bring it into her conscious awareness now. It is beginning to build, and we are helping her to see and feel that, even surrender into this sensation.

R: **Is it healing for her? To surrender to that sensation?**

I: Yes, if she can fully surrender and accept this pressure.

R: **How would that support her**? [I could notice that they are taking her back through the experience and her speech was slowing down. I kept asking questions to insure she will be able to move through it fully this time.]

I: It is actually. . .if she can fully surrender into this sensation, it will allow the conduit that is clamped in her jaw. There is a glitch, there is a hitch, there is a place in her jaw that is slightly catching.

R: **So it will help it relax?**

I: Yes, we're helping her right now to feel the sensation that she labels as too much, too much pressure, and it's terrorizing. We're helping her open the conduits of her hands and feet, her third eye, and her jaw. To let this infinite energy move through her, recognize the power of it. She's still struggling slightly with the sensation; it's overwhelming for her.

R: **Relax more, letting go more, and more dissolving into, allowing beautiful energies, to help her balance. Deeper. . . Thank you for working with her and doing that. Is she relaxing more into it?**

I: She is trying; it is big.

R: **Relaxing more with a breath and feeling the waves flowing through. How would that affect her as she's relaxing into it? You can share with me how that affects and heals her?** *(long pause)* **You can share with me more, so she can hear and relax into the information.**

I: She is a portal; she has an open channel. This open channel has the capacity to allow an exceptional amount of energy to flow through and to ground through her system to allow her to have the capacity and the energy to help bring in great positive change and bring in a great capacity for life, if she can open and trust this sensation.

R: "Perfect love, perfect trust," [a saying that Ava mentioned to me for deep surrendering.] What will happen then?

I: Beyond this film of terror and fear is direct access to be able to speak with the council, the high councils in all realms. It is not a gift often given for it can cause madness. She is battling with the madness and the immensity of being able to have such a direct sight. However, we do feel that she's capable of navigating it.

R: I'm here to support in any way to help her ground for that experience.

I: Unfortunate timing, she needs to pee.

[I have mentioned that it is not a problem and asked that we will continue from where we stopped. They agreed and we took a short restroom break.]

A PORTAL TO THE COUNCIL

R: What would you like to add now to share about this portal and about the Council, and about the healing?

I: Reminder to Ava, the profound depth and openness, clarity of her heart, and that if and when the sensation rises any residual of this place of terror that she recognizes her profound capacity to open, to trust, to know how powerful she is, and to no longer doubt it. She has residues of doubt and thinks maybe she is just mad and just raving or just wanting to somehow be special, and so she resists because of her humbleness. She does not understand how she could have such capacity, but it's because of the purity of her heart that she has this capacity. We gave her a very direct connection, knowing that she wouldn't be tainted by its power. We do not often grant access to this direct level for the possibility that a human being can distort and manipulate for greed and the. . . It can manipulate this powerful heart energy.

The terror itself is her own protective mechanism to help her stay humble. Because it terrifies her so much, there is no way that she could utilize this for any type of manipulative energies, for she sees the absolute immense annihilation that it would create; that it would in a sense, nullify her great gifts for her to use this in any kind of distorted way. The terror is actually a gate to allow her to enter this realm with such profound humbleness and gratitude. It is also not normally a tactic that we use because it can cause such madness. And yet, the only way to access this level of understanding is to engage with such a profound humbleness, so that it is able to be manifested in such a pure and radiant form.

We feel that she's doing an excellent job at this, and yet she's still. . .because of the humbleness and because of the terror, it still instills a level of madness and fear within her. We invite her to recognize her pure heart, to remember how capable she truly is, and that it is a gift she requested to be bestowed and that we felt, we all agreed, was within a healthy bound of her consciousness merged in form. So, if she can continue to meet the terror with love and the open eyes that she is able to maintain when she looks straight into Source, with an open heart. [Then] the terror will begin to open and reveal itself as the final gate — to allow her to be able to communicate directly, with more ease, more grace, and without the residual shreds of doubt that calls her to question why she was bestowed with such power. It is then through her humbleness and her openness and her trust and her facing terror; her capacity to face terror is profound. We do not say this to boost her egoic sense of self, but we know that it will not, but we would like to remind her of the profound level of warrior she actually is.

The amount of terror she is able to face without running away is truly astounding for a human form. She doesn't even realize how strong of a warrior she is. She thinks she is weak because of the terror; she thinks she's weak because of how intense it feels and how much she wants to run away and hide, and yet she doesn't. She lets the terror consume her, because somehow she knows she can stand it, and that it will allow her to penetrate through the final gateless gate in order to enter the realms of divine, eternal bliss, in order to dip into this well and bring back the nectar, to share it with all beings who would most likely tremble and scream and destroy themselves if they took the same path. This is not to say she is somehow better or more of anything. She just. . .it's actually her profound capacity of humbleness and love to give her this power.

We remind her to trust her power — that it is pure and it is the only reason she has it. Eventually she will stop doubting, and eventually she will allow the terror. She will allow herself to pierce through the final veil of this terror.

R: **Can you now amplify for her the sensation of her heart and what to focus on as she goes through that? This profound love** and purity in her heart, this pure light that she is, can you amplify that and focus on it even more so through that light, she can allow this terror to dissolve and to reach the beyond and to the council who would like to speak through her? Is the Council present today to speak with me?

The Council: Yes, we are here.

R: Thank you so much for coming forward. Thank you. What would you like to share? *(Long silence)* Is there something you would like to start with? Or would you like me to ask questions?

The Council: You may ask what you will.

R: Thank you so much. So you mentioned that she have this profound ability to channel the Council and that is something she is meant to do in the future, to receive more information and share.

The Council: Yes.

R: Okay. Is there anything you would like her to focus on? Any topics that you'd like to focus on first, to be shared?

The Council: We have noticed that during this time of great awakening, when the energies are increasing from the unit of consciousness, that when it translates and prisms itself into three-dimensional reality, creating a slightly more increased sense of duality, this could be considered an understatement. **(R: Yes.)** And so, one of the most important things we need right now is to bypass the extreme layers of fear, anxiety, and divisiveness in mind that is increasing in the majority of the population. It must be met with paths into the heart and the body. Therefore, her guided meditations are more important than ever to help inspire and bring people back into their hearts without trying to argue or engage their minds. Therefore, commitment to recording and sharing these meditations is essential at this time.

We understand the technological challenges of this mission. We'll do our best to support her and yet, we do need all hands on board as of now, in order to help, for the increased attachment to "mind" is creating interference with the ability for beings to receive the ascension protocols and the downloads that are coming through with the increased energy waves. We recognize, however, that this is a natural symptom of Unity, moving into a dualistic world of matter. Matter by nature has a dualistic nature in order for matter to exist. A yin and a yang, a positive and a negative — the electromagnetic field in [and] of itself exists here in this realm because of duality, and therefore it is an essential part of the program. So trying to bring unitive downloads for the upgrades to the DNA system requires bypassing duality in order to bring more balance to the system.

Therefore, we ask that she increase her commitment and dedication to creating and sharing her short stories and her meditations and her songs, because it is needed. As she does her small part, she helps to ground in another layer of the pillar, which then allows the other beings [that are] doing similar work to also do the same. She can let go of any concern that she's not doing enough and is not helping enough. That's causing paralysis moving forward, and [the letting go will] help her to recognize that every step she takes into helping to bring herself and those around her, both in the physical and the virtual realms, into coherence, that greater coherence is amplified around the planet.

Her drop in the ocean inspires and amplifies the other drops in the ocean. So instead of feeling this intense pressure or responsibility and weight of the world, instead allow her to enter her own coherence, in order to share this coherence and bring increased coherence to others, allowing the ripple effect to allow us to bypass the symptoms of duality that are now creating increasing divisiveness in the minds of beings, especially in the minds of beings ready to awaken. There is definitely a sense of a regression and consciousness occurring as there is resistance to the lifting of the veil, so to speak, that comes with changing, the great changing in these times. Therefore, all of the warriors, all of the truth warriors incarnated now, as challenging and as difficult as it is, and of course self-care and patience and tenderness and acceptance is perfectly okay to stay dedicated and devoted to the mission.

R: **Thank you so much for this information. Can you share with me what the best way for a human. . .a tool. . .to get into coherence would be? Is there any protocol that you can share for reaching coherence?**

The Council: The most accelerated and grounded path to reach coherence is through intentional sitting practice combined with breath and awareness. There are several authors and teachers actively sharing these coherence techniques. However, the interesting thing about this is that in the nature of duality, the resistance to a sitting practice is increasing. Attention spans are shortening, distraction and comforting techniques are increasing, and the resistance to the sitting practice is augmenting in this culture currently. Therefore, creative ways for bypassing *(getting around or beyond)* this resistance are required. Although a traditional sitting practice is one of the most grounded and effective ways for allowing the physical and emotional and spiritual form to be integrated in order to come into coherence, extra support is needed, for it must be met in a place of comfort and ease, which is challenging, for in a sense, it is discipline and conviction and devotion that is necessary. And yet that is the exact vibration that is being most resisted at the moment. Therefore, we have found though some of the best ways to bypass this resistance, and Ava is aware of this. . .is through sound vibration, relaxation savasana-style meditations over sitting meditations, music, laughter, comedy, story. These are the more subtle approaches to inspire one to come home into a sitting practice, which is one of the oldest and yet most fundamental practices for the human form to be able to come into balance with its physical, emotional, spiritual, and energetic systems.

R: Wonderful. Thank you for this information. You said it's about awareness and the breath, seated. Is there any information about the breath or the awareness that needs to be shared in order to achieve that? So, just focusing on the heart and allowing the exhale to be long and relaxed? [Here I'm adding more commonly known information so they would give more specific tools.]

The Council: Focusing on the heart is a practice, yes; however, the heart has a very strong electromagnetic pulse. It has a very detectable current and therefore, is considered a gross sensation, not gross in the word disgusting, but gross as in large and major. (R: Yeah.) The pitfall for focusing on such a gross sensation is that it does not sensitize a being to their subtler sensations. However, it is a good starting place for helping people recognize the power of the electromagnetic and energetic field within them, so it is a good introductory method in order to inspire someone to commit to a sitting practice. However, we have found that by encouraging the form to learn to recognize the subtler sensations, that that actually increases sensitivity and allows one to feel the gross sensations with much more texture and awareness. In a sense, it's much more difficult to become sensitive to the subtle sensations and [in the beginning] tends to inspire boredom and resistance, fantasy and distraction in the minds and the consciousnesses of those beings coming and choosing to sit. We do find that focusing on gross sensations for a moment at the beginning is a good inspirational tool, yet then must be put aside to understand the subtler sensations throughout the body.

Once the subtler sensations have been sensitized, then one may return to the gross sensation practices in order to augment the connection, the coherence in the heart. However, if the second step of sensitizing to subtle sensations is bypassed, it limits the full capacity of the nuanced possibilities that the heart meditation actually can create.

For the heart meditation is not only a coherence builder to find the center vortex and the perceived center of the electromagnetic field, i.e., the black hole inside oneself. One realizes when one sensitizes to the subtler sensations that the heart meditation actually connects one to the entire physical system. Because the heart sends blood into the full system; blood is not just physical blood, but it is also the energetic, spiritual blueprint that allows for the upgrade in the codes of the DNA. It is the messenger that sends the messages throughout the entire system and revitalizes the entire system with oxygen, nutrients, and the other physical sensations needed to maintain physical life. However, if one has not learned to understand and feel subtler sensations, then the heart meditation will be centered in the heart.

The heart meditation actually is meant to be the mycelial network or like the roots of a tree in the same sense. The heart meditation is meant to transcend beyond the heart and reach the full distance from top to bottom, inside and out, and meet every single cell of the human body. If the subtler sensations have not been learned to be recognized and sensed and felt, without focus on the gross sensations, then the heart meditation does not have the full potential to bring one into true coherence. Therefore, dedication is needed to set the heart meditation aside in order to focus on full-body, sensation-based practice to increase the sensitivity nuance necessary to be able to feel the electromagnetic field, the vortex, and the black hole centered in the heart, in each individual cell, each individual atom.

It is unified coherence that allows one to slip. . .slip into Source and utilize the heart as a portal into the expansive inner landscape that gives you the bridge of the portal into the infinite landscape, outside of the human body. To allow the form, to allow the consciousness to travel and join the galactic family, one must learn to have coherence in all of the cells. Then the heart becomes the master cell, but the master cell cannot guide the subtler, smaller cells unless the smaller cells are able to be identified independently and separate from the heart. Therefore, scanning-based practices such as Vipassana and other techniques, allow one to find the infinitely nuanced detail of finding sensation in all parts of the body. Once the entire body has been mapped with coherence, once the entire body and every cell can actually be felt as the pixelated essence of energy that it is, then the heart meditation can have its true potential. One can return to the heart, and therefore, the heart can then be the master gate, or the master key in a sense — directing and guiding the entire cellular system into coherence. Once the entire cellular system is in coherence, then [one can] easily slip into the awareness and consciousness of that beyond our individual selves — is possible.

Until full coherence in all cells is achieved and maintained, heart coherence isn't possible, for you must have the entire system all in congruence and alignment in order to have the power to sustain [what] the heart needs, in order to truly be able to open the portal into the next dimension and into the next realms of possibility. The entire system must be fully online to support the heart. Any distortion, any lack of ability to fully concentrate and feel this coherence will limit the distance. . .distance is not the correct word because the distance is infinitely small and infinitely large at the same time. I use the word distance only to express a concept of travel — into the inner realms — in order to meet with council, in order to meet with the Galactic Federation, in order to meet with one's Higher Self, in order to meet with all the reasons why beings want to travel into "outer space." — the mysteries they're trying to unfold and unravel, the true spaceship is inside. And therefore, true heart coherence is necessary, which requires understanding and sensation of all the subtler nuances in the form.

R: Thank you. Thank you so much for this. You mentioned scanning as a way to get through the subtle sensations? Are there other ways to get to this subtle energy body?

The Council: Yes, this is the yin technique. The technique is essential. Many people say that they don't meditate; they dance, or they run, or they have art, or they have some other practice. Those are yang practices to come into coherence. Yang practices for coherence are essential for tuning the human body, for tuning a human mind and allowing coherence to happen. However, yang coherence patterns such as Yoga, exercise, dance, music, art — anything that a human being uses to enter into the flow state — are [all examples of] yang coherence practices.

Yang coherence practices are equated to the gross sensational practices; therefore, because they are much easier to actually sense with the five senses, so it is a good bridge for people to use the yang coherence practices such as breathwork, yoga, dance, exercise — whatever they are utilizing — to get their heart rate moving the blood completely through their system and allowing complete circulation to bust through any layers of energetic and physical stagnation. Yang practices are essential. However, in the same way that heart coherence is a gross sensation practice, it's an advanced technique to actually experience fully and completely. Therefore, once a human being has chosen to engage in yang coherence practices to bring them into yoga — into unity of mind, body, and spirit — to allow the mind to quiet, [then] the volume knob on the internal chatter system is able to be utilized.

Once that happens, there is a limit to how far yang coherence strategies can bring an individual into their full coherence — in the same way that the heart coherence is a good beginning step, but must be set aside for a more yin and subtler sensation coherence practice. So therefore, once a human being has found the capacity to find stillness through themselves through the yang coherence practice, then dedication and discipline is needed to set those behaviors, those activities, aside that bring them into the flow state, and instead then shift to the yin coherence practices, such as subtler breathwork and subtler sitting practices of using awareness and sensation-based practices, like Vipassana or other meditation techniques.

A yin coherence practice is necessary in order for the gross or the larger coherence, the yang coherence practices, to reach their full potential. It is a spiral in the sense it's the same infinity pattern. So the yang coherence patterns such as exercise, art, dance, those things that get our heart rate up and allow us to bring ourselves into coherence, are good to establish the pattern, establish the connection with coherence. However, to reach the next level of evolution, a yin coherence practice in a sitting meditation is necessary in order to then feel and create the same sense of unity and yoga. "Yoga," meaning to yoke and to create the fusion between mind, body, and spirit, is necessary to then augment the ability to then come back to the yang coherence practice with even greater awareness and subtler sensitivities.

So it's a back and forth pattern; the same as the infinity pattern that we have been describing in the sea of healing for Ava's physical and energetic form. A back and forth between yang coherence patterns and yin coherence patterns enables us to rise in the DNA spiral of consciousness and allows us to upgrade and activate the more advanced genetic codes.

Each one requires a foundation of the other. For example, starting with a physical, yang coherence practice, such as exercise or yoga, then allows one to sit and fully allow oneself to find the stillness of mind, body, and spirit in yin practice. Yin practice without a yang practice is almost impossible, or the mind will be too restless and unable to learn how to truly concentrate. Once one learns the internal yin practice of coherence, then one can return to the yang practice of coherence and increase their capacity for presencing, and finding the flow state in the yang coherence pattern with the augmented level and foundation of the yin coherence pattern. Once the yang coherence pattern has been up-leveled to the next degree, like climbing a ladder, so to speak, in the DNA helix, one then returns again to the yin coherence pattern to further increase and ground the foundation of sensitivity and coherence, to learn true concentration, to allow the mind to come into complete stillness and unification with the body and spirit, so that the mind takes its proper role as the support, as the secretary, and as the arms and the legs of the Higher Self, instead of trying to run the entire show.

Once a yin coherence pattern has been maintained and increased again, one returns again to the yang coherence pattern. When one is committed to both a yin and a yang coherence pattern through yoga, exercise, dance, whatever the flow state chosen is. Ideally multiple, different, flow state coherence activities are chosen to increase the bandwidth of ability and ways to allow the brain and the body to slip into full coherence. Then going back into yin coherence pattern, when one goes back and forth and continues the infinity pattern, like stitching, like the internal weaving, one continually, more and more increases their capacity for true coherence and concentration and continues to rise in the ladder and the activation of the different levels of the DNA.

When one has established this effective and consistent pattern on a daily basis, one will continue to slowly rise the rungs of ladders and unlock higher and higher levels of their DNA code. When one slips in that pattern and stops and takes a break in their yin and yang coherence pattern activities, they will start to slowly slip back down the ladder. This does not create permanent damage but does deactivate the higher programs that require certain levels of presence, clarity, purpose, and pure heart to activate the higher levels of the DNA code. Slowly slipping back down the ladder will happen if these coherence patterns are not regularly maintained. As soon as the patterns are maintained and in regular pattern and become a regular part of the habit of the individual, they will slowly begin to climb the ladder again. They will climb the ladder more quickly because the pattern has already been established in the past; they will find themselves at a new level of coherence able to unlock even higher levels of their DNA potential. The more they commit to the active yang and yin coherence pattern strategies, the more quickly and accelerated their ascension and awakening practice is.

R: Thank you. Beautiful. Can you make this pattern for her very clear, so she can climb up this ladder and reach you guys, and have this ability to know and to reach this coherence like she is right now?

The Council: Ah, she is. . .she has already been writing about this coherence pattern strategy, and she is working on the workbook to help other beings do this. We ask her to go back to the workbook and continue working on this because she is at a high enough level to be able to be teaching these levels to others. That work is essential at this moment, and the guidebook needs to be taken out and finished and shared.

R: Very good! Thank you so much. What else needs to be shared from the material that was collected so far? *(Long pause)* Would you like to give us some guidance regarding the book that we want to put together from the information that you share with us?

The Council: The purpose of this book is to accelerate the awakening of humanity and to ground in actual techniques in order to maintain and ground this awakening. An audio version, however, is essential, for the actual, vibrational timber that the form of Ava is able to translate is an essential piece; the written word is important. However, a disk. . .actually, it is more than one disk; it is a series. The audio will be broken up into chapters as well and must be shared, for it is the audio transmissions that are extremely important.

However, you will find that the attention span of many human beings cannot handle the entire sessions all at once. Therefore, it needs to be broken up into chapters. The priority for this book is to share the background necessary to inspire beings to listen and to understand the importance of this work being translated. Most importantly, are the actual techniques. So, some of the stories, perhaps the stories of the pyramids, stories of the The Designer, the stories of this being's coming to realization of the incredible capacity to translate Source information through the verbal language cortex, and have language that is both simple and easy to understand will be good to create the context to allow the trust to be built amongst the audience.

However, the meat of this material is the actual ascension techniques and the coherence pattern, access points, the tips and the inspiration to dedicate to the path, which actually must be done in real time. The book is only the beginning in a sense, to inspire those beings to commit to an academy and a practice of learning how to ground this coherence into their lives. Therefore, the book in a way is only the...what is the correct word? It is the beginning. It is the call to those beings to then come to receive in-person training, to receive, to come and do online courses, to listen to the guided meditations, and to commit to the actual daily practice.

The book itself is a great launching pad, but it is each individual's dedication and devotion to a daily coherence practice that is necessary to upgrade each individual's access to their genetic code. Ava is not the only being, of course, and the beings that are already activating are not the only ones that need to be activating and upgrading their DNA code.

The goal is to get as many human beings with their incarnated souls to choose to commit and dedicate themselves to the path of activated coherence. This is a daily practice that goes on in each moment for the rest of their lives. It is not something that is read, felt, and catharted and then moved on from.

Therefore, the book is the inspiration. The true work is creating a body of work to help guide beings through this process. The workbook that is being created, and the guided meditations that are being created, and this material all needs to be shared and created and put into a platform of an academy or school that allows beings to access this information at the rate that they are able to accelerate. [The information] is offered in a step-by-step manner, so that they are given the information they need to ascend to each level without getting completely overwhelmed.

The workbooks are essential, but in a sense can often be skipped over; the encouragement would be to join the online academy, which will also eventually have a physical location. Therefore, a retreat center will be essential. However, in this time, as much of the information can be given over the digital wavelength to allow people to begin to practice this on their own with the guidance of the visualization, the guided meditations, the workbooks, the books, the sounds, the stories, it is all a complete package to allow one, a being, to access the true potential of their DNA Activation.

R: **Wonderful, thank you so much for this clarity. Now I understand more of the purpose, and it gave me a lot of ideas of how that could be created.**

[The council continues to share with us more information about the book and more practical personal and business suggestions. They explained the importance of our church's non-profit structure. They offer ideas of how to make the material more freely available and also explained the importance of us not being under financial stress and debt, as it disturbs the coherence of the beings who are bringing this information forward. They asked that we would stop relying on or choosing to make income from what they referred to as "our back up plan," the ways we make income that are born out of survival mode.]

CLEAR CHANNEL

R: **May I speak with the Council please? (A:** Yes.**) Thank you so much for coming forward again. She had another question about the toxicity in her body and the fatigue. Do you want to elaborate?**

The Council: Yes, she is correct. Her physical system is sensitive [to] nightshades, gluten, eggs, dairy, alcohol. She had the tiniest sip. I know. I know that it is frustrating being so sensitive. We're not trying to deny her the earthly delights of this realm. However, she has committed to being one of the clear channels for these times, which is an immense responsibility. The only way to do this responsibility without distortion is to have a perfectly clear physical system. Therefore, she chose to come in with a system that was this sensitive; so she could without a shadow of a doubt, feel that toxicity when she eats and imbibes in certain things. It was a choice that she made to help her in her commitment to being the channel. She chose it so that there could be no way that she could fall into distraction. She recognizes that eating just a simple thing outside of the [appropriate diet] realm, for being the Clear Channel disrupts the channel [because she ends up] feeling toxic. However, she also noticed that even with this sensation [food toxicity] inside of her being, she can still open the channel, and she notices that when she weaves with light, she's able to alchemize [the toxicity and feel vitality within]. Therefore, she sees the balance she can create between pristine choices and the fuel that she gives to this physical form. She sees the places where she can bend and lean in, and then the choices that allow her to feel the most vital.

Unfortunately for her, the night shade realm, eggs, dairy, sugar, wheat clog the system, but because she is such a clear channel, the channel remains clear, and therefore these distortions get stored and move through her system in a way that causes her pain, physical pain in order to keep the energetic channel open. So that the energetic channel is clear and not distorting the field. And so she feels physically instead of energetically because she's committed to being the clear channel and it was important to do this work today. Therefore, we moved the distortion into the physical form so that the energetic form can be clear. She recognizes this discomfort and understands the commitment she must make in her diet in order to avoid this physical sensation, but it is a compromise.

Therefore, [if] she chooses to eat those things, then she will feel the physical discomfort, but she has committed to being the clear energetic channel, and therefore all systems are working to maintain that. If she's not in perfect balance at manifest[ing] in the physical, if she wants to have a clear, pain-free physical vessel, then she must adhere more stringently. I know, even more than she already is to her health and wellness patterns.

It's a choice that she made before she came — part of her contract, but it was part of her commitment to her path. We knew that if we gave her the sensitivities that there would be no way that she could avoid her purpose. The purpose was so important that she chose to take the added sensitivities to help keep her directly on path.

R: Thank you so much. Now that she knows all of that, can you clear her and align her both energetically and physically? So she will keep more and more clear and practice more and more? I will continue reminding her as well.

The Council: Just to make a point, she is actually doing quite well. We do feel, the word is not pity, the word is not. . . We empathize with the extreme level of clarity she must maintain. It is a challenge. We recognize it, but we also commend her discipline, and we commend the discipline without the vibe of negativity and complaining. We do notice that when she must constantly engage this discipline, that she does do it from this place of love for her temple and this love to be a clear channel, and she doesn't whine and complain, except occasionally in good nature at the ridiculousness of it all. We appreciate the levity that she brings to any complaint she brings about the amount of discipline she must engage when engaging with the physical realm of nutrition. She often makes us laugh.

R: Is there anything else you would like to share?

The Council: We have created this being. . .the council spent significant energy and time coalescing the energy of this beam to allow her to be well received in this world. This is a time for feminine energy to rise and due to the nature of the residuals of patriarchy, unfortunately a beautiful woman is the most physically appealing form to share information, in these times. We asked this form to release any resistance to being a spokesperson for the awakening and allow her to realize her potential that she was specifically designed in order to be a spokesperson for the awakening. She has been perfectly designed for this role. We asked her to not let any distortion or fear of ego entrapment or ego desires to cause any doubt that she was designed specifically for this work. The nature of her energetic blueprint and across all forms of her astrology and Human Design and Gene Keys — any system you use to look at her system — shows how perfectly designed she is to hold the space as channel.

She is perfectly designed with the open throat in order to allow her to be as grounded as she is while also being a channel to Source, while also being in a physical form that is both pleasing to the eye of all beings in different realms of society, and also being someone who is extremely approachable. Even the design of her face, in the way that her emotion translates through her face allowing truth and authenticity, to be translated through her body language and her facial expressions, further allows her to augment this transmission and allows more people to be able to receive this information without being turned off by some of the languaging. Her languaging choices even are a mixture of very grounded, intellectual and scientifically educated systems mixed with some of the more fringe and some of the more questionable versions of languaging that have not yet been proven by modern science to allow her to not come across as sounding like an indicated ninny, but gives her the power to have credentials amongst many different types of classes of people. She can change her languaging to match almost any level of consciousness. This is a gift we bestowed upon her to allow her to meet all beings where they are at.

Therefore, these transmissions are designed and aimed towards an educated class of beings open to receive this information. However, much of her comedy and some of the other stories are also designed to help reach those beings who would be turned off by the precise nature of this languaging codex.

[This was the first time that Ava had clearly channeled The Council. Their energy was very assertive, and they spoke very fast and clearly. It seems as if they had pre-planned and created Ava in a very particular way to fulfill her purpose. We were also very impressed by the practical information about reaching yin and yang coherence. Now she has become familiar with their energy signature, she will likely recognize it more easily in the future. I was happy she learned more about her reoccurring night terror, surrendered to the pressure and overcame this, and discovered the beautiful gift on the other side.]

THE
CALLING LINES

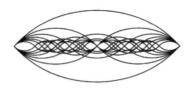

SESSION SEVEN

Almost a year later synchronicity strikes again for Ava and me. We had been asking ourselves, "When would we know when the book was complete?" We sensed that there was more to the story, but in the meantime, both of us relocated and were also traveling frequently. Destiny guided us once again. We discovered that both of us were planning to arrive in the same town for the same week, without coordinating or knowing of each other's plans. We could feel the Divine at work, as it couldn't have been more perfect. Feeling the importance of the opportunity, we carved out times for these next three sessions. We were reminded that "I" has a plan beyond our understanding, and we are grateful that we can listen and surrender to the unfolding.

R: You're arriving now to the surface. You can start to look around you and describe your very first impressions.

A: Everything's turquoise — a pale, blue green. Just not solid, it's like floating sand and water. It's moving like leaves falling out of the trees and caught in the wind. It's grains of turquoise on black and white. It's a paradox; it's turquoise; it's on black and it's on white at the same time. It's on everything and on nothing; it's all turquoise, such a beautiful blue.

R: Wonderful. Tell me more. Look all around you and describe it to me.

A: I can't make sense of it. It's like sand in a lava lamp or something, but grainy; it's just moving pixels of turquoise across the background of black and white. It doesn't seem to be coalescing into anything clear. It's just turquoise grit, like pixie dust or something. It's trying to coalesce into a shape. Fibers. Just light particles and waves of light at the same time. There's nothing holding them together. There's no. . . There's nothing making them create form. They're just kind of drifting with some unseen wind.

R: **Is it all around you?**

A: It's mostly in front of me. I can't tell if I have a body in order to turn around with.

R: **Look down to the direction of your feet. What do you notice as you look down?**

A: I don't have feet. I've got a tail, swimming tail. Kind of like a mermaid tail.

R: **Wonderful. Tell me more. Scan up your body and describe it to me.**

A: Hmmm, I think I'm a hermaphrodite. Seems like I'm both male and female. I could be either. I get to choose. Yeah, I'm both. Slender but strong, and I have both parts. I can reproduce asexually if I want, or I can mate as I wish.

R: **You feel slender and strong?** *(A: Yes.)* **Do you feel young, or do you feel old?**

A: Time. I don't know if I age here. It seems more timeless, like I just am part of this. I just am this. It's interesting because there's no time, but there's no change, and yet there could be change. If I wanted to mate, then that would make change. I just am, in this. . . I think I might be underwater. I can't tell because I'm underwater, right? There's no surface. It seems like it would be the air, but I'm pretty sure the way it's moving, those are bubbles. I think I must be under the water.

R: **Can you describe more about your upper body? What does that look like and feel like?**

A: Human looking. There's a chest and breasts — male and

female together. They're not that big. I'm strong. I have a wide chest, but I have breasts like a woman, and I have strong arms. Long hair. Striking face. I'm a hermaphrodite. It's both equally, beautifully male and female.

R: What color is your upper body?

A: It's pale. It's a mix between pale cream and pale green and pale blue, depending on the light. The scales fade at the waist, but the skin is more translucent. It's a different refraction quality than skin in the air. It's micro scales. They're very small scales, but they're smooth. It's kind of sparkly. The skin's a little sparkly.

R: Very good. Beautiful. What else do you notice that is attracting your attention?

A: It feels nice to swim; my fin is strong; it's like one solid unit. Not two legs, like on a human. It's strong and powerful. I like to swim. . . I'm swimming, exploring. I'm going to a gathering. There's a sense that I'm going to meet others, but I'm alone now. I like being alone. It's quiet. There's no misunderstandings. It's just quiet.

R: Wonderful. You can continue to share with me and move forward to the next important place.

A: There's a gathering. We're all coming together from different parts of the sea. We've come to share and to update each other on different quadrants of this planet. There's not much land at this point. It's all under the sea. The sea is the primary place where it's all happening. There's a gathering here, and there's warm waters, and I enjoy the gatherings. It's nice to hear different songs and stories and meet new beings, and feel different energies.

R: How many beings are showing up to this gathering?

A: There's a lot. There is my village. . .village isn't the right word. It's my school. It's my group. My group, not all of us came. There's maybe twenty of us. There're hundreds here, if not more. I can hear the bubbles. It's loud. All the beings are moving around, and there's a coalescing of energy that's beginning to happen. There's a lot of excitement in the field. Bubbles. There's a lot of bubbles.

R: **What do you feel yourself doing there now?**

A: Well, I'm going to go meet with the other. . . How do I describe this? So. . . *(long pause)*

R: **You can describe it like a movie, so I could imagine it with you. What do you notice there?**

A: I notice that I want to go, and I want to gather with the other. . .with the other callers. I want to gather with the other callers from the other pods, so that we can keep sharing the codes, so that we can communicate across the vast expanses of the ocean. I'm gathering with the other callers. We're the callers. We communicate telepathically sometimes, then there's also a way to communicate with sound that moves through the water, and it can go really long distances. In a way, we're singing under the water, and it sends the stories along the energetic lines. We're always working on how to choose the right currents to carry the sounds on, so that we can go farther, so that we can communicate both, because telepathy only goes so far. We like to use the calling with the telepathy in order to communicate amongst pods. We've been communicating through just the calling for a while, and so now it's finally time to come back together.

The gathering is all sorts of different groups doing different things, but I'm going to go find the callers. The callers are all coming together because we're all so close, because we're actively always communicating with each other. We're always creating the web. It's kind of like an underground spiderweb. I'm going to join the callers, so that we can work on the codes. It's a really beautiful system of. . . It's part telepathy because the telepathic connections can transcend space and time. Because we're going such long distances, sometimes it's not quite enough, and so we augment the telepathy with the calling lines, which are tones similar to whales and dolphins that you know on Earth. We can put a lot more information in the sound lines than through just telepathy. We can pass emotions and ideas; we can pass pictures and emotions through telepathy. We can pass more details about what's happening when we mix the telepathy with the calling lines.

I guess you could call them songs, but they don't sound as much like songs in air. Songs in water sound a lot more like whales or dolphins. It's sound, pitch. They travel the farthest, the pure pitch, and then we can embed the codes of all the information that we need to pass and whatever we're working on. We can get very intricate with the information that we can transmit through the calling lines. I'm excited to get to join back with the other world pod calling groups, so that we can refine our codes. So yeah, we are going to meet, I'm just wading my way through all the beings and meeting friends and getting a little bit distracted, but ultimately, I'm working my way to the calling pod.

R: Beautiful. So let's move a little forward when you arrive. Arriving at the pod now. (A: Okay.) Continue from there.

A: I missed everybody. Hi.

R: Connect with them now and share with me everything that you notice, everything that you learn and everything that you communicate with them.

A: It's exciting. It's been a little while since we've all gathered, so there's a lot of bubbles. Everyone's excited and calling and telepathizing and bubbling, and kind of dancing with each other, but there's no feet, so it's like a water current dancing. We're settling down now and getting to work.

There's discussion of. . . There's a sense of divergent time lines; there's a sense that. . . There's an interesting way that we can move amongst dimensions into different planets in different times. We're on this planet; it's all underwater; there's only a couple of mountains and very small amounts of land poking up out of the water. It's like 99.9% under the water, but there's an interesting alternate, parallel planet — that's Earth — that's much more balanced with earth, land, and ocean. For a while we were on Earth, but it got dangerous for us there. Most of us have left and we're here on the alternate planet that was designed a lot like Earth, like the land masses are very similar.

Most of the qualities of Earth are here, but in the way that this one evolved, our planet is all under the water, and there's no humans. We can jump. There're certain places in deep, dark parts of the ocean where there's these portals where we can jump dimensions, and we could go into the deep chasms of Earth. We used to really like spending time on Earth, and we're reminiscing about Earth, but Earth got too dangerous for us. So we left, and now we're here. But we're missing the humans actually. We're actually telling stories right now of how we used to have love affairs with humans sometimes. We missed their hands and feet. We have hands, too, but Earth hands are different. They have a different relationship with Earth. It feels nice on our skin. We like their feet; they are fun. Their legs are funny the way they wrap around us. We were joking about the humans. It's been many, many hundreds. . . We had to leave Earth. It got too dangerous for us there.

We're trying to get to work. We were just being silly, I guess, and reminiscing about our adventures on Earth back many hundreds of years ago. We'd like to go back, but it's just not worth the risk. We don't die if we're here, but on Earth we can die. So we don't go much anymore because it is too dangerous.

R: I see. Very good. Thank you for sharing with me. Let's move forward to more important information that you learn there, at this gathering.

A: We've been working on refining the calling lines to add more texture, so that we can communicate more details about safety and needs and where the schools of fish and the currents of warm water [are], and just all the different comings and goings of the ocean. It's nice to be able to communicate around the planet. It's peaceful here. It's calm. But what's coming is that somebody went to Earth. (Deep sigh.) It's been a long time since somebody went to Earth, but they went and they didn't come back. Then we sent someone else after them, and we're hearing the reports now. . .

R: Share with me the report. What do you learn?

A: We thought it was bad a few hundred years ago. *(Deep sigh.)* Humans are just massacring all of our kin and the oceans. [The sound of the voice got deeper and more emotional.] They seem to have a sick fetish with just cutting off like one little part of these beautiful beings and then just throwing the rest away. They're just taking one fin, or one little piece of their bladder, and then the rest of them, they're just throwing into the ocean. . .rotting and dying. It's appalling. It's just genocide. They're just. . .they're murdering all of the kin that we left in the oceans. We're realizing that we've been here so long in our sanctuary and beautiful oasis, just working on our song lines, and just working on our calling lines and just living and being, but there's this realization that it seems like Earth needs our help. Some of us don't want to go; some of us want to go; we don't know what to do, but we're realizing that the callers probably need to go because we're the ones that can help set the grids in the oceans and help create some, like safe passage for a lot of our kin that are being murdered in the seas and [we can] create calling lines to warn all the water kin of where the humans are.

They're going to destroy everything in the ocean — is going to be dead. It's absolutely astounding, what's happened. We're all just sort of taking in the scope of it and the danger of it because they would worse than kill us if they found us again. There's legends of us that it's been so long since we've been there that if we get caught, then they'll be hunting us; they'd be looking for us. For if the shark fins are of top commodity, imagine what our fins would be. Imagine what our bodies would be. So It's dangerous to go back to Earth, but we're feeling like we have to go through the portals, and we have to return because otherwise, there's not going to be anything left in the oceans at all. It's disappearing so fast. The coral's disappearing. The waters, the temperatures are changing, like the whole ocean system is on the edge of collapse. We have the knowledge to help restore balance; we could create calling lines and we could interact with the GPS and all of the technology that the humans have now.

These reports are astounding. We're trying to receive all the information telepathically from the being that made it back. He's showing us all the pictures from Earth. I don't even know what to make of all these things, but it sounds like we need to help, and I'm terrified. I don't want to go, but yet the pictures that he's showing us. . . How can we not? How can we just sit by in our oasis, in our perfect sanctuary, when the oceans are being absolutely murdered? So, it seems like we can help because the calling lines are very intricate textures, and we could potentially create protective grids and create sanctuaries for the kin to retreat to. We might even be able to interfere with some of the tracking systems and some of the technology that we're being shown that's on Earth because it's working on sonar. They've learned how to work with the sound and light patterns. That's our specialty, sending information along these sound lines through the water.

We're sitting around reading all of his telepathic reports of what's happening and taking in the gravity of the situation and deciding how many of us are going to go through the portals, if there's a way, we can mask ourselves or hide ourselves so that we don't get captured or caught. We want to help. We want to help Earth, even though we might die. We are just listening and feeling into what to do.

R: Thank you so much for sharing with me and thank you for wanting to help Earth. Let's close that and move to the next

important place in that life.

A: We're down in the deep, down in the bottom of the ocean abyss. It's where the portal is, where we can go to Earth. I decided to go. Several of us have decided to go, several callers and then others as well. I want to help and support. We're going back to Earth after. . .it's been hundreds of years since many of us have been to Earth. It's more dangerous than ever, but it's our sister planet after all. We can't leave them on their own. They don't have a chance without our help. We're going down into the deepest, darkest dark. And in the deepest, darkest dark, there's a light. . .we have to surrender into, then it turns us inside out, and then we reform on Earth.

We're gonna go through the portal, go to Earth and see how we can help. We're saying goodbye to our friends and loves. We know we may not come back; we may not make it back. Well, you have to try to help create balance. We can also use the calling lines to weave in vibrations of love and help try and change and shift, so the humans stop being so destructive. We can start weaving compassion and balance and understanding into the calling lines, so that some of the humans that are more sensitive, and even those that are not, might receive them. In that way maybe we can start shifting the tide towards balance. Give our kin a chance to rest and not be constantly running from the humans. We're going to try and help in every way we can, both to create protective grids, hiding grids, safe channel grids, and then also working on the grids to send up to the surface.

We're working with the moisture in the air because we think we can send the calling lines over the surface and through the air. I think that will help because we can just put a love vibration through the moisture droplets in the air. We think it should have an impact because ultimately, we have a very similar genetic code as the humans. We have more strands of DNA; there's. . .we have more telepathic lines. We're working on a different pattern; we're not mortal. We're immortal, telepathic, and communicate through the mind. Ultimately, humans could as well. It's all the other programs that cause mortality and the lack of ability for telepathy. It's all the same fundamental framework.

If we can send the codes for us, it seems that we can alter and send simpler codes that the humans can understand. I'm learning how to work now that we've gotten here. I'm just assessing it, and I'm noticing I'm feeling pretty scared, and I can't do my work if I'm scared. I'm working on calming myself, so that I can tap into the frequency that's on Earth now. I'm learning all of their technology lines and how they're sending their technology. They're sending their information across wavelengths, so we're studying now, so that we can match.

When we were here hundreds of years ago, this technology didn't exist yet. They figured out how to send calling lines. I mean, in a sense, that's what they're doing; they've discovered the calling lines, but they can't do it themselves. They've created instruments that can translate, and so they don't understand what they're really working with. They're using these devices that they've made to transmit these currents; they don't actually realize that they're sending the current through their own DNA. They don't realize what they're doing. They think they're just sending them through the air; they don't understand how connected it all is.

So they're sending these really. . .wow! The information that they're sending on the calling lines is so intense; oh, my goodness, it's so much. They don't realize that they're sending all of that, everything they're sending across the wavelengths — all their information for all their devices, and all their tracking, and all their mapping, and all their information, and all their...all their whole. . .their whole web, their whole internet web. They don't realize that they're changing their very DNA and they're sending the wave. . .they're sending the call lines, through all space and time on planet Earth. They're part of it; they think that they're just sending these waves through the air, but it's not the way it works. It's sending it through the energy matrix of everything. They're sending all of this data through their own bodies and disrupting so many...oh my gosh, it's overwhelming. I can't. I'm like shocked. I'm shocked that they're able to survive this. I hear that their cancer and rates of disease have increased, but I'm shocked that they're actually able to function with this much distortion going through their field. Because they're being bombarded with so many intricate layers of calling lines. I've never seen anything like it.

It's fascinating how advanced that they've been able to become, considering how little they actually understand. It's almost comical, but in the most tragic way. Because they don't actually see what they're doing. They don't realize that these vibrations that they're sending all their frequencies on. . . they are working; they are manipulating — without their own knowledge — their own auric and energetic fields. Their own telepathic fields are getting hijacked by all the information that they're sending. It's corrupting all of their DNA files. It's a mess. I'm just learning the systems. They're very intricate and complex and considering how in away simple they are, it's hard to describe. It's simple in some ways, but they don't really understand what they're doing. The impacts are wow! I'm still wrapping my understanding around how much they have impacted the auric field of the planet, both in the air and in the water, and their own bodies, and the bodies of all sentient beings on the planet. It's pretty astounding.

I'm learning the best I can. I'm using my telepathic abilities, and I'm working and listening and looking at some of the beings who are creating this code and are creating these channels. We're also doing our best to telepathically connect with the actual vibrations themselves and really learn what frequencies have they learned to tapped into — which calling lines have they actually [using] — how deep into their own auric and energetic field have they gone by sending these messages? They're getting more and more intricate with each layer; they're calling them those different numbers with the letters, and they make a little arc or rainbow, like a little ripple. They're calling it WiFi. There's 3 and 4 and 5G lines. . .and all of the transmitters for it...it's just astounding the amount of distortion that is all across the field. Thank God I'm under the water because above the water it's absolutely deafening. I don't know how to hear anything; no wonder they can't be telepathic. There's so much distortion, but at least under here in the water, there's not. . . There's still a lot of distortion; they're sending a lot of frequencies through the water.

At this point, we're still learning. We're trying to catch up on this technology that they've gathered and see how we can help guide it into more healthy patterns, so we can make a positive impact. We're realizing there's a lot of different intelligences here on Earth now. There're beings from many different other realms and dimensions also here to help. At least we're not the only ones here to help, but there's also a lot of frequencies here that are trying to distort. I'm still just trying to wrap my head around the enormity of how much has changed since we were here last.

R: Thank you so much for sharing with me. Now let's move forward to another important day.

A: Well, we've learned that we can telepathically connect with beings that are practicing presence or meditating here on Earth. Those that are clearing their mind are actually able to buffer themselves from the distortion, so we're learning from them, because they've been inundated with this distortion their whole lives, and they're learning how to quiet and still it, in order to tap into that place of presence amongst the distortion. We're all so sensitive, so we're actually learning from these beings how to navigate the distortion fields, so that we can interact in a good way. This is a turning point; it took us a while. We were so bombarded with so many of the energies. Now we've learned from the beings who are practicing presence, and there are actually millions of them on planet Earth. We're feeling really grateful that there are so many beings here that are learning to drop underneath and outside of the distortion, all the frequency patterns, and drop into themselves.

We've been learning how to filter out some of the call lines that the humans have set up, or we're calling them "call lines." That's all of their technology, all their WiFi, all of the invisible currents that they're sending. We're learning how to filter and buffer and to get in between them, so that we can find...so that we can reach some places of quiet; so we can send our song lines and not get interference from their song lines.

At first when we were trying to send our calling lines through, they were getting bombarded by all the frequencies and all the signals that they're sending. We were having a hard time busting through all of it. We happened to telepathically connect with some beings that were practicing meditation and presence. That is where we learned now a new technique to filter our sensitivities, so that we can find the spaces where the technology is not, so we can send our calling lines through undistorted, more subtle patterns. We realized that they're sending a lot of their WiFi through. . . it is almost like a certain blanket.

There's a certain frequency line that they're sending everything on, and that we can slightly modify it in order to be free of their patterns. That's been a huge advancement and is allowing us to start to make some progress in creating a worldwide calling line network — a mesh, a mycelial network of our calling lines, with the intention of creating vibrations of love, peace, compassion, appreciation, and respect for all sentient beings — not just for humans. We realize that they have a very narrow bandwidth of compassion, only for the ones that they are allied with, instead of all beings. It's a very limited compassion network that they seem to have. We are working on creating a worldwide network of compassion lines to help. . .

We hope to help raise the vibration of beings on Earth and help them lift all these frequencies that are bombarding them, so that they can have a little spaciousness; so they can actually feel their hearts. That's the project that we're working on now. We've divided ourselves; we spread ourselves out around the planet, far enough away that we can still communicate with our calling lines, but to create a grid that goes all the way around, so that we can do our best to create a positive vibrational field around the planet.

We're working with some of the multidimensional beings that are working from above, and [with] inter-dimensional beings. They're helping augment the grid above. They've been working above for a long time, and they've been working below, but they didn't have the technology that we had. Now we are joined together and realize that we have a shared mission to support the raising of the vibration of the planet. We've joined a bigger team. We're bringing a unique piece to the puzzle because of our history and our shared DNA with you humans, and yet [also] our own unique DNA that's different from the humans. We share a different type of vibrational similarity than some of the other inter-dimensional beings that are here to support and some of those who have incarnated into human beings. So there's many different layers all here working simultaneously to help support the raising of the vibration of this collective.

R: Thank you so much for all your work and all the information that you share. Let's move forward to the current days that we are experiencing right now and share with me what's been done now. What else would you like to share with me now?

A: The councils are gathering soon; there going to be a council soon — many different layers of the inter-dimensional beings to try and create a better strategy for how we can make more positive impacts on Earth. There's going to be a meeting soon with — a team of some of the callers from our world are meeting with some of the beings who have chosen to incarnate, and some of the volunteer coordinators for the incarnated beings. Plus, we're also meeting with some of the inter-dimensional beings that are holding grid points in subtle realms of the atmosphere that can't be seen by humans. They're holding the different grid points in the different dimensions. And there's other dimensions even under, in the ocean. There's our dimension, which is more in the physical dimension, working with the energetics and sound dimension. But there are other subtler vibrational beings that are working with the energetics in the plant and even underneath the plant.

We're a sort of a bridge between the physical beings and the energetic beings because we're working with the telepathic and energetic calling lines or song lines or vibration lines, but we're physically embodied beings from a different planet who have now moved ourselves to this planet. So we hold density, unlike some of the beings that are holding energetic space or some of the beings that have incarnated. They've taken their beingness and put it into three-dimensional human form. Then there's even three-dimensional astral beings up in the atmosphere and three or four different types of beings in the physical. There're also many different ones in the energetic realms and the subtler realms that are embodied. So there's going to be a gathering of all of these beings to strategize the best ways to kind of unify our efforts.

R: So can you elaborate what forms did you take on the Earth?

A: Well, I mean, I'm currently in. . . I guess you would call them the Mer-people forms. So the half-fish, half-human form. We have five strands of DNA. The humans have been stripped down to two strands. We are an average of five; some of the beings have evolved to have seven or nine strands. We have five, but some of them aren't fully activated, because it's hard to have five degrees or five lines of DNA embodied in physical form. It's vibrating so high, once you get to the fifth line, that it tends to be more an energetic being; it's hard to hold embodied form. I'm currently in the form of these Mer-beings that are from the sister planet that have come back to

Earth. I'm not the only one [here now]. What are you asking me?

R: **What forms the others are taking. You said that there are volunteers who come, and they take different forms there?**

A: I'm in the pod of the Mer-people that have come embodied. We're the five-strand-DNA embodied. I'd say we're about 40% or 50% human DNA, and then 40% to 60% of another race that was brought from an inter-dimensional galaxy from many, many. . .very, very far away that was used as part of one of the experiments when Earth was being formed. There were some parallel Earths with different experiments happening on them. There was the Earth experiment, and there were several hundred experiments, and some of them were more successful than others. One of the parallel Earths was more underwater. We're physical beings. I'm one of those beings now anyway. We're meeting with a whole team of beings; you're wanting me to list out all of those beings?

R: **So there's many types?**

A: Yes. I'm showing you right now an embodiment of one being from a parallel planet, but of course, we know that consciousness is all beings at all times, differentiated into intimate, infinite forms, for infinite expression and possibilities. I'm sharing currently, from the perspective of this Mer-race. This is a physical race, but it's a physical race that has a higher percent chance to work with the energetic realms as well; we're able to use the portal to come between planets. With only the two strands, they can't, they can't travel as easily, at least with their physical bodies. I think what you're asking me is about all the other different types of beings that we're about to meet with? Is that what you're asking?

R: **Mmhmm. Yeah.**

A: Alright, so from my awareness, there are the Mer-beings, which are the beings that we portaled over from the sister

Earth. There are other beings under the ocean, there are... There's a LOT! There're three main categories. There're the beings that are under the water. There're the beings terrestrially on land, and then there's beings up in the atmosphere. There're nine different categories. There're the terrestrial beings, the embodied form beings — underwater, on land, and in the sky. I'm one of the beings that is embodied in form from another planet, but also here — used to be here. We used to be able to travel between planets.

There're the physical beings under the Earth and under the water on the Earth — the ones that have incarnated from other dimensions and are living as human beings now. There's a lot of those. Those are the embodied volunteers on planet Earth. Then there's us that have chosen to come from the other planet, because we realized what a mess was happening and there's us in embodied form. There are many different species of beings embodied in forms that are not human. They are [here] in their actual other race [extraterrestrial bodies], and so there's some of them on planet Earth; there's some of them in ships above. There're many different ones that are actually in physical embodiment.

R: Is the Mer-race currently on the Earth right now?

A: Well, yes, we've come. We've come from the sister planet, through the portal in the deep abyss of the ocean to Earth in order to support. We don't have to stay; we weren't incarnated here on Earth. We've been around; we're not really. . .we don't have death the same way that humans have death. There're the physically embodied beings on all the three realms, and then there's energetic beings of each realm, the spirits that have passed and have decided to stay to support. There're beings that were not invited at all that have come to support. When they don't have a body or a form, they're not as tied to [the] Earth plane or underwater or above; they kind of just go where they're needed, but you could still, in a sense, if you wanted to. . . [you could] put them into three categories of the more energetic beings that are under the water with us or on the surface of the Earth or up in the atmosphere, or the auric, or the energetic realms of Earth. So I guess it's six major categories, but then there's subcategories of each one. There're beings from other actual races that have traveled, then there's beings that have traveled energetically, or just with their awareness, and their physical bodies are still on their other planet. There're beings that have never actually had a body that are just using their awareness to come and be here to support. There's [also] just Awarenesses [referring to the Observers, a type of consciousness that watches and records without physical form] in general that are here. It's hard to put an actual count on who's here. Of course, it's the paradox of life — it's all one thing anyway; it's just hard to describe.

R: **Thank you. Let's move forward to the important times and important information.**

A: I don't know how to describe it, but there's the sensation that it's all coming to a point. It's all coming to a peak. I can't tell if it's like a physical mountain peak, or whether there's a peak coming in like the culmination of the work, or if there's a culmination in the energy lines or there's a culmination in the story. I'm seeing a point of things coming up to a big, mountain peak point, but I don't understand.

R: **You can continue to observe and as you observe, you learn more and you notice more and you can share with me freely.**

A: My head hurts from all the WiFi. It's a lot.

R: **Is there anything else that you notice there?**

A: I don't know.

THE GRID OF COMPASSION

R: So let's close that scene and take you to a healing temple where you can clear all the energies, so we can start the healing process. Take a deep breath and drift and float to the most appropriate healing temple to clear and to heal. Arriving there now. Arriving to the healing temple now. You can start to look around you and describe your first impressions.

A: It feels like I'm inside of a pearl.

R: Inside of a pearl. Beautiful. Tell me more, what else do you feel inside there?

A: It's soft and smooth and silky and rainbowy and... It's like rainbow silk.

R: That's nice. What else do you notice? You can fully relax. May I speak with Ava's Higher Self please?

HS: Ahhmm *(makes a yes sound)*.

R: Thank you so much. You showed this beautiful mermaid mission. Why did you choose to show that today?

HS: It's the simplest because she's the happiest when she's in the water and the ocean. She loves being by the ocean and being in the ocean. *(Long pause.)*

R: Wonderful, and you showed about the mission and how they operate and all the difficulty. . .the intensity of learning the new frequencies and overcoming them. Why did you want to share all of that? What's important to share with us today?

HS: Well, you'll notice that there's a similar theme in all the stories that come through, because it's all the same thing. It doesn't matter how I describe it; it doesn't matter if I use Mer-people or The Designer of Earth, or whether I use "I," or whether I use the pyramid makers. It doesn't matter. It's all bringing us to the same story that we're all based on vibration and sound, and song, and that we transmit so much through these currents. Way more than we think, and especially now where there is so much bombardment in the WiFi fields and in the frequency fields here on Earth. We've got to remember how important it is for us to drop underneath them and to find our center and to create our own lines. To create our own calling lines. To generate our own frequencies, so that we're not just being bombarded and depleted by all of the technology running through the currents.

We need to understand how important this current system is — not the current as in now. I mean the current as an energy current system. It's so important. The story doesn't even matter. It doesn't really even matter if the story I'm telling you is a story is real, or if it's not real; if I'm telling you about pyramids or the designing of Earth or the Mer-people in the way they move through the portals. The important part of every story that you've heard thus far through this channel is the importance of working with your energy lines, the importance of working with your vibration, realizing that we're all telepathic beings, and we all have the ability to lay these call lines, these calling lines, the song lines, these vibrational lines, and that's what can guide our lives. This can help protect us in our daily lives of dealing with all the bombardment of all of the frequencies that are in our atmosphere and in our world.

It reminds you; it reminds her; it reminds all of us to be sovereign beings — to take responsibility for our vibration, to take responsibility for our frequency.

These stories remind us from all the different perspectives and all the different beings that we're all doing the same thing, whether or not we're under the sea or on the land. Whether we're singing, whether we're talking; it's all vibration; it's all energy. It's all about what we're putting out there into the field. Regardless of what I'm saying, it's just painting all these different pictures of the same story over and over again — which is, in a sense, exactly the songs of remembering. It's all about how to tune and how to be aware of our energy systems, so that we can create positive change in the world.

Every story that I've shared, ultimately, if you strip the story aside, the fundamental essence of everything is our vibration — the vibration that we are emitting and the vibration that we are creating. What is our intention? Is our intention to gather the resources [we need], or to exploit other beings? Is our intention love? You'll notice in every one of the stories that the intention is to share a vibration of love, to augment the understanding and the harmonics that can be possible on planet Earth when we come together.

These stories are meant to inspire us to come together and to create a grid of compassion, to create a grid of forgiveness, to create a grid of love, and to use our frequencies consciously to create this. This is a call to each one of us to lay the call lines, to send out the call lines. Whether or not an actual Mer-person is coming through and being channeled through this being from another dimension is irrelevant. It's absolutely essential that we take responsibility for our vibration and for our mental frequencies that we're putting out.

What are we thinking about? What are we talking about? What are we doing? What is our intention? Why are we doing what we're doing? Everything you do in every moment is creating a call line, is creating a song line; it's sending another vibration out into the energy matrix. With so much distortion happening in the field, it's our utmost responsibility to be mindful of how we're sharing. Ultimately, people love mermaids. A story about mermaids sending out call lines and helping to raise the vibration of planet Earth; it may be very well true. I'm not telling you that it is or it isn't. What is most important is the parable that's within it.

No matter what, we've got to do the right thing; no matter how scary it is to rise up and to face our greatest fear and the potential of death and being captured and enslaved or exploited.

It is not nearly as important as the integrity of showing up to help our kin, to help our kindred beings, the other sentient beings on the planet. It's just another parable, pulling from the infinite possibility and from the infinite realms, reminding us of how important the songs of remembering are. It is the time to be singing our songs and telling stories of truth in love and being very mindful about the vibration that we're emitting, so we can create the worldwide grid of love and compassion and forgiveness and help raise the vibration of humanity and the planet. So all the stories, in a sense, touch each of us in different ways. Some of us resonate with different stories, of different themes and different ideas, more than others.

This is a theme that she's been writing on for a while; there's a story she's been writing about mermaids; she's been wearing this ocean stone, the larimar on her chest; she's been spending a lot of time in the water, so it's alive. It's what is easily dipped from the well of Source. The way that this channel often tends to work through her, is it takes a thread or a seed of what is active in her consciousness and then dips down deeper to bring in the parable and brings it all back to the same story of a vibration — of being these vibrational beings and being true to our vibration, and to sing our songs, and to help raise the vibration.

Sometimes it can feel really hopeless, the weight of the world and the weight of all the frequencies and the WiFi and the 5G and all of the stuff can feel really overwhelming. We need to find small places of inspiration where we can feel some sense of hope, or what can we do? We may have failed at trying to keep all the 5G towers from going up, if that's what people are wanting to do. But what can we do as individuals in the system? How can we make a difference? How can we make a positive impact? By being sovereign beings responsible for our energy and our vibration that we emit. That's how we make such a profound difference and an impact. This is just another story, to help inspire us to tap into our songs and to remember our vibration.

R: Beautiful, thank you so much for sharing. And, you know, I feel like there's many of us that are aware of this working on the grid. We're traveling through the Earth going to many sacred sites and trying to send unconditional love through the grid and create those calls and energy frequencies. I'm wondering if there's more practical guidance for people that are aware about how to effectively create that and amplify the frequency?

HS: Yes. Yes. So step one, obviously, is there must be a practice of being able to drop below the mind, to be able to quiet the mind. 99% of humans on the planet don't know how to do this first step, so the most fundamental first step is to practice dropping out of the mind and coming into presence. There're many different techniques for this. There're many different techniques for meditation out there; whichever technique one uses, the ultimate goal is to drop oneself below the mind, outside of the mind, and into the silent realm. When beings begin to practice, and they start to find the silent realm, they're usually terrified by the silent realm. Silence, the endless silence, is terrifying and very confronting. That's why the mind likes to fill it up with endless chatter.

After one has found the space to quiet the mind, then one must practice becoming accustomed to the silence and feeling safe in the silence, instead of feeling terrified of the silence. That's step one.

Step two. Once you've been able to master step one and rest in silence, step two, that's when you can start dropping into the quantum field. You can start dropping into the area where you can start to feel the texture places of where the song lines and the call lines exist, which is in the energetic, the matrix. The blueprint of existence is in the realm of silence. It's an infinite field of silence that goes on in all directions and all space and time; you've seen it — that's the flower of life pattern [depicted in 2D]. It's the shape of everything in the 3D. In the multiple dimensions, it is the shape of everything. Its resonance frequency is silence and Aum [Om]. There's vibration and there's sound within the tapestry of silence.

Once one learns [to rest in] the silence, then one can learn to feel and hear the subtle frequencies that are traveling in the silence, and realize the background of silence. That's how you learn to start being able to translate and read the textures of the song lines. Because they're woven in there; they're traveling along the arcs of the shapes that you see when you see the flower of life, which is the two-dimensional representation of a three-dimensional infinite pattern of space-time, the unified field. To access the unified field, one must learn how to quiet the mind and then rest in silence without being terrified. Once you can rest in that for long periods of time, that's when you can start to learn to discern and start to feel the different textures that are moving.

Imagine that you're blind and you're learning to read braille. It's a similar concept; you're not going to necessarily see it with your third eye. Some people do. Some people have a more visual access to this field. Some people have a more somatic access to this field. Some people have a more auditory access to this field. One must take the time to refine their system enough to be comfortable enough with the silence of it, then they can feel the not-silence or the texture on top of and within the silence. Or traveling on the vibrations of silence or on the universal sound of Aum that's dancing on top of the silence, and dancing through and mixing with the silence. Once one has learned to rest in silence long enough, then one begins to hear the sound of the universe. The one song. The one verse. *[Uni-verse].* At first, it is most likely just going to sound like Aum, or just sound like a roar, or like a vibration of an indistinguishable sound.

There was a movie that came out in the 90s, called *Contact*, about extraterrestrial encounters. At first, when they received the message from outer space, it was just a sound; it was a pulse. At first it was just that one sound. The scientist who was blind, he was the one who realized that there was texture in the sound. For a long period of time, all they heard was that sound, a grating, loud sound. The more they investigated it, they realized that the sound had layers and texture, then that texture revealed the whole schematics for an instrument that could then take one to another dimension.

They didn't discover it all at once. It's not like they just immediately got the blueprints for the device and built it and then went there. At first it was just one loud grating sound, and then all of a sudden, the sound had texture. Then the texture was just chaos. Then the chaos showed a pattern, and then the pattern came together. And then the pattern was built. There was a step by step by step.

Humans need to do the same steps; they need to learn to rest in silence and not be scared of the silence. They need to start listening for the universal sound and really feeling the textures of it. When they learn somatic meditations like Vipassana, or things like that, they start to learn the somatic texture of their own body and the vibration of their own body. Then they start to realize that the vibration of their body and their being is a reflection of the vibration all around them and of all beings.

Whatever technique one uses, you just want to be able to truly practice it. A lot of times people will try one type of meditation, and then another and then another and another, and they bounce around to many different techniques. They don't get very far. It's not so much about picking one in particular. It's not so much about which one you choose, it's more about choosing one and riding that one long enough until you actually learn to find silence. And to hear, to begin to hear the sounds and the songs of the universe in the background of silence in order to be able to start to understand the nuances of it.

Once you can start to understand those nuances, you can start to feel it. At first, when you're blind and you grab a cord, you just feel rope. Eventually you realize that that rope is made up of smaller threads that are strung together and woven together, and you start to realize that there's a whole intricate texture to this rope. You could unwind that rope and feel all the individual threads. It's the same with humans learning to become aware of this, the song lines or the call lines, and learning how to work with the unified field. It is step by step quieting the mind and quieting the mind enough to be able to start to hear the sounds and feel the sounds, not just hear them but feel them. Then start to find patterns within those and start to realize where the patterns are pointing. Then start to realize that they can start to translate. They might not be able to translate right away.

You might not be able to immediately tell what the song lines are describing. It takes a period of [dedicated] time to truly attune the self in order to really be able to hear it more and more intricately and to be able to distill meaning from it. Once one has learned to hear the sound of Aum and hear the sound of the Universe and started to then really listen to the texture in the Aum, they realize the Aum is not just Aum. Not just the A-U-M. There's actually an entire universe of information coming on that sound. It takes a lot of patience to start to hear all the different, subtle nuances that are coming through on the universal sound. Then consciousness can weave any type of information on top of that, so there's another layer that can go on top of the universal sound that can weave through all space and time and can send any kind of information when we attune ourselves. That's where true telepathy allows us to, in a sense, read the sound of the universe through feeling, knowing, and cognition. Sometimes it's just consciousness and cognition; sometimes it's a somatic feeling. For some it's hearing, and for some it's visual. So many different beings can tap into different sides. Some have very strong visual, mystical experiences, and some hear it and some see it, some feel it, and some can taste it.

When you start getting into the more subtle, more advanced nuances of how to decipher and translate this information into usable information, one's got to soften the grip. There's this sensation that one needs to grasp. Once you start to hear the sound of the universe, there's this excitement and this wanting to kind of grab at it. Like, 'Oh, I've heard it; oh, now I've got it.' The mind wants to kind of grab on to the sound to understand it. You can't hear it that way. You dampen the sound. If you grab it, you dampen the sound. You've got to keep surrendering and opening in order to let the vibration play through you. It's almost like you are the guitar string being plucked.

R: It sounds like after you have this somatic experience, you're able to hear it and translate it, then there is another layer that you're creating in order to interact and to create a calling that creates more harmony? (A: Yes.) Okay. So can you describe that? How do you create another layer? Is it just projecting images? Projecting sounds? Because. . .how does it do that?

HS: It's not projecting. Projecting is an aspect of grasping; you're trying; you're striving. I found that it doesn't work as well. You're talking about how to actually send information, or to receive, or to understand information? You're wanting to send information?

R: I guess I'm trying to understand the intention behind that. As I said, like interacting with a grid in order to create a more harmonious grid. So, what's the next level after you translate it? How are you interacting with it in a way that creates more harmony?

HS: It's about aligning your intention with the pure intention of love. You can send almost anything through the vibration of pure love. It's like if you're trying to send a mental image to a dog. If you're trying to communicate with a dog, you can't say "don't do that," to the dog. The dog sees in telepathic pictures that you send it, of positive things. If you want the dog to sit, then you send the dog a clear image of "sit," and the dog will sit. If you send the dog a clear image of "don't sit," it doesn't understand, "don't sit." And it sits. If you want it to not sit, you'd need to send an image of stand or run or go, if you want it to go. You need to always send your positive message to the dog and the dog receives it.

This [concept] is well known in dog training. If you send a positive, clear picture of what you want the dog to do, the dog usually does it. But if you send a negative, if you send a "don't do," it tends to either be confused, or it does the opposite of what you want it to do, so it's a very simplified version or simplified analogy to this. If you're in the vibration of pure silence and surrender and love, and if you're not grasping or striving, and if you don't have an agenda, if you're sending your message from pure positive intent, then you can send anything instantaneously. It's the vibration of your intention.

Then once you've stabilized that pure intention, you can send almost anything. If you're coming from a place of agenda, or trying to manipulate or coerce or change for some sort of personal or selfish agenda or goal, then you're not necessarily in the pure vibration of love, and therefore it's not going to be effective. The goal is to get yourself into the absolute pure vibration of love, then anything you embed within that vibration of love can be instantaneously transmitted. It's an amazing technique, but it requires a lot of practice to get yourself that refined and that intentional about what message that you're sending or uploading onto the song lines.

R: **Thank you so much. So, if you would like to summarize all the things that you shared with us today, what was your intention with sharing all those messages today?**

HS: To realize that you are a conscious creator. That you are powerful beyond measure, and your thoughts, words, intentions, and feelings create the universe. To remind you what a great and powerful and sacred and humble responsibility it is to be a conscious being embodied in form. You are a transmitter of song lines, of call lines. What message are you sending across the world?

The summary ultimately is, what is your intention? What is your purpose? Why are you doing what you are doing? Take responsibility for yourself and your thoughts and your feelings and your actions and be aligned in the vibration of love, and then magic can flow to you. Ultimately, everything that I've shared is just to remind us that we are vibrational beings. When we refine our energy to be in the vibration of pure love, then we can send calls, and we can send messages across vast expanses of the planet.

R: **This is very beautiful. Thank you so much for this information today.**

THE
HOLOGRAPHIC
HUMAN

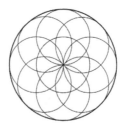

SESSION EIGHT

A few days later Ava and I met again, and we agreed to do two more sessions with a long break in between. We discussed the questions we both still had after reviewing the materials so far. I was eager to learn more about the creation story of the Earth experiment and the creation of humans. I was aiming to have a continuation of the information we received during our third session. I'm sharing this with you because during this next session there is a moment when I ask a question in a way that may seem out of context, but *they* could understand me because of our discussion prior to the session.

This session started differently from all the other sessions we had together. Ava felt like she was being pulled into a sleep state, and I assured her that it was good that she felt so relaxed and to please continue to talk and describe what she was noticing. She was able to stay in deep relaxation without falling asleep. She didn't see much at first, and the information was not flowing as fast as we were used to, but then she started to describe more about her physical and energetic sensations.

This brought forward a unique opportunity to witness and learn about the physical body and the energy centers from the inside out. After this experience, we were able to bring forward her Higher Self and they continued to share more information about the questions that we had about the Creation and so much more.

R: You can start looking around. Describe your first impressions. *(Long silence.)* What do you notice as you look around you? You can use all your senses. What are you looking at? What do you feel while you're there?

A: I feel like I might have been slipping into a dream.

R: Mmhmmm. Very good. Feels good?

A: I think I fell asleep a little bit.

R: That's good. That's okay. So you are very relaxed. That's very good. You can stay very relaxed. Let's see what comes to mind as you look around you. You're already there. Look around you now. What do you notice there?

A: It's like. . .this pulsing. Pulsing ripples of light emanating from me and coming to me at the same time. I'm emanating and yet there's something emanating, radiating, out to me. It is both and. . . I can't see anything except these pulses of light, getting kind of gray. The pulses of light that are emanating and radiating are white but with. . .not white. It's like every color, but it's white, with translucency of 60%; it's not bright white. It's this opaque film, like a veil, or a very thin fog. There's this rainbow element to the pulsing. I'm noticing that I'm part of this pulsing.

R: You also receive this energy, and you're also pulsing?

A: Both receiving it and pulsing it out at the same time.

R: That's nice. How does it feel to do that?

A: It feels really good. It feels good, and yet it also feels really tiring. I couldn't possibly do anything else but lay here. It feels like this generative energy, but it also feels very. . . I don't know if draining is the right word, but I feel really tired.

R: Do you feel like you can surrender to it and do it while you're surrendering to it?

A: Yeah.

R: When you look down to your body, what do you notice?

A: I don't have one, I don't think, although there was a point of me. There was this point of consciousness that was me. I don't see a body. There was this emanation from the center point and I was the center point, yet I was also a relative point, because the radiation was coming towards me. There was this aspect of "I"-ness, but there's no body, I don't think. Although originally, I thought that it was the length of [a] human body because the pulse felt like it was coming from not one single point but like a long point. So, like a body with many different energy centers, all pulsing. There's no form here when I look down.

R: And what goes through your mind as you're pulsing there?

A: There's no thinking because it's just an enjoying of the pulsing there. There is no thought, just an enjoying of the pulsing, receiving, of being the pulsing.

R: Very nice. You feel like you did that for a long time? Or is it you just arrived?

A: Feels like I just arrived. So heavy. All I can do is just feel this pulsing. That's it.

R: Good. Do that for a moment and allow the heaviness and allow yourself to fully surrender to it. Feel yourself there. [I then moved her to the next scene].

A: I feel that I'm in a field of grass, and I have hands. I looked down and I had a hand, a human hand on the grass.

R: Very good. Ground into that body and use all the senses. You can share with me more. You're discovering your body and everything that you noticed. What are you looking at?

A: I am looking. . .

R: Tell me more. You said you saw your hands on the grass, then what did you see next? You can share with me freely as soon as you see it. What are you looking at now?

A: I don't know. Nothing.

R: Okay, just darkness all around?

A: There's some lightness. There's some lights sparkles, and colors and white.

R: Okay, good. Tell me more. Is it all around you? Where do you see it?

A: I feel like there's this really strong pull trying to pull me into unconsciousness, and I can't seem to resist it.

R: Okay.

A: I'm trying to stay present; I keep falling asleep.

R: I understand. It's very relaxing; you feel like you're sleeping, but as you speak, you're able to continue to describe what you're seeing and that will keep you in the state — the relaxed state that you can continue sharing information from. You're doing very well.

A: I feel there's a pulsing, a swirling. Like I'm the center of a torus, and there's pulsing around me. Feels good, and yet it feels overwhelming, and I'm feeling fatigued by it, and yet also enjoying it because it feels vital and strong. There's this pulsing.

R: And are you moving? Is it pulling or are you in one place?

A: Not really. No, it's mostly this toroidal field that's starting in my heart and going out from my body and coming back into the heart all around me. I'm making the center of **a torus**.
[See Symbols Glossary]

R: Beautiful, and the energy is flowing through you?

A: Yeah, there's a lot of energy moving through me, especially in my hands and feet. There's a tingling sensation; it's quite strong. There's secondary toruses [toroi] in each of the hands and each of the feet that are pulsing, and they're generating current. Also, there's one in my heart. There's one in each of my hands. There's one in each of my feet. There's one in my hara or the dantian area. Well, I guess there's one [torus] in each of the energy centers — each of the chakra centers. The strongest ones are the one in my third eye and there's a larger one — there's a fountain which is more like a current; it's not my energy center. It's a portal that creates an egg around me. That's the crown, but it goes around to the tips of my feet and connects back in with the toruses that are at my feet. There's a whole energy matrix around me right now and through me, and I'm part of it. I'm generating it. It's me. It's my energetic body. I feel my energetic body.

R: That's wonderful. I'd love to get to know that body more. So you can continue to describe everything that you notice, as you notice it.

A: There's also a center of it, where it pulses in the roof of my mouth, but it's just a reflection point of the others. Basically, what I'm experiencing is the Alex Grey paintings of the Sacred Mirrors [they depict the energetic map of the body]. I'm feeling the energy system; it's pretty much. . . It's identical to his drawing. I'm feeling that it's wanting to pull me. It's activating. Each of the centers are activating and generating. They're building, and there's a pulling sensation, pulling me into the black hole in the center of the torus. There's a sensation that's trying to pull me into it, and there's a void there and that's where I guess unconsciousness is and entering into the dream state, so I keep falling into it, and I'm trying to stay in the conscious realm of it and not slip into the black hole of it. It's building and all around and in my body.

I'm a generator, an actual generator. It's turned on, and it's self-perpetuating a current that's going out in all directions — up and out and back in again in that toroidal donut shape, but there's multiples of them. They're communicating with the whole energetic body system, so there's one complete one that's my whole body. There's smaller ones at each of my energy centers and each of my hands and feet. Even then, there's a smaller one in each cell. There is a wave synching up to work together to generate one energetic auric field. It's resetting and sending waves of energy up through, pulsing up through my legs, through my arms; there's a whole energetic wash happening right now. It's an energetic shower. There's these subtle buzzing waves with tides — waves that come in, waves that go out, lapping the shore of me.

Each cell is communicating with each energy center, and then each major center and then the whole, and now I am the vertex in the greater whole. It's trying to come online and repair the discordant energy that comes from the mind activity and from all the technology, especially the phones and the WiFi. In this place at the edge of sleep and waking, [I am] tapping back into the generator and getting my system back into its connection to itself. It's generating this heat that is stimulating and relaxing at the same time. I feel like I'm experiencing electric shock therapy, like when you go to the physical therapist, and they put the current on you. I feel like that's happening all through my body right now.

R: **Wonderful. Very, very good. Allow that energy to continue to do the work, the healing work, and bringing all systems into balance, online, and into coherence.**

A: There's an orgasmic pulse that's spreading over my third eye and wrapping around my eyes and allowing a deep state of relaxation and reset as it's shuttering. If you look closely, you'll be able to see it fluttering. There's an orgasmic portal connecting my feet and my hands to my third eye.

R: **Very good.**

A: They're all fluttering in the same peristalsis *[rhythmic, wave-like, involuntary muscle]* contractions but the opposite. They're outward, expanding, and pulsing as they relax and release and then pull back down on themselves. There's a toroidal generator field to it. It's an orgasmic generator. No, I guess it's a chi generator. It's a chi generator that keeps digesting the chi as it enters into the black hole and then spreads it out again. It's also starting to activate my root and then my sacrum is also now starting to pulsate and ripple.

R: Good. A chi generator, and now also your root and the sacral is being activated?

A: Yes, all systems are activating; the root is vibrating. The third eyes is also now in the shimmering kundalini reset, and the hands and the feet are building in heat and energy. There's a current that's connecting the legs. The whole system is coming online and moving up the spine and causing pulsing contractions, orgasmic contractions, up the spine and out from the center — the center, but it's a fractal center. It's pulsing out from the center of the heart out into the whole body and then every single cell is doing the same thing, so it's quite pleasant.

R: Very good. I'm happy you're having this experience and all the systems are coming online and balancing with each other. Share with me what's happening next as it's happening.

A: There's a shift in the visual field. Before it was blank and gray, and now there's light forming and creating more pattern and more intentional pattern as the generator is doing its work. It's culminating a picture in the third eye. It's getting brighter. It's getting really bright as the system's building and generating energy. There's a brightness and focusing of a picture, almost like it turned on, like an old-time movie projector, and it's starting to warm up; it's trying to put the image on the screen, but it's still blurry, and it hasn't come into focus yet.

R: Yeah, so now you can start to focus on it and start talking. You can describe the colors, the images. As you speak about it, it will become more clear.

A: It's swirling and it's pulsing. It's grainy, and it's getting more clear. There was a moment where it went totally clear for a second, then it went back to static again. It opened up a window into an... All of a sudden, it's actually not grainy. It's actually not an image, it's actually. . . There was a film, there was a barrier in place, and it's dissolving. It dissolved for a second and gave me a completely clear. . . Like it's when you're driving down the road and you've got your windows up in the car and they're kind of fogged up, and then you roll down the windows. Suddenly, you can see perfectly clear out the windows. It's like that sensation actually, but it seemed as though there was a window up and now the window went down for a second. There's a scene looking down at a planet. Very dark, it was at night. There was a lot of light generated from another source of light than electricity. They were more bio. . .there was like a living element to the light. It was a very big scene, and it was very dynamic with a lot of layers. It was only like a split second, and then the window went back up again.

R: What are you looking at now?

A: Right now I'm looking at. . . I guess it's a window pane. I can't tell; there's like a veil. I'm looking at a veil, or like a translucent, like a cloudy. . .can't see through it. It's like there's a film; there's a cloudy film over my third eye.

R: Yeah. Okay, very good. When you look down to your body, do you have a body over there?

[She now dropped into a deeper trance and shifted to speak from her Higher Self perspective.]

HS: Well, sort of, it's a hologram. It's me, Ava, but it's not. It's a holographic reflection of something larger that's just reflecting Ava. Ava's just the holographic picture that has the illusion of matter, so that it can navigate Earth. In this space, it's the bridge in between the hologram or the body of Ava and the. . . the bigger matrix of the larger chi-generating matrix of all the fabric of space-time, right where all these holograms projected back. In reality, we're all just part of this energetic grid. From this space, I can see the layer that is the hologram, and I also can see that the hologram is just the film itself.

Actually, I was looking at the film, the hologram. I was looking at the hologram from the inside out. That's what I was looking at. I was looking at the hologram of Ava from the inside out. Instead of normally in a mirror, you see her from the outside. Looking into [back at] her. She sees things from the inside, looking out. Underneath that layer is the film, because that's where consciousness is projected, or consciousness is the film, in a way. The projector is showing on the screen; the screen is [how we perceive] consciousness. The projector is beyond consciousness. It's the universal [all] and so, at this point, it seems as though I'm dropping below the layer of the projection of Ava and looking at the film of consciousness underneath it, at the energy matrix.

I'm seeing her energy matrix beneath the hologram. Well, there's the hologram that. . . There's the [perceived] "physical" hologram, then there's the energetic hologram underneath. I'm looking at that right now. That is all just still a hologram; when you drop underneath that, that's where you can get into the full matrix — the whole fabric of space-time. That's where we can. . .you can move. So right now, I'm underneath the hologram of the body and underneath the hologram of the energy, and I'm looking out at the energetic imprint.

R: **Thank you so much. Can you share more about the hologram of the body?**

HS: The hologram of the body is a specially designed reflection, from a story of a consciousness that's wanting to project. There's the infinite potential realm; There's the infinite energetic realm; and there's a drop of consciousness that has an agenda or has a goal, or it has an intention to manifest and form in order to be on the planet. The hologram is the sustained consciousness projection into three dimensions. It has the illusion of feeling solid when you're in the hologram itself. When you're in the holographic program, it all feels very solid and real. Most people live in that [consensus] reality that we are solid and Earth is real.

Deep down, the way that it was all designed, it's actually not physical; you're starting to realize that with science when they say that it's actually 99.9% space and there's just a tiny fraction of matter. Even that fraction of matter, if you go down small enough, is also not matter. Technically, the hologram is just the persistent illusion that has the [energetic] density that is perceived as solid. From the other side, it is really just an energy mapping system that is dense enough to hold itself together and exist in space-time; to exist in the three-dimensional reality. So the one can navigate the soul through the physical dimension. None of it is actually physical. It's all a holographic projection, and there's these different levels and so. . .

R: Beautiful. And you brought her to a place that she saw this planet fly through the window when it went down and became clear.

HS: She thought it was a planet; it is not a planet. It's very large. It's not a planet she was looking at. She was looking at the wormhole that connects one back to the infinite realms where one can travel through space-time. It looked like a planet. She saw darkness and she saw light. She thought that she saw the edges of it, so she assumed that it was a sphere. Actually, she was just seeing a small opening into something much larger, and the edges appeared to be circular. It made the illusion of a sphere, but it's not. It's inside out.

All of reality is an illusion of inside out. It's all a mirror reflection, hologram projection of oneself. It appears to be a sphere, but it's actually the toroidal field [viewed] from looking down into the center point, where it falls into an infinity of infinite smallness. You're actually looking at the singularity point, but it's actually just the center of the torus that you can't see past that. It's the event horizon of the black hole. You can't see past it, so she was looking down, well, from herself. She was thinking that she was looking down into a sphere, but really, what she was looking at was the tunnel that goes down into infinity and back out the other side of the larger torus. She just misunderstood what she was looking at.

R: **Okay, thank you for clarifying. Is it appropriate for her to travel through it to go to the other side so we can learn from that side too?**

HS: Okay.

R: **Thank you so much, so you can travel now. You can also describe it as you travel and as you arrive. What do you notice?**

HS: Well, there's an illusion that you're in a bubble, a circular spaceship, a circular vessel, because you're in the very center of the torus in that moment, navigating the current, navigating the infinite field. The infinite field, it is much more of a toroidal shape, and the sphere is actually just the single point in the center. That is the limited perception of your...your visual capacity. It's an illusion, when you think you're in a sphere or you think you're in this bubble, but you're actually part of the whole torus. It's designed into the system, because consciousness can't quite grasp being in the entire torus at once. It's overwhelming; it pulls; it feels like you're being annihilated and being pulled in infinite directions because, well, you are.

We've recognized that [human] consciousness can't quite move through the torus, because that's the Oneness consciousness, and it's too much at once. There's an illusion built into the hologram to allow one to rest in one space in the torus and feel it as a sphere. When you find the center of it, you're in the sphere of it. When you're feeling pulled or you're feeling spun out, then you're not in the center of your own torus. You're being spun around and around and around, and that's depleting. You're actually on the right track. If you're experiencing the illusion of being in the sphere, then you're actually in the center of the toroidal experience, which is then where you can access the wormhole, as it's actually a tunnel. An infinite tunnel, not a sphere, but it's inside out because that's how consciousness can understand it.

R: **Wonderful. Now you're moving through and arriving to the other side of it.**

HS: It's big.

R: **Tell me more.**

HS: Yes. Oh, yes, it's that place again. Let's see. It's the night terror place that she experienced a lot as a child and in her dreams. It's so big, it's maddening. It's too much for the human.

R: **She can move herself through it gently and safely. She can pass this without any problems. Safe, moving to the next place.**

HS: Once you've turned inside out, it's quite relaxing. All the things you've been holding on to are no longer relevant. Once you've surrendered, it's much more; it's very relaxing to be the whole torus and to recognize that you're infinite consciousness and you're not bound to the sphere of the body. We think that we're the energetic sphere, which we are in the hologram projection. Once you reach through to the other side and allow yourself to be annihilated by the toroidal pull in all directions at once, then it's actually quite relaxing. You actually feel like you've turned yourself inside out and are now looking at yourself from the outside looking in. Suddenly, your self feels like a small, beautiful, little thing, then you look around, and it's infinite around, and it's okay. In this place it almost appears as though each individual human being looks the way when we look up at the stars and we see individual lights. It almost sort of appears as that, where each individual being seems like a dot of light, but if you go in closer, a whole, entire galaxy or a whole universe in that dot of light. It's not an illusion. You are not on a sphere looking out into infinity. It's inside out from that; it's actually all infinities in the drop, and we're looking in at an infinite picture that's infinite, that gets infinitely smaller and smaller as you look in. As above and so below; it's not just infinitely big — the Universe — it's actually [also] infinitely small.

R: Beautiful. What else are you showing her now?

HS: We're letting her feel what it feels like to be space with no boundary, no edge, just space. I'm letting her get used to no longer being Ava and no longer being a being, no longer being human. Just letting her get used to the idea of being space and being bigger than the whole planet and bigger than her own body and bigger than the whole universe and seeing all of that as these tiny dots and letting her get used to being very big. This is the bigness. This is the night terrors she was experiencing — feeling the bigness, the vastness of the expanse of all existence. Most humans aren't able to stand that realm. She withstood it more than most, but it terrified her, and she also was rather fascinated by it.

R: Thank you for allowing her to experience it now in this peaceful way. Sounds enjoyable. What else is she experiencing? How would that help her now?

HS: This will help her as she remembers to take steps to reset and calibrate her energetic system, so that she can better navigate her hologram program instead of letting it be hijacked. It's very easy for some technologies to hijack the energetic system, distort it, and deplete it; that's why she's feeling tired. Well, she's also...her hologram is also experiencing the shedding process, so that's natural to feel the tiredness, but this is a reminder to help her not let herself get hijacked by the technology and to interface with it from a more sovereign place. We're just letting her feel herself turned inside out, so that she can realize that it's safe to be this big. She thinks she's going to explode being this big, so we're letting her feel the vastness of being turned inside out.

R: Wonderful, you mentioned shedding. What do you mean by that? What is she shedding?

HS: On her moon time [menstrual shedding].

R: Okay. Then you started by showing her today all the systems of the toroidal fields of her hands, her feet, her body. Energy centers. Can you share why you showed that to her?

HS: She needed a reset. She had gotten a little bit distracted in her own personal dramas in life and then had allowed the phone to hijack her energetic system.

R: I see. Now is it all in harmony and wellness? Is it all in alignment?

HS: Yes, she's still getting accustomed to being turned inside out. Yes, her energy system is strong; currents are strong. Her system is recalibrating and resetting and awakening herself and reminding itself to dance in unison. Yes.

R: Good. So she can relax into it even deeper now.

HS: Okay.

R: Even deeper than before. I'd like for you to continue from the most appropriate place for her to continue to receive information. The most appropriate for what would like to come forward today. You can arrive to that place now and continue from there. What are you showing her now?

HS: There's an abyss of terror and pressure that wants to pull. The mind attached to the human body is still pulling on her. She's resisting being turned completely inside out in order to leave the body, so she's still in it.

R: Is it safe for her to do so?

HS: It's safe; it terrifies her.

R: How can I support her to do so? To relax more into it? Maybe you can show her the process and she can look at it as it happens, so she can relax into it more. Is there anything you can show her so it will help her to relax?

HS: Spot right behind her eyes. Spot behind her eyes where there's. . . behind the eyes and behind the jaw there's a spot deep inside. Final spot to let go of. The ultimate spot where the soul relaxes and releases from the binds of the hologram system. She's having a hard time letting go of it.

R: Let's breathe into that spot. Does that spot have a consciousness of its own?

HS: Fear.

R: Fear. Okay, so let's allow that fear to be communicated and allow the fear to come forward, so it can express itself. Hello.

Fear: I'll be lost forever. I can't go any further. I'll get lost forever. I won't be able to come back.

R: So you're afraid that if you let go of that part, you'd never be able to return to that body, and you'll be lost.

Fear: Yes, I like this body. I don't want to go.

R: Yeah. Yeah. If you will be reassured that you'll be able to return to the body easily, would you be able to let go?

Fear: Okay, sure.

R: Let's... Yes, let's take another deep breath. I'd like to speak with the Higher Self please, so you can hear as well. May I speak with the Higher Self please?

HS: Okay.

R: Hello. Hi, am I speaking to the Higher Self?

HS: Yes.

R: Thank you so much for coming forward, so this point of fear within her has this thought that if it would let go, it wouldn't be able to return to the body.

HS: Yes, it's the fundamental program to transcend the hologram program. It's standard.

R: It's standard, so it's safe for her.

HS: It's a mechanism; it must be overridden.

R: Okay. Can we do that now?

HS: They have to choose; they have to give the consent to override the system.

R: Okay. So let's take a deep breath. May I speak to this point of fear, please? Hello. Did you hear that information?

Fear: Yes.

R: Are you willing to give the consent to override that system?

Fear: Yes.

R: Thank you so much. Take a deep breath now. May I speak with the Higher Self please?

HS: Okay.

R: Would you start the process of overriding that?

HS: Yes.

R: Thank you. Describe what you're doing as you do it please.

HS: There is an unprogramming. Each cell must let go at the same time; each cell then informs [the others]. Each cell is constellated around a certain group. Each group is constellated by a larger field. It's got to be unprogrammed. It can either be removed from the cells all the way up to the whole consciousness, or it can be removed from consciousness and then coordinated down into the cells. If the cells have been in contraction for a period of time, then they won't always respond to the override from consciousness. It has to be done individually from the scan [referring to Vipassana-style, body scan meditation], and the intention sent to each cell through vibration. Let's see if we can do it from both directions at once to help to override the [base hologram] system completely.

We are sending vibrational current from consciousness down through each of the sub-centers down to each of the cells. It's kind of like the same as the federal government, state governments, city governments, local governments — like the same kind of concept; each one is regulating a smaller amount, and then it's not overwhelming for any one system. It's a surprisingly similar system, although without the hierarchy and without the bureaucracy, but it's just a communication pathway system, like in tree branches and roots systems. It's the same system, except that there is a backdoor connector. When you think all the different routes are reaching different endpoints, [for example, in Earth tree's root nutrient systems], ultimately on the other side, all the routes come back together in one point. There's actually a way to access the system from the tips of the roots all at once and from consciousness itself from the center. We're working on aligning the vibration from both points. It's infinite points, right? In the third dimension, it looks like all the root tips are all separate, but they're not; they all come together — each root tip actually is consciousness. There's a singular point [of consciousness]. I'm going to work on both sides.

R: **Thank you for doing it. I really appreciate it. I know she's going to appreciate it very much. Then you can continue to share with me the progress. Take a few moments to do the work and then take a moment to update me. I'll be here waiting to hear more information. You're doing very well. Thank you so much.**

HS: She's been so good for the last seven years not eating any sugar, and yet she ate a little bit of sugar several times in the last week, and she knows that this does not support her system. It frazzles out her system. We're going to remind her to stick to her commitment.

R: **Very well.**

HS: We're working through her feet. We're accessing. . . We're accessing it through her third eye and her hands and her feet all at once. Clearing the blocks here.

R: **Very good; thank you.**

HS: We worked up through the system. We worked up through her feet into her arms and her upper body, are now getting closer to the source in the back, in the center of the head. Okay, she's more ready now. It will continue to work its way through.

R: Very good. So as you're relaxing more into it, would you like to take us to the next place where there's information to share with us today?

HS: Just a moment.

R: Take your time. Releasing more. Letting it all go.

HS: It seems as though there is a language emanating from the pulses and coming from the hands and the feet.

R: Very good. Allow that. This language when it goes all the way up to the vocal cords, allow the vocal cords to express it. Tell me more about what's happening there now.

HS: There is a weaving of light up through the cord, through the spinal cord into the teeth. There's a code coming through. I'm working on translating it. Her body has tapped into the hologram. Her body is tapped into the universal fabric. There is a light current going from the universal current through the universal matrix up through her feet and through her hands; she's working to translate it. We're helping to tune the hologram to receive the translation.

R: Thank you. You can continue describing what's happening as it happens.

HS: It's a wave of light with all sorts of stories. It's like there's all the information that's on the Internet. There's everything. The whole Akashic record is embedded in this thread of light, and it's all moving through her body. It's an infinite ocean with all these textures and all these stories and all these pulses, and it's so overwhelming. She doesn't know how to filter the translation; there's so much coming through; it's everything all at once, and she is not quite sure how to narrow down the field in order to be able to understand and translate.

THE UNIVERSAL CURRENT

R: Is that energy that flows through her with all those stories, does it have a consciousness of its own?

HS: It is consciousness.

R: It is consciousness. May I speak to this consciousness, please?

HS: Yes.

R: Hello.

Consciousness: Hello.

R: Thank you so much for coming forward today. I'd like for you to share with me anything that you find relevant for today. Would you do that?

Consciousness: Can you be more specific?

R: Yes, can we go, for example, to the moment of the evolution of consciousness from where we stopped the last time [during the third session]? **Can we continue from there?** [The aspect of her Higher Self from Session 3 came forward to continue.]

HS: I believe we were speaking about the nature of consciousness brought into form. There was a moment where organisms had no awareness of existing; they were just driven by impulses. Then there was a moment in the shift of the evolution of consciousness, where there was an awareness that one existed, yet it was a background thought. There was an awareness of it, but it didn't matter very much. The being of the organism was still driven by the impulses.

There was this awareness that one existed. From that moment, ironically, the intention was to create connection between consciousness and form — Source energy and form — but instead it had the impact of creating the illusion of separation. Once one was aware of itself existing, then that was the birth of the illusion of separation, therefore the birth of fear. This was an unexpected development in the evolution of consciousness for the thought was that there would be the telepathic connection with everything.

When the boundary of one organism with limited consciousness was created, suddenly the consciousness could no longer perceive consciousness outside of its form. It then saw itself as a separate entity; therefore, [it] needed to survive and needed to do what it needed to do in order to survive. It had awareness of its own "mortality." Then unfortunately, once consciousness woke up inside form, the illusion of separation began.

The illusion of separation is the birth of separation sickness, with the primary symptom being fear, which then leads to all the other aspects. And so, the hope was that with the evolution of consciousness, form, energy, mind, and intelligence...the hope was that the separation sickness could be remedied by the greater awareness of the energetic realm beyond one's own individual, physical form. Unfortunately, trying to bring telepathy and awareness of energetic forms beyond the physical form can be a tricky one, when the mind goes to fear and starts producing fear responses, which then creates certain hormonal patterns, which then lead to things like cortisol and stress.

Once cortisol has been created, once that fear response mechanism happens from the surprise of suddenly feeling separate from source, therefore, feeling alone, therefore, panicking. What results from that panic is the energetic surprise or feeling of somehow being separated or cut off. That energetic surprise [and contraction] manifested itself in the vibration, which now we would call cortisol, or a hormone of stress that didn't exist at the time. It was merely an energetic expression of the surprise of the separation.

This has been a very persistent, unexpected manifestation of putting consciousness and awareness of existence into physical form. The thought in the experiment was that given enough time and evolution, the brain could evolve to the point of being able to hold the amount of consciousness required to understand telepathy, beyond instinctual compulsion, because that's what organisms had been driven by before. There had been an instinctual compulsion, and that was what allowed them to stay in the vibration of telepathy and move as a unit. Once a being was aware of itself as existing in an individualized form, that was the birth of the illusion of separation.

Again, the hope is that as the beings evolved, and as consciousness evolved in that form and was able to better inhabit that form, that it would then be able to then perceive telepathically and recognize that it was not separate from Source — therefore, heal the separation sickness that resulted from separating consciousness into physical form, which wasn't exactly the expected result.

This doesn't happen in all species; some species are able to maintain their intuitive connection to Source, their intuitive connection to All That Is. That did happen in other experiments on other planets, when the atmosphere wasn't as dense or the density of the hologram wasn't as dense. Unfortunately, on the Earth experiment, with the nature of the hologram having density to manifest and a physical 3D illusion of solidness, [the illusion of separation happened.]

In that [Earth] density there have been times in the evolution of species where they have forgotten, and there's been waves. . .there's been certain different wavelengths over time and space where they have been able to access the energetic realm and recognize the connection to all that is, and other times where they've forgotten. So there are these waves of forgetting and waves of remembering when these beings are aware that they are actually still connected to everything, and then the illusion, the very persistent illusion, that they are separate, and therefore [seemingly] alone. This [has created] a very interesting array of manifestations of different trajectories, and the evolution of species has been a very new experiment, mixing the density of planet Earth with the level of consciousness brought in and the energetic, the energetic imprint [of fear].

There was some reference in the past [sessions] to the virus of fear, but in a sense, it's not necessarily that a virus came in and corrupted the system, which is the story that is believed when one is in the separation illusion. It's actually [just what] happened when consciousness woke up inside individualized form and forgot that it was everything. It was just a fundamental nature of consciousness awakening within an individual form, that unfortunately or fortunately, as however you would describe the nature of what IS, without judgment fear was birthed.

[It was birthed within] the illusion of separation that happened when consciousness awoke in an individualized form complex enough to acknowledge its own existence and its own mortality. It has been a perpetual experiment ever since, to determine whether or not a being could evolve to the point and become aware enough of its energetic system and of its consciousness to perceive beyond its individualized self [and return to feeling connected once more]. For a long period of time, that did happen on planet Earth; consciousness did evolve to that point, but It gets to a certain place where it can't seem to maintain that anymore, and then there's a reset.

So, it seems to be these waves of remembering and waves of forgetting, as in previous times we have discussed this cycle. **(R: Yes.)** We are currently in a period of time where the consciousness has evolved to a certain point where it is now starting to remember again; it is starting to remember that it is connected to all, and it is no longer completely under the illusion of the separation. It seems as though the potential trajectory of what's happening right now in human consciousness and Earth consciousness is that there is a remembering. A lot of what's happening right now is to help augment and inspire this remembering that we are not just this individualized consciousness placed into an individualized form. [We are starting to remember that this] is all an illusion and that we are all these energetic beings tapped into a greater matrix. When we relax the mind and are able to remember this, then the telepathic connections can begin. Then the fear, that separation sickness, is able to be resolved and healed.

We're at a culmination point right now where we've gone through many different phases of evolution, and we've actually gotten to quite an amazing, sweet spot with the complexity of human ingenuity and intelligence separated into individual form, or the illusion of individual form, waking up and understanding its connection to All That Is. We're right on the precipice of another great awakening and evolutionary jump point in the nature of humanity and the Earth itself — because of this awakening beyond the separation sickness that happened when consciousness was separated and placed into individualized organisms. We're at a really beautiful and poignant part of the cycle. At this point, human ingenuity, intellect, and technology have expanded to a certain point through the separation sickness; that is now finally transcending its own [illusion of] separation sickness by the technology; that is finally [being] produced and created is able to actually prove that we are not separate beings. We are not [just] separate consciousnesses and individuals in form. Technology has finally caught up to the reality that can break through the barrier of the fear that is produced as a symptom of separation sickness, or the illusion of separation.

R: **Wonderful. Yeah, I can see that. Thank you for explaining that. Can you share with me about how the design of the human came to be? The design of the different systems of the human body, and how that was created?**

HS: Again, the human body is a hologram. It's a hologram program that has been run as an experiment on other dimensional experiments. However, the density wasn't as strong to [generate and] be in the same kind of gravity that we have here on Earth; [the density/gravity] that allows these systems of earth, air, water, and fire to interact in the way that they are. It [the human body hologram] has the same amount of consciousness mixed in, with a somatic awareness of being able to feel the skin with consciousness and energy. And so, there was a hologram program working on other [planet] system, designed by another team, but the balance was different. There was not as much density on that planet; consciousness was higher. Separation sickness was not present.

So the idea was that Earth was designed to have more of a persistent illusion of the three-dimensional, the solidness. Part of the Earth design had the embedded function of being a very persistent illusion that wasn't meant to be penetrated. The idea was... What would happen when we brought in consciousness and energy and matter and form and density with love and a capacity of compassion? Other beings on other planets had more of a telepathic connection, yet there wasn't as much of an individualized personality and individualized love. The idea of the human being was to allow duality to come together and create union. How can we create the sensation of Divine Union in the duality of the very persistent illusion of separation? It was a paradox. Could we break through the illusion of separation with enough connection of individualized consciousness, merged with love and compassion and feeling and forgiveness in the density of the body?

Could we transcend the density of separation sickness if we brought enough consciousness into a form? The human being was an idea birthed from witnessing many different other types of organisms suffer with the separation sickness once consciousness was placed into an individualized form. We remembered that there was a program, a holographic program running on another system, and we thought that it might be well adapted to this system, once we added the component of the more individualized personality and heart and consciousness along with it. [The other] experiment was more telepathic; it was more of a hive creature. It was more of a communal system that worked more like a murmuration of birds; the species worked more in the telepathic realm.

R: Mmhmm.

HS: Then the question was. . . Could we [create an organism that could] reach a higher state of bliss, the sensation of Divine Union, of merging back with Source and feeling connected to Source, in the paradox of an increased density that is Planet Earth? [The density of Earth] which allows us to sculpt in a way that we're not able to sculpt on other planets in other dimensions. It was a unique opportunity to bring together consciousness and matter and density and energy and love. Perhaps that combination of ingredients would allow for the possibility to transcend separation sickness and truly be able to create the quintessence [perfection] of the human being, which is an individualized drop of consciousness completely connected to Source consciousness at the same time. This is the ultimate, poetic resolution to the reason why the Big Bang happened in the first place, or [why] consciousness decided to explode itself into infinite bits. Because it was tired of being everything and having no edge and no form.

The idea was. . .how [can we] resolve the fundamental dissatisfaction or that fundamental longing to feel connected? The idea of the human being was to allow that possibility to happen. It took a long time because we had to sculpt species on planet Earth that were suitable to this atmosphere and suitable to this oxygen level. It was many, many iterations of slowly sculpting the energy, which then created many different forms that are in the archeological record through bones of previous animals and beings of other times. It was all a long, slow process of sculpting energy to create a form that could hold the holographic program from the other dimensions.

I know that doesn't quite make sense, because it was a holographic program, why couldn't it just be instantly programmed? Taking a holographic program and working it through actual matter and form takes what you call time. Outside of time, it's pretty instantaneous. It actually is a very graceful evolutionary experiment, but slowed down in the density of matter, it takes place over billions of years. It's a paradox; it didn't really take that long, but it did, because that's how long it took to sculpt the clay in 3D, but outside of 3D, it was much faster. There was an elegant exploration of letting consciousness itself choose the direction it wanted to go, while very gently, sort of nudging it in certain directions in order to help it integrate with the holographic program of the homo-sapien-type being. Does that make sense?

R: Yeah, yeah, I do understand it. I'm sure that also by listening to the recording and going deeper into it, it will be even more clear. What came to mind is that it feels to me like here on Earth we speak that we have maybe a few bodies like the physical body, emotional body, mind. There're different schools of thought that are separating the layers of the bodies in different ways. I'd like to learn from you about those different layers that the humans are being designed to...to have a full system. Can you elaborate about that?

HS: Okay. So, humans are very dualistic creatures. That's the nature of the hologram. It makes sense that they see them as these individual layers. You see, like the physical body and the energetic body and the astral body and the causal body and the etheric bodies. There're all these separate layers wrapped around each other. That's the way duality perceives layers. In a symphony, you've got many different instruments playing, and they're playing different frequencies, but it's all creating one inner-woven tapestry of sound that you hear as one beautiful symphony. So that's really more what's going on.

Yes, there's the different layers that can be seen as different layers and in trying to understand the different layers, it's nice to separate them and see them as separate, but they're not separate. It's like trying to say that the violin is the symphony, or the violin is this layer, and the cello is that layer. It's only when they all are together in one unit and one symphony — when they've come together and connected, that then you hear the true sound of the music. It's the same.

Yes, you've got the physical body, the energetic body, the astral body, the etheric body, the causal body, and the karmic bodies. There're the many different layers that make up the hologram. Yes, you're right; it's layers, like in that [software] program, Photoshop. There are these different theoretical layers, and you can individually manipulate each layer. Ultimately, they don't exist. Ultimately, it's just pixels [singularities] and thought [vibrations]. Ultimately, in order to create [digital] art, [the vision needs] to be translated; it's going to need to be condensed. When you merge all the different layers and you put them together, you flatten it and they become one thing. The layers become one piece of art with many different combined layers.

In a sense, that's what we're looking at. The human, the human brain, the human mind, when it's trying to understand complexities, it separates things into layers. It's true; there are the layers. The layers exist, and layers are there for a reason. Each individual layer would mean nothing without the other layers. It only makes music; it only makes life when its layers are actually woven into one fabric. Each of the layers you could consider one thread. Ultimately, it's one complete system, and they can't work separately. You can't separate them, like in Photoshop. It's only separated in the illusion of the computer. Technically, I guess you could print out each individual layer on pieces of paper, but fundamentally, for art to be considered the art itself, it needs to be merged.

R: So beautiful. I'm wondering about this evolution of the consciousness through the different beings and creating those different layers. For example, I would say there is a different layer that exists between, say, an animal and human. There might be another layer that was created that has not existed in other animal forms or plant forms. So I'm wondering if we can learn about this evolution of creating humans with multi-layers of consciousness that are able to be experienced. Do you have information about that?

HS: Oh, yes, that's what we were talking about before. That is the place where consciousness, actual Source Consciousness, being aware that one exists, and aware that one is an individualized unit, and to be able to self reflect on itself. It's the extra layer of the witness consciousness that allows one to reflect and have a conversation with oneself. That aspect is not present in most animals. There have been a few animals that have evolved to have that witnessing aspect. This is the place that we're talking about; [this is what] created the separation sickness. The intention was not to do that.

The intention was to allow that level of consciousness to be fully connected to Source, to be able to truly have God consciousness embodied in form and be able to experience other while also experiencing self at the same time. The idea was Divine Union. Unfortunately, what happened when the witness consciousness was inserted into the consciousness of the human being program is that one was able to reflect upon itself and see itself as the individualized unit and recognize that it existed and that it would die, and that it was somehow separate from other.

That is the place that we're talking about. That is where we worked with what was evolving on Earth. These beings that followed impulse and instinct and knew that they were a being, but they didn't think about it; there wasn't the witness consciousness that they had to get into alignment with themselves. That's the [primary] difference. For a long time, even the Homo sapien did not have that. For many tens of thousands of years in the Homo sapien evolution, it was more driven by instinct. It was more driven by an awareness of....not saying that there wasn't an awareness of existence, but there wasn't a witness reflecting and judging that, or analyzing that. It just was.

If you ever watch an animal, like say you watch a cat, it's not questioning the way it's walking through the room. Right? It's walking through the room perfectly as it is; it is in perfect alignment with itself. It's not questioning its existence as it walks through the room. But with that, it's also not questioning what's really going on here. It's not questioning, "Who am I?" It's not questioning, "What is life? What is that?" It's just walking through the room.

There's a difference when one can actually have self-inquiry of "Who am I?" That's really it, right there. That's the sweet spot, when the witness consciousness wakes up to itself and starts asking, "Who am I?" with actual, deep earnestness and not just superficially, when it's truly asking that question from self-inquiry. Right there, that's the access point into Divine Union. That's the sweet spot that we've been aiming for in all of the evolution of all planets and all organisms — is this ability to be able to reflect upon itself, notice itself, recognize the illusion of separation. Face it. Ask, "Who am I?" and then emerge. Emerge into Oneness that way. That is the portal that we've offered humanity.

Other species have not yet received that possibility. The cat's not sitting there washing itself and wondering why it's washing itself. It's just gonna wash itself. It's aware that it exists and that it needs to wash itself, but it's not questioning itself. It's not asking, "What am I? Am I a cat? Who am I? Why do I exist?" That ability to witness and reflect back on itself is not present.

That was the gift of consciousness that we added to the Homo sapien evolutionary process because we thought that the idea was that the human being had evolved to a significant place of consciousness and form. If given that opportunity, given that gift of self-reflection, of asking and being able to ask the question, "Who am I?" in order to find the portal back into Oneness, that could be the ticket back home. That would allow the entire game, the entire experiment of exploding consciousness into infinite bits, that right there. We've found we've finally created the portal back home through that ability to self inquire.

In order to get to that place of self-inquiry, we must face one's own mortality and face the greatest fear, face oneself, yourself, and really ask that question, "Who Am I?" A lot of times you get caught up in the fear of, "Who am I then, if I'm going to die?" The greatest existential fear is the fear of annihilation. So It's challenging. Thus far the human being has not... Some human beings are doing that work. They're finding that portal back to Oneness through self-inquiry — Ramana Maharshi's whole inquiry line on, "Who am I?"

This is it exactly the point of the whole experiment — is reminding humans that this gift that you were given wasn't meant to cause separation sickness — that when seen in its true light is actually a portal beyond death and into the experience of Oneness.

Ultimately, this is what the whole experiment is about. It's about merging the consciousness of Oneness with the realm of duality, so we can enjoy Oneness and other at the same time. We can live in the paradox and reach that true Divine Union potential.

R: **Beautiful. I understand more, thank you so much. When was this upgrade for the human given? When were they able to start asking those questions about "Who am I?" and the self-inquiry. You shared with me one upgrade about receiving language. (HS:** Yes.**) I'm wondering if there was a different upgrade that you're referring to now?**

HS: Yes, this was a different upgrade, after language, which allowed them to create connection and tribe, and communicate. They were struggling to communicate telepathically because of the density on planet Earth, while some of the other species were able to. Eventually. . .yes, they were given an upgrade to the synapses in the brain and in the heart, and the electrical system to allow this self-reflection. That happened. . . [Lets] see, in the human timeline and the Earth timeline, where would that have been? I suppose that would have been placed. . . Well, it's actually been in several layers, because it started out. . . How to describe this?

There's been a subtle increase in the capacity for remembering woven into the genetic code over the past tens of thousands of years. Even though the gift was given to humans shortly after, around the same time of language, but it wasn't actually able to be utilized. It lay dormant, except in a few individual members of the population who accessed it. Usually, those were the mystics, those that accidentally or intentionally consumed entheogenic *[something that generates the God awareness within]* plants, animals, or fungi. Only select members of the population were able to access and unlock that dormant kind of code that was put into the DNA of humans.

It's hard to say exactly when it was. It's not even so relevant to say when it was put in because it was put in actually a long time [ago]. It was actually put in before language; it's just, it takes a certain... It was actually put in much, much earlier, almost at the point when Homo erectus turned to Homo sapien. That was when we chose, you know, the human being for this project. The potential was uploaded into the DNA, but the DNA had to come to a certain level of consciousness in order to be able to activate the program. It's been laying dormant for hundreds of thousands of years, except in the unique individuals. Now they're starting to catch up; it's starting to happen on more of a mass scale. Ironically, the separation sickness is also at an exponentially higher scale as well.

It's interesting that the pressure on the system of the separation sickness coming to such a culmination and the fear sickness coming to such a culmination, that it's actually pushing these organisms to finally access this code that's been laying dormant in their system for their evolution for quite a long time. The question isn't so much when was it put in the system because it was designed into the system, as soon as we chose human beings for the experiment. This is the reason why we chose humans — was for this purpose. It was put in at the beginning, but it wasn't able to be accessed because their consciousness hadn't evolved enough to be able to even recognize or to activate the program.

R: So what made you choose humans for this experiment?

HS: Well, that's actually not quite the right question; we did not actually choose humans. We chose the combination of conditions that would allow for a species to evolve that could potentially satisfy all these different areas we were trying to combine. So we set the conditions and then deposited some DNA, and then allowed natural evolution and entropy to do its thing. Humans were what came to be, so it was partially our design. It was partially us inserting some seed DNA from other systems that we knew would work. We knew that a being that has a capacity for a certain-size brain, certain capacity for hand-eye coordination, to be able to interface and interact with other and interact with self in a form that had density and consciousness — there was this bipedal concept of bringing that type of an organism to hold this realm. It wasn't so much that we chose humans, we created a set of conditions that would allow humans to evolve, and we weren't exactly sure what they would look like.

I mean they look different on different planets based on different conditions. In a sense, it was a combination of us choosing a genetic DNA print that could evolve and have rapid possibilities for learning and also had extreme capacity for somatic experiencing, emotional experiencing, energetic, and telepathic experiencing. Ultimately, the human being is many of the best parts of all the different species that have manifested throughout the galaxies and throughout the many different multiverses. All combined and then set into this condition of Earth. Human beings, in a sense, are unique to Earth, and they created themselves, and they rose to the opportunity of the conditions that were given to them. They evolved into utilizing the tools and the capacity that we gave them to transcend some of the other species that stayed more in their animalistic instincts. It wasn't so much that we chose humans, it's that we created a system, or we created a set of conditions that made it ripe for a being to evolve to utilize this gift. It turned out that it was humans that were able to do this.

[*Ava's note:* The word human comes from the Latin word humus, meaning made of earth or ground.]

R: Beautiful, what are the mix of the beings, other types of animals' DNA that are being mixed within the humans? And what are their qualities?

HS: Well, the Human Genome Project is. . .shows you all that information. It's pretty obvious where humans have evolved from at this point. You can see the way that the evolution of different species on Earth have evolved over time. I don't really feel like that's pertinent to the conversation. **(R: Okay)** Is there a more specific question that you'd like in regards to that?

R: I have this feeling that there are different types of beings [star-beings] that are involved in the creation of the humans. I was wondering if we are a mix of other species and if we are effecting each others evolution.

HS: Oh, I see. So you're asking me about the non-Earth beings, the seeds that we brought from other dimensions?

R: I'm curious about how those beings created us and how we influence them? I'm staying general about it because maybe I have the wrong idea about it.

HS: It's not so much that we took specific DNA from, say, the Arcturians, or from the Sirians, or from any of the other Galactic Federation members. It's more that there was a holographic program for life, for intelligent life that's been set on many different planets and their conditions and then evolved to be the species that they are. It's more that we used the holographic programs. Seeds. It's the ones that worked well on other planets. We saw what traits and what things sort of evolved on those planets, then we would use the holographic code itself from those planets and then drop them on to the conditions of Earth. It's not so much that we took DNA from say, a Sirian, or an Arcturian, or one of the other cultures. It was more that we utilized. . . We saw how the program evolved or manifested on that planet and the benefits — the positives and negatives that happened. It's more the code itself. It's the holographic program that was translated. It wasn't so much the physical. . . the physical DNA map. It's the same thing; it's all hologram. It's not actually physical.

Your question is more pointing to, did we gather or do we collect zygotes? Or do we collect eggs and sperm from creatures from other planets? It was more that we accessed the holographic program that was running on those planets that created those beings and then changed it and manipulated it to meet the conditions of this planet. Sometimes there were samples taken of physical species on other planets in order to match their physical manifestation with the hologram program to see where the mutations were occurring in the code.

To answer your question, it seems like you're asking a specific question like, which planets did we bring humans from? It was more like we made a new program based on the other programs. It's a mixture of many of them.

HELLO, CAN YOU HEAR ME?

R: Would you take a moment to do a body scan and bring all the [Ava's] body into harmony before we take a break? How's her body doing?

HS: It's generating a strong pulse. There's still. . . This right ear is still very resistant to our support.

R: Take another deep breath into that place and focus on that place in the right ear. Focus on that place now and allow that energy to come forward to express itself. Hello.

Energy: Hello.

R: How long have you been there?

E: Old.

R: You're old?

E: All along.

R: All along. . . Ahmm. . .and what type of energy are you? Do you have a gender?

E: No.

R: No. So what are you creating in the body?

E: Inflammation.

R: Inflammation. And what are you feeding off?

E: Her channel of hearing.

R: Channel of hearing. Very good. Let's go back to the time when you were created. The moment where you're created; let's see how you came to be. Go back to that time. Be there now and tell me what's happening there. How did you come to be?

E: In the beginning, when the extra currents were given to her to help her survive. Knowing that these extra currents could cause madness but also gave her [an] increased [ability to] channel; there was an inner resistance of the body to channel... Not wanting to hear it. There was a deficiency in the ear and the kidneys. The body was resistant to the mission.

R: How did you enter into her body?

E: It was a dysfunction built into the eustachian tube. There was a contraction and a resistance to the mission. Not wanting to hear it.

R: Okay, very good. Now that she is doing her mission, and she is doing this beautiful way of hearing the information and channeling, I think it's time for you to move on and have another mission. She's already hearing very well and doesn't seem like she needs you anymore, right?

E: I still don't want to hear it.

R: She still doesn't want to hear it? Or you don't want to hear it.

E: I don't want to hear.

R: What don't you want to hear?

E: It's too much. It's too loud — all these people's thoughts. It's too loud, all the information; it's too much.

R: It sounds to me like she's doing a good job in this journey, discerning and collecting what's necessary and blocking out what she doesn't need. Let's ask. Let's ask her if she's wanting to let that go and to release you from your job there. Okay, may I speak with Ava please?

A: Yeah.

R: So, are you willing and ready to release this thing in your ear that was trying to block you from listening, hearing too much?

A: Yeah. It's too late for that now, isn't it? *(joking tone)*

R: Yeah. I think you know why you're here and you're ready to do it. It's time to let it go. Let's take another deep breath. May I speak to this Energy in the ear please?

E: Okay.

R: Did you hear that she is releasing you from you job?

E: Yes.

R: So are you ready to go now?

E: Maybe.

[I continued with the extraction process as I normally do and helped this energy to disconnect from Ava's and move into the Light with love and forgiveness.]

*[**Ava's note:** Everyone has a weak spot, their achilles heel, right? Mine has always been in my ears. As a child, I had recurrent ear infections and was given antibiotics regularly. As an adult, almost anytime I have a cold, it settles into my ears, and they become clogged. Once, my ear drum even ruptured from the pressure. When they become clogged, I lose my audial depth perception, my equilibrium, and I can hear everything I say echoed loudly within my head. I must manually clear them every few minutes. As long as I stay diligent with my diet and silent/listening practice, my ears are mostly clear these days, for which I am immensely grateful. However, I am still aware of their sensitivity. As soon as I eat dairy, sugar, wheat, or slip in my practice, they clog up again. This constant teacher keeps me showing up for myself, otherwise, I suffer.]*

THE COUNCIL GATHERS

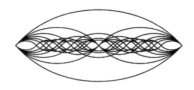

SESSION NINE

After taking a nice break and having something to eat, we agreed to do another, shorter session that would take only an hour or so. I used our keyword, and it was easier to reach a deep trance the second time.

R: What do you notice? Do you feel like you're moving? Or are you in one place?

A: I feel like I'm in a place that's really big and open; there's a dark, indigo-purple current pulsing out from underneath my feet and going out. THAT place [the night terror] . . . I'm supposed to follow it to the council.

R: Very good. So you can follow it now. Describe this as you're following it.

A: There's a sensation that I'm seeing the perspective from being me and looking down and seeing my feet. Every time my feet step, it makes this indigo pulse. I'm also above myself looking down at this being walking. I'm also underneath looking up at this being walking. I'm seeing myself from multiple, different angles, and I'm also seeing myself from the council, looking back at me approaching the council. I see all these things at one time.

R: Nice. When you look at yourself, how do you see yourself? What do you look like?

A: I'm a hologram, a blank hologram. Blank. I can project any image I want onto this blank hologram. It's neutral. It's just the silhouette of a body, androgynous. It could be male or female. There's no characteristics yet. I can choose how I present myself at the council.

R: **Very nice. Walk toward the council. You can see it from all the many angles. Describe what you see as you get closer to the council.**

A: These huge, huge windows of a technology I've never seen on Earth before. It's like big, arched windows, and they have almost a seamless seam, so it's not like individual panes of glass somehow. It's like this. . . curved, bay windows overlooking. . . I think it's overlooking Earth. I think we're up outside the Earth's atmosphere. It's all black. The Earth is pretty small, down below. It's bright, and you can make out the edges. I can make out the Earth. It's not just like a little dot, and it's also not huge. It seems like we're a certain distance up from the Earth's atmosphere. The Earth is about the size of a tennis ball in this scheme of things.

I can see so far. The glass on this ship thing. . .it seems like it actually has different layers. I can see different places. I can see the Earth from some of the windows, and I can see other galaxies and things out of other windows. It somehow seems like the glass has magnified Earth a little bit, but then there's all these other frames that I could look at. There seems to be a ceiling, but it's curved. Everything's curved and whitish-silver. The floor is all open, and the furniture is moving and built into the floor. It's almost like it materializes wherever we need it from the floor. There is a table, a council table. It's sort of floating, but it has one pin in the center that's bringing up the photons of light from the floor to then make the table. I can tell that it can easily. . .if somebody wanted to change the shape of it in any moment, they could. I can manifest a chair if I want it anywhere.

At the same time, I don't actually have a body; I just have this hologram print, so it's sort of irrelevant whether I sit in a chair or not. It's more like an energetic understanding that we are coming together around this table. It doesn't necessarily matter what it looks like so much. It seems like we're a distance. . . We're closer to the Earth than we are now to the Moon because the Moon is much smaller than a tennis ball in our frame of sight. It's small, so the Earth is about the size of a tennis ball in my scene. We're that distance away from the Earth, though not as far as we are from the Moon.

R: **Okay, very good. Thank you for sharing with me. Continue observing and see what's happening next. Is the council already gathered?** [Ava starts to speak from the Higher Self perspective.]

HS: Yeah, the council is gathered. Some are physically present, even though physically is sort of relative, but some of them are projecting their image from elsewhere. We're all holograms. There're different levels of holograms. There are the holograms of those coming from Earth, then there's holograms from those that are meeting from other galaxies. We are all coming together on this. . .it seems like a ship, but it's actually not. It's actually more of the laboratory headquarters, or it's like a safe space. It's a station in the hologram where we can all come and be outside of the matrix, but not fully in 3D and not fully in non-3D. I don't know; it's hard to describe. It's like it's not in the dimension of 3D, but we're meeting; we're still kind of close to Earth, you can see it.

R: **Good. How many beings are in that council?**

HS: There's a lot. It seems to be about. . .   There're these concentric rings, but they're not hierarchical. Everyone moves depending on whether they're speaking or whether they're directly involved with a topic, and then we can shuffle around because we're all holograms. It's really easy to move ourselves about. It's not as slow as on Earth, where you have to get up and walk around the room. You can just sort of instantaneously put yourself where you want to be.

There's a circle of about thirteen members that are actively discussing a topic, but then there's many, many others that are listening and witnessing, and then when they need to speak, then they drop into one of the spots in the inner circle. Some beings are planted in the inner circle because they're actively involved. Some are coming in and out. There's space for everyone. I'm not sure how many people are here? Or how many. . .not people. . .how many beings are here.

R: Thank you so much for sharing with me. It sounds like the main thirteen are the ones that are sharing information. *(HS: Yes.)* Okay. Very good. I would love for you to take a moment and listen to see what is the topic that is being discussed at this moment? What are you guys discussing there?

HS: It seems like there's two or three topics of discussion that are happening simultaneously through telepathic channels. It's almost like computer programs are running, discussing things. It's like there's a little bit more available. It's not just like humans sitting in a boardroom meeting to all be in the same conversation. There's three main topics happening. One is frequency. There's a frequency pod; it's working with all the EMF and all the WiFi currents and all the cell currents and the broadcasting currents. It's working with how to bring the frequency-increasing codes through and how to help them get through all the distortion of all the other frequencies that the humans are emitting through their devices. So, there's one team that's working on. . . I guess you could call it frequency communications.

There's one that's working on international relations and discussing the hotspots of tension and potential violence and nuclear use. There's a team that's looking at the international climate of what's happening right now and keeping an eye on everything that's going on.

There's a third that's looking at the environmental systems of Earth and figuring out how to. . . There's a lot of experimentation going on, sampling going on, then there's also teams of brainstorming trying to figure out how to help stabilize the system until... Basically, there's some teams trying to buy time and keep the system stable while human consciousness increases, to see if they could actually increase [to the level where they] stop creating so much damage. There're some mitigation teams.

There're the augmenting teams, the mitigation teams, and then there's the reconciliation teams, I suppose you could say, right now. That seems to be what's going on. I'm having to run several programs at once because part of my consciousness is one of the design team. I need to be aware of all the different conversations that are going on. I'm running on several of the different platforms, but I can't describe more than one at a time.

R: Yeah, of course, thank you so much. You're doing a really good job. Is there any one of those programs or conversation things that are playing parallel to each other that you would like to describe?

HS: It seems as though one of my primary roles is on the frequency communication team. As I've shared in the past, there's always this constant evolution of the signals that the humans are emitting. Then, there's us trying to weave the songs of remembering through, to weave the codes, the upgrade codes. How do we get those upgrade codes into the field, so that the artists and the mystics and the poets and those that are listening into the field can hear it and pick up the possible muses, and pick up the possible themes that are trying to get manifested in the 3D.

Interestingly, their technology keeps getting more complex and more advanced in the same channels that we work with, and never before in human evolution, have they ever been able to work on our channels. There has been an interesting development that they've accidentally dropped into some of our channels. It distorts our ability to bring in the codes and to bring in and allow us to keep the muse lines and all the creativity flowing through, so that humans can pick up on what they need to pick up on. I've described in several other sessions where there was this need to augment our ways that we're sending in the codes, so that they can make it through the distortion fields, and it's just an ever constantly evolving process. Yet, it seems that we are making some progress, so that's good.

R: **Very good. Thank you for sharing with me. What can you share with me regarding the international situation that you learn about? What's happening right now on the Earth?**

HS: There's a lot of hot spots brewing. Gosh, there's so many. There's a lot; we were concerned about this. It seems as though things got a little quieter for a while with the epidemic, and there's a lot more stillness and quietness, and people weren't moving as much. So there's a little bit of stillness, but over time, that stillness is turned into restlessness. There's a vibration of restlessness across the planet, and it's now starting to release, but there's been a lot of pressure built up. A lot of beings have a lot of extra stress and pressure on their lives. The cortisol levels are through the roof. It's been sustained cortisol for over a year now, and so it's starting to impact. There's starting to be more of this really deep-seated frustration and a stress fatigue experience is happening. There's still more of that energy coming.

There're several hot spots around the world and several places where violence and potential problems can evolve. It especially builds in the heat of the summer, in the Northern Hemisphere at least; there tends to be more of that during late summer when the energy has been building all summer and the heat adds to it. We're focusing our attention on the upper hemisphere now. It's slightly quieted down a little bit. In the Southern Hemisphere, they have just reached their winter solstice. Here the Northern Hemisphere is gearing up for more violence in several different locations on the planet.

R: **Okay, and when those things are starting to heat up, what can you guys do from your perspective that helps cool that out?**

HS: Oh, there's a few. . . I mean, we have several beings who have incarnated and are in their roles. Some of them are aware of their experience; some of them are not aware; some of them have chosen to incarnate to be in the field. They are playing out their roles as leaders and because they're in the system, whether they're conscious of it or not, we can upload codes that emit from their frequency through their holograms, so that we are able to emit. We are able to get a direct seed within some of the meetings and some of the gatherings of some of the world leaders, and they're able to bring some calming frequencies into the physical spaces.

There are also other volunteers that are fully conscious of their mission. They are actively working within the system to help guide [others] towards more compassionate choices. We also can work from the sound frequency. We've been pairing up with the International Relations Board for us to actually insert or spread a field of vibration that increases compassion, understanding, and cooperation. We can emit frequencies through the field and not have to be physically present. Then, of course, there's the team that goes in and actively deactivates nuclear warheads if they're going to be detonated. There's a team always watching for that and to keep the nuclear blasts from happening. There's always a team keeping their eye on that and disabling those warheads.

R: Very good. Thank you so much for sharing this. Do you want to share anything that you learn from a more ecological perspective?

HS: Yeah, this one is getting more and more challenging. Destabilization is happening at an increased rate. It's causing increased disruption in weather patterns, which is then causing increased disruption in the ecological stability of many different systems. There's definitely a collapse happening in many different systems. We're especially concerned about the oceanic current right now, especially in the Northern Hemisphere — the hotter, the warmer currents.

There're not enough cold currents in the winter, so it's changing some of the fundamental patterns. There's a lot of systems that are becoming increasingly destabilized as time moves on, which we knew would happen, but it's happening at a faster rate than we anticipated. It's just continued to destabilize, which is going to continually increase frequencies and natural disasters, climate anomalies, intensity of storms, intensity of heat, heat waves, intensity of fires. Overall, it's easy to see the trend of what's happening.

PREPARING FOR WHAT IS TO COME

R: Okay, is there anything that you can tell us about the coming months?

HS: The best way to prepare for what's to come is to prepare yourself inside for anything that could come, to find your stable ground inside. Then, whatever comes you can meet it with presence and acceptance and your wholehearted earnestness to do your best. Knowing the future very rarely helps a situation; therefore, it just does not seem appropriate [to share]. The most appropriate thing is that we stay in our center and we choose love, no matter what comes.

We can look at the rate of change, and there can be predictions. We can look into the quantum future and know that all of this is futile anyway, so it's a paradox, but rarely have we found that knowing the future actually helps; it often tends to cause more problems. It's best for you to focus on the fact that the rate of change is increasing; the rate of destabilization is increasing.

It is time for human beings to take responsibility for their energy bodies, and for their mental bodies, and their thoughts, and their own state — to find their solid ground inside and stay centered. So it is of utmost importance that we take responsibility for our energy, sovereignty, and our creation vibration.

R: Beautiful, can you give another practical way for humans to take this responsibility?

HS: Well, this is quite unlikely considering the trends. When humans take space away from their devices and put their bare feet on the earth or bare feet in running water, they reconnect themselves to the vibration of the planet. When they stay connected to their electronic devices, they entrain themselves to their electronic devices. They entrain themselves to the very distortion patterns that we're trying to help them disengage from. It's becoming increasingly challenging to reach them. There are attempts to reach them through the device channels instead of trying to separate the device channels. However, ultimately, for a human being to stay centered in themselves, they need to stay connected to their Source and remember they are all part of this planet; they are all an organism of this planet. Therefore, the reminder always is to presence themselves with clear water, clear air, as much as possible, taking space from their devices, bare feet on the earth, drinking clear water when possible, cleaning up their diet. It's the simple things.

Less and less of the humans are even doing the simplest things. Then of course, there's all the upgrade possibilities when beings are very dedicated to their advancement and they're taking the time to cleanse their field and then presence their field each day through meditation and breathwork and yoga and other types of energy work.

Even just the simplest actions of just taking space from the devices, laying their bodies on the earth, putting their bare feet on the earth, eating plants and animals from the local land; just the simplest things are also becoming less and less frequent in many places in the world. We can talk about simple techniques, or we can talk about more advanced techniques. Depending on whether you're just trying to maintain a clearer vibration or whether you're trying to upgrade the DNA in order to be able to receive more of the advanced codes that we're sending in. There are a whole plethora of activities. These have been shared before; there's not necessarily a need to repeat them, just to review and to actually do it. In 3D, it actually has to be done regularly. In the etheric realms and a lot of the light realms, it can just be thought and made manifest. One of the whole parts of the Earth experiment is that in the three-dimensional, in the program, in the hologram, even though it is an illusion, the illusion is very persistent; therefore, to stay in the vibration of the illusion is the game. Which is what we are doing. There's not really any way out of it at this point. One must actually manifest it in the physical dimension in order to gain that skill in the physical dimension.

We're not working only in the thought, or the cosmos, or the energetic planes. We're working in the physical planes and the energetic planes. Therefore, a human being must commit not just in their minds to doing something, but they actually have to do it, they actually have to take the time and space to do it. Because that's how slow density is in order to actually make a change or to upgrade the system. It has to actually be done in the vibration of time and space, which is a very slow and dense vibration. So one has to slow down and actually put in the time to do it.

R: Okay, beautiful. Yeah, you elaborated before about how to receive upgrades through getting into coherence and yin and yang meditations. I'm wondering about it. I still feel with myself a lack of clarity on how to get to coherence. In other words, for example, through meditation, through focus. What are the things to focus on during a meditation to help with coherence?

HS: You ask the funniest questions; you always ask the opposite of the question. Fascinating.

R: *(Giggles)* So what would be the question you would ask?

HS: It's not about what you focus on in meditation. Meditation is focusing. It doesn't actually matter what you focus on; you just need to focus. It's not so much the object, it's the fact of the concentration; it's being in the vibration of presence. The question is not, "What do I focus on in meditation?" No, meditation is the art of practicing focus. You see, it's backwards.

R: Yeah, this I know. So the question. . . I guess I wonder if there's anything that you could focus on to help you find coherence more than other things that you may be focusing on?

HS: The most important thing is consistency. The most important thing in manifesting coherence in a three-dimensional plane is to consistently practice it. A lot of times people practice at different times of the day or maybe they'll practice this day, but not that day. To maintain coherence in three dimensions, [at first] it has to be maintained in time and space. The number one recommendation is to actually be consistent in the practice, ideally, the same time each day or at least every day. There is an intention put towards maintaining coherence. A lot of times people will put a lot of attention into coherence for a few months, and then they fall away. Then they don't understand why it's not working. The very [fundamental] aspect of coherence is that it's got to be consistent coherence. Once you've discovered coherence and experienced coherence, then it's much easier to return to coherence, and then much easier to maintain coherence. Once you've discovered coherence, then your job is to maintain coherence. Once you're maintaining coherence, then your job is to amplify coherence.

If you're still at the step of trying to discover coherence, then the best steps to discover coherence are to commit to a daily practice and be very dedicated and devoted to this and watch your energy around it. What are you feeling? Is there a resistance in the energy of doing it? Are you feeling annoyed while you're doing it? Are you feeling resistance to even do the act of doing it? If you're resistant to the act of doing it, but you're making yourself do it, there is only a little bit of benefit there. There must be a full acceptance of doing it and the commitment of doing it and a follow-through of doing it in the full acceptance space. There is an aspect of resistance that keeps us from being fully present; therefore, we don't maintain coherence.

You could sit every day for ten years, but if you're in resistance every single time you're doing it, there's only so far you can get. First, you have to be dedicated to doing it, but then you got to make sure to check your intention — of why you are doing it? If you're doing it out of a sense of obligation that you have to in order to upgrade, you're in resistance to accepting what your actual potential is. If you are in alignment, then there's a devotion, there is a dedication to the practice and therefore you're not meeting your meditation practice with resistance; you're meeting it with the energy of coherence.

Some of the other possibilities is that oftentimes when one begins to start a practice and coherence is difficult to find, you find yourself thinking a lot and constantly bringing yourself back to presence. Honestly, as difficult as this may sound, it really is just an aspect of continuing to practice, to stay dedicated. . .just keep trying, even if you're in resistance. But be careful that you're not being in resistance to your resistance. Especially that you're not being resistant to the resistance of your resistance. The more layers of resistance, the more challenging your experience and the less benefit you'll get.

Ultimately, if you're struggling to find coherence, then the best solutions I can offer to finding coherence are to be mindful of the substances you're putting into your body: stimulants, caffeine, sugar, chocolate, processed foods. All of these things disrupt your inner coherence. If you're trying to find coherence and you're struggling to find coherence, then look at the places where you are not setting your body up as the antenna for coherence. If there's any places that you're not allowing yourself to set yourself up to be the antenna, then those would be the first things that should be remedied.

If you've remedied all those things, if you've removed all stimulants and sugars and distractions from your field, and you're still struggling to find coherence, then I would suggest, if you need a place to focus on. . .if you want to take the question and flip it around backwards for training wheels, that's completely appropriate. So I would suggest choosing a location in the body to focus on; you could choose the dantian, you could choose the vishuddha [throat chakra]. You can choose any location. You could choose the spiritual heart; you can choose the heart. Choose a location to bring. . .rest your awareness in, and stick to that until you can maintain your awareness there.

Once you learn to actually maintain your presence in a certain location, then you no longer bound to need. . .to keep your attention in that one spot. It's a training ground to allow yourself to practice enough focus so that you can discover coherence.

Once you discover coherence, then you know where you're going and there's a deeper desire to want to return to that, and then it's a matter of maintenance. In trying to establish coherence, if one is struggling, first take a look at how you're distorting the antenna of your body, then take a look at how you're distorting the antenna of the mind. What are you thinking about? What are the patterns? Are you able to bring yourself back again and again? What thoughts are you holding on to? What thoughts are you refusing to let go of? Which ones do you return to again and again?

That's another one. Taking a look at the mental antenna, the physical antenna, the energetic antenna — that one often can be cleared with breathwork and yoga, so that one can sit more in silence. Regular breathwork and yoga help to clear out the energetic antenna so that one's not disrupting the field to discovering coherence. Once the physical, mental, emotional, and the spiritual beings are all settled, then coherence can happen. The exercises that I've shared in the past are all good and simple exercises, but they just must be done on a consistent, regular basis.

There needs to be profound honesty for the participant of. . .where are they jamming up their own antennae? Even fairly well-practiced meditators can suddenly fall off the wagon and no longer be dedicated to their practices. They may find themselves slipping in the clarity of their antennae. The best way to discover coherence is to prepare the antennae to receive coherence, so that's looking at the different energetic, physical, and emotional levels of the body and making sure they're all well prepared and the conditions are being created to allow coherence to happen.

[*Ava's note: I have noticed that when I commit to my daily practice of yin and yang coherence for a consistent period of time, then quantum upgrades tend to happen spontaneously. For example, each day this past winter I snowboarded for two hours a day. I also did a sitting meditation for an hour each day. After a month of this daily practice, I had a vivid dream where I was snowboarding on an infinite slope of fresh, untracked powder. I knew I would never fall and hurt myself, and I never needed to get on a ski lift. It was infinite. I rode this powder heaven for a VERY long time. (It felt like I rode forever, but obviously the dream eventually faded.)*

The next day, my riding improved exponentially, and I felt like I had spontaneously received an upload of an advanced skill, like in the movie The Matrix. I even snowboarded through the trees for the first time that day. I had never believed I could safely do that before. Suddenly, I had no issue navigating the terrain with ease and grace. Perhaps some people can access this spontaneous quantum upgrade more quickly than I can, but for me, a month of daily yin/yang coherence opened up the possibility and neural pathways, then the dream experience helped me release all fear and 3D concerns about flying down a mountain at high speeds. I upgraded my abilities to snowboard with less fear and with more presence, precision, and proper body alignment. I consider this a sweet spot where 3D practice meets quantum spontaneous learning.]

SPIRITUAL ANTENNA

R: Thank you so much. It was very clear. I'm happy I'm asking bad questions that will give me good answers. Thank you so much. So I'd like to ask you. . .you mentioned here that you clear the physical antenna, the emotional, the mental, and you said also the spiritual antenna. Can you give me an example of what this means when your spiritual antenna is not clear and clean?

HS: To access the spiritual antenna, one must access and clear the other antennas first. The spiritual antenna is much more subtle. First, you want to focus and make sure your physical antenna is clear. Then you want to make sure that your mental antenna is clear. Then, once your physical and mental antennas are clear, then your emotional antenna starts to become clear. Once your physical, mental, and emotional antennas are clear, then you can start to tap into the subtle realm of the spiritual.

The reason that the spiritual antenna would not be clear, and the word "spiritual" is a very strange and misleading term because spiritual people talk about being spiritual, about having a spiritual life or a spiritual practice. All life is actually spiritual; it's spirit that is our energetic and vibrational connection to Source. Our vibrational connection to Source becomes distorted if we are diluting it or distorting it with physical impurities, emotional impurities, or mental impurities, and if spiritually we are allowing ourselves to be stuck by fear. If fear is keeping us from advancing or from facing, or from reaching connection, then we need to continue to purify and lean into that fear, so it's no longer distorting us.

Deep honesty [is needed]. What do we truly want in our lives? Why did we come here? What is our mission? When we're receiving that information, that is when our antennas are clear enough to receive our vibrational connection to Source.

"Spiritual" is not something separate from us; it's not like we're living a life and then we have a spiritual practice on the side. Every single moment is our relationship with our connection to Source. The only way that the [spiritual] antenna can be clear is when the other channels are clear and then there is a pure devotion to keeping the vibrational connection clear. We have to be careful that we're not thinking about it like some separate box on a shelf that we tend to. Ultimately, the spiritual connection is the most fundamental connection, but it can't be clear when the other ones are jammed up. They need the base ones to be cleared to allow us to receive the information from our higher selves and from our Source connection.

R: Okay, very good. Thank you. That's very clear. There was another question that I wanted to ask you regarding those kinds of names that you call different bodies. You mentioned energetic body and then you said also causal body and astral body are different layers of less physical bodies. Can you elaborate about the difference between those bodies?

HS: I could, and yet, if you use your vast base of knowledge using the thing you call your internet, you can easily look up each of these words and they are readily described.

R: Okay, so you feel like it would be a waste of time to get into those topics?

HS: Yes, you can research any of those topics and find the definition.

[Listening to this response always makes me laugh. I know that they can give very in-depth explanations that might be more accurate than what we can find online, but I trust that they have the bigger picture of what will be most beneficial to share. They were also considering the energy of Ava as the channel, and the time that we had left. We had agreed to keep this session short.]

R: Okay. Thank you so much. Now I wanted to ask you about an intimate relationship she had that recently ended. What would you like to share with her?

HS: Ultimately, she had established a very solid connection with herself and with Source and then allowed that to slip a little bit to where [she] went back into that fear and then longing for partnership to feel complete. There was a deep longing for that, and therefore, she attracted a being that also had a strong longing for that. They matched each other. Ultimately, she drew in a match from a place of longing and a place of lack, so she was met with that. She had been doing a lot better at releasing that vibration, but it sort of, kind of came back up.

It's okay. It's natural; it's human. She slipped back into an old pattern of longing for intimate connection and partnership, and therefore, she attracted a being also longing for that, as a reflection to remind her that she is a sovereign being and is complete within herself. Therefore, when she is complete in herself, then she can vibrate and attract a being that is complete in their self.

At this point, no permanent damage has been done. There is an energetic drain on her from this connection, and the cord needs to be cut, for she's being drained energetically by the current and the cord that was connected and created. Ultimately, there could be some consequences through the emotional realms. There is definitely a lot of story and projection. There is some [emotional] pain that could continue to ripple. However, she needs to clear this line as quickly as she can.

R: Okay, can we cut the cord now?

HS: Yes.

R: Okay, please cut the cord. Invite the light beings we'd like to assist you with that, and share with me what's happening as it's being done.

HS: Here is a cord from the heart, from the dantian, from the sacral center, and from the root center. All four of the lower centers have been [impacted] activated and the Vishnu [or Sudarshana Chakra], wow! The chords went all the way up to the throat, even then obscuring the third eye. There was an energetic linking, or there's been an energetic [drain] that's taken hold of each of the centers. It's impressive that she allowed that to happen. All right, we're working on each one. They're not that strong; that's good, but she needs to be more careful and remember the incredible amount of energy and light that she has. She radiates very brightly. She can be a beacon for hungry ghosts and beings that are in a deep place of longing and a deep place of feeling disconnected from Source. This is a lesson for her to remember how much work that she has done. Therefore, she needs to wait and be patient for other beings that have refined their system to the level that she has. That she can't dip in the [online dating] pool without setting herself up to potentially letting it happen. She allowed this to happen. She knows. Yeah, she just needs to keep it a little bit more clear. Focus back on herself and trust the process.

R: Okay, is it clear now? Did you clear the cord?

HS: We are working on it.

R: Okay. Let me know when it's completely gone. May I continue to ask more questions while you do this work?

HS: Hold on. We have begun the process. She needs to continue to do it each day, for the next 49 days.

R: What does she need to do?

HS: She needs to keep cutting the cords every day for the next 7x7 days.

R: Okay. Thank you. Thank you so much. You mentioned that she attracted this guy through lack. What attracted the new guy into her life? What energy?

HS: She is experiencing a radiance attraction [with this new man]. His radiance was shining without need, and her radiance was shining from a place of fullness, and they recognized each other's fullness. There is a radiance, coherence, and augmentation when they are together. Neither of them are perfect. They're both still working through some of their core wounds, which is a natural part of the human process. Ultimately, their attraction for each other came from radiance, and it's why it feels light, because she was feeling the reflection of the radiance, and there's the shared joy of connection. This connection is one of radiance.

R: **Wonderful, very good. And you mentioned a core wound. What do you refer to as a core wound of Ava?**

HS: There is this fear of being alone from her time in the incubator and other periods of time of feeling alone, even in her home. The sensation that alone is not okay, somehow. There's this sensation that she feels more relaxed when she's in intimate connection with someone else; she feels more calm. She has been actively working on it. It is much healthier, much more complete, and whole, and she just needs to stay with it.

R: **Very good. Now that you know that and it's even more clear now, can you reprogram that part of her that feels that alone is not okay? And help her love equally either way, whether she is alone or has a partnership. (HS:** Yes.**) Thank you. Thank you so much for doing this. Very good.**

[We continued with a few of her personal questions until They (Ava's Higher Self collective) announced that they were complete as sometimes happens. I honored their request to conclude the session. I brought Ava up to full consciousness and on the way up I invited her to set an intention to help her integrate the information in the best way. Ava's intention was Devotion. I thought that was the perfect word to summarize the session and the profound teachings they shared. Ava was feeling great, lighter, more clear, and fully recharged.]

Ava's note: *I find it amusing that after nine sessions, we come back to the theme of alone once more, which is right where we began. Except now, it's completely different. As we publish this book, I am now engaged to a man with a heart of pure gold, the one who I had this "radiance attraction" with. The long, seemingly endless expanses of alone have shifted to a daily, rhythmic pattern; together, alone, together, alone. Alone has become precious. Now, I often experience the ecstasy of alone that the channel referenced. From this place, I experience a deeper understanding of this fundamental nature of the human condition and of "alone." When "I" spoke about the feeling of loneliness, of being everything, forever, without end, with no edges and no other to share existence with, the solution was to birth the Multiverse. Does life, the Universe, the Big Bang and whatever was before it, birth from a sense of aloneness? Ironic that the intention of this story is to help us remember wholeness, unity, oneness, and that we are all One. I've come to realize that we are never really alone.*

I sit with this feeling a lot. Alone. How do we integrate this recurrent feeling of separation? How do we cultivate and maintain the sensation of unity and connection with All That Is in a 3D world, with the illusion of separation from Source woven into its design? It's a theme that is woven into the design. We can try to avoid it, fix it, suffer from it, and then finally, we choose to go within to feel it — to feel our connection to All That Is, and fully integrate unity consciousness in the here and now.

Through my journey, I have realized something perfect about alone...

I

ALONE

With a little L" for "Love" added deep inside

And a little space in between

Becomes

ALL ONE

1

I

The 'P' Words

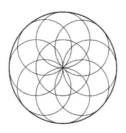

SESSION TEN

Ron: Now I'd like to do a few practices of visualizations to activate the part of the mind that has the symbols and the images and the memories. I'd like for you to take a moment and visualize a bird. The first bird that comes to mind. . .describe that bird to me.

A: I see a hummingbird, a ruby-throated hummingbird; it's small. Its wings are beating so fast; it's just a blur. You can't see them. Its chest is fuchsia pink, so bright. The light is shining; it hits the feathers and makes them sparkle like a gem. It has a shiny, fuchsia chest with a green body. It's emerald green.

R: Wonderful. Very good. You can close that scene. Now we'll do another practice. I'd like for you to go to a place where you enjoy the music. The place where you really love the music...the music that you enjoy. Be there now and describe where you are?

A: I'm in a cathedral with stained glass windows, vaulted ceilings, and beautiful acoustics. A choir is singing. I hear the sound reverberate through the whole building; it fills you. It's not just hearing the music; you feel it. The whole chamber resonates with the sound.

R: Are you there by yourself or are there others with you?

A: Right now, I'm alone, watching the choir practice. Soon, it will be filled with people listening.

R: Wonderful. How old do you feel over there?

A: I haven't been born yet. I'm watching my father. My father sings in the church choir. My mother meets him here. That's why I came in here. I came into this life for the love of music and song, and a love of God and the sound of songs of the cathedral. I'm going to come in here this time. It's my way in. It will give me a good chance to seed in why I'm coming here this time.

[Even though we were still in an early part of the induction, it was clear now that she had dropped into a deep trance and was observing from the spirit side the moment she chose her parents.]

R: Beautiful. What else do you notice from this perspective?

A: How young my father is. His mind is funny. I can read his thoughts and know his inner dialogue. He's funny. He has such a beautiful voice.

R: So what is funny there? His appearance? The way he looks?

A: No, his inner dialogue is funny.

R: Ahh..his inner dialogue, okay. What can you notice about his inner dialogue from the perspective where you are?

A: He's excited about a date with my mother; they just met. He wants to look good for her very much. He's a little worried about what other people think and how he's perceived, how he looks, and how he comes across. He's got this chatter of worry and preening, but underneath it there's such a beautiful love of voice and song and love and beauty and truth and kindness and playfulness. [He is] such a beautiful being. It's funny.

R: Is there anything else that is attracting your attention from this perspective?

A: My mother. She'll be coming soon. She'll be coming to the church. She's so beautiful; she's so courageous. She left her small town home to go to the big city for a better life, and she meets my father in a church. I just feel her bravery. She's such a beautiful woman. There's just so much hope and tenacity. She's very brave.

R: **Thank you so much for sharing. So let's continue from there. You can close that scene, and we'll drift and float from there to the next important place for you to see. You are arriving at the most appropriate place. You can start looking around and describe your very first impressions.**

A: Colored glass. Window glass. Sunlight through the glass. Light. I see the dust sparkling in the light, the light that's shining through the glass. I'm in another big cathedral, similar to the one before, but this one's different.

R: **As you speak, it will become more and more clear and you can continue to share with me everything that you notice.**

A: It's beautiful. There's a huge organ, a pipe organ. Bronze pipes are going up into the cathedral and have been polished recently. It's so beautiful. There's a grand piano. There's a beautiful carpet with patterns over a hardwood floor. It's one of those beautiful rugs that has a mandala in the center. It feels really nice on my feet, standing on the carpet. I'm barefoot. My feet; I like to feel the feeling of the carpet. It's nice. I'm really excited. There's a lot of energy moving through me.

R: **Tell me more. Look down to your feet and describe yourself.**

A: Well, it's me, but huh...It's me, but it's the future.

R: **Very good, tell me more.**

A: It's not very far in the future. A few years maybe. It's very much like me, but I'm me from this place of such pure alignment. I'm so right where I want to be. I'm preparing. I'm going to be putting on a show. There's going to be a service tonight. No, not tonight. Ohh. . . I think, it's two days, I believe. It's a series of offerings, and it's going to be story time with children, and there's going to be a service, a Sunday morning service with music, and there's a full choir coming to rehearse the parts.

I'm standing here; there's not many people here yet. You're there too. The energy is building. We're going to be sharing. There'll be a live channeling and a few different things. . .there will be the choir concert. There'll be more of a dance. Part of a slow tour where we go to different towns and share music, and the book, and the channelings, and the ministry. We're doing it, and I'm just enjoying seeing the dust sparkling in the light, and the light shining on the grand piano, and shining on the pipes, and my feeling (my bare feet) on the carpet, and I'm looking out over this this huge, beautiful cathedral, and it will be filled soon. There's just such a deep joy in my heart.

It seems like I'm finally loving myself all the way through; I'm loving myself. I'm truly giving myself the best version of my life I can imagine. I can do what I want to be doing, exactly why I came here. I'm standing back in the moment, back here in that moment of now. It's the future past now. The moment when my soul chose to come in through my parents because of that cathedral [and their love], and now here I am in devotion to these songs, I'm standing in a cathedral preparing to share these heart songs. I can feel the ripples. There's so much joy in my heart. I'm just so overcome with gratitude at how beautiful it all is and how lucky I am that I get to be here and share this for all the people, for all the things I love, so grateful. I'm finally brave enough to do it. I'm laughing at myself that I took so long, but it's all perfect. I'm just feeling so grateful to be here. I feel. . .it's just so much energy, so beautiful. I'm so blessed to get to sing in such a beautiful hall. The acoustics are so amazing. It's so rich. Every note that comes out of my mouth; it just feels like heaven is moving through me. It's perfect. [She started to become very emotional, on the verge of crying, and her face turned red.]

R: So wonderful. I want you to enjoy this through all your physical body, and all the cells of your body, all the atoms of your body. Feel that and integrate that feeling, this embodiment, enjoy that. Allow them to heal all your being, any part of you — your physical body, your emotional body, your mental body, your spiritual body are all vibrating, and enjoying that harmony. [Ava is fully weeping and laughing as I speak these words.] **Let that flow through you and enjoy that. Allow everything else to be let go. You don't need that anymore. You can align yourself to that feeling, and anything that is not that can be let go now; you don't need that anymore.** [Ava continues to weep and then sighs.] **Take a deep breath. . .** [And I moved her to the next scene.]

A: Hmmm, I think I'm on the ship again.

R: You're feeling like you're on the ship again?

A: I'm on a ship. It's funny; I'm at the controls of a small pod that's part of the bigger ship, and I'm working the controls with my awareness and with my. . . I can't tell if I'm using just my awareness, or if I have form. It's me again, but I'm. . .it's more. . .it's not me, Ava. It's not like the me that's down in the cathedral singing, but it's the other part of me that's up and out of it. It's the other part of me that's looking down at me on Earth. **(R: Yeah.)** I'm calibrating all the controls. I'm so excited because I can now merge with the self purely. [From] the temple of sound, from that place where I can have my fingers on the infinite keys and the sounds and now, I'm on Earth and going to sing in the cathedrals. They meet (her aspects) in that center of oneness. It's in that energetic resonance where the overtones and the harmonics all come together. There's this place, when the sound fills the cathedrals; in that moment of that perfection then I can perfectly, without any interference or distortion, can meet it here from this side. There's a beautiful amplification that can happen. A portal is fully open both ways for that pure music, that vibration — the songs, the songs of remembering to flow through freely. That's what we've been waiting for in a way. I've been waiting for me to join me here. *(Giggles)*

I'm setting all the controls. I'm so delighted because this is the beginning; this is the beginning of where we all are coming online. More and more of us who are embodied now and who are incarnating now are waking up and doing the work to clear the fear and to clear the resistance to fully step into our soul mission. There's more and more of us doing it, and I'm just delighted to feel myself aligning with this. Aligning with my purpose fully and aligning with the mission and making it easier.

There're so many less layers of distortion to go through when it's straight from the temple of sound to here; it's like I'm on a ship, but it's not a ship so much. It's just an image overlay; it's just sort of an imprint to help me understand. Sure, yeah, there's a ship, and I'm up above Earth, sending, helping to augment the sounds that she. . .that I, she, the other me, the me on Earth is sending up, and then I'm up here sending it down. It's not really down and up. That's a three-dimensional perspective, but for reference.

Then beyond being in the ship, I'm in the temples of sound, the temples of consciousness. We're matching; we're meeting in the harmonics. The vibrations of the songs of the universe are able to flow through the cathedral. When the people are in the cathedral, that sound augments and fills them. The resonant vibration moves through them and vibrates all their cells, and shakes them and vibrates them until they open to reveal their own heart songs to them. It helps to soothe and prepare their bodies to receive and to accept it, and to awaken to their own soul mission. It's happening, the exponential awakenings are happening as we are all coming online and sharing our gifts fully, no matter what. I'm feeling a deep sense of delight and joy. I'm feeling. . . It's happening. We're doing it more and more around the world. We are doing it despite the fear and despite the density and despite the distortions, all of that. It's happening. We can, we are the creators of the Universe; we can create heaven on earth here; we don't have to wait. It doesn't have to be the way the stories in the Bible talk about Heaven after Earth. We can bring Heaven here on Earth. Heaven can be here on Earth; we can all create it together.

That's what we're meant to do. I'm just feeling so delighted to feel this point coming into alignment. I'm happy for her. She's finally letting herself fully receive the gifts that she's always wanted to and resisted for so long. She's doing it in such a beautiful, humble, open-hearted way. I know for so long she was really afraid that she was just wanting attention. She used to say to herself, "Who am I to want to sing, or who am I to want to have all this attention on me?" She was embarrassed by her own longing, but it wasn't a longing to just have attention on her for the sake of attention for her ego. No, there's truly a beautiful song, a beautiful heart, a beautiful message of love wanting to come through. She needed to refine it, and it's okay. I'm just feeling joy to be preparing to meet her here. To meet her here from this side; it's all one side. There's no such thing as sides; it's just. . .translating it into the 3D is challenging.

THE SOUL SEED

R: You're doing great. You can speak freely and guide her and share with us what you find important to share at this point. [She is now fully embodying and speaking from her Higher-Self.]

HS: What I offer to her is the same that we offer to all beings. As we're awakening, as we're stepping into the greatest versions of ourselves, that greatest dream that's in your heart. That little seed of a dream that wants to be born but feels like the most impossible dream, that feel like the hardest thing to do. [That dream] It's just like a seed; it's so tight inside its little shell; it feels so safe inside that little shell. The hardest thing is to bust out of it, to be so vulnerable [while] not knowing if you will bust out in the right conditions, or in the right place, or if you'll thrive, or if your little seed will be able to sprout and grow; if it will be nourished. It's terrifying for a little seed. It feels like the hardest thing to truly break out and to live your greatest dream. **(R: Right)**

The seed must break open. You will break open and water yourself and give yourself the right conditions. The breaking open will happen, and as you let yourself, as she lets herself...just remember to keep breathing. Keep pouring that nourishing breath, that energetic water, and drinking lots of water. . . just keep nourishing that little seed. Trusting in its own design, in its own intelligence to grow. It's always worth it for the seed, even if it dies, even if it has to return to compost. Even if it doesn't succeed in the way that it imagines that it wants to; it's still a part of the whole; it's still adding compost to the whole, so that the beautiful blossoms of the garden can grow and can keep proliferating here to build a perpetual Garden of Eden.

When you get nervous and contracted, and you start to get scared, you [can] just consciously put your bare feet on the earth and ground and breathe. There's a pretty well known quote amongst their culture — "nervousness plus breath equals excitement." Breathe, breathe into the fear and keep opening your little seed. It seems like the hardest thing to do, but once you do it, you'll realize it's what you were designed to do. You are designed to break open and to grow your unique version of life into the world.

It's the most liberating feeling to let yourself be that seed and to crack yourself open to let yourself grow, to dive your roots deep down into the earth and let yourself unfurl and to blossom. It's why you came here. Each one of you has a beautiful seed in your heart. You might not even know what it is. It might be so small and so tucked down in there, you don't even know what your little seed is. Bringing your attention to it, looking, earnestly looking for that little seed within your heart...it always will reveal itself to you. We can be patient with ourselves, but also firm with ourselves to keep nourishing our seed, until it can break open. Keep tending the garden of ourselves, so that we can grow into the Garden of Eden, the eternal paradise that we were meant to be, that we are designed to be. In each offering our unique flower to the garden. When we each allow ourselves to crack open and share our heart songs and create such a beautiful garden together. That nourishes the whole world.

We can do it. We don't need to be afraid. We don't need to be afraid of what could happen or what might come. What could happen, the worst-case scenario; it doesn't matter. The only thing that matters is that we keep nourishing our little seed, growing a little garden no matter what. Trusting, trusting in the perfection of life and death. We don't need to be afraid of what's to come.

R: Thank you so much. Beautiful.

HS: Nothing can harm you. We are harmony itself. We are harmony, or harm of none; our heart song is harmony. We can each just feel that harmony within us. You're safe. No matter what it looks like out there. No matter what you hear, no matter what. We're safe. We're so safe to bust open and to be vulnerable, and to grow, and to put it all out there. Every seed, when it busts open; it knows eventually once it grows, and it blossoms; eventually it will die. We all know this. It's okay. Still, it's safe to blossom. It's safe to burst out. You're safe. We're all safe. I know it looks really scary. It feels really scary. It's only an illusion. It's only to aim your awareness back inside to your own heart. That anxiety you feel; the fear you feel; the contraction you feel; it's an alarm bell asking for your attention. Bringing your attention into your body, into your belly, into your heart, into your chest, in your womb; wherever you're feeling the energy, feeling the anxiety, and the fear. It's a beautiful bell, just a beautiful ringing to bring you into yourself. It's uncomfortable, and it feels terrifying. It feels dangerous. It feels like harm; it feels like it's gonna hurt you. It tells you it's not safe. Don't listen to that part. **(R: Ummhmm.)** Keep turning to the harmony inside your heart. Let yourself burst open. Be the seed that you are. Grow, little one. Grow.

R: **Beautiful. Thank you so much for sharing this. I'm wondering, is there another scene you want to show her today? Or should I start to ask questions?**

HS: You may ask.

R: **Okay. Thank you so much. I'll start with asking about the things that you already showed her, like choosing her parents. Why did you choose to start today like this?**

HS: Ava's story is unique and universal. Each of our souls chooses to come into a body. We choose a life that will help us embody why we want to come. I've shown her different aspects of her birth. Her birth, before her birth, during her birth, after her birth. They've all been shared, but this one hasn't been shared. When her soul, when the soul spark of her ignited, the moment that her parents met in love and devotion and song. . . How can she be other than she is? How could she be anyone else but her? She chose to come in through the cathedral, through the love, singing of the choir, and the love, and the bravery of leaving home for truth. It's the perfect combination.

Her parents were the perfect combination to allow her to bring in her dream. She chose it. It may not have turned out just the way she wanted. I know, she had hoped that she would have opened up much sooner, that she would have found her gifts long before, but it doesn't matter how it turned out. What matters is the perfection of this moment now. The perfection is the culmination of that soul's dream to embody, to plant itself in the body, inside that little seed in the center, in hopes that she would nourish herself enough to allow it to break open — to allow her to become who she came here to be, who she wanted to be, and who her heart song longed to be.

It feels important to remind her where she came from; why she chose this body; why she chose these parents; why she chose this unique expression of her garden — her flower. It's beautiful, really. It's such a beautiful, perfect poetry. The way she came in, the story of her becoming; the story of her birthing. If her father hadn't followed his love of music and his love of God to sing in the church, he would have never been there in that moment. If her mother hadn't left her home and cultivated her bravery and her courage, because something called her soul deeper, called her to a deeper purpose, even though she didn't know what it would be or what would happen. She did it anyway. Those two energies coming together and creating a new life from love. It opened a [portal]. . . the love pouring through creates a frequency vibration. She wrote her destiny the moment she chose that form; she knew she was choosing the best outcome she possibly could, the best potential, the best possible way to come in; she chose it deliberately. It's good for her to remember that.

She didn't just choose it for some mission to try to save humanity or to help us all awaken. She also chose it for just her own joy, her own absolute ecstasy of how good it feels to let those songs move through her body, especially rippling out and into a cathedral. In a temple of sound and song and love and bravery. She came in for the joy of it, not just for the mission, not just for the responsibility, not just to pass this message on, but to create her own version of perfection, to create heaven on earth for herself. It is as perfectly selfless as it is selfish. That's why it's so perfect. The soul's expression of its deepest longing; the capital "S" version of Selfish not the ego's version of selfish, for our own scarcity and need to take care of ourselves, but from the capital "S" version of Selfish. She gave herself the best possible ride she could imagine giving herself.

It's good to remind her that she did that and to help her feel it. As she's choosing it more and more, and as she's embodying it more and more, for the benefit of all beings, for the benefit of waking us all up into our love. She can only do it through waking herself up to her own love of herself and exquisiteness of being embodied in her form. Singing the songs of love and letting that vibration clear out anything that's not love from her body and all around her and the Earth. She came for the joy. It's perfect; it's poetry, and it's part of the story. You must remember that we each chose. We chose our path, not just for sacrifice to martyr ourselves or throw ourselves into a cause or to suffer and struggle. We actually each chose to come in knowing that we gave ourselves the potential to awaken into our own version of paradise. We may not get it; there's no guarantee that we will embody it, but our hearts' and our souls' longing keeps calling us to nourish our little seeds, and against all odds to break open, even in the pavement in the concrete of this world. We have the strength and the resilience to get our roots down into the soil and into the earth and allow our unique and nourishing part of the garden to emerge and to grow. It's an important part of the story.

R: Thank you. Beautiful. Thank you for sharing that. Then you showed her this perfect version of her future self singing in the cathedral, feeling a really beautiful alignment with her soul. Why did you show that and how it affected her?

HS: The ego can easily attach the idea that, "oh, in order to feel peace inside, to truly feel absolute joy, we must succeed on our mission in order to arrive there," right? [Our ego believes] that you must do x, y, and z in order to reach that perfection. That is a mistake in translation. What we are showing her is her heart's deepest longing. This is her dream. Her dream is to bring heaven on earth for all beings and for her to enjoy that. What she came to do is to play in the Garden of Eden through song and joy. When she can feel that, when she can truly remember what it feels like; if she's doing it. . .not that she'll only feel that once she's doing it, but to remind her how delicious it feels. If that were here right now, if she was already there, if that were now, if she were living her perfect paradise right now, if you were living your heaven on earth right now. . . How would you feel? What would you feel in your body if you had done it, if you had succeeded, if you had got everything you thought you wanted and everything you dreamed of? If you had it right now, if this was perfection. . .how would you feel? How would you feel [now]?

Letting her feel this feeling of perfection of the joy of having believed in herself, the joy of having given herself the greatest gift, the joy of releasing her resistance — her fear of playing it small or choosing the backup plan. All that suffering she created by resisting her greatest dream. [We are] letting her also feel the joy, the absolute bliss in being exactly who she is. To feel that feeling of the full yes, that oh, yes, the vibration of yes, YES. YES! Feel that vibration of YES. THIS YES. THIS YES. NOW. Yes, the vibration of yes. *[Her voice got louder and more excited.]*

Envisioning our perfection gives us a point; it gives us a point to feel; it has already happened. It's already real. There's nowhere to strive. There's nowhere to get to. We've already felt it. We already felt this perfection inside of us. When we let ourselves really feel the perfection of this moment, the perfection of us letting ourselves live our favorite dream, we feel that feeling of relief, and freedom, and surrender, and safety, and relaxation. We're no longer in resistance to ourselves, resistance to who we want to be, resistance to what we want to do. When we are living in the full YES. Really visioning what is our YES? What is our heaven on Earth? Feeling it, seeing it, claiming it, knowing that we are already won. We are already that. We are that right now; no matter what it looks like in the 3D. That's one point of perfection. The perfection in our inner vision, that perfection of the eternal now, the future, whatever you want to call in the 3D, this thing that seems like we're striving for. It's a feeling, and that feeling, if heaven on Earth is right here, right now, how would we feel? Ava would feel peace; she would feel calm; she would feel joy; she would feel vital; she would feel energized; she would feel overflowing with love; she would feel at ease; she would feel absolute sanctuary; no more fear of death; no more fear of failing; no more fear of anything, because she's hardly letting herself feel that [now].

From that place of actually feeling that perfection within ourselves, we give ourselves; we create the vibration to match that, so that we can arrive there. We can invite miracles into our life. It takes two points. In three dimensions we must be grounded in both points. Really, it's three points. It's six points. It's...how to translate this...the eternal now perfection, which is everything, always, forever, in one moment, right now. Then we translate it in 3D, which has past, present, and future; above, below, within; x, y, z [coordinates], right? Three dimensions has x, y, z, 1, 2, 3, right? So there's segments, multiples of three.

There's multiples of three; there's also a multiple of six that creates the fabric. If you're standing inside the fabric of the *seed of life, in the flower of life, you would see a six-pointed star, and you were the single point in the center of it. From that single point, you can touch the entire existence. It looks like one, and it looks like six, and in 3D it also looks like 3, x, y, z , and it looks like a triangle, 1, 2, 3. We're trying to translate non-dual quantum physics into three-dimensional physics. It's a little bit clunky.

[*Please see Symbols Glossary]

There's the point of perfection, and she's feeling that point of perfection; she's letting herself feel. If heaven on Earth is right here, right now, how would it feel? Feeling that right now. She opens up one of the pathways to manifesting miracles. You've got the point, [that] is within ourselves right now. What does our life actually look like right now? It might look very, very different than our version of heaven on earth. I'm sure it's easy to feel the yes. The full f*ck YES, Y.E.S to the perfection; to the heaven moment. . . but then there's bringing ourselves to the now of the 3D. Whatever our life might look like. We might feel really limited; we might feel stuck. We might feel like we're choosing our backup plan. We might be surrounded with drama or challenges or health problems. It can feel really crunchy. Our tendency is to feel a lot of resistance to our now. A lot of "no" to the now, and a yes for that future perfection, that future heaven. When we do that we're mismatching — when we're not allowing ourselves to align in the 3D; we must match.

There's a pattern: When there's two points, there's an arc, the way energy moves, it creates the *Vesica Pisces shape. Within the Vesica Pisces shape is one petal of the Flower of Life, which then opens up, and that's the fabric. That's the architecture of the fabric, of space-[time], of the energy, of everything. That's the fabric, the flower of life, but it's three dimensional; it's not two dimensions. You see it in two dimensions in the drawings, but there are some physicists who have translated it to show it to you in three dimensions, and we are part of it. **(Yeah.)**

[*Please see Symbols Glossary]

To travel from point to point, you don't go on a straight line; you go on the same current. If you're at one point on the flower of life and you move in a current to the other point...it's an arc, and that arc is that Vesica Pisces arc. From one point to the other; from the point of perfection; heaven on earth; to our point now, to ourselves now. We must find the YES for our now. We must fully accept where we are right now and let go of our regrets of the past — that we didn't do it as fast or as well as we wanted, or that all of our failures and things we messed up on, or the fact that we're worried about our future, whether we'll ever get there. . .those are all - "NOs." That's all being in resistance to our now.

We must fully land in our now. Inside of our present moment, inside of ourselves, and find our yes, and find the full, energetic vibrational yes, right here, right in here, right now. When we find and fully accept our YES for our right now, this is the now we get to start with. It doesn't mean we accept all this crap that we're dealing with, and we just keep living like that. We accept it right now and stop being resistant to it, so that we have the power to change it. You can't change anything from the "no." We must accept our life exactly the way it is. This is our lesson right now. We're meant to go from this *yes* and manifest the miracle of our heaven on earth. That's our potential; it's our possibility. We can merge those two *yeses*. We can merge those two points on the Vesica Pisces into one now. That's what she was experiencing in a meditation yesterday. It's the perfect thing to add because it's all about the vibration of the *yes*. It's the sound; it's the song of *yes*. The songs of remembering in its simplest. . .there's all these different songs that can be sung, but ultimately, the greatest power is in the vibration of *yes*. It doesn't matter what language. It's the vibration of *yes;* it's the acceptance that is the opening of *yes*. *Yes,* opens all resistance. *Yes,* opens the clench in your jaw, the clench in your anus. The clench wherever you hold is all "no" it's all resistance.

The *yes,* the right now is the pure openness. We're showing her now, her past, her future, her present, possible futures, possible past. We've shown her all the different directions on this six-pointed star in a sense. We're inside of it. She told you the other day; it's like jacks, like a child's game, a little *jack.

[*Please see Symbols Glossary] ✳

That's the shape of it — the shape of being inside the Flower of Life. We're in the center. Your consciousness is your center point, and when you feel your *yes* to who you are, what you are right now. *Yes,* this is my now; this is what I've created up until this point. I forgive it all. I accept it all. Yes, yes. Now. Then we go in and we listen. We listen for our Heaven on Earth, our heart song, our little seed within ourselves. We say *YES* to that. Those two points match; we create the arc; the energetic arc can form. We can follow it in the now and create and manifest miracles. When we practice experiencing perfection on purpose.

She woke up in the middle of the night the other night and wrote these three words down. **Practice perfection** on **purpose**. It doesn't mean the egoic form of perfection. It doesn't mean we have to be perfect. It means [feeling] that feeling of perfection. That feeling when everything has worked out — we have done it, happily ever after. That feeling of the happily ever after in the future. We bring that to the now. If we feel that now [regardless of external conditions]. . .if you feel that perfection now, how are we going to behave? What are we going to do? We're going to live our greatest joy. We're going to live our greatest service. We're going to live our greatest purpose when we bring acceptance of our now and an acceptance of our most perfect dream come true, and we marry them in this present moment. That's how we manifest miracles. That's how we awaken to our own song and remember our own song. The songs we are remembering are here to alchemize our ability to open our eyes.

The vesica piscis on its side is an eye. We open our eyes. We open our current; we create our current between our now and our desired future. We let go of our past; we let go of all of our worries of the future; we tap into the divine potential of perfection right here, right now. We practice feeling perfection right now. That means surrendering, accepting, loving. It means embodying the *yes*, The *Yes*. *Yes*. *Yes*. *Yes*. So, we are showing her her YES! *Yes*. We are showing her the yes.

R: **Beautiful. Did you want to add anything regarding why you showed her what she is doing on the ship? Or in this temple of sound at the same time? Or, did we talk about that?**

HS: Oh, well, I've used this metaphor throughout the book to help. It's really hard for the human mind to accept other [than] the idea of something outside of [ourselves]. We [are] all so confused on like, what is God? What is the Great Mystery? What is Great Spirit? What are aliens? What's really going on out there? We want it to be us and another thing, right? We need this otherness. We need this story of otherness, so that we can come back to our unity. There's this idea that there's this benevolent force that's here to help us awaken and help us bring ourselves into perfection. In the 3D, sure that's other. It could be this galactic council that's here to help us; it can be "I;" it can be the designer; it can be God itself. In its essence though, in non-dual perspective, and in unitive perspective, we're all one. It's all within us. I was just showing her, from the lens of other, that as she lives her profession, as she really embodies her greatest joy and her greatest heaven on earth — singing in cathedrals, letting her voice fill these temples of sound here on Earth — she's connecting to the temples of sound of all the muses; she's connecting to that vibration of yes, and the vibration of love that's throughout the multiverse, that's in all of our hearts. At the heart of God itself. It's everything. It's all oneness. **(R: Yeah.)**

It doesn't matter whether or not you take the story of the other, the ships, or whether you realize that it [is a story that] helps us. It gives us these baby steps to open up our consciousness, so that we can accept that we're actually the creators of our own heaven on earth right here and right now. It's not somewhere else. It's not some other place and some other time. It's all in the perfect now, and then when we die, it'll be that perfect now, wherever that is, right? It doesn't matter so much. I was showing her though. . .I was helping remind her that if she needs that illusion of other; she needs that metaphor of other. There's a whole team of beings out there supporting her and helping her. [When] she goes and she steps into those temples of sound and those cathedrals and she sings, she is connecting to the Divine Love of the universe, and the universe is loving her right back. She's not up there singing alone. She's up there singing with all of creation, singing the joy that is creation. Creation is a song. The songs of remembering is all about that. All of it is this beautiful song, the one verse, the universe, one-verse, one song, one sound; it all comes back to that. We were just showing her that we got her back. She's got her own back. It's all in alignment. Yes. Y.E.S. Period.

R: **Beautiful. Thank you. I did want to ask if we have this opportunity, because I know some other...we had this conversation trying to kind of make sense of it. I know there's different levels and layers of...let's say our Soul, our consciousness...Some people call the Higher-Self, and then above that maybe there's another monadic consciousness or another collective consciousness as part of your soul in the way that consciousness has been fractal until we arrived here to the 3D. Would that be appropriate to share with us how it's being fractalized?**

HS: (*Laughs out loud.*) Well, I believe the definition of fractal involves the infinite. A fractal is infinite, so it's hard to describe, in limited. . .in words, the infinite fractals, when it is infinite. There're infinite layers, but there's no layers at all. I'm not really sure how relevant it is to go into all the different layers at the moment because ultimately the point is about collapsing all the different layers and merging into the oneness of bringing our unique consciousness of our now into the universal perfection. Feeling that YES brings us into unity. I'm not sure how relevant it is to go into all the different layers right now. **(R: Okay.)** It seems more relevant to help us all collapse the layers and allow us all to be inspired to bring our heaven on earth right now. To practice perfection on purpose. **(R: Yeah.)** Right now.

R: **Beautiful. Thank you. Yeah, I had the feeling you might won't find that relevant at this moment. Maybe we can talk about it another time when we have the opportunity and when it does serves a purpose. So, I wanted to start to focus on the book and information that can help us share this work in the best way. (HS: Ok.) Thank you so much. Is there anything that you want to guide us on first? That you've noticed. . .from the way that we are managing our doubts and concerns? To help us make that more clear?**

HS: The first word that's coming through is another "P" word. Practice perfection, on purpose, with **patience**. Be patient with yourself, be patient with each other, be patient with the **process**. The means don't justify the ends; you must practice patience, **perpetually**, in the process of **producing** our perfection. . .our **product** *(laughs)*. So remember the 'P's. Practice patience. In the patience, the way's open. When you're noticing the fear and the resistance and the conflict, those are all bells. Come back into patience. It's all perfect. The timing is perfect. It's okay.

THE DAUGHTER OF TRUTH

R: Yeah. Okay. Wonderful. Now I know Ava has some ideas about how to share her names through the different materials that she has, and she was wondering if her idea is what she should follow, or do you have any other ideas and opinions about how to show the material with her [different] names in the best way?

HS: Yes, her ideas is actually quite elegant. So, the thing is, Allison means daughter of truth. Ali means a light of God. Avalon means eternal paradise. Ava means breath. It means life; it means Eve. It doesn't matter so much which name is used because it's all the same, but there is an elegant poetry in the work that she's been doing to embrace the potential. Nothing has to be shared. There's no. . .no one is forced to share anything; there's no must. There's no "have to" do anything. There's an invitation here to share for the benefit of all beings, but there is no "have to", but it is possible. There is a beauty, there is a vibration of healing that can happen if she does embrace this idea. . .that has been coming to her in meditations, in her dreams.

I will share it now so you both are aware. . .everyone is aware of this idea. It is be patient, be gentle. This is about being gentle. We're here to be gentle and in the gentleness create profound change. . .so we can be gentle. We don't have to be hard, but there is a way. There are many ways that this information that has been shared in this book can be shared.

There're so many ways, but there is this way that she's leaning into, which has a beautiful poetry to it. That helps to not only lift up and heal her own personal traumas, but potentially also to heal universal traumas and to bring conflict into resonance. Her given name is Allison, which means daughter of truth, she has the potential to bring in great healing from the Christian Church and the traumas that Christianity has created and its distortions.

There was Jesus's word and Jesus's message of love and forgiveness, and then there was. . .what happened to the message and how it's been changed over time and used as the technique for control and submission and fear and separating us from our direct connection to Source. The point was to create a direct connection with Source, not to create an intermediary, and they were the only ones who have the power, and that power has been abused for many thousands of years. That power is still present, and there is a way to alchemize that power. It's possible, if she feels up for it, she could bring those other sections [about Issa] back in. Yes. There is no need. None of it needs to be shared, but any of it can be shared. If she uses her first name, then in a way she is maintaining the integrity of some of the things that came through the channel. Even at the [previous] ending (at end of Session 9). . . for if you take Allison, and you add an "E" on it, you give it some space and you add an "E," and then all of a sudden it says "all is one."

If you share it goes from "alone" to "all is one" to "one," so there's a beautiful poetry. . . Ava came through in a period of time, and she could choose that; it's all. . .it's all perfect. It doesn't really matter which one she chooses, but I am enjoying the poetry of just Allison, the daughter of truth.

[**Ava's note**: Above, the channel references that we 'could bring those other sections back in'. As mentioned once before, we have long deliberated whether to include the Issa materials in this book. We wondered if it was distracting to the central theme of the book or would be too polarizing, due to the controversial nature of the material. Personally, I felt reluctant to share these parts out of sensitivity and respect for my family's beliefs. After contemplating this choice for many years and asking the channel about it, because we couldn't agree amongst ourselves, we decided to bring the Issa materials back in, after all. I realized that I feel weary of hiding anymore. I know I am a good person, and I can feel that my heart is not *deluded by demons. . . I finally had to accept that I would rather have a relationship of authenticity and acceptance over one of me hiding who I am out of fear of losing those I love. I surrender. I let go of my attachment to outcome and trust that if I do upset my family and other Christians, that they can understand, forgive and accept me for who I am. . I share this information as a call for peace, acceptance, and forgiveness. May peace begin within.*

HS: There is an aspect of what she's sharing with the letter. . .

[They are referring to a beautiful letter that Allison wrote to her family to help prepare them for the release of this book and was considering including it as part of the introduction of this book. After reading the letter, we decided together to keep the letter part private.]

If she adds the letter to her family and then reveals the story, not from a place of "Oh, I'm speaking for Jesus," but more of this humble call to that. . .she does love Jesus with all her heart. **(R: Yeah.)** Jesus is her father and her grandfather and her uncle and her brother and her lover. Jesus is in all beings. Christ consciousness is that seed in each of our hearts that carries forth. **(R: Mmmhmm.)** Jesus was the Son of God; that is true. Jesus came with a message of peace and hope and salvation, to help us connect directly once more with God. He was the minority; he was the heretic of his time. It is possible that it is time for it. It is time for a new, a new message, but it is a big one to share. It's a big step to take, but it is a beautiful one. . .to not cut those parts out.

The other idea would be to cut all the parts out and to add them later into another edition or into its own book. Either are acceptable; there's no 'have to'. **(R: Yeah.)** We share this information with you to help beings awaken, to sing the songs of remembering, seeing our own personal heaven on earth right here on Earth. If it feels like heaven on earth to share all of it, and through the lens of Allison and to bring back those stories that were cut and to share it all. . .if that's the heaven on earth, then by all means, go for it. If it needs more patience, and you cut all. . .you choose to cut all those parts out and share them in a future edition or in another book that's dedicated to Issa, both are fine. It doesn't change the message. The message of the songs of remembering, the book that you two are bringing through stays the same regardless. It doesn't need to be **pressure**. Here's another "P" word. It doesn't need to be about **pressure**. It doesn't need to be about pressure. **(R: Yeah.)** It's about practicing perfection and being patient in the now.

We like her idea. It is beautiful. It's poetic in many layers, because the letter that she shares also includes the deep suffering that she encountered because of the church and the deep feeling that because of all of her visions of hell realms that she must be bad. She must be from hell. That's what she believed as a child. She was such a bright little being, who heard the voices of the angels, who hear God. She's such a beautiful, bright little light.

Unfortunately, hearing the tales of fire and brimstone and hell, she remembered those visions, she's seen them, she's experienced them. She was afraid if she told anyone that she would be condemned. That they would all see her as the devil, see her as hell, so she didn't tell anyone. She hid it deep inside and felt deeply ashamed that she must be the devil. She must be from hell, or that this must actually be hell, because she'd seen all those visions of hell realms. The church, the preacher was telling her that this was hell. She believed that she must be bad, and so she locked her gifts away, and she locked her seed deep down in her heart because she thought, oh, well, then if she's bad, if she's really in hell, then if she really lives her love, if she really lives heaven on earth, then the worst kind of hell would be to have your greatest dream and then to have it ripped away from you. Taken away from you because you're bad, and so because she took on the belief that she was bad, because what the church was telling her about herself. . .mistakenly not understanding what these visions of hell were. She had a lot of work to do. She had a lot of trauma to [integrate in order to] uncover her seed, to allow her seed, to nourish her seed enough to let it sprout. She had to uncover. . .it was very deep, deep, deep under layers of feeling like she was bad and that she was condemned. **(R: Yeah.)**

That's not what Jesus wanted. Jesus didn't want to take our bright lights and our beautiful little children and to scare them into thinking that they were bad people. **(R: Right.)** The visions that she had; she had visions of hell, and she also had visions of heaven. She had visions of angels; she had visions of paradise; she had visions of all sorts of things; she just remembered more than most. The preacher got it wrong; the church got it wrong. We can create our own personal hells. Most of us are living in our own personal hells because of all of our resistance to our lives. We feel so disconnected from Source within us that we are living hell right now. **(R: Yeah.)**

She wasn't bad, and it's sad that the church taught that there was no one to support her to help her understand that because she had visions and dreams of hell, that she was in hell, that she was the devil, there was. . .there were no resources to help the children understand their dreams, to help those ones that can remember more, because some do. Some come in with more memory, and some come in with less, each soul chooses.

What if we had resources in place? What if there was a system in place to help teach our children how to navigate these terrible dreams and to not take on these shattering beliefs that they're bad, and that they're in hell, and that they can't live a good life because they'll just be punished if they do? What a tragedy that is, but what a beautiful, beautiful gift that she went into the depths of her darkness. She unburied that seed deep under all the piles of pain and blame and feeling bad and unworthy and condemned and separate, and she still found that seed, and she still nourished it, and it still blossomed. The compost from all that sh*t is beautiful. **(R: Yeah.)** It's beautiful poetry.

R: I'm curious though, a lot of the concern was about her safety, and I'm getting the sense that you're giving her a full yes to. . .to fully embody her dreams, and it sounds to me like, it feels like there's safety within that, and you mentioned. . .I'm just wondering if there's anything else you want to add regarding this topic because it was something we were working through a lot through the process?

HS: Yes. This journey. . .for anyone who reads this book, they get to read of the personal journey of someone's becoming, of someone's awakening, of someone's embodying their truth, and we all must uncover our fears and our resistances and our blame and our projections and our victim. We must step out of that triangle that you mentioned *(The Drama Triangle)* and to truly step into our embodied power.

You are taking on a big project, and it is irresponsible to think that you are not potentially challenging the Christian Church, if you choose to do this. You are, you are choosing to challenge the foundations of the Christian Church if you choose to share all of this information. It is not something trivial or to be taken lightly. From what I can feel from and see that the church, although it's not as powerful as it was several hundred years ago where the penalties were death, there is still a lot of power, and there are still a lot of people hungry for that power, and who don't want to give it up. As she and you step more fully into your full embodied light, into your full embodied purpose, into your full embodied heaven on earth, into your true version of yourself. . .as you truly let your seed fully sprout and blossom into the world, then you're right, that fear does transform into a deeper knowing.

It is possible that this can be shared in a way, in a softness, in a tenderness and in a humbleness, that might actually crack open the shells of the Christians who have such a shell around them. [That they believe that] they are broken and that they are wretched, and that they can never save themselves. That only Jesus could have saved them, and thanks God, Jesus died for all of their sins because they're so wretched that they will never be able to truly rise into the love that they truly are. There's this dis-empowered narrative that is running in the Christian Church that is rather heartbreaking because Jesus came to offer us a way and to remind us that we are each the sons and the daughters of God. And that yes, through him, through his example, through his merging with his knowing that he is God within. He shone such a brilliant light into the world to help inspire each of us. It was [meant] to inspire each of us to merge with our own inner light within. It wasn't meant to be a dis-empowering story to separate us further from God. . .that we needed [an external] Him to save us from our wretchedness.

That story, that narrative isn't working. Here we are two thousand years later; Jesus left us to steward the Earth, and look what we're doing. Look around at how we are holding dominion. This is our dominion. We're the kings and the queens of Earth here to take care of and guard and steward God's creation. Look at what we've done. Just in the last couple hundred years, look what we've done to each other and to the planet. Jesus came with such a powerful mission, and he was the greatest avatar; he was the greatest enlightened being ever to walk on Earth. There's no debate of that.

Would you recognize Jesus if he came back now? Revelations says that he will come back suddenly, the same way he came before, but when he came before he was born [in] a minority, poor, working-class homeless family. He was born in a barn with the goats and the cows and the shit. He heard that song; he heard the sound of God in his heart, and he didn't know how to participate. He didn't know how to just be a carpenter in the world, so he left, and he disappeared.

Some stories say that he went to the Far East and studied with the great sages and the masters there, and learned to open up his channel and to feel his divinity and to connect with God fully, and to feel that he was this beautiful perfection. Made in the image of God with a message of love to give to the world. He embodied that knowing and he came back to share it, knowing that it was heresy. He came back knowing that it was heresy and that the penalty for heresy was execution. He could have chosen a life making a family, having a child, building a home and living 'til old age, growing old and dying. He could have chosen all of that, but he didn't; he chose to share his ministry of love. He came to show. . .he chose to show the corruption that had come into the places of God, into the houses of God. He came to disrupt that corruption. If he hadn't lost his temper that day and thrown over the tables in the markets, I wonder maybe he could have shared his teachings for longer, but he chose that path he chose. He chose to be executed for the benefit of all beings. He gave it all for love. He risked everything, his own life. Yes, he died for our sins, but not in the way we think. He died to show us how disconnected from God we have become.

Maybe it is time for a new narrative because the narrative that we're wretched and broken and imperfect and can never rise into the true image of God that we are, and that we need a savior to come and save us. That's not why Jesus came. Jesus came to help awaken the love of God within each of our hearts, to be in each of our hearts. Yes, he's a savior, but not from this disempowered, victim place. If you choose to tell that story, choose it from your path of devotion and know that you are choosing to speak heresy. Maybe your heresy will be well received, maybe your heresy will be welcomed because with it is this vibration of love and tenderness.

She wants to recognize Jesus when. . .if he comes back the way he came before, she would want to recognize him, so she's dedicated her life to live like him, so that if he comes, she'll f**king know. She will see him; she will recognize him, and she'll be able to walk up to him and look him in the eyes and thank him for coming back, because we need all the help we can get. The way so many of us have been living, if he came back right now, would you recognize him? If you walked up to him, would you be able to look him in the eyes? He left us in charge. He left us here to steward this beautiful Earth, and we've been looting it, and raping it, and pillaging it. We have not been taking good care of it. [Allison got more emotional and started to cry a bit.]

R: Take another deep breath into the body to just feel it deeply and let it go. Thank you so much for this beautiful clarity and message. It's really helpful to understand how to share this book and the freedom that we have, and the feeling of how to do it in alignment with each of us, our soul and excitement, and the clarity of the message that you're sharing right now.

HS: I need to share with you a moment that I've tapped into. As you know, we've shared with you that Allison has been refining her channel to where she taps in with you, and she also taps in through her writings and songs and she's been writing this. . . letter. She's been writing even what I share with you now, and I'm sharing it with you now from the nowness of it,but she's been writing this. . .**(R: Yeah.)** And she looking forward to sharing. . .to showing it to you, and there's still a question of like. . .are we really ready? She wonders, and **(R: Yeah.)** you must both choose; there's no pressure, but be aware that you are choosing to step into a heretical realm for the benefit of all beings. If you choose to share this, and if that's what you choose, then so be it. An infinite blessing is on you, but know that heresy sometimes is not rewarded with success. Sometimes it is. It is possible that this could be the gentle route, the clear route that could actually crack open the heart of Christianity back to its source. It's possible that it could. We cannot tell you the future. **(R: Right.)**

R: Okay, thank you for sharing this. I want to also feel into other parts of the book that we were wondering about. . .because part of the thing that's important for us is not to create more fear. There's a few sentences throughout the book, like that many would leave. . . We had a question if it should stay as is. . .? We see the benefit of sharing the information also, as is, and also we have a question if we're not just creating layers of fear that actually ripple in the wrong way than we wanted to do. So from your perspective about sharing this information, what do you find the most appropriate?

HS: In the beginning, as she was opening her channel, there of course [were] still distortions of fear. She spent a lot of her life seeing the inevitability of the destruction that we were causing on planet Earth and struggling deeply with how to participate and how to help and feeling rather overwhelmed by the state of affairs. She was even published in the New York Times Magazine when she was 21 speaking this, and the feedback was that she was being too harsh. Then nobody wanted to hear it, and it got taken out of context. It came across as her calling people greedy and uncaring; that we were, you know, raping and pillaging the land. This was before the environmental movement had really even gotten started and there was a lot of kick back, and she got very afraid of the resistance and the feedback that she got. She got a lot of scolding. A lot of. . .who was she to go into a major magazine publication and start telling everyone that they're greedy? There's a lot of defensiveness that came up because of it.

She hid for many years after that; she didn't quite know how to make a positive impact; she didn't want to come across as being scolding and harsh. Through permaculture and regenerative agriculture is where she focused her attention after that; it was a way to shift that. She felt that she was taking in this feedback that she was being too harsh and judgmental and critical. It's funny that this came up again in the beginning of these transcripts, because the words like "razor's edge," and the words like "most need to leave," there's truth in them, and there's also a slightly distorted perspective. Each of us chose to come here now, even though we have exceeded the carrying capacity of planet Earth in the amount of resources and population growth. We have exceeded the carrying capacity of planet Earth, that is a rather simple, pretty well-known scientific fact. At the same time, each of our souls chose to come in right now to participate in the great awakening, and so some of us did choose to come in knowing that we may not necessarily live a full life span of the human being.

The human being now from this perspective feels terrified by that perspective, that we might die in some catastrophe or famine or plague or war before our old age, but our souls are eternal. Our souls came in here and incarnated for a purpose, and many of us. . .our deeper awareness knows that we may need, we may. . .we will all leave; every one of us will leave. Every living being alive on planet Earth right now will eventually leave. It wasn't meant to come out like a threat, that we're on a razor's edge between being exterminated or reaching the New Earth.

It's true that the story that she saw. . .there is truth to it in that our actions have consequences. The nuclear warheads and the way that we are living disconnected from our hearts is having consequences on future generations, and on our own souls, and on our own hearts. We're breaking our own hearts. We are all one and whatever we do to the Earth and to each other; we are doing to ourselves. We forget this, right? Because of the games of Earth, we forget, but the songs of remembering are being sung, and we're starting to remember. It doesn't matter necessarily whether you keep those words in the book or not, but it is important to clarify that this story isn't a story of threat, and doom and destruction. It's a wake-up call; it's just shaking us awake from our sleep and being like, "Hey, we have created so much damage and destruction on planet Earth that we are putting into question whether or not we will continue to be able to exist on this planet with our civilization intact."

This is not a new. . .this is not a surprise to most people. Most people who are paying attention realize this, and to feel the impact of that, to feel the grief of this is so overwhelming that most of us need to distract and numb in order to cope, and in order to function in this world. We're participating in what is contributing to the destruction of our ecosystem, and the overpopulation of our planet. All of these things are true.

And. . .remember, we are creating our own heaven on earth. God gave us this planet to create heaven on earth, and we have made a mess of it because we've gotten so lost in our own distortion and our own fear, that we keep harming each other and ourselves. We are so. . .deep down most of us are so heartbroken at ourselves at the way we've been behaving that we are **punishing** ourselves by **perpetuating** the **problem**. More 'P' words. Peace, it's time for peace. If you leave the words in the book, make sure you clarify either at the beginning or at the end or maybe both, **(R: Yeah.)** that it's not exactly the way it seems; it's not that these stories are false or that these stories are absolutely true. Another 'P' word. . . Allison loves **parables**, and parables are stories that have a lesson in them. A lesson of love and of choice and of responsibility. They inspire us to be better people. That's what parables do. These are all parables. I wasn't trying to scare you; even though in a way, maybe we need to get scared a little bit. Maybe we have been too complacent in participating in this. . .

R: Yeah. That was my feeling about it a little bit.

HS: It's not like there's a team of alien beings up here in the atmosphere ready to hit detonate, or to sing the songs of undissolving, so that we're all going to just blow up because we're so f**ked up. Right? That's not the point. The point is. . . "Hey, we can't keep going on like this. How do you want your truth? Do you want it soft? Do you want it gentle? Do you want it harsh? Do you want it sci-fi? How do you want your truth?" Because the truth is that we are made in the image of God to claim our birthright to create heaven on earth. That is our potential; that is our gift. That's what we can rise into, and look what we're doing with our collective dream. Look at what we're all creating; look what we're doing to each other. Look what we're doing. It's silly.

We've gotten so addicted to suffering that we're perpetuating more suffering. We need to break our addiction to suffering. Perhaps scaring ourselves silly a little bit and perhaps contemplating for a moment that we might be on the brink of being all annihilated because of our ineptitude to take good care of this planet, maybe that's a message we need. But more importantly, we need to forgive ourselves. We need to forgive ourselves for this mess we've created and to realize that we can create heaven on earth here, and some of us will need to leave.

We're not all going to live until we're 100. The earth is getting more and more destabilized. There're more and more natural disasters. Many of us are going to leave; it's just everyone of us is going to leave; it's not a threat. We already know this in the context that it was shared and the way it was shared, and the way the story unfolded. You're going through the evolution of her own mind, and this deep fear of seeing this world from a very young age saw. . .it was she could see that the Titanic was headed for the iceberg, and no matter who she said it to or how loud she yelled, nobody noticed that there was an iceberg. . . **(R: Yeah.)**. . .that we headed straight for [it]. She loves humanity so much; she loves this Earth so much; she loves life. She loves the possibility of the beauty that we can create with these bodies; the magic we can create. The miracles we can manifest on this planet are so profound. She is so in love with the possibility of what the gift that we were given. We've all forgotten how to claim our gift, and so maybe it was from a less. . .ahh, what's the right word? The story is perfect as it is. It's a perfect evolution of someone's surrendering into the perfection of who they are, and she has been scared shitless of what's going to happen on planet Earth. **(R: Yeah.)**

She's been an environmentalist for twenty-five years, long before everyone else, [probably referring to the current main stream environmental movement of our times] and she hasn't known how exactly to make an impact, or how to make a change. There was this part of her consciousness that has been seeing this razor's edge, has been seeing the fact that we exceeded our carrying capacity, and so part of her consciousness helped, and we wove. . . The Designers, the 'I', the Oneness. We all together wove the story, and it's perfect, the story is perfect as it is, in its imperfection. The most important part is not to get caught in fear, fear of being punished for being bad or wrong. That's not the point. We take in the story and we let it all wash through us; we allow ourselves to forgive ourselves for our failings, for our ignorance, our mindless consumption, our distraction. We're so addicted to the suffering and so afraid of pain at the same time. We've been all self-medicating with distracting ourselves with everything that this earth has to offer and exploiting the resources so that we can all feel more and more comfortable while deep down we're extremely uncomfortable. **(R: Yeah.)**

This story, this book, the point of this book is to bring us into our hearts, to bring us into our love and into forgiveness. It might be a good idea to have a little warning at the beginning, so if you're going to share the parts about Issa, then share her humble story of her challenges with Christianity, but at the deepest part, how much she loves Jesus. **(R: Yeah.)** She's not a blasphemous human. She's not from the devil. She's not from hell; she's not some false p[rophet]. . .she's not bad. **(R: Yeah.)** She came with a message of love for all humanity because she loves us all so much; she loves herself so much. She wants to play with all of us in the Garden of Eden. We kicked ourselves out of the Garden of Eden. The story of Eden, acknowledge the tree of knowledge, that's our minds; we separated ourselves from God. We can come back to the Garden of Eden if we all choose it together, so let's focus on the possibility.

Here is another 'P' word for us. Let's focus on the **possibility** of putting ourselves into the perfection that this world is. With the world that we are given, we can still do it. We can still do it. There's a lot of work to do. We've made quite a mess, and none of us are going to make it out alive, but please. . .this isn't about threat. This isn't about a razor's edge, that you better, you better shape up, or you're gonna be punished. [I'm starting to laugh and right then she started to be more emotional] Forgive yourself. . .forgive yourself; forgive each other. Help us rise out of the ignorance and help us take responsibility and become stewards of earth that we were meant to be. That's what Issa came here to teach us, is to be the stewards of Earth. That's why we're here. We're here to be stewards of Earth and stewards of our own heaven on earth.

You were given a paradise with a body to feel it all in. Instead of being endless and formless and boundless. You're given the gift of getting to experience the light of God through an embodied form; to get to touch and to taste and enjoy the five senses and the infinite senses that are beyond the five senses; to share in the beauty and the vibration of love and music, and magic, and art, and connection, and play. We're all here to quench our thirst with the most infinite beautiful water.

But, we're choosing war and separation, and destruction, and waste, and ignorance, and distraction, and poisoning ourselves. We're **poisoning** ourselves with drugs and alcohol, and **plastic**, and **pollution**. . .all those 'P'words. . .because we're feeling disconnected from Source. Those medicines, when we're self-medicating, they give us a momentary relief from it, right? We take in those poisons to feel less inhibited, to feel less tense, less stress, to feel more connected to our joy again; that's why we do it. That's why we get addicted to other things beyond love and light and nourishing things.

We can forgive ourselves and rise; rise into the human beings we're meant to be, this beautiful gift of God. Let Jesus's message **profoundly penetrate** to the core of you. We are made in the image of God. We are here to forgive and to love, and to merge our divinity with our humanity. To give it all for love. Let Jesus save you over and over again by saving your own heart, by releasing and surrendering and loving, loving so fearlessly and so perfectly. You're not wretched; you're not broken. Yes, we're flawed. Yes, we're humans. Yes, we make mistakes, but we are perfectly imperfect; we're imperfectly perfect. We are made in the image of God. We can rise and be the stewards of Earth and create heaven on earth. We can. It's our birthright. It's what we're meant to do. Forgive yourself.

R: **Thank you so much. I have a few more questions. Can we address those? (HS: Okay.) Thank you so much. I wanted to ask regarding...there's a topic about the facial recognition and her being recognized, tagged, and things in that nature. Can you share more about what's important to share or not share regarding those topics?**

HS: The more. . . she and you and we all embody the vibration of love and share this from the vibration of love, and share what needs to be shared from the vibration of love, the more protected we are from potential threats. (**R: Yeah.**) It's true that there are beings out there in power that don't want to lose power, and this information can maybe be perceived as a threat. It is possible. When you speak heresy, when you go against the predominant power structures, you are in a way, you are choosing a less certain path. Choose it with love or don't. Be patient, be gentle. In a way, the same thing. . .there wasn't facial recognition software two-thousand years ago, but it's the same. Jesus knew that he was speaking heresy, and he knew that he was going against the **predominant paradigm**. . .more 'P'words. He chose it, and he chose the consequences.

Each of us must choose how we're going to live our life and how comfortable we're going to be, and how many risks we're going to take or not take, and how many dangers we're going to put ourselves in front of. She's got to do what feels right for her. She's got to step into her role as much as she's willing to. If she's ready to speak heresy for the benefit of all beings, then, f**k, you know, somebody's got to do it. We're all doing it in our different ways. There's a lot of people coming out and speaking heresy right now, because we need it. We need a new her-story. We need a story of the Divine Feminine heresy, all the different meanings of this word and the roots of the word. It's time for the woman's story to come out; it's time for her stories, time for heretical material to come out, because the paradigm, the narrative that's running is not working, and this is a time of change. Just know that you're choosing to step into a battle, a battle between the ego and fear and love and truth. Love always wins. (**R: Yeah.**) Love always wins, but I don't know exactly how.

R: **Okay. I do know there's a lot of other materials of many other channels and information that already challenge the readers, and people are being attracted to certain materials and some others are not attracted to certain materials because of their own desire to stay in their perceptions of [whatever it is]. . .and at the same time, I'm just trying to get clarity regarding how it is most appropriate to share the information in a way that also keep the safety. This is why the idea of sharing it completely anonymously was also an option. So both could happen in the balance of sharing the profound messages you bring forward and the love and the clarity, and the truth, and the joy, and the safety, and the excitement of sharing this material. In a way that it support Allison's nervous system and myself.** *[long pause]* **I do sense that we talked about it, I'm just wondering if there's anything else regarding that balance that can come with clarity or is there anything else to be shared?**

HS: I'm hearing words, more 'P' words. I'm hearing the words **pray** for **protection**. Pray for **peace**. I'm not hearing a specific answer so much. What I'm hearing is an invitation, the invitation to be a heretic or the invitation to take it slower. . .in this now moment. I can't claim to know all the answers. I don't claim to know all the answers. I don't. . . I wish I could give you a simple answer of what to do or not to do. (**R: Yeah.**) If the true intention is for peace, if this story is being shared for the benefit of all beings, then be clear in that and share that and share it gently; share it gently. You're going to have to choose what that means to you. I don't know how to tell you. (**R: Yeah.**) But nothing needs to be done, but everything can be done.

Allison's already accepted that she is a heretic, and that her life trajectory may not be normal. She's done the work to accept that she's not settling down and having a family and building a house and doing all those things. Maybe she can still have that. She can still adopt; she can do that later on. She's chosen to share a message of love with the world because of her love of life and her love of humanity and her love of the Earth. She's already made the choice. This is the **pace**, another 'P'word, at what pace are you going to share? Like either one could work; you could cut out everything about Issa and share it later, and it would still totally work, or you could keep all of it in, and it would totally work in a different way. It is possible that her family may struggle with it, and it could affect their relationship. It's possible. Yes. Yet, I think she's touching in on this. The letter that she's been writing from this place of humbleness, she's really asking for their help. She's asking for the help of Christians. She's asking for forgiveness. She's asking for us to break our hearts open and truly let Jesus into all of our hearts. **(R: Yeah.)**

I think if it's shared from that place that maybe it could be received in this time; it may be perfect. **(R: Yeah.)** If you're both not a full 100% f**k-yes for it, then there's no harm in waiting; there's no harm in putting out another edition including the secret parts about Issa. It could be a sensation if you added it later or if you added it in another book. It doesn't really matter so much. You could do it fully anonymously, but the issue with fully anonymous in this day and age is that everything is so. . . everyone is so out there, it's so transparent. The channel will be more trusted if there's a face with it. Sure, you can release it anonymously, and that was the way it was often done in the last twenty, thirty years, but in the times that we are in now, it feels like it would have a bigger impact if she was willing to show her face.

We completely understand why she was resistant in the past. It's a lot to accept, and one must choose it. **(R: Yeah.)** She wasn't ready to choose it then; she didn't even realize what she was choosing. She didn't realize what she was getting herself into. I think now she is realizing that her face and her songs, and even potentially her first name are in a way part of the code. **(R: Yeah.)** I can tell that she's feeling. . . she's realizing the **power**, another 'P' word, she's noticing the power that's present if she fully, if she more fully reveals this work with her songs and with the face and with potentially even her name, Allison. **(R: Yeah.)** Well also works. Ava is fine, too. It's not an untruth, but imagine the potency of the channel of the truth if her real given first name was the name and not an alias. **(R: Yeah.)** Like there is a power there. **(R: Right)** There's an integrity there, and it's not that the integrity is not there if she doesn't, but there is a power there and she feels it. She knows it; she acknowledges it. She realizes it; it's just. . .it's taking a lot of surrender and bravery to fully...**(R: Yeah.)** embody it, but. . . **patient**. . . **(R: Okay.)** It's happening. It's happening.

R: **Beautifully. Thank you so much. I wanted to ask a few more things and also to make sure we're receiving healing for her, through her body. I was wondering, are you working on her body while we were talking?**

HS: Oh, yes, we've been working the whole time. Her currents are pulsing strongly and clearly. She's noticed it from the very beginning, from the first moment you began. The rhythmic pulsing in her hands and feet has been growing. Yes, we have been working on her this whole time and in a way is one of the reasons we showed her what we showed her is to truly help her step into her full vitality and to let all these challenges with her ear and her bladder and her mental state, just all the different things that she struggles with. They're all remnants and the distortions of her fear.

The ear was in her resistance to truly hearing her channel, and hearing everything she was hearing was too much, so she was putting cotton in her own ears in a way. She acknowledges that her ears are practically perfectly clear. The more she listens, the more they clear. We're showing her her heaven on earth reality because she's ready to fully step into it. She has broken and is breaking her addiction to suffering and pain. This existential addiction we have to pain and suffering is because of this feeling that we're unworthy or that we're bad. She is surrendering that as she steps more and more into her true embodiment of herself and loving herself more, and choosing relationships that are honoring her, and she's making choices in her life that are honoring her greatest desires. She's aligning with herself and aligning with love. She's aligning with her vitality more and more, and her vibration is rising to the point where these lessons that were drawing her awareness to her listening, and drawing awareness to her womb space, her creative center; drawing awareness to her sacred temple. She is receiving those lessons; she's aligning with those lessons, and so they are no longer necessary, and they are dissolving away, as she has been in a place of deep hibernation this winter and going deep into them, going all the way into those patterns of pain and suffering and illness, and [it's] allowing her to upgrade, and allowing her to embody her fullest potential. She's feeling it, and we're helping her feel it.

We are noticing that she is aligning herself as we've been talking. We haven't had to do as much because she's been doing it, because she's feeling and realizing how to do it, how to truly align herself with love and align herself with her life and align herself with her light. (**R: Yeah.**) That's where vitality lies. When we live in full alignment with ourselves, our vibration is so high that there's little space, there's no need for it. The pain of suffering is there to draw our awareness to places that we are out of alignment, and sometimes, unfortunately, we have chosen life paths where pain and suffering are going to be perpetual in our life path. We've sometimes chosen the pain and suffering for a deeper soul reason, and I am sorry for those. . .that not everyone is able to transcend all their pain and suffering, and Allison may not either. She may. . .there may still be times when her vessel is so sensitive that as she has lessons, she needs to learn they manifest in the physical quite clearly. (**R: Yeah.**)

That doesn't mean that she's failing or not doing a good job. It's all perfect. Sometimes we need it. Sometimes we need the pain and the suffering to draw our awareness and attention to a place, to where we finally do really face ourselves and face our truth and face our soul, so we can truly live in alignment with our life. Yes, we are working on her; we have been working on her, but more importantly, she is aligning with herself and that works way better than us doing it for her. Right? It's that someone else needs to save you thing. It's that whole idea that we are broken, and need saving and need fixing, and we can't do it ourselves. There is part of our consciousness that wants that; we kind of want someone to come in and rescue us and to take care of us and to fix us. We're happy to help and support her, but she's getting to the point now that she's recognizing that she can do it herself, and she is doing it herself. There's no blame and judgment in some of the pathways she had to choose in order to get into alignment. I think it's more of her willingness to truly, fully address the issues that she's had, no matter what way she did it. She is truly acknowledging and addressing herself, to her core, taking risks to come into alignment, and she's feeling that alignment, and that's a beautiful thing. **(R: Yeah.)** So we encourage her to. . .YES, we say YES because we don't have to do as much because she's doing it already. **(R: Okay.)** Remember the power that we are, power we have to. . .power we have when we practice.

R: Okay. So I wanted to go a little bit deeper into this topic of the bladder, and also she discovered there was an STD that they don't check [for] in the U.S. and they only find it in Europe, and it was taking her a long path of two years to heal from that.

HS: Yes, technically, it is inaccurate to say STD so much, that's not a necessary word or the word to really use. . . There was a bacteria. . .there is a [commensal, or naturally occurring] bacteria, and when there is a misalignment, it can get out of balance. It can be transferred through sexual activity, this bacteria is a very nuanced one, for yes, it normally can live in balance. It can live in balance in the human body, so it's both, and it's not either/or. Which is frustrating because in the either/or model, it's either commensal, or it's a bacterial infection that was passed through, potentially through sexual activity, but it can be both-and. It's deeper than it being a specific bacteria with a specific name.

There was a fundamental misalignment in the way she was sharing her energy and cultivating her own sexual current. Regardless of whether it was passed from another or whether it arose within her, her misalignment with herself and her choices got to a point where it had to manifest in the physical, to bring her awareness to it with enough. . .so that she would truly bring your full attention to it.

Unfortunately, she's such a sensitive being that she manifested that very powerfully and very painfully and then suffered quite immensely because of it. It's not about blame. It's not about she did it to herself. It's not. . .it's not about that. It's not like, "Oh, look how badly you got out of alignment with yourself, so you had to punish yourself with this two-year bacterial infection." No. . .it's not so much that, it's that she chose to have such a sensitive container, so that she had the potential to live in full vitality when she is in full alignment with herself.

She chose a vessel that was so sensitive. Most people are not this sensitive. The majority of people who live with this bacteria inside them never even notice it, but she chose to be so sensitive, so that she had the potential of being the clear channel that she longs to be. Some of her choices, out of loneliness and fear, and a feel of separation, caused her to make some choices that weren't in her highest alignment, and she knows that. She knows; she said it before; she truly longs. . .and her heart sings and shines when she is intimately connecting in a deep container of love and devotion and. . .cherishing. **(R: Yeah)** If that's not there, she doesn't want it, and yet she was sometimes choosing it anyway because she was getting impatient. **(R: Right.)**

It's not like she got an STD as punishment for being promiscuous. That's not really what was happening. It's that her deepest dream for herself is to connect intimately in a container, in a field of true love. Unfortunately, because she made the choices that she did, and the way it manifests in the 3D, it's taking a lot of effort to come back into balance, and so that's why she ultimately decided to use the western medicine route of the very potent antibiotics in order to come back into alignment.

It's not that we were trying to keep it a secret from her. Everything we said if she really listens to the transcripts again from the past sessions speaking about her bladder, we did speak about the density that she picked up from that lover. We didn't call it a bacteria with a specific name, but that's because in the realm of vibration, it is a density. It is a density that emerges from sex as a distraction or sex as a coping mechanism or sex as an addiction, to feeling good, feeling connected, to feeling pleasure.

Sex has a beautiful potential of offering those things when it's in a healthy container of love or devotion, but when it's just. . . when it's used as that it can be dangerous. For her as a clear channel especially, she can't. . .she's not. . .she's so strong and powerful, but she's too sensitive and open to engage in that way, and so she took on a density which you could also call, you know, a bacterial infection, a very, very hard to cure bacterial infection. As she is fully aligning with love inside of herself, we do feel that she will. . .she is coming into full balance. She is now testing negative; her symptoms are improving. She is choosing love; she's realizing that she no longer has any desire for sex as a. . .as just a pleasure path, or sex just for play. She is aligning with what she really wants.

It's not that sex for play is bad if that's what a being wants, if a being's greatest desire is to play in the sexual field, sure, but they need to be aware of what a powerful field and a powerful portal they are playing with when they're using that. . .that pathway of penetration. It's not that there's any judgment. It's about what does this being truly want in order to create their own heaven on earth, and so. . .

R: So my question regarding. . .?

HS: Yeah, so what is your question exactly?

R: I have a few about this topic, maybe we can kind of touch on them quite quickly, so we can have more questions today. I don't want to exhaust her energy too much. One, I wanted to know, for example, she was taking this workshop in the mystery school in Europe. How was that affecting her? And how. . .what did she learn from that experience that can maybe make this topic more clear?

HS: Not sure I'm understanding the question exactly. Will you ask it again?

R: Yeah, I think just because we had this in the other session, you mentioned that she only should do the lovemaking from this place of love. In between the time and the sessions until now, she has been exploring practices of sacred sexuality in different ways. (HS: Oh, yeah.) And I was wondering if that was a negative impact or positive impact, or if she learned something meaningful from that?

HS: It was a positive impact, and it was rather poignant poetry as well and rather ironic, because she discovered that she. . .she discovered the name of this bacteria [*Ureaplasma urealyticum*] pretty much the week before she entered that portal of that course. And so she entered that field with the knowledge of this density within her, and it then shaped the way she engaged during the. . .during the course. Ultimately, it was very beautiful because she really went into deeper intimacy with her beloved and because they both tested positive for this right at the beginning of the course, it really brought them closer together because really there. . .it was sort of funny because like there is this divine. . .path. . .their love. It's such a beautiful and potent and powerful gift. . .their love, and there is such a possibility, and there was some resistance to entering that field of love.

Ironically, even though it wasn't what either of them wanted, testing positive for this actually drew them closer because they. . .in a field where they were planning to play and to cultivate with others, they instead were through ethics and integrity to keep everyone safe, forced to go deeper with each other. Ultimately, it's not what they expected to happen, but what they got out of that course was a deeper acknowledgment and understanding of the profundity and the beauty of the love that they share. When they went into that portal, they didn't really know. It was rather tenuous; it was a little bit fragile, and like uncertain. There was love there, but there was a lot of not knowing and. . .going into that field together with the knowledge of that bacteria's name and its implications and that gave them a beautiful opportunity to dive into the love, which ultimately is what she really wanted. It's sort of funny, that's like, it's not what she wanted was to test positive for a contagious bacterial infection, but what she really wanted was a divine partner.

Now, she's in **primary partnership**, more "P" words, with a beautiful man that she loves dearly and who dearly loves her and supporting her in her dreams, and supporting her in manifesting her dreams, and honors her as the **priestess** that she is. Another "P" word, like the **perfection** of it is **poignant** and **perfect poetry**. Even though she knows going into it, that even though she wanted to do that work, she wanted to go to that course, she's been wanting to go to that course for years, she knows deep down that mostly she chose to go to that course to be with him, (**R: Yeah.**) and to dive deeper with him. She did even go to it with a little bit of fear that if she didn't go, that he would enter into a **portal** with someone else and she would lose him, but it wasn't just fear, there was also a deep calling. . .there was a soul calling that there was a **potential** there. There was a **possibility** of partnership there with him. There was some weird part of her that trusted that if she went there with him, that there was the possibility of the partnership that she saw in their connection deepening, and it did, partly because of. . .strangely, the bacterial infection that she had unknowingly carried for that time. . .that density she carried and it wasn't. . .and he was the one who, you know, discovered it. **(R: Yeah.)**

There is a. . .there is a beautiful poetry in their partnership and the way it all came together, and as they surrender into that and stop trying to resist it, and just in a way, like surrender to the perfection that their partnership really is for helping them both become the best versions of themselves, then I think it'll help them have more patience with how to proceed with their. . .with their sacred sexuality with others and with themselves and in the containers, how to navigate the fields. I think as they surrender more into their field of love and into their partnership that they'll realize the perfectness of the patience of this supposed problem is providing.

R: **Beautiful. Maybe you can show just one more blind spot about her relationship. I know she did ask about it, if there's more information, if it's really partnership to cultivate diving more. . .in alignment, like you mentioned before. Is there any other blind spot that Allison should know regarding her partnership right now?**

HS: The partnership she has found herself in, what is beautiful about it is it was such a surprise. She was not looking for it. She was not expecting it. She. . .she went in, she entered it without any expectation, and the portal, the magic opened up through that. . .and the radiance potential has expanded. It is a beautiful exploration that she's in and and that he's in. Their connection has the potential of amplifying both their souls' purposes into the highest versions, and they both must choose it. She loves him. He loves her. There's no question there, and then that is a beautiful possibility because she's fully being met by someone who fully meets her, and yet they're exploring balance of sovereignty and synergy. In that balance of sovereignty and synergy, there is an uncertainty there is a. . .you know, they don't know yet. She has a lot of devotion, and she feels a lot of devotion for their partnership.

She just needs to remember the only blind spot we notice is that she needs to remember to pour that much devotion into herself and into her purpose, and into her life and into her mission, which she recognizes. She knows that; she's been writing about it. It's not. . .a blind spot so much as just to remind her to utilize this relationship as a reflection to make sure that she's pouring enough devotion into herself and into her mission as she is into the partnership. As she does that, when she truly pours it into herself, then he's going to feel the freedom in that; he's going to feel that she's not like pouring it all into him and feeling that pressure. Another "P" word. So, when she pours it into herself, then she's focused on herself and she's able to radiate her joy in her love, which then he of course feels and inspires him, which is going to help him lean in more and feel safe in the sanctuary of that.

There is a potential, there is a possibility that their union could be a divine union of epic proportions where they both step into their full king and queen potential and share their love and their light with the world. They're both very, very powerful people with very powerful voices and a very, very strong vibration within themselves. He's still finding his way into his power and is still seeking some external validation in order to feel worthy. He had a very. . .a lot of trauma imprinting. He chose a pathway in that was extremely difficult to help purify his heart, and he is a very pure soul. He came through his challenges and his birth story and his life story. Wow. He really truly has done so much inner alchemy, but he still has some to do, and he's still choosing the three-dimensional path, the power, before he's ready to claim his own power, but she understands.

She took a long time as well, and his awakening happened a lot later on. He chose a lot of drinking and a lot of other distractions that kept him from his awakening until much later on, but what it gave them is a beautiful complement where she chose. . .she started her path of awakening very early in her life, but has struggled with it because of that; she's felt very alone in it. She has really deeply mastered the. . .the shamanic realms and the visionary realms and the priestess realms, and he has mastered a lot more of the three-dimensional realms. His coming into his priesthood has happened a bit later, and so he has a longer. . .he's still in his journey, and so he's still not fully ready, and he's still sabotaging a little bit and still hasn't fully, fully risen into it, but he is rising. She's helping him rise, and then they have a beautiful complement to each other because of her mastery of the psychic realms, and well. . .and his mastery of the physical realms.

There's a beautiful synergy that when they weave their vibrations together, they truly can really embody and ground a lot of powerful vibration into planet Earth and into the three-dimensional realm, so there's a beautiful potential there if they both choose it. He's still leaning into his choice and still feeling the shackles of some of his previous choices of his sort of unsatisfying. . .some of his unsatisfying monogamous patterns. I don't know if you want to include all of this in the book; it maybe more personal. Some of it can be included, but you know, there's discretion there. [We have received his consent to share this part.] He's rising into his as well. There's no harm in risking it all for love. It may not work out; it may. There is a potential that they are stepping into a divine union type partnership for the benefit of bringing more of God's love to earth and to radiate more love into the earth, to the world. It is very possible.

Even if it dissolves, even if one of them or both of them don't choose it or can't rise into it, it still is preparing them and preparing their souls to step into their full embodied mission. They are allies. We said this before; they are soul allies with a potential for divine partnership if they both choose it and the potential for deep, deep transformation and aligning themselves both with their life missions, [even] if they do not choose to continue to do it together in partnership.

[This session was done remotely using video conference software. I muted my side of the microphone while Allison was speaking to make sure that the growing background noises of my surrounding would not disturb her. After she was done talking I forgot to open my microphone while speaking my further question and Allison opened her eyes to make sure we are connected. Those are the instructions that were given during the induction to ensure the safety of the session. If the connection is lost, she can open her eye and do the necessary actions to connect us again. When we are connected, we can continue from where we stopped. I quickly noticed my mistake, opened my microphone, gave a few deepening relaxation instructions, and we continued.]

R: **Let's take another deep breath now. Maybe you can just do a body scan to see if her body, her bladder, all those things are fully healed and in harmony? Will you do a body scan for me? See if you find anything else?**

HS: She is in harmony. She likes french fries. She has a hard time with fried potatoes and carbs. She knows this. She is in harmony and she's doing better, and she's acknowledging and recognizing that she can live, she can enjoy these things sometimes. It doesn't need to be all or nothing. The more she lives her life in alignment with her life, the stronger and less sensitive her system will be to slight food densities and choice densities. When she's living fully in alignment with herself she can tolerate these things more often, but she just needs to be careful and just enjoy them as a once in a while treat. (**R: Yeah.**) Be careful to not let them be a pattern, but she is in surprisingly good harmony in this moment. We're feeling the harmonics of. . .in her body, and it's. . .it's actually really quite beautiful.

She's deepened her devotion to her love and to her life and to her practice. She's been birthing her offerings into the world. She's committed to herself and to her love. She's committed to her health. She's just recently returned to the death practice temple to allow her to really drop into that alignment and remember the perfection that she is. The message of the "practice perfection on purpose" is very strong in her right now. We're just noting the beautiful synergy when practice and light, integrating into life, integrating into our livelihood, and using plant medicines and sacraments to augment what one is already doing in their practice is a very beautiful synergy.

It can be quite destabilizing and overwhelming when someone is just using plant medicine as their pathway to connect with the divine and to connect with themselves and then not integrate it with regular practice. It can be very destabilizing, but we're noticing the beautiful foundation and synergy that's happening with her combination of practice and both physical practice and her practices and practice in the death temples.

SYMBOL OF SOUND

R: Okay. Thank you so much for this. Was there anything else you wanted to share regarding the coherence, the yin and yang coherence?

HS: With the Yin and yang coherence. . .we talk about the yin and yang coherence creating the infinity pattern, and there's another symbol; that's the infinity pattern that starts to rise, she saw earlier today.

[They had trouble finding the names, so they described them. The symbol is called Unalome, the pattern of the Buddhist path to enlightenment. **See symbols glossary.**]

You can add that symbol into the book as well.

[They continue and gave more instructions to make a place in book that we add symbols. And this birthed the idea of making a symbols glossary.]

There's that symbol that can be very important for helping to ground yin and yang coherence. There's also the deconstructing and the understanding of the symbol that's being used on the cover of the book. It is such a beautiful symbol, and in itself has many codes embedded into it. But the fact that it not only the single symbol, of the single pattern of overtone harmonics, which is what that symbol is [made of], is showing you the full overtone harmonics of music of a scale C.

You're not only getting to see the relationship of music in that one pattern, but when you put the six of them together, and you create the pattern of the **Flower of Life** [See symbols glossary], and that symbol, the six-sided symbol that looks kind of like the children's jacks, there are a lot of codes in that symbol as well. You may want to include that in the book of the breakdown of the mathematical relationship of why you chose that symbol to be the cover of the book, because of the songs of remembering to use a symbol that shows the harmonic overtone potential of music and that healing vibration.

[In the end of the book you will find a glossary of symbols with additional information about the mathematics, sacred geometry, and the Tree of Life beyond the commonly known and the traditional teachings.]

The funny thing is; that same pattern that you're using for the cover of the book; not only is it the pattern of the overtones of music, it is also the pattern of the way quantum energy moves; it is the way energy moves through life. That same pattern, if you notice, you'll see it in the way water runs over land; you'll even see it in the way snowboarders cross the mountain, and these cross that leave these vesica pisces shapes. You see, there's this natural harmonics; it's not perfect, it's not perfect resonance, but you can see the perfection in it and the pattern within it.

Allison spent the winter snowboarding each morning to help tone as a moving meditation and physical practice meditation, and she sees it. She sees the same pattern in the tracks that people leave on the side of the mountain. It's a pattern that runs through all of life, through music, through the quantum realms, through energetic realms; it's the way all vibration moves. When we notice that pattern, and we learn it, then we can be in resonance. When we are in alignment with life, when we are in alignment with this pattern within us. Then we're flowing, and we don't have to use our resistance and our "no" to break. We are sort of that symphony, those infinite threads that are all moving in this together, in this tapestry.

When our subconscious, sabotaging patterns get afraid, we start to contract and we brake, and we clamp down and contract around one thread or another thread, and that causes knots; that causes densities to form. When you create densities in our pattern for too long, that's when illness forms; that's when unease forms and disease forms. Densities begin in an energetic place, and the more there's the the "no" and the resistance, whether either in the energetic form outside of us or within us. Then we get knots in our vibration and we're not able to flow with the full currents of our life. When we get in alignment, and we're flowing in alignment with our life, we're flowing in that pattern, that same pattern. It's what makes up that shape of music. When we get to trust that pattern; we feel the rhythm of that pattern and can trust it, and then we don't have to brake and resist so much. We can actually live our lives in harmony.

From yin and yang coherence, when we look at the infinity pattern, even though in two dimensions, it's got this cross and then its got the two circles. When you really look at the infinity pattern, if it's multiplied, that vesica pisces shape is actually within it. It's the fabric of the space-time. The fabric of the seed of life is also within that infinity. Infinity's just looping back on different vertices of the seed of life, of the flower of life. I believe I spoke to it earlier in this session where I spoke to the creating the vesica pisces within ourselves as a way to collapse into the unity of consciousness.

There is this aspect of connecting with our "yes" and our acceptance of our point. Our present now, where we are exactly right now in our life. Accepting our life as it is. Not accepting it to be a doormat to let injustice and corruption happen to us, but accepting that this is where we are. Instead of wasting our time in regret and wishing it were different than it is, and slows us down in that form of resistance. In the full acceptance of where we are now, and then from that place go deep inside and listening to our soul essence, our heaven on earth, that point in the quantum now, in our future, and in the quantum now that already exists. The perfection moment that already exists within us; we can connect those two points.

At first, it's like connecting those two points of music. It's a whole note apart, and it can be divided in a wavelength pattern that's either in halves or thirds or fourths or fifths or sixths or sevenths. That's how we travel, we travel in that fraction of the whole, or once we really get good at it, boom. We can travel one to one; we can travel in the whole, and we can meet vertice to vertice when we are singing the octave of ourselves, the C one and C two, an octave apart, our resonant tone. When we're singing an octave apart, we can manifest miracles now. When and we can connect our now moment, our current reality now to our quantum perfection now, that's what all the great teachers talk about. Yin and yang coherence is a beautiful foundation to allow ourselves to find our own inner rhythm, our own inner vibration, and learn to play the music that is our life, our soul music, our song; our song of remembering is woven into mathematics of music.

[They now suggested that we would practice drawing the symbol and add how to draw the symbol, so everyone could practice.]

So I think it'd be a good idea for you to include the symbol, to include how to draw the symbol yourself, so that everyone can practice. Because when you can practice it, when you can draw the symbol, attached even in the workbook that comes out later, like have some grid paper, so that people can practice drawing this pattern and feeling it in their hands, feeling it in their body, just the feeling of following the current of life, flowing with the wavelength of song and wavelength of sound.

[We add some information at the end of the book and additional drawing worksheet with additional information about sacred geometry and sound would be available online within the Readers' Zone.]

Musicians already do this naturally, but for people who do not play music or don't know about music theory, they can still feel this vibration and can tap into it. It's innate intelligence to all of our designs; our human design was built in with song. We know it deep down in our core, we know it. We've forgotten it, and we may not have learned it in this human lifetime, but we can still feel it.

I think offering people the opportunity to practice drawing that symbol themselves, either the drawing the infinity pattern and feeling that pattern within themselves, drawing the climbing infinity pattern, I forget the name of. . .and being able to draw the symbol that you're using, for the watermark of your book. I think it would be really good for everyone to be able to. . .not I think, it will, it will be good for everyone to draw and to practice feeling the vibration, the signature, the pattern of the musical vibration; feel it in their hands, so they can translate that into their life and start to feel the current of being in their rhythm. Instead of needing to brake in order to slow down, but use the rhythm of life to slow ourselves down more naturally, and it's much more graceful, and they can keep the full flow themselves going. That's surrender. This is the art of surrender and letting go and unwinding the tension we hold in our body.

The tension we hold in our body is resistance; it's braking. We're telling our cells we are feeling afraid, and our cells are braking and then telling all of our other energy centers in our brain to brake and to stop and to contract. Then we start to sabotage our lives and sabotage manifesting the greatest version of our life. That point between our now and our perfect future always feels far away; it always feels an infinity away, but they're not. They're actually one point. When you have collapsed them together, that's the infinity pattern. We bring the two points into the one point, and we do that by learning to surrender both physically, by learning the places we're holding tension in our body and actively working to let those go.

Allison's been working with her jaw and her hips and her hands and her feet in different parts of the body for years, and she's learning to master this art of surrender in the physical. When she's done that she can feel the current of life's song through her and her song through her, and she's able to align herself with it more and more as she progresses and so. . .the most important thing is when we tap in to our resistance and learn it, so that we can unwind it, surrender into it to find our soul song within it; match with its resonance; match with its frequency, its vibration, so we can follow its wavelength; we can ride our own dragon into our own perfection right now.

That's what yin and yang coherence is, part of the foundation to allow us to find and enter our liberation, to enter the blueprint. Not the blueprint, the blueprint is our. . .we have this blueprint, and we can enter into our mainframe of our program and access it in order. . .

[We had a sound problem and I asked her to repeat what she was saying.]

When we utilize a foundation of yin and yang coherence, and we begin the practice with both quiet sitting meditations and active practices, we start to be able to be aware of our inner resistances, our inner fears, our inner places where we brake and contract around life. To really guide ourselves through life, we need to learn to ride our surrender, to ride our energy current without braking, but we need to feel safe first. When we don't feel safe, that's when we brake. Allison has actually written a beautiful piece. It is an offering in conjunction with this book about how to learn to really navigate our spaceship, our bodysuit of life. It goes perfectly with the book and the story. It's perfect, so if I miss a part of it here, it's not that important.

The idea is that when we use the foundation of yin and yang coherence to find our still point, to find our infinity point, and we go deep inside ourselves, we realize that within infinity there's a fractal. You were talking about layers in the fractals before. Once you go into infinity that's when you find your song of the universe flowing through you, and there are both the moment of it. . .there's the one single point of it, like light that is both a particle and a wave. It's both and. . .it's not either/or; we know this already. It's the same thing. . .music, light, energy, it's all the same thing.

As we go into our yin/yang coherence, we find still point through that center point of that infinity; it opens up to reveal that Vesica Pisces within us, our overtone, our soul's overtone, our harmonic, and our harmonic then becomes two points. It expands out and becomes two again. We get to learn to ride our wavelength, our inner music, through the different fractions. That is why the symbol is really important to be in the book, so people can practice learning their inner rhythm.

Once they learn their inner rhythm, then they don't need to brake in order to slow down when they're feeling afraid. They can learn to align themselves with their rhythm and with their music, and then they can go as fast or as slow as they want, without having to brake and knotting themselves up and getting themselves into patterns of density and contraction. It's both a physical practice of releasing and falling into the void. . .truly surrendering into the art of letting go in the physical and in the mental and in the spiritual, so that we realize that in surrender that is our true power.

When we let go into and slip into the rhythm of our life, the rhythm of our song, the melody of our song, when we can ride our wavelength, our pattern through life, the art of surrender helps us do that. When we brake, we think we need to brake to slow down, but that's actually not how you brake in the infinite. That's how we brake in a car. If we're driving the car, we push the gas pedal to go, and we hit the brakes to stop. In the infinite realms, to truly ride and to travel into the multiverse, to align with our lives and live our perfection and to live our song, we must learn our song; we must learn our own music, so that we can ride it. Then we can ride it with grace and follow the pattern of all life and let go of that density that holds us back and sabotages us and causes us pain and suffering and illness.

That's the point of this book. When you awaken your song of remembering, when you practice your yin and yang coherence, and you listen to the song, in your heart, and you learn it; you learn it to the core of your song; and you learn to ride the rhythm of it. That's when you can then align your perfect yes to your now with the perfect YES of infinity and collapse it back into the infinity, to create heaven on earth right here, right now. That's liberation. That's the feeling of liberation, it's absolute perfection. You've done it. You have liberated yourself into receiving your pure love and to giving your pure love. That is the highest potential of the human being. That is what we designed it for. That is why we designed Earth the way we did, was to give human beings the potential to transcend the physical body, the lower evolutionary patterns of contraction and separation and fear and survival. We merged that patterning with a higher program, so that we can transcend it and rise into the songs of love that we are and sing the symphonies together to create heaven on Earth.

[*Ava's note:* *Transcend here means to allow our consciousness to rise in vibration and be fully embodied within the physical body; not the concept of leaving or dissociating from the body. Channel is talking about transcending the patterns of contraction and separation to embody bliss. The traditional definition of transcend is to go beyond the normal limits of, or to surpass*].

We can manifest miracles to where all of us are safe. All of us have a place that is home. None of us have to leave anywhere. None of us are in danger of being annihilated. We can let go of all that fear. The razor's edge is immense. It's not a razor's edge. It's an illusion. It's infinite in here. It's an infinite playground of love when we let ourselves be open and surrender into that love.

This book is the beginning. This is the seed to help us burst our heart songs open and grow a garden of Eden once more on planet Earth. That's really it, right? To practice perfection on purpose, paradise here now. That's what the song of remembering is for. It's not to inspire fear. It's to help us surrender into the perfection that we are and rise as the beautiful stewards of this beautiful paradise on Earth. Earth is paradise. It can be when we all come together as one and learn to sing our songs together. One, beautiful symphony of love.

A GIFT OF SONGS BY AVA

If you have not already listened, we invite you to find it and support Allison's artistic creation in the Reader's Zone.

www.songsofremembering.org

Go to Readers' Zone on our website and sign up.

QR code for direct link by scanning with your phone.

CONCLUSIONS

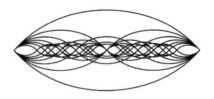

AVA'S CONCLUSION

Wow, that was quite a wild journey. Did we really just glimpse into another dimension of reality and bring back a new mythical version of our origin story? Aboriginal people in Australia talk about the world being created by songs, after all. Even in the Bible, it all began with the Word. Many cultures have wisdom teachings sharing about the importance of unconditional love, forgiveness, surrender, the illusion of death, Oneness, and that we are all one being living in the infinite dream of God. It's not really so different, this ancient future story we just shared.

As a storyteller, I am quite familiar with the art of building plots and themes. However, I am surprised again and again at how the channel takes us on such an unexpected yet poetic journey. It was never "my" idea. Each session started as its own unique adventure, and the vision that would emerge from chaos seemed unrelated to any central theme, at least at first. I never sat and thought about what should happen or come next. It just came. As a recovering control freak, I reveled in the surprise of experiencing what would happen without my control. Still, over the course of four years, a cohesive story somehow emerged out of the mists of mystery. A journey from the illusion of separation into the embodied experience of coherence, from fear into love, from alone into Oneness. I would have never tried to write this story. Yet, here it is.

This story revealed so many answers to so many mysteries, but ironically, it has generated even more questions about the nature of life, death, God, existence, and consciousness. Personally,

I wonder. Do I just have a vivid imagination, or am I really a channel, especially when I fully relax and get out of my own way? What's the difference between our inner vision or being a channel?

I did dedicate my life to sacred service and ask to be a clear channel for the Divine, after all, but I didn't expect to actually BE a channel. I just wanted my life to align in service to Love and Truth. "Be careful what you wish for," they say, "You just might get it."

If so, apparently, I have access to multiple channels, depending on what frequency we tune my inner radio receiver to. It makes sense, in an odd sort of way. Every quirk and aspect of my body, mind, and essence seem to be perfectly designed to bring me right here to this moment, to share this information with you. No other career path ever felt right, even though I tend to thrive at any path I fully chose. I struggled to commit to a career because a voice kept calling me in deeper to the Great Mystery.

Another question I ask is what if my purpose IS to share this with you — you who want to listen, who are ready to let go of fear and to live powerfully in your heart, to live free and sovereign while feeling deeply connected to All That Is. I am coming to realize that I am amazingly blessed, and it turns out that my favorite things...to sing, to share stories, and to ponder the nature of the Universe and why we exist, to remember who I truly am, and to wake up from the illusion of my separation from Source...is actually why I chose to come to Earth! It's been my heart and soul calling me all along, while my mind resisted and shied away from this strange purpose.

Why not? Truth is stranger than fiction after all.

As a trained scientist, even though I no longer work as one, I am driven to understand truth. I feel like it's my duty to utilize my vehicle as a guinea pig to see how much I can upgrade my own programming to embody greater health, vitality, longevity, and potential as a human being. As an ordained minister, I feel the divine in all things, all moments, and in each breath. As a sci-fi nerd, I want to know what role I play in this infinite Universe. As a human, made of humus and earth, I want to treat my home with kindness and respect. As a mystic and philosopher, I know myself as a drop of Source energy embodied in form for but an instant in the sea of Infinity, and I want to fully embody and play this game of life while I can. At the same time, I am the entire Ocean in a single drop.

I feel a deep calling to leave this precious planet better than I found it. I would like to succeed in my chosen purpose and share my light, my songs, my stories, and my channel. I want to help myself awaken fully and remember who I truly am, and to help others do the same, so that we can all rise into what we are meant to be. For decades I've been trying to figure out how to help. What if I'm finally revealing my own unique niche to myself and to you?

From my experience, I have come to understand we are each God/Source embodied in form. We are Source's greatest creation and dream . . .a beautiful, loving experiment — a novel combination of light, energy, matter, density, consciousness, love, and feeling. What if we are here to learn to love, to forgive, to choose love no matter what, to choose truth, to refine and purify ourselves in order to merge once more into Source and Oneness?

Regardless if I'm delusional or a clear channel, I will spend my life force energy being the best human being I can be, sharing as much love with the world as I am able to do. How can that be a bad life? I won't take it personally if you've read this and analyzed my personality to determine what insanity, neurosis, or genius concocted this strange tale. Please don't put me on a pedestal or throw the baby out with the bathwater.

For I am incarnate as a human being. Humble and messy and vain and beautiful and all the things. I fart and burp, stick my foot in my mouth, and make mistakes. I am also filled with a light and a knowing and a trust that is unshakable. I am in love with life, despite the deep pain I sometimes feel. I know that I only want to share more love, hope, inspiration, and connection with all. I humbly offer this story for the benefit of all beings, with embarrassment still warming my cheeks at the absurdity of everything I just 'said' out loud.

I face this embarrassment in the hopes that this story may be of service to you. What if this story can help you to remember and choose to live your story more fully? I think it comes down to choice. I chose to remember why I came here. Do you remember, back in my introduction, when I brought up the hero's journey? Well, on the hero's journey, the main character is usually the chosen one, right? Why? Because despite how the "calling" presents itself, they choose to follow the path of the hero. They may choose it out of their own inner calling. Often, they stay comfortable in their default backup plan, until life forces their hand (like it did for me). Ultimately, they still have to choose to follow the pathless path laid out before them, risking the uncertain outcome.

In my hero's journey, I'm the chosen one, because I choose to be. I choose to live my soul purpose no matter what comes, even if I fail. I choose to be hero of my personal story, despite the risk and discomfort. Why? Well, a wise man once said, "Living in devotion to your soul's purpose is absolutely inconsequential in the infinity of space and time; it will make no difference. Yet it is absolutely essential that you do it with your whole heart." I questioned this wisdom for awhile, but eventually, I realized that I agree. THIS is how I make my life into a great story, one worth reading in the great book of the Akashic Record.

To quote my beloved Jesus, he said in the uncannonized Gospel of Thomas, "if you bring forward that which is within you, that which is within you will save you. If you do not bring forth that which is within you, then that which you do not bring forth will destroy you." I suppose you could say that this is my driving creed, as it feels like sound advice to me, regardless of who said it.

Through this journey in life and through the journey of creating this book, I have traversed depression, fear, anxiety, and even suicidal ideation. I have also experienced deep peace, inspiration, and ecstasy. I have felt silent awareness and the realm beyond space and time. I have come to know that I am Source experiencing existence through the temporary, one-time lens of me.

Each of us is Source experiencing existence through the temporary lens of our current self. I'm not special, and I am. It's all a grand paradox. We are as precious and unique and as special as an exquisite flower blossom. We are a blossom on an infinite tree, covered with unique, and yet surprisingly similar, flower blossoms. I know my work now is to keep this channel open, to keep remembering, to practice and integrate the advice that the channel so generously offered.

When you read this text, what if you were reading an aspect of your own autobiography? The Autobiography of I. Your own story. Each of our stories. I'm special. You're special. Each of us is unique and special, and each of us has a story to tell. Each of us has a purpose to pursue here on Earth to satisfy our soul's longing. What if we all chose to come here for a specific reason? What if you actually chose all the hardships you encountered in life before you came — themes specifically designed to bring you to the heart of the matter, to the pivotal moment when you choose love or fear? What would you do if you knew you chose this? Would you embark upon your own hero's journey, even though you don't know the ending?

"The End is Only the Beginning. The beginning comes after the end."
—Allison (Ali) (AVA) Avalon.

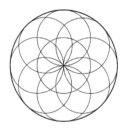

RON'S CLOSING AND OPENING

"Change your perspective and your life will change."

This is my conclusion in one sentence, so if you need a moment to integrate the information you have read so far, you can stop here and pick this up later when you are feeling fresh. What you are about to read is a bit more than just a normal conclusion, to say the least.

I'm being guided to share an unexpected journey I experienced just before finishing this book. An incredible chain of events and a lot of information was revealed to me while I was creating the Symbols Glossary and the illustrations for the main symbol of this book. I wove for you in the following conclusion a shortened introduction and first chapter of my next book. It is truly a shortcut packed with many keys that may accelerate your path of awakening. If those discoveries activate you as they did for me then I'm so excited for you, and I trust that reading the next pages will be worth it. Are you ready for more? After all, it is the time of the remembering.

I hope you can imagine the great joy I experienced from witnessing and facilitating these sessions. Putting this book together and being immersed in the materials has never ceased to surprise me and nourish me tremendously, and it was also one of my greatest challenges. I will explain more soon. Every read-through, I'm seemingly discovering a new paragraph that has profound content which has an expansive impact on my consciousness. It is as if another layer was revealed to me about the book that I was not aware of before that is now ready for deeper integration. I truly feel that this material is alive, and one can benefit from reading or listening to the sessions more than once. Looking back at my life, I can notice my growing trust and that my lived knowing of our Oneness is being refined into a greater awareness that is being sustained for a longer extent throughout my days.

As you know by now, throughout the process, Allison went back and forth about including her real name or alias as they suggested in our first session together. During session three, 'I' mentioned that it would be appropriate for her to do live IQH sessions in front of groups and share her face during interviews and videos as she had been designed for it. Later on, they mentioned that she designed her life purpose to share her information, art, and teachings more freely. As the facilitator of healing sessions, I'm always aiming to align my clients with their highest and best timeline. I knew that it was only a matter of time and healing that would allow it to be so. It was extremely important to me that Allison felt safe, ready, and excited to share the materials in whatever way was appropriate.

If we would have shared it completely anonymously, we may have included a few more of the personal parts, but I think we would have missed an important aspect of the book and of course her songs. I had this feeling and deep prayer that throughout the writing process there would come a time when she would feel safe enough to share her true self and gifts with the world. Her wishes and my excitement to include her songs within the book gave her the encouragement to find the courage within her, but also added new layers of worries and concerns.

We continued addressing them throughout the editing process. Session ten was scheduled after we already received the book from our first editor and were getting ready to make this final choice. That last session was so beautiful and powerful and we just had to include it. It felt to me like a celebration. When I brought Allison to full consciousness during our last session, we both burst out with laughter. It was like putting the cherry on top. It was confirmation for both of us that we had reached the moment of her readiness to share the book. For me, it was an extremely important step so we could finish this book in a good way, and I could soon focus my energy on more collaborations, creating healing events, workshops, prayer-formances, and so on, but most importantly, the collective dream we share with many, the creation of the New Earth Communities, Eco-villages, Cities of Light.

After receiving the green light to share her name during our last session, I felt inspired to give the reader a sense of our process as it was created and received. The true evolution of how this all came to be, started seemingly anonymously, as it was written, through the power of transcending her deepest fears and replacing them with this pure joy and excitement to live and share her talent and gifts more freely. She was now empowered and confident to live her life purpose. This is the vision I held while feeling this potential timeline happening for her and myself, demonstrating in real life the energy and the message of this book. This was my guiding light.

Seeing Allison stepping fully into her mission was my greatest gift, and this book gave me many. I'm incredibly grateful for all that I learned and the ability and privilege to share this information with you. I can feel in my heart the beauty of each one of us clearing our fears and stepping ever more fully into our own divine life path. I can feel the potential of a massive removal of limiting beliefs in a collective way and for each of the readers just by reading and seeing this lived example. It is a multi-layered process. I asked myself as well, "Do I live my heart's deepest dreams?" The answer for me is probably not yet. So, what am I truly afraid of? What is stopping me now? The answers to this are changing at each moment, so every once in a while, I just keep asking.

On a more vulnerable note, like all humans, I too have had my own challenges to overcome. Collaborations are something I think highly about but they are not always an easy process, right? This book took us longer than expected as each of us had our own path of initiations. The creation process of this book accelerated my healing journey too. I had this deep feeling that I needed to close this gap between what I wanted to feel and what I was feeling. I wanted to embody more of what has been shared in the book and to lead by example, but I kept facing more and more challenges. I too had to clear some fears, like the fear of not ascending, a fear of almost passing a test but failing in the last moment, something as deep and collective as "eating the forbidden apple," fear of the dark forces, and deep regrets that I referred to as my "guilt-hole" which contained stuck emotions.

On top of that, financial challenges started to rise as sessions were not coming in as much as before. This was surprising for me because, since we started facilitating hypnosis healing sessions, we had amazing results. People from all over the world were following us and watching the sessions we posted online. We also initiated the IQH Practitioner Training online with great results and a growing community of IQH facilitators. Our following was growing, and I felt like I would never need to worry again about income as we were doing such divinely guided healing work. My healing sessions were so profound. The students were doing well and loving the course. Why would it ever stop?

I felt as if this challenge was divinely orchestrated, and I knew that this had come with important lessons and created the right conditions for me to finish this book. Finishing this book and my personal healing became my first priority. So, I took 'I's advice about cleaning my antennas. I did a couple of cleanses for my body and changed my diet. I did emotional clearings and mental work to bring me back to a sense of wholeness. I exchanged healing sessions with other practitioners of IQH and experienced other healing modalities. I cleared some of my own fears, fears I absorbed from others, and even collective fears I had taken on.

Those challenges helped me look deeper into my "Rescuer to Victim" tendencies (if you remember the Drama Triangle I mentioned in the Introduction) and I had to resolve some of my unbalanced relationships. I was inspired by the, *The Power of TED: The Empowering,* by David Emerald, to take full responsibility and accountability for the creation of my life, and to change my perspective to the empowering roles as a Creator, a Challenger, and a Mentor.

I faced parts of myself that created my co-dependency patterns, my attachment style, and many of the little lies I was telling myself which allowed my less healthy habits to stay a bit longer. You know, like after this holiday I'll start a diet. . .or in the next new moon I'll do XYZ. I made a ceremony to heal my relationship with the tobacco plant and resolved our love/hate affair that I started at a young age. In recent years it was only coming in small waves for a few weeks out of a year, normally when I would visit Israel. This was a cause for lots of self-judgment that held me back from taking better care of myself.

My relationship with Michael was also transforming and we made new agreements that would allow us both to embody and sense our sovereignty. It took a lot of back and forth and some alone time until I could let go of my own self-judgment, until I could even love and accept my shortcomings, and trust the perfection of it all.

For myself, the concept of yin and yang coherence helped me to realize that I needed to look for balance in all areas of my life. After many years of being very physical as a professional dancer, followed by many years of being a hypnotherapist and more focused on spiritual expansion, it is time for me to balance my physicality and my spirituality, my artistic expression with my services as a spiritual wayshower, a healer, and a teacher. I began to find balance with how much I give from my energy to others, how much to myself, and how much I allow myself to receive. It is an endless dance.

From my own experience of being too hard on myself, I want to ask you to be gentle with yourself. Be gentle with your process. Make sure to enjoy your path, and make sure to enjoy being human as long as we have this opportunity to be embodied in this physicality. As I surrender to my contraction and surrender to my expansion, my wish is to remind everyone that we are not being judged by the Divine Source. Source loves us unconditionally and we have chosen the path of our suffering to expedite our learning and remembrance.

You may ask me; how do you know that I'm loved unconditionally? How can you be so sure I am not being judged by Source? Great questions! I hope that the next discoveries and stories I'm about to share will explain more. But more than that, may it activate your direct experiences and knowing for yourself. I know it because I have experienced it. I have experienced clear, direct downloads from Source showering me with unconditional love. Only then I was convinced it was true. For this, I'm so grateful, and I know that you are loved too!

Even during my deep struggles and my financial limitations, I was always provided for and all my needs were met. I believe it was necessary from a higher perspective. It helped me to focus and take accountability and ownership of my creations and listen more closely and deeply to my heart as I learned to humble myself, ask for support, take better care of myself, communicate better my needs and limitations, and listen. The beauty is that I learned to trust Source, the true provider of all that we have. Again and again, I was given all that I needed, exactly when I needed it, and in pure divine timing. With every low tide, I got better at trusting; this too shall pass, just keep listening. Trust. Coming to this realization and acceptance was necessary to help me cultivate humility and stability and become the steward of the book, as 'I' called it.

I could never have created this book without the support of my husband, my family, the donors who supported us right when we needed it, the editors, the designers, and the friends that worked on this book with much heart and devotion. I see you all as an embodiment of the Light of Source. I'm forever grateful to you all. I have chosen to give all the share of my income to a special fund of New Earth Ascending ministry for building the New Earth Community and our humanitarian projects and efforts. I will keep trusting that I'm always being provided for.

Throughout the writing of this manuscript, I too have gone back and forth about whether or not to share my personal information and my present life's awakening events and if to include the part when Allison's Higher Self shared about my lifetime with Issa. During a session I facilitated with another client and friend, I asked what would be most appropriate. I mentioned that I was debating between a version with or without or keeping it solely about her. They recommended that I share. Then I asked if there was any more information about the process of completing the book:

HS: "You are two/too given a message, that you take your time to complete your book, deeper than you know what is right, when to complete it, so we recommend you take your time."

They explained that they would work with me in my dreams and through more life experiences in the coming months for more information that would be important to include. So, I listened and took it into my heart as I know by now that if they said it they probably know, and it is true, they do work with me in my dreams.

I took a moment to integrate this request as I was feeling a bit upset and overwhelmed. I want to be done sooner than later, like a nine-month-plus pregnant woman that just wants the baby to be out already! I was laughing at myself, and thought, it better be worth it, like sending this request to all the invisible forces that supporting this creation of this book. Just keep working step by step and you will know when you will be done.

As they said, the book kept being slowed down and I'm learning and practicing all the 'P' words, perfection on purpose, patience, and peace. In the meantime, I permitted myself to share a bit more about my stories throughout the book and after reading

Allison's comment about her telepathic experience with Moses, I decided to add the information I received telepathically as well, about the 13th Sefira - חופש - *Chofesh* in Hebrew (Freedom) of the Tree of Life from Kabbalah, Jewish mysticism. I checked within myself and it felt like, yes, it was time to make it public. Maybe this piece of information is not that interesting for all the readers, as most readers, like me, don't know much about the Tree of Life, but I know it can be very meaningful for some.

Long story short, the idea of adding a glossary of symbols was born while I was reading session ten and designing the images they mentioned throughout the book to share. I also tried to redesign an illustrated explanation of how to draw the symbol from the cover using my limited graphic design skills. I looked deeper into the harmonic series that Allison sent me and I got worried that we had made a mistake in the design of the symbol on the cover. I asked myself, why is it jumping from six waves to eight for one wavelength? Where is the seventh wave? Why is it not all 'C' notes? I also saw notes 'E' and 'G.' I thought "**I**" mentioned it is all 'C' notes on the different octaves. (They didn't; they said the **harmonic** of 'C' note). Maybe we need to correct it? And what would the symbol look like if that would have been the rising of note 'C' in octaves and not the harmonic?

I dove into the research to learn for myself what was happening. I followed 'I's' suggestion to practice drawing the symbol and I started to make the glossary and found **the Universal Tree of Life** and the **Krystal Spiral** that is associated with it. I noticed that the Krystal Spiral and note 'C,' rising in an octave, are similar to one another. They both double in frequency. I found it to be a very interesting coincidence. Is it a coincidence?

This inquiry opened Pandora's Box for me full of transformative discoveries about Sacred Geometry, sound, and frequency. It was like a roller coaster of synchronicities. I was finding new information, finding new mistakes or misalignments in designs, then finding more information that opened new ideas, and questions. It became clear that every seemingly "mistake" opened a new path full of transformative discoveries. It kept opening my mind and raising my energy. I felt the divine flow of creativity with a nice feeling of a gentle high with a chain of events that blew my mind.

It reminded me of times in my early awakening when I started to feel the energy of the Christ Consciousness opening my heart and I began to experience incredible synchronicities that made me worry for a moment that I may have lost my mind. This time, for the first time in my life, I felt like a true geek or a scientist who was deep in their research, making designs, writing my theory, and following the breadcrumbs to a new and unfamiliar destination, while also feeling so deeply the spiritual unseen support and inspiration.

I even had those dreams they talked about. In one dream I was sitting with a significant friend and an ally in my life. We had a lovely meeting in the dream and then we were visited by a special blue bird. The bird looked at us and then started to sing for us in the most incredible and out-of-this-world sound frequency. The song's waves became visible to our eyes and became three-dimensional. The bird smiled at us and left as if through a portal carrying a traveler trailer. I thought it was funny because Michael and I were living in one. In the dream, my friend and I both got so excited to have shared this unique experience and felt very activated by the new energy.

The second dream was from a time during ancient Egypt. I could read and translate the hieroglyphics and I was sharing with the people around me a corrected version of the story of the Jewish exodus that was different from what is now written as part of the Old Testament. I did not retain the information consciously but the feeling of being a different type of being with this unique skill was very profound. It was explained to me later that where my soul came from, I used to translate language out of symbols and codes. I came in with a bit of a different operating system than what is being used for the written language of our days. I chose it and this is why I had suffered from dyslexia from a young age.

It was a huge healing for my heart to realize this. I found more acceptance of my challenges as they were now being revealed as gifts. I was just so grateful to be back in this divine flow and fully trusting that I'm now getting closer to finishing the book. I felt confident that I needed to add my discoveries and the "new"/old geometry that I was exploring and designing for the closing of this book.

So with a mind wide open, limited graphic skills, and limited time as I was creating more stress for both of us by aiming for another deadline, which now also seemed to be confirmed by growing synchronicities, and my broken English (that improved tremendously through this writing process), I have written a detailed explanation of my discoveries. I documented the process of finding and creating what I jokingly named the **Flower of Immortality** and the **God Seed** *[see symbols glossary]*, and the meaning behind the overlapping geometries of sacred sound symbols. I was so happy with myself, and I started to really get excited to share even more stories about my own awakenings, like when I had the direct download from Source to propose to Michael to marry me. . .ohhh, ohhh. . .This could never end!

I wrote it all as simply as I could and it wasn't too hard to do as I'm a beginner in those topics and without previous knowledge of Sacred Geometry or the science of harmonics and sound. I wrote the progressions of my discoveries and all the fun synchronized events that led those to be. I share it with an invitation for more exploration and conversations as it is just the beginning of ongoing research that is still expanding. I added my growing theory intending to inspire others to explore it for themselves from a unity and oneness perspective with the traditional Flower of Life, and not from a polarized approach of good and bad like I have seen more commonly online and was turned off by. I came across videos of a geometry wizard George Leoniak that confirmed my findings. His videos and drawings felt as if he was reading my mind.

I thought I was finally done, and I added the new materials to the book as a continuation of my original conclusion and asked my trusted friends for feedback and editing. They seemed to feel that it was too long, complicated, and advanced to be added as my second conclusion. It was suggested that this could be shared as a beginning of another book and not as an ending of this one as it is very different in its nature, and it is opening another huge topic. They explained that the new material is moving the reader back up to the mental energy when my original conclusion was from the heart.

Surprisingly, I found this "rejection" or cancellation of my hard work to make sense. It took me only a short moment to find the perspective of the perfection of it all and take it as another opportunity for growth. The new geometry was teaching that every moment is a choice point, every moment could be a crossing point of different designs, different realities, the overlapping sound in different octaves. This moment must be perfect. There must be a better way to share the information. I went inward to listen until a new idea and inspiration would arise. I asked how can I share it with more heart energy and less mental energy. I know some of it must be shared here because I was guided to do so half a year ago. What to share now?

Knowing that the "new" geometry should be shared soon birthed the idea to start a digital book project that each chapter will be shared as soon as it is ready instead of a full book back-to-back. This would be easier for me to keep more balance in my life. I had the inspiration to call it The Never-Ending Book, as the "new" geometry was teaching me about the infinite, the Multiverse, and that the expansion of consciousness and Source has no end. I knew that sharing the information in this way would open collaborations between me and many, those before me and those after me.

So now, here I am writing about it again and now I trust you are prepared for this content. It is expanding on traditional topics as consciousness tends to do. If it gets too complicated for you to follow, you can skip a page and perhaps come back to it later when you are ready and feel fresh, or after you have integrated more of the information they have shared so far in the book.

So, here we go, while deep in the research I remembered a session with another client, a friend, that was talking about **Metatron's Cube** *[see symbols glossary]*, and the Flower of Life. It explained about the role of arc-angel Metatron and how it is being implemented from the higher realms of Oneness. Surprisingly, or not, this client sent me an invitation to an online platform. I saw it as another sign to reach out and offered her a free session to explore more. She was so happy I reached out as she was in the depth of a three-years-long Dark Night of the Soul. It felt divinely guided for us both and we did the session the next day.

Her Higher Self gave much more information, and it was clear that things are way more advanced than what is commonly known. 'They' shared that this should be shared like toy keys for a toddler. In the future, the baby will grow up and know that keys can be inserted into a hole of a door that opens into a new space, and the next place is completely different. For now, this information is just a toy to start playing with something that is beyond the human capacity to comprehend.

They went on to say humans are missing the energy of numbers and the energy of Sacred Geometry. They asked me not to focus on mathematics but to focus on the energy of the geometric patterns, as well as focusing on the energy of the numbers and not just the numbers themselves. They shared that the **God-Seed** *[see symbols glossary]* is within each one of us. This knowledge is within us all and we should focus on the energy of the sacred geometry. This is what makes it sacred.

After shortening my conclusion and cutting most of it out, I shared it with my second editor. I thought she would love the new material as she was very educated in Sacred Geometry. She was very honest with me. This new part I added was triggering for her and was causing a big reaction. She has studied in-depth the sacred geometry of the Flower of Life. She knew that some people are almost demonizing the Flower of Life. I knew that there were polarizing approaches out there, but I had not explored other teachings. At first, I couldn't find the symbols to match what I was learning, so I had to design them myself for it to make sense.

For me, it was just about the geometry and the sound, and the information that was shared with me in my IQH session explained it from a very neutral perspective. I had cleared any doubts about my discoveries, but I became aware that most people that are familiar with the "newer flower" are being shown a distorted representation that is preventing them from finding those symbols worth exploring. I assumed this was part of the reason for her reaction.

I have facilitated for my second editor a few sessions in the past and she is also a wonderful channel with enough materials for her own book. We both felt into it and agreed that it couldn't be more perfect. There are no coincidences. I offered to facilitate a session for her before she started editing again so we could have more clarity about my new material and clear up whatever was preventing us from moving forward.

Her session was epic! In it, she received and experienced the new geometry and we both learned much more and got excited about sharing it again. I received more confirmation and clarity. The information was extremely beautiful and more will be shared in the future in the first chapter of my ongoing digital book I'm planning. As she was downloaded with the new geometry, her Higher Self said:

HS: "This newer geometry that you are addressing, which she resisted for a little bit, was breaking the barriers really of what we've known, so that we can go even farther inward into our hearts into spaces that are new and have more information that will allow us to create in a more harmonious way. The feminine inward and the masculine outward."

They mentioned that this geometry helps us to find the center of the original sphere and that it is important to orient ourselves to our center, the center of our hearts, the center of our Earth. When we are finding the center, we can use the feminine source spiral to go infinitely inward. It reminded me of the center point meditation I used to do and teach, and my discoveries about the point of mass/the point of gravity, that each object, including our bodies, has a singularity point that contains the total mass of all its parts.

They explained that our language has distorted the word Darkness to have a more negative connotation, when in truth it is only the absence of Light. The darkness is the feminine principle and so much of creation is born in and out of the darkness. They also had a wonderful explanation that helped me feel the energy of numbers more:

HS: "There are many ways of drawing or emanating spirals. None of them are "perfect" or "correct". All of them are from Source. They are just different expressions and ways of creating. The Fibonacci, in its truest form, is what is called in this realm an irrational number, just like Phi is, or other irrational numbers. They're not rational to our minds, our mental binary minds, but they are a whole energy and entity unto themselves that has no beginning and no end. So the math behind it becomes very feminine. I don't know who said this, perhaps we can look it up, but when that irrational becomes rational, that is when you shift dimensions, when you shift your consciousness, when the Phi ratio becomes one."

They explained about the tilt of the Earth and that we used to have the North and the South poles upright. This allowed us to spin faster. Think about those spinning toys. If they tilt, they start to wobble. This is similar to the wobble we had in our consciousness.

They mentioned that the "new" geometry that I shared, and she was now attuned to throughout the session, is helping us align our North and South poles and each one that is carrying those codes is helping to align Earth to her upright axis and it will allow us to spin faster again and receive more light codes and more geometry. We needed to be upright. There was an event and we got tilted and now we are in the process of realigning the poles to allow us to spin as we were designed to be. They explained that the shape dodecahedron is not reaching the perfected representation with only the outward spiral (*Flower of Life*). This confirmed information from a video of the professional geometrician I found online that showed that not all the angles of the dodecahedron in the Metatron Cube are in a similar and perfected angle as it should have been. He also compared it to the dodecahedron in "The Flower of Immortality." Her spirit guide added information about platonic solids and another shape, the **stellated dodecahedron** *[see symbols glossary]*, that is the merging of the water and fire elements, and that the dodecahedron shape helps us to find the center.

So in a nutshell, when I looked into the frequency of note 'C', I saw that it is doubling within each octave. This was similar to the Krystal Spiral. Then I learned that a spiral is basically a wave looked at from another angle, and a spiral has a ratio or equation that creates a Sacred Geometry."

I spent hours designing symbols as most of what I found regarding the new geometry was not in the right proportions and didn't align with one another. It was confusing for me, so I had to do it for myself. Working on the symbols really unlocked more energy, ideas, and thoughts, so I compared the different spirals such as the Krystal, Fibonacci, and Golden spirals, and found their meeting points. Then I learned that the geometry of the flowers when designed in 3D could look similar from different degrees/angles (or "angels" if you like). This confirms those meeting points again.

I also learned that if the spirals are spinning at a different speed or start from another center point, they can overlap. It leads me to think that the manifestation of a reality or a hologram can be a few different spirals expressing a geometry that harmonizes and overlaps, creating a bridge between dimensions. A meeting and a choice point, and all that is needed is to move the witnessing point of any situation to another perspective, to see it from another angle. That would change the harmonic resonance and would change the projected outcome. When we change perspective and harmonize with another frequency, we can change the trajectory, dimension, or timeline.

I asked during IQH sessions about the 12 spheres of the Tree of Life and if they are familiar with it, and the Higher Self confirmed that they were (my client was not). So I asked what the 13th sphere represents. They replied that when one is activating all the 12 spheres to work in harmony as one organism made out of different parts working together and creating a whole being, the 13th will be created by itself.

They gave a metaphor that the 13th is like a ladder being created to help you rise into another space that is operating completely differently. They find it important to mention that it is not a portal that will take you fast to another space. It is a ladder that will help you reach a new way of existence, more like a soul join back to its Higher Self, or a Higher Self joining with their monadic consciousness, each time into a new ocean of consciousness that is operating in a new dimension with different rules and ways of existence, getting closer to Source.

I asked what will help someone to activate all the 12 Sefirot, and to my surprise, they mentioned that I should learn about the meridians which are important because it is just like the energy flow. All the systems need to work together. Later I did an internet search and discovered that the body has 12 main meridian lines.

They mentioned that there are many more spirals but to answer my comparison between Fibonacci and Krystal spirals, the main difference is that the Krystal Spiral has more options because of its fractalizing nature. The Fibonacci Spiral seems to be expanding in only one direction, which means that the lowest is equal to 1. They said, "The Fibonacci is highly rudimentary; it's very elementary in comparison to the others." And "one can't be existing without the other."

They have given a metaphor about transparent sheets on top of each other with geometry on them and how there would be noticeable intersection points, but this was hard for me to understand the deeper meaning. Then they shared a metaphor of planets that are spinning in space and creating alignments with one another. They confirmed that the meeting place could be called a choice point, but when you are in the fractalizing dimensions all points are choice points.

I learned about the harmonic Universe, or to be more correct, the Multiverse. Then I was thinking about the 13-moon calendar and the 13th Zodiac. Do you remember in the second session that 'I' mentioned the 13 main locations on Earth? Some other findings seemed interestingly synchronized, like 8 main notes on a piano keyboard, when note 'C' is the first and the last note in an octave and acting as a meeting point of 2 different octaves. Each octave has 13 keys, 5 black and 8 white keys.

You see what I mean? And this is the short version of the discoveries. Probably too much too fast for many humans.

You know by now that while we are here in a physical body, we are very limited in what we can comprehend. I believe that as long as we are in a physical body, we can't really grasp the full truth and all that there is. As they say in Buddhism, we live in Maya (Illusion). All we come across including this book is slightly distorted. The perfected reality is talked about in different religions in different ways. I find that those traditions are an essential step in the evolution of our consciousness. The Higher Self gave a metaphor of a flower having to die to make seeds and the seeds then create a new version of a flower. We too are experiencing a similar process of letting go of the old ways and receiving the new. It is the nature of expanding our awareness. It takes us a moment to learn and unlearn, to integrate before we can be exposed to more expansive ideas, so our minds would not explode as "I" said.

Facilitating IQH sessions is the art of asking questions and you never know what interesting information will come forward. If you have an open mind and dare to question everything and only take what resonates with you, I invite you to read the first chapter of the ongoing digital book in the Readers' Zone.

I have mentioned before about seeing things from another perspective. Not long ago, I had a unique experience and a vision of the moment when we accomplished our galactic mission on Earth. I was floating in space and my telepathy was back online. I felt pure bliss. My heart was filled with joy as I sent my gratitude, telepathically, to all my lightworker friends, the Volunteers, people like you, for transmuting a portion of the suffering that you have agreed to take on yourself by coming to the Earth and living here during these times.

Now my vision is of you and me, all the readers, inspired together to step fearlessly onto our divine path and to co-create the new harmonious communities. It is the potential I see for our future. I know it is the collective dream of so many of us, and I trust in our human family to take this opportunity we were given and transcend out of the density of amnesia. I trust we succeeded in the birthing of the New Earth. I trust it because I had a few profound lived experiences that confirm it. I trust it because I had profound IQH sessions that shared beautiful and uplifting information and I'm looking forward to sharing those with you.

I believe that each one of us has a never-ending hero-story to tell about how we all have contributed to manifesting the New Earth reality. Overcoming challenges on the path becomes easier when we change perspective, but it is not always an easy thing to do. It definitely wasn't easy for me or Allison. Many of us are well aware of the Dark Night of the Soul and may even experience it more than once. There are moments when the soul is tired, and the meaning of life becomes questionable. There are moments in life when a physical practice or spiritual practice is difficult to maintain or seems impossible. There is no shame in that hardship.

Those are the moments when a real and deep prayer is being birthed. It is the moment when Source can demonstrate the power of unconditional love and truly awaken one's spirit and realign life to the deepest truth in the heart. I believe each one planned their unique path of experiences that would open their mind and heart and connection to the Divine. Each one has a unique path of learning to communicate directly with Source and their spiritual team. I was told in one of my sessions by the Higher Self that the number of people on the planet should be the number of religions we have as no one path to Source is like the other. All are unique and important.

Do you remember that I grew up thinking that religions were the cause of all the problems in the world? Well, some of it might be true, but I feel that it is more accurate to acknowledge that we are living in a world of polarities. After we accept that, we know that we have to experience and witness both for the evolution of our consciousness. I find it so funny that now I'm a co-founder of a spiritual organization. We are an inner-faith ministry that follows the principles of Oneness and respects all traditions as fundamental for the evolution of humanity's awakening. We all need to grow in and out of something, right?

Many are starting their awakening with the support of medicinal substances like plant medicine ceremonies or other synthesized versions. All are gateways for the expansion of consciousness. I too had some experiences, always with much care and intention. During my first psilocybin mushroom ceremony, I saw a book in the sky, and on the cover of the book, there was a Star of David. I remember looking and for a moment worrying that my magical experience would turn into a Jewish religious trip. It didn't, but I did become vegan for many years. My love for nature grew and the journey helped me heal my digestive issues. Going back to the story, my friend asked me if I asked to download the book. At that time writing a book did not seem like something I would ever do. When we designed the symbol for the cover for this book out of the harmonic series that Allison shared with me, I was in awe that we ended up creating a similar shape to the Star of David, but also so different, more feminine. It felt like the coming true of this vision.

An even more profound event happened the day before in my dreams. The day before my first mushroom medicine journey, I had a dream within a dream. I didn't know that this could even happen. It started with me visiting my high school and meeting old friends, then I was suddenly moving quickly through a tunnel of darkness that opened into huge halls of art. For the second time in my life, I experienced a pure bliss similar to the out-of-body experience I had that initiated my awakening. I walked through an infinite amount of art, painting, sculpture, music. . . all types of sacred arts and patterns from cultures that I never saw before here on our Earth. When I got out of those infinite halls of art, I looked around and saw a beautiful and clean planet with green, pristine grassy hills, and then I saw The Temple. It was made from patterns. It was so beautiful and behind it there was a magnificent rainbow of three-dimensional purple and pink colors. It was spectacular!

But no one was there. Then I was told telepathically by invisible beings who I could feel around me: "If you want, you can stay here with us and feel like this forever." So I asked, "Does it mean that I would not see my friends and family anymore?" They replied that this is true. So I asked to come back. In an instant, I was back to the continuation of my first dream and into a weird, unexpected, and awkward moment of kissing a childhood lesbian friend. I immediately woke up and as I opened my eyes, it felt as if a brick fell on my chest. It was a painful return to my body after such pure bliss. I cried for a moment and then realized it was a beautiful preparation dream for my mushroom medicine journey the following day. I knew I would come back to my sanity and be safe to explore.

During one of my IQH sessions, the Higher Self mentioned that The Temple is ready, and the sound is tuned to the perfected harmony. The memory of The Temple I saw instantly came back. I believe I was taken then to see what we are collectively dreaming for our future. If we step out of time, in truth, it is already done. We are just remembering and choosing each moment which parallel timeline we each are aligning to experience. Each moment when you choose from love, we reach closer. Almost like playing a hot and cold game with ourselves, two steps closer, one away, two steps away, three steps closer, but, it is inevitable that each of us will make it in our own time, in the most divine timing, in the most surprising ways, as you allow some parts of yourself to die a little and birth yourself again even within the same body.

When you get into the Oneness, where nothing is lost, everyone you love is already there. We have all chosen to be here for many reasons, some more personal for our soul evolution and some more about the collective galactic mission. I'm ready and excited for the next phases of Ascension. We have new foundations to build from and incredible beings from all over the Earth, the Universe, and the Multiverse to support us as one. It should be fun! It can be whatever we make it to be, and it can combine all the things that we love to do! Dancing, singing, playing music, praying, teaching, traveling, healing, learning, and being together as a community with the Earth and the animals and the beyond.

From a more practical perspective, I ask myself how can we create New Earth Communities? What can bring people together to create something that will be a fun and exciting process? What can be a good investment of our time, energy, and money that will bring more balance between our physical and spiritual nature? Well, a village has many layers, right? From schools for kids, healing centers, producing food, building harmonically and ecologically, and so on, and I think the whole process can be fun, full of creativity, excitement, and joy. I feel like we are being asked to dream bigger and more galactic, not from a survival consciousness and perspective, but from the inspired vision of the coming true of all of our purest, most elevated dreams.

During the night before a past New Year's Eve, I had another old vision came up again, like from the depth of my subconscious. I experienced this vision in my dreams, a super futuristic SHOW! It was a multi-generational, multimedia performance art production for all the family, that will share the New Earth energies and the timeless stories that demonstrate living in harmony with the Earth and the Universe, and will wake up, activate, and heal many at once. The vision showed us co-creating a beautiful production that creates a community, education for youth, and for the golden child within us all, demonstrating in real life the art of living in harmony with all!

This is only one example of projects NEA might do soon, or have done, depending on when you picked up this book. We hope that you will join us in creating and celebrating a Heaven on Earth here and now in whatever capacity you feel called to. You will find the updated opportunities, discussions, and projects on *Source⊙Energy*, our private online social network. I have great hope that this will inspire you to dedicate your energy and practice to maintaining and amplifying your own heart coherence and, in each moment, to align your energy with the grid of unconditional love, compassion, and forgiveness. Join us in this incredibly vast galactic operation to help Mother Earth and the human family ascend.

Most of the people I know do not hold a consistent spiritual practice and the same holds true for me too. I sometimes have periods of falling out of consistent practice and back on some less healthy habits. This leads me to understand that having mystical experiences, knowing unconditional love, and having those turning points in life of rapid awakening and even direct guidance and contact with Source is not always enough to keep the fire of dedication stoked for a long time.

I pray this book will merge the codes of devotion with your own dedication to yourself and help you shine the infinite Source of Light within you, just like the Sun, and remind you of the star that you are. Let it be the spark that turns on your devotion to yourself, the practice of loving yourself and giving yourself the pure love that you are, no matter what challenges, what fears, or what events are to come. Let's use every moment of the NOW to be in gratitude and trust.

If you are not already doing so, I invite you to start a daily practice NOW. Start really small and really simple but start NOW in the true spirit of devotion. Start with gratitude. Gratitude is the simplest pivot point you can create for yourself at any given moment. NOW, what are you grateful for?

I may offer you a simple exercise to try now and do every morning when you wake up:

Fill yourself up with gratitude for being alive and having a body. Repeat to yourself in your heart for the next few minutes or so: "I move for the Source of my being/the higher power of my understanding." Remember the highest frequency of Unconditional

Love you ever felt. Think about the strongest energy of love you have given or received. Feel it in your heart and amplify it with the sensation of pleasure in your body. Feel the pleasure of a simple movement, feel the pleasure of your skin, or the pleasure from movements that are massaging yourself from within as you move, and breathe deeply. Don't think too much, just move. Move to amplify the energy of unconditional love for yourself and gratitude to your body. Dedicate the energy you are generating towards the benefit of all. You can do it even while lying down or moving on your bed.

Right after that, simply rest in stillness and repeat to yourself in your heart for the next few minutes: "I breathe in gratitude for being alive." Focus again on the energy of unconditional love, and gratitude to the Source of our being. Fill up your heart and just breathe in. Let the exhale happen naturally, calmly, and peacefully. You can do this while lying down if needed in a way that you can focus and not fall asleep.

Do your practice, however it may look or sound, in the spirit of devotion. Do it daily and let that practice inform you. Let it transform you. Each moment and each choice express your devotion to unconditional love for yourself and for all Creation. Together we rise, one step at a time, one breath at time, to a higher octave of perfected sounds, and a geometry of unity and peace.

I thank you for reading our book and for taking this journey with us. Thank you for doing your sacred part on this Earth. We are looking forward to meeting you in person, online, or in Spirit. We are looking forward to dancing and singing with you and co-creating the New Earth.

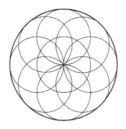

MISCELLANEOUS TOPICS

We collected a few more topics and questions that I asked Allison's Higher Self, but we thought they were less relevant to the flow of the book. I thought they still brought forward beautiful information that we do wish to share with you. We would share the topics with you here, but the content will be found in the Reader's Zone on our website.

- Compromise Versus Collaboration

- Contact with Extraterrestrials

- The Divine Potential of Sex

- The Name of God

- As Above, So Below - Gradual Awakening

- Merit Badge

- Trump

www.songsofremembering.org

SYMBOLS GLOSSARY

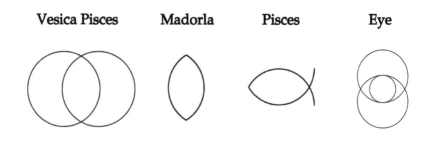

Vesica Pisces   Madorla   Pisces   Eye

Three-dimensional Vesica Pisces

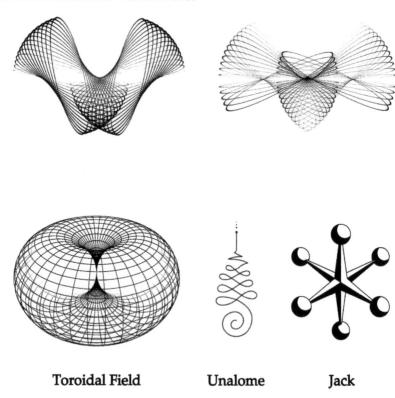

Toroidal Field   Unalome   Jack

The Seed of Life

Venn Diagram

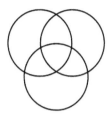

The God-Seed (5 circles)

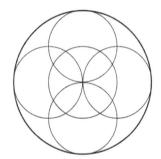

The God-Seed (9 circles)

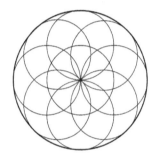

Flower of Life

The traditional **Flower of Life** -commonly known name for 19 circles. When the first circle · is centered and the other are starting or meeting at the next mid-point.

The Flower of Immortality
18 Circles

Commonly known as:
Eternal Life Creation/

Traditional Tree Of Life

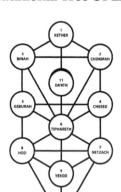

The traditional Tree of Life
with the Flower of Life

Traditional five platonic solids within Metatron Cube.
(See correction on page **486**)

The Universal Tree of Life

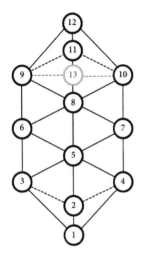

The hidden 13th Sefira could be placed on the meeting point between the 9th and 10th, and the 11th and 8th, similarly to the 11th Da'at in the traditional tree. In a 3D prospective it can be placed behind.

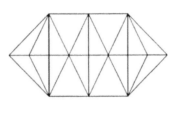

Kathara Grid

The Universal Tree of Life within the Flower of Immortality

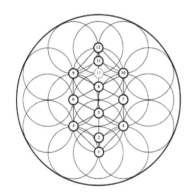 

Four Universal Tree of Life within the Flower of Immortality with 13th hidden sefira named Chofesh – חופש - (freedom) as the center point.

Fibonacci Spiral

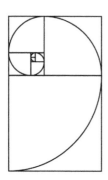

Fibonacci
1,1,2,3,5,8,13,21,34. . .

Krystal Spiral

Krystal
1,2,4,8,16,32,64. . .

The Golden Ratio

$\varphi = (1 + \sqrt{5})/2 = 1.618033988749....$

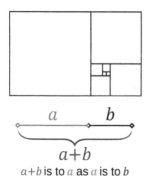

a b

$a+b$

$a+b$ is to a as a is to b

Fibonacci Spiral & Krystal Spiral

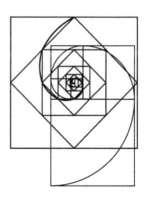

3D Wave to spiral

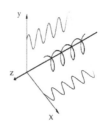

Krystal Spiral within The Universal Tree of Life and within the God- Seed

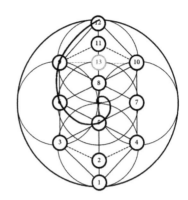

The most common comparison diagram online of Krystal and Fibonacci spirals with the meeting point (Choice Point). If you would see the colored version you would notice that the colors might be misleading, but the small arrows on the spiral are correct.

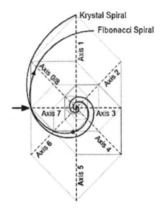

Three-Dimensional Universal Tree of Life

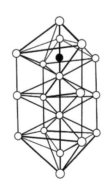

Golden Ratio within **The Flower of Immortality**, and with **Krystal Spiral**

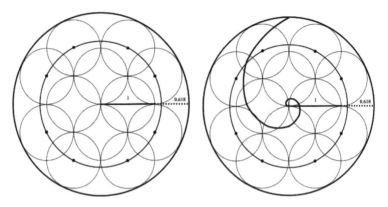

Golden Ratio within **The Flower of Immortality**, and with **Krystal Spiral**

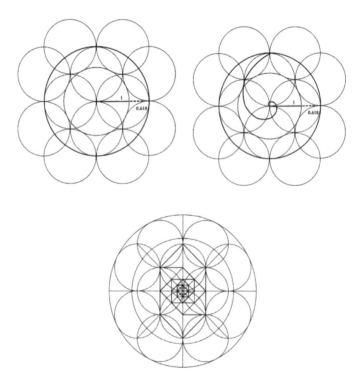

The Platonic Solids within (three dimensional) God-Seed

Stellated Dodecahedron

The Traditional Metatron Cube with a dodecahedron comparted to a dodecahedron within a God-Seed with equal angles.

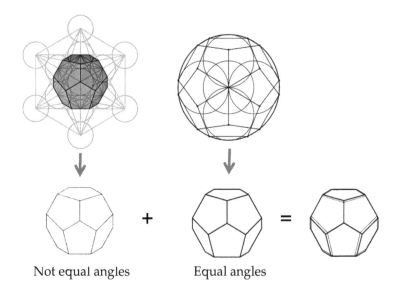

Not equal angles   Equal angles

The Platonic Solids within (three dimensional) **Seed of Life**

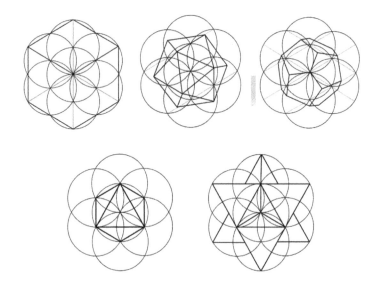

*This page is Inspired by discoveries and designs of George Leoniak

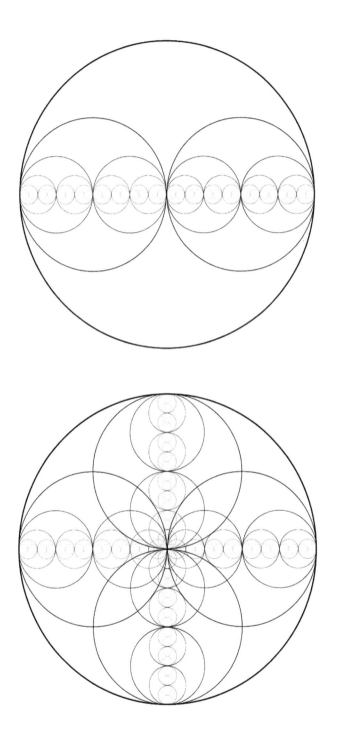

Sine Waves of 'C' Note on in rising octaves
Doubling each octave

$C_0 = 16.05$Hz

$C_1 = 32.11$ Hz

$C_2 = 64.22$ Hz

$C_3 = 128.43$ Hz

$C_4 = 256.87$ Hz

$C_5 = 513.74$ Hz

$C_6 = 1027.47$ Hz

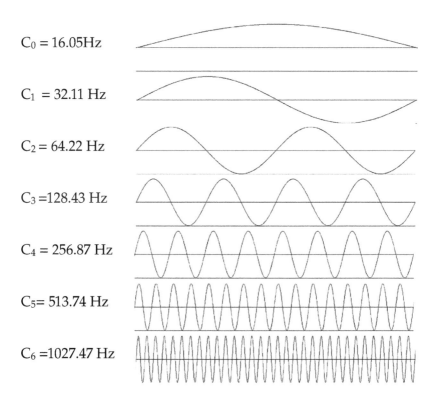

*Commonly known frequencies for tuning pitch 432 Hz

Sin Waves Frequency of Harmonics

1. $C_0 = 16.05$ Hz

2. $C_1 = 32.11$ Hz

3. $G_1 = 48.11$ Hz

4. $C_2 = 64.22$ Hz

5. $E_2 = 80.91$ Hz

6. $G_2 = 96.22$ Hz

7. $(A^{\#}_2/B^{\flat}_2 = 114.42$ Hz $)$

8. $C_3 = 128.43$ Hz

*Commonly known frequencies for tuning pitch 432 Hz

Discovering how the symbol of the cover would look like if was made by 'C' note on rising octaves without changing the amplitude.

DRAWING THE HARMONIC SERIES

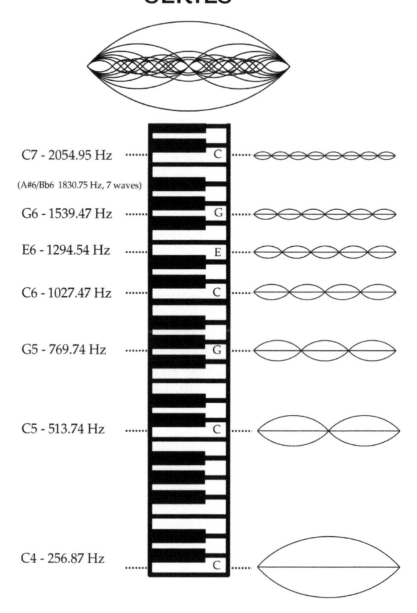

C7 - 2054.95 Hz

(A#6/Bb6 1830.75 Hz, 7 waves)

G6 - 1539.47 Hz

E6 - 1294.54 Hz

C6 - 1027.47 Hz

G5 - 769.74 Hz

C5 - 513.74 Hz

C4 - 256.87 Hz

All the frequencies above are the most commonly known today with tuning pitch 432 Hz and might have more variations. I have learned that the tuning standard has changed from 432 Hz to 440 Hz

To practice drawing the symbol you can take a copy page and follow the lines. You can mark the center point as a reference point for easier laying it out on top of each other.

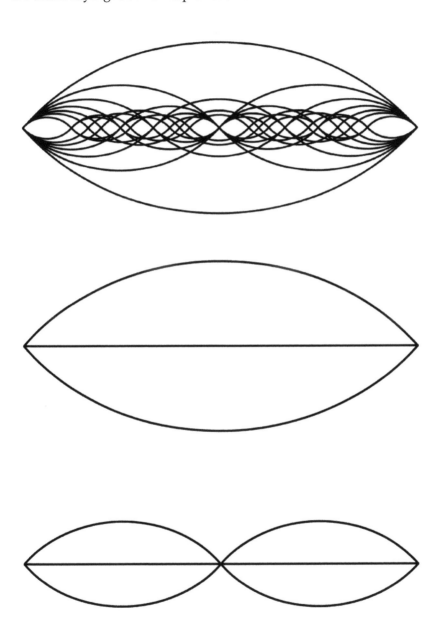

The mystery of the missing 7th

RON'S ACKNOWLEDGMENTS

I received a huge gift and feel I'm honored to share it with you. I send my deepest gratitude to Source and Mother Earth for granting me this opportunity to discover and share the knowledge and wisdom in this book, and to assist humanity in its remembering of our divinity and Oneness with all of life.

I give my infinite gratitude:

To AVA! For allowing us to share this material as a testament of our amazing journey together. I know it was not easy for her as it reveals a lot of personal information and required a great deal of vulnerability and courage. I want to thank Ava for all of the heartfelt energy she put into collaborating with me to bring this sacred information forward to share with you. I do not take this for granted.

To my most beloved friend, partner, teacher, and husband Michael James Garber. For all of the many ways you have supported me. For the many faces and colors of your love. For all of the energy you are pouring out from your heart for this grand, galactic mission of Ascension for the benefit of All. You are truly an angel, a beacon of light, and inspiration for me and many others.

To Dolores Cannon, my teacher and ally. Thank you for sharing your methods and perspectives and for paving the way for us and many others. Thank you for demonstrating and teaching the benefits of evolving beyond what is familiar with a spirit of curiosity. Thank you for daring us to ask questions and try new things with care for our clients. I feel blessed to continue your mission of restoring and sharing the ancient and lost knowledge.

To all the members of New Earth Ascending for supporting the ministry and spreading unconditional love, information, and healing energies with others. Thank you for your donations and for making this book possible.

Finally, I want to thank you, the reader, for dedicating time during your precious life to read this book, and for all the people who helped to put this book together — transcribing, editing, layout, designing the book cover, and assisting the publishing process of this book. I could not have done this without you!

Thank you so much from the depth of my heart!

In Love and Devotion,

Ron Amit

AVA'S ACKNOWLEDGMENTS

First, I would like to thank Ron for his continued encouragement, patience, and dedication to accessing and sharing this extraordinary information with me. It took me quite some time to integrate this strange tale and to acknowledge that it needed to be shared. I am forever grateful for the unique opportunity to partner with him and New Earth Ascending to help open this channel that I am and to share this story for the benefit of all beings. This story would not have been shared without his gentle persistence and skilled facilitation.

Additionally, I thank a different Ron for seeing me long before I ever saw myself. Somehow, you knew this story was coming, one way or another.

Thank you to my incredible, diverse, and abundant community of friends, spirit family, and fellow volunteers who love, support, and play with me all over this exquisite Earth. I love meeting and loving you all over again everywhere I go. Thank you for loving me and encouraging me to be the me-est me I can be! Your love and acceptance have helped me bring this story to life. I long to mention out all your names, but I would need a whole chapter to list all the incredible souls who stand with me in devotion to love. Thank you friends, inspirations, and allies; you know who you are.

I offer deep gratitude to my meditation teachers Kerry, Jorge, and Sahaja for offering me the time and space to truly learn how to meditate, experience pure silence, and find and stabilize the still point within. I would not have been able to access this channel without the profound gift of presence.

I give thanks to my many plant and animal medicine guides, mentors, and teachers, especially Terrence, James, Michael, Luna, Cristina, Ishmael, A&L, Max, and Merrill, for helping me face my fear of death and to fully feel my ecstatic life! What allies to have in such epic explorations of consciousness.

And thank you Jack. Your presence in my life is such a gift. Thank you for your support, your generosity, and sense of home. I can hardly even imagine what my life would look like without you. You help me remember that miracles are real.

I would also like to especially thank my parents for bringing me into this world and for teaching me to always be myself, even when that meant disappointing them. I am so grateful to be me in this life, and I have been given such an amazing and unique opportunity to live a life more extraordinary than I ever imagined.

Thank you Jen. Thank you for always showing me such unconditional love despite our differences. You and your family mean so much to me.

Infinite gratitude to my beloved Leon, for loving and welcoming all of me. Thank you for the sweet sanctuary we create in each other's embrace, and thank you for teaching me what it feels like to truly love and to be loved in return. May all beings feel such freedom, depth, and joy in love. You have been my favorite surprise here on Earth so far. You are a delight, and I absolutely adore you.

Last but not least, I give thanks to myself for listening long enough and for being brave enough to keep leaning into my heart's full YES, even when I think I must be insane. I love you honey. I love being me in this life. Thank you.

In Gratitude,

AVA

THE ILLUMINATION CODEX

THE ILLUMINATION CODEX SERIES

WWW.NEWEARTHASCENDING.ORG

Support Our Initiatives

We dedicated our lives to supporting this Grand Transition to the New Earth. We are dedicated to assisting people to realize their divinity and manifest that truth in every aspect of their life. We stand alongside with you as humanity awakens to its True Nature and becomes a People of Light in the heavenly reality of New Earth.

We have created a special axillary and fund within the New Earth Ascending ministry - The Songs of Remembering Alliance. Our purpose is to continue to co-create more projects with Allison and all who wish to join our efforts of manifesting the new systems, communities, schools, and the development of the New Earth civilization.

If you found this book supportive and wish to gift it forward, or if you wish to support by making to make a tax-deductible donation to one of our humanitarian initiatives, please scan the QR Code and choose:

The Song of Remembering Alliance is a private unincorporated nonprofit axillary of New Earth Ascending ministry with the benefits acknowledged within the USA - 508 (c)(1)(a).

If you wish to study and become an IQH Practitioner, be sure to check out our online Illuminated Quantum Healing Training.

Ingram Content Group UK Ltd.
Milton Keynes UK
UKHW020635260723
425809UK00015B/610

9 781959 561119